Constructing a Social Welfare System for All in China

The China Development Research Foundation is one of the leading economic think tanks in China, where many of the details of China's economic reform have been formulated. Its work and publications therefore provide great insights into what the Chinese themselves think about economic reform and how it should develop. This book sets out the general objectives, principles and framework of a proposed new social welfare system for China, putting forward relevant policy recommendations. It provides a comprehensive overview of China's current welfare services, including retirement pensions, education, health, employment, housing and social security payments, and goes on to cost the proposed new social welfare system and assess the government's capacity for implementing it. It shows how the new system will, within an integrated framework, provide comprehensive welfare for all, including rural and urban citizens, migrant workers and disadvantaged groups such as the rural and urban poor. It also shows how the new system will aim to balance economic and social development whilst maintaining China's high economic growth rate, increasing domestic demand and promoting economic restructuring.

China Development Research Foundation (CDRF) is a civic, nationwide non-profit organization founded on the initiative of the Development Research Center (DRC) of the State Council. The mission of the Foundation is to advance good governance and public policy to promote economic development and social progress in China.

Routledge Studies on the Chinese Economy
Series Editor Peter Nolan
University of Cambridge

Founding Series Editors
Peter Nolan, University of Cambridge and Dong Fureng, Beijing University

The aim of this series is to publish original, high-quality, research-level work by both new and established scholars in the West and the East, on all aspects of the Chinese economy, including studies of business and economic history.

Constructing a Social Welfare System for All in China

China Development Research Foundation

Routledge
Taylor & Francis Group

LONDON AND NEW YORK

First published 2012
by Routledge
2 Park Square, Milton Park, Abingdon, Oxon, OX14 4RN

Simultaneously published in the USA and Canada
by Routledge
711 Third Avenue, New York, NY 10017

Routledge is an imprint of the Taylor & Francis Group, an informa business

British Library Cataloguing in Publication Data
A catalogue record for this book is available
from the British Library

Library of Congress Cataloging in Publication Data
A catalogue record for this book has been requested

ISBN: 978–0–415–58470–8 (hbk)
ISBN: 978–0–203–83126–7 (ebk)

Typeset in Times New Roman
by RefineCatch Limited, Bungay, Suffolk

MIX
Paper from
responsible sources
FSC
www.fsc.org FSC® C004839

Printed and bound in Great Britain by the MPG Books Group

Contents

Boxes

Figures

Tables

Team members

Advisor:

Wang Mengkui Former President, Development Research Center of the State Council of China; Chairman, China Development Research Foundation

Project Coordinator:

Lu Mai Secretary General and Research Fellow, China Development Research Foundation

Project Director:

Tang Min Deputy Secretary General, China Development Research Foundation

Authors of the Master Report:

He Ping Director-General, Institute of Social Insurance, Ministry of Human Resources and Social Security

Li Shi Professor, School of Economics and Business, Beijing Normal University

Wang Yanzhong Director-General, Research Center for Labor and Social Security, Chinese Academy of Social Sciences

Authors of the Background Reports:

Kong Jingyuan Director-General, Department of Economic System Reform, National Development and Reform Commission of the State Council

Wang Zhenyao Director-General, Department of Relief and Rehabilitation, Ministry of Civil Affairs

Jia Kang Director-General, Research Institute for Fiscal Science, Ministry of Finance

Zheng Bingwen Director-General, Institute of Latin American Studies, Chinese Academy of Social Sciences

Zhang Li Director-General, National Center for Education Development, Ministry of Education

Zhang Zhenzhong Director, China National Health Economics Institute, Ministry of Health

Ren Xingzhou Director, Institute of Market Economy Research, Development Research Center of the State Council

Mo Rong Deputy Director, Institute of Labor Sciences, Ministry of Human Resources and Social Security

Liu Minquan Professor, School of Economics, Peking University

Gong Sen Senior Research Fellow, Social Development Research Department, Development Research Center of the State Council

Tian Xiaohong Research Fellow, Institute of Politics, Chinese Academy of Social Sciences

Wu Huazhang Director, Office of Health Development and Policy Studies, China National Health Economics Institute, Ministry of Health

Yu Jiantuo Research Fellow, Center for Human and Economic Development Studies, Peking University

Zhang Shifei Associate Research Fellow, Institute of Sociology, Chinese Academy of Social Sciences

Wang Min Associate Research Fellow, Research Institute for Fiscal Science, Ministry of Finance

Luo Chuliang Associate Professor, School of Economics and Business, Beijing Normal University

Wang Xiufeng Assistant Researcher, Department of Information Studies, China National Health Economics Institute, Ministry of Health

Project Officer:

Du Zhixin Program Director, China Development Research Foundation

Preface

Establishing the goal of building a 'moderately prosperous' society marks a new era in China's socioeconomic development. This goal also puts improving our social welfare systems squarely on the agenda. Social welfare systems are an important component of China's current stage of systems-building; they are necessary for coordinated and sustainable socioeconomic progress.

'Reform and opening up' over the past three decades has brought about miraculous economic growth, a moderately prosperous standard of living, and significant improvements in social welfare, particularly the widely recognized achievements in poverty reduction. However, China is still a developing country. In terms of social welfare, it is still at a low level, with inconsistent development and pronounced disparities between urban and rural, and among various regions. Improving social welfare systems and increasing welfare benefits for urban and rural residents in proportion to our economic growth is imperative if we want to address socioeconomic imbalances and narrow the urban–rural and regional gaps. They are essential in our efforts to build a stronger and more prosperous socialist country. Indeed they are crucial to realizing the mission of modernization.

This work presents the substantive conclusions of research organized by the China Development Research Foundation (CDRF). Like two previous annual reports published by the Foundation, namely *Development with Equity* and *Eliminating Poverty through Development in China*, this report focuses on key issues in socioeconomic development. As the title indicates, this report is about building a developmental social welfare system that provides China's people with universal access. 'Universal access' indicates that the system is meant to cover both urban and rural residents. 'Developmental' means that the process is incremental and needs to facilitate, and in turn be promoted by, economic growth. This report proposes general goals in constructing such a system at the current stage and maps out a basic framework. It elaborates on key contents of the system, including pensions, medical and health care, education, employment, housing, minimum living allowances and social welfare for special groups, and it provides policy recommendations accordingly. Social welfare could well incorporate a broader range of subjects, but we regard these as the most basic and most important. China is trying hard to raise domestic demand right now, and to increase the ratio of its consumption in GDP. Issues raised by the report in this regard are crucial policy considerations.

A philosophy and practice of 'social welfare' has long been a part of China's cultural makeup, but in its modern sense this 'social welfare' program comes as a response to social problems associated with industrialization and a market economy. The positive as well as negative aspects of other social welfare policies and systems in the world have provided us with very useful material to use as reference. In the three decades before China's introduction of 'reform and opening up' policies, as well as in the most recent three decades, unremitting efforts have been made to improve social welfare and these too have provided us with invaluable experience. The proposals and policy recommendations in this report start from the standpoint of China's current situation, and take into consideration both these domestic and international contributions. It should be noted that this report also makes preliminary estimates of the public financial support that will be necessary for the social welfare systems that are discussed. The estimates are based on the principle that social welfare must match the economic development and financial resources available to a country, and must not only facilitate a balance between economic and social development but must help sustain that development. The estimates made in this report rely on the assumption of continued economic growth, and also on reform of and improvements in our public finance and taxation systems.

A great amount of social-welfare research has been done in recent years in China. Little of it is of a comprehensive nature. The comprehensive, systematic, and empirical analyses and policy recommendations in this report should make a considerable contribution to the goal of improving our China's social welfare system and policies.

Wang Mengkui
Former President of Development Research Center
of the State Council
Chairman of the Board of Trustees of China Development
Research Foundation
February 18, 2009

Foreword

It is great that *Constructing a Social Welfare System for All in China* has now been published in English. This book reviews the evolvement of China's social welfare system and discusses in depth the key challenges for Chinese endeavor to restructure the current system. The book proposes to establish a welfare system which brings benefits to all social groups, adapts to China's social and economic context, and lays a solid foundation for China's economic growth in the long term.

Apparently, China today is experiencing critical transition of its development policy. If we conclude economic growth was China's core task of development policy during the first two decades of reform and opening up, China has shifted its priority to social development during the past decade, as well as the coming one. This adjustment is in essence a long-term, lasting and fundamental effort, which thus exerts far-reaching effect. Since the Chinese version of *Constructing a Social Welfare System for All in China* was released in April 2009, China has made remarkable achievement in strengthening her social welfare system, which covers the following major areas.

1. Old-age Security. The State Council launched the *Guidance to Establish Pilot Programs of New Rural Old-age Insurance* in September 2009, deciding to conduct pilots of farmers' social old-age insurance in 10% of Chinese county-level administrations, while planning to expand the pilot areas to universally cover all the eligible rural residents by 2020. In September 2009, the State Council also announced the *Tentative Measures for Transferring and Continuing the Basic Old-age Insurance of Urban Enterprises Employees*, which means that old-age insurance programs for urban workers, including migrant workers, are portable across different provinces. In addition, all the provinces had established a unified basic old-age insurance fund system on a province-wide basis by the end of 2009, which helps to mitigate risks on a broader scale and realize effective fund allocation.

2. Health Security. The Chinese government keeps increasing the standard of subsidy for the new rural cooperative medical insurance, from 100 *yuan* per person per year in 2009 to 200 *yuan* per person per year in 2011. By the end of 2010, the new rural cooperative medical system covered 96.3% of Chinese farmers, or 835 million people. As for urban residents, the government promoted

the system of basic medical insurance, which focuses on the medical service of unemployed urban residents, particularly junior and high school students, children, seniors and the disabled.

3. Education Security. In June 2010, the Ministry of Education released the *Guidelines of the National Program for Medium- and Long-Term Educational Reform and Development (2010–2020)* and spelt out the goal of education development by 2020. To be specific, the popularization rate of one-year preschool education reaches 95%; the gross enrollment rate of high school reaches 90%; the students of secondary and higher vocational education amounts to 38.3 million; extended education of employees reaches 350 million person-time. In addition, this *Guideline* clarified the institutional arrangement to forge ahead with the balanced development of nine-year compulsory education between rural and urban areas, increase the national budget for education and secure the equitable access to education for children of migrant workers.

4. Housing Security. In June 2009, the Ministry of Housing and Urban–Rural Development jointly launched the *Planning for Guaranteeing Low-Rent Housing (2009–2010)* with other ministries and defined its target of basically solving the housing problem of the current 7.47 million low-income urban families by 2011 and further improving the low-rent housing system. Therefore, 900 billion *yuan* will be put in place for this purpose. China will build an additional 36 million subsidized housing by 2015, increasing its coverage to 20%.

5. Adjusting the Rural Poverty Line. By the end of 2010, the Chinese government decided to adjust the rural poverty line and increase it from 1196 *yuan* person/year in 2008 to 1500 *yuan* person/year so that the poverty alleviation policies can benefit more people as low-incomes.

6. Labor Market Policy. Chinese local governments increased the minimum wage one after another from 2010. By March 2011, around 30 provinces have raised the standard of the minimum enterprise salary, most of which see an increase of around 10% while some even see 25%.

7. Enacting the Social Insurance Law. The Eleventh National People's Congress passed the Social Insurance Law in October 2010. It witnesses China's active effort to integrate its social welfare systems. It is the first time that China confirms the basic framework of a social insurance system, as well as portability of old-age insurance, and medical insurance in the form of legislation. This law also proposes the target of 'national coordinated' basic old-age insurance for the first time, making it a milestone in the history of Chinese social welfare system.

Except for the above-mentioned fundamental systems, China further launched the *Regulation on the Relief of Natural Disasters*, modified the *Regulation on Work Injury Insurance*, improved the budgeting and supervising system for the social insurance fund, and intensified financial input for social welfare in the second half of 2009.

In the newly-released Twelfth Five-Year Development Plan (2011–2015), the Chinese government is to establish a social welfare system fully covering both rural and urban areas by the end of 2015. The top priority is defined as filling the holes of systems and reducing segmentation of different institutions, such as advancing the reform of the old-age insurance program for public institutions, and constructing the work injury insurance system which combines prevention, compensation and rehabilitation of work injury. Based on these efforts, China will gradually expand the coverage of the social security system during the Twelfth Five-Year Plan, increase the social security level and narrow down the welfare gap between rural and urban areas as well as across different regions and groups.

The Chinese government believes that improving the social welfare system not only means all the citizens share the fruits of reform and development, but also boosts Chinese economic restructuring and enables long-term and steady economic growth. A better social welfare system is regarded as an effective tool to narrow down the gap of income distribution, enlarge domestic demand (particularly consumption demand), and address the internal and external economic imbalance.

In fact, the development of the social welfare system is also the requirement of Chinese citizens. During the first two decades of China's reform and opening up, China suffered from a relatively low income level and low living standard, so economic rights was put at the top of the people's requirement, such as the rights for property, employment and market access. However, this has changed during the past decade and will continue to do so in the years to come. In the face of the remarkable Chinese economic growth and increasing social income, Chinese people will focus more and more on their social rights about education, health, pension, employment and housing. If the Chinese government is able to face up to such changing appeals, share common views with its citizens and maintain benign interaction with them, it is expected that China will be able to sustain its rapid economic development.

Although China's social welfare system is faced with several crucial challenges for further development, such as converging different social welfare systems caused by massive rural–urban migration, as well as the problem of financial sustainability caused by expanding coverage and rising welfare standards, we have every reason to be grateful for China's remarkable progress in improving the social welfare system over the past decade, particularly the last five years. China's achievement in evolving the social welfare system is as impressive as the economic growth, while the former is no less significant than the latter.

The readers of this book may find that many concepts and policy recommendations proposed exactly conform to the development of China's social welfare system over the past two years. There are many reasons for such a seemingly coincidence. Firstly, the authors of this report are all leading experts in this area from government departments and research institutes. They are quite familiar with the latest policies for social welfare and fully aware of their development trends. Some of them are even engaged in drafting these important government policies. Secondly, this report depicts the panorama of how China's social welfare system developed over the past decade, and records the thoughts, debate and consensus of Chinese and foreign academic and political circles in this regard. In this sense, although the Chinese social welfare system has made considerable progress since this report was launched, its analysis of the status quo and challenges for the system, and its policy recommendation about principles, priority and orientations of restructuring the welfare system, are far from out of date.

I sincerely hope the English version of *Constructing a Developmental Social Welfare System for All* can help those foreign friends who care about Chinese development to have a more thorough and fundamental understanding of China. Such an understanding entails not only Chinese achievements over the past decades but her challenges, difficulties and options, so that they can contribute their wisdom for China to cope with these challenges. We also believe that as a large country undergoing fast-paced transition, China's challenges, options, experience and lessons are highly relevant for other countries, particularly developing countries.

LU Mai
Secretary General
China Development Research Foundation
April 12, 2011

Acknowledgements

After more than a year of hard work, we present this volume: *Constructing a Social Welfare System for All in China*. Three decades of reform and opening up have brought massive changes to China's people—to their economy, their society, their way of life. In the course of these changes, economic and social structures are undergoing profound adjustment This report, commissioned by CDRF, proposes to establish a 'universal-access developmental social welfare system' as a strategic initiative to meet future social and economic challenges. Moreover, it argues that such a system is critical to meeting our goals of 'maintaining growth, expanding domestic demand, making structural adjustments, and improving people's well-being'.

The smooth completion of this report would have been impossible without the dedication of the entire team and the generous support of numerous experts and entities. He Ping, Director-General of the Institute of Social Insurance of the Ministry of Human Resources and Social Security, Li Shi, Professor at the School of Economics and Business at Beijing Normal University, and Wang Yanzhong, Director-General of the Research Center for Labor and Social Security of the Chinese Academy of Social Sciences, took on the task of writing the main parts of the report. The report benefits greatly from their rich theoretical knowledge and profound understanding of China's policies and practices. In the course of creating the framework for the report, and discussing and drafting it, these three built a solid foundation for its final form. Wang Mengkui, Former President of the Development Research Center of the State Council of China and Chairman of the Board of Trustees of CDRF, provided constructive criticism and detailed advice after reviewing the draft three times. This greatly improved the final results. Tang Min, Deputy Secretary General of CDRF, helped compose and revise many chapters.

The field of social welfare touches on many disciplines, and this report also benefits from interdisciplinary perspectives. To provide a solid scientific basis for the analysis and ensure the feasibility of policy recommendations, CDRF asked scholars from universities and government-affiliated research institutes as well as policymakers to write twelve background reports. Much of the data, analyses and recommendations of these background studies is incorporated in the main part of the report. These background reports and their authors are: *Welfare Systems and*

Practices in Foreign Countries by Zheng Bingwen, *A Comparative Study of International Social Welfare Systems* by Liu Minquan and Yu Jiantuo, *Minimum Living Allowances in China's New Social Welfare System* by Wang Zhenyao and Tian Xiaohong, *China's Old-age Security System* by Kong Jingyuan, *Public Education Service in China's New Social Welfare System* by Zhang Li, *Healthcare Security in China's New Social Welfare System* by Zhang Zhenzhong, Wu Huazhang and Wang Xiufeng, *Job Promotion, Job Assistance and Unemployment Protection Systems* by Mo Rong, *Housing Security in China's New Social Welfare System* by Ren Xingzhou, *Social Welfare Systems for Special Groups* by Zhang Shifei, *Fund-raising and Public Funding for Social Welfare* by Jia Kang and Wang Min, *The Management Framework of China's Social Welfare System* by Gong Sen, and *Analysis of Urban and Rural Welfare* by Li Shi and Luo Chuliang. Our gratitude also goes to Du Zhixin who provided a report on the research team's investigation in Europe. All authors of the background reports also participated in discussions at various stages in the writing of this report, and offered valuable suggestions.

During the research and writing process, many other experts also participated in discussions and offered constructive criticism, including Lu Xueyi, Yu Xiaoqing, Zheng Jingping, Fan Gang, Han Jun, Bai Chong'en, Li Daokui, Cai Fang, Li Peilin, Wang Chenguang, Wang Xiaolu, Gao Shiji, Chen Huai, Du Yang, Wang Sangui, Bai Nansheng, Liu Jitong, Li Xuejing, Xiong Yuegen, Wang Ming and Wang Xiaozhuo. Appreciation should also go to the National Bureau of Statistics of China and the Public Finance Scientific Research Institute of the Ministry of Finance, for their generous support in providing data and research analysis. This made our estimates of the total public funding needed to establish such a system possible, as well as our estimates of the State's actual public finance capability. To draw on the experience of European countries and America in building and reforming social welfare systems, the research group made a trip in May 2008 to Europe, and carried on in-depth discussions with European counterparts. The Denmark-based Copenhagen Business School very kindly made arrangements for the study tour and seminars. Ove K. Pedersen, Sven Blondal, John Campbell, SøRen Kaj Andersen, Ole Beier Sørensen, Bent Greve and other scholars offered their comments and expertise on European practices. In September 2008, the CDRF convened a video conference on social security and public funding with the International Labor Organization. M. Cichon, J. Woodall, A. Hu, Florence Bonnet, E. Saint-Pierre Guilbault and Zhu Changyou shared their ideas on the report's framework and contents.

The CDRF has undertaken all the work of organizing this report. Under the leadership of Tang Min, CDRF officials involved in the project include Du Zhixin, Feng Mingliang and Du Jing, who not only undertook specific projects, but also collected and compiled necessary materials, provided research assistance, and edited drafts when the report was being finalized. In addition, Ke Yilan, Chen Xiaolong, Yang Junxiong, Hu Ziqiang, Gao Guoqing and Zhang Yan were most helpful in a great variety of ways.

In order to facilitate ongoing research for the annual Development Reports, the CDRF established a China Development Fund. The Starr Foundation and Vodafone provided very generous support for this Fund in 2008. Germany's GTZ sponsored part of the research and publication costs of this current report, and the Ford Foundation funded the preparatory work.

On behalf of the CDRF, I would like to take this opportunity to express my heartfelt gratitude to all members of the research team and to other entities and persons who contributed to this report's successful completion.

Lu Mai
Secretary-General of China Development Research Foundation
February 20, 2009

Executive summary

Setting up a social welfare system that fits the context of China and its stage of development is key to ensuring the fairness of our socioeconomic development. It is also vital if we want to take a scientific approach to economic development. Since the 16th National Congress of the Chinese Communist Party, the Chinese government has increased its overall investment in social welfare systems, and its call for more creative approaches has led to significant progress. In order to improve our institutions and build a well-regulated and sustainable social welfare system for all, CDRF set up a research team to work on this topic. The research findings and policy recommendations of the resulting report, *China Development Report 2008/09: Constructing a Developmental Social Welfare System for All* are summarized below.

1. Definition of 'developmental social welfare system', and purpose of this report

Aimed at China as it will be in 2020, this report introduces a new concept in social welfare systems. It incorporates two main innovations. First, it emphasizes universal access to the system. Second, it highlights the 'development-oriented' features of the system.

'Universal access' is one of the most significant manifestations of 'fairness' or 'equity' in the social welfare system envisioned for China in the future. The most prominent feature of the system is full coverage of 1.3 billion Chinese people, including in particular the vast number of rural residents. 'Full coverage' incorporates three layers of significant changes. First, it requires formulating new rules and regulations for social groups that are not yet covered by any social security system. For example, this includes pension insurance systems for farmers and rural migrant workers, and old-age security and basic medical services for the unemployed urban elderly. Second, it requires expanding the coverage of existing institutional arrangements so that more social groups can benefit. These include urban and rural employees of small and medium-size enterprises, and people who are partially or 'flexibly' employed and self-employed. This means eliminating various barriers that currently prevent these people from being covered by the social security system, and it means lowering contribution rates as necessary to adapt to their financial capacity. Third, it requires gradually improving the standard of social welfare and improving its degree of fairness, so that all citizens can maintain a normal life and enjoy adequate public services. In doing these three things, it will be necessary to set up mechanisms that allow adjustments in the level of social welfare provided, depending onto the degree of inflation and on changes in people's income and government revenues. The objective is to ensure that all people across the country share in the benefits of socioeconomic development.

'Development-oriented' implies that the system is human-oriented, that it is China-specific and gradual in execution, and that it is strategic in its objectives. First, it emphasizes the need to put people at the center of the new welfare system, and to stress and promote the notion of 'comprehensive development' of the people. This implies including 'upstream' intervention in the system, such as the development of health, education, and employment assistance. Second, the term implies opting for a process of gradual development, rather than precipitously trying to accomplish everything at once, and also rather than simply transposing or copying the models and methods of western welfare states. We must realistically take into account our government funding capacity at different stages of the process, our demographic structures, income levels, degree of marketization, differences in regional development, our duality between treatment of urban and rural residents, level of urbanization, labor mobility, diversifying employment and the traditional Confucian aspects of our culture. In opting for 'gradual development', we must make sure that the system matches the different stages of China's socioeconomic development. Third, our social welfare policy should be formulated with an eye to mid- and long-term development, that is, it should have a strategic perspective. We must strengthen the 'social investment' capacities of our system and gradually transform a model that emphasized 'compensation' into one that emphasizes the mutual reinforcement of economic development and social welfare.

2. Basic principles of the developmental social welfare system

Basic principles underlying the policies advocated in this report include the following.

a. A firm resolve to make sure that fairness or 'equity' is tied to 'efficiency', with 'equity' as the primary consideration. The main goals of the system include: enabling all citizens to enjoy social welfare, reducing the polarization that has occurred in the process of industrialization, and promoting social equity and stability. Universal access to social welfare should be realized. The system aims gradually to eliminate inequalities related to the household registration, gender, occupation, status and other forms of 'identity' discrimination. In particular, children from poor families should be provided with equal access to education and other developmental opportunities in order to prevent ongoing perpetuation of poverty from generation to generation. While emphasizing 'equity', the system also takes into consideration 'efficiencies', and the ability to maintain dynamic economic development, so that it can assure sustainable economic growth in the long run.

b. A firm resolve to assure the sustainability of the system by making sure it is geared to our ongoing stages of economic development and our country's financing capacity. In setting up a sound national welfare system, our first task is to address problems arising from starting the entire system 'from scratch'. From initial steps, we have to extend coverage from a very limited section of the population to a broader section and then indeed to the whole population, as we also progressively raise the level of benefits. On the one hand, we deal with the most pressing needs, but on the other hand, we look to the long-term sustainability of the system in terms of benefit levels and the ability to pay for them. Since China's social welfare system is still in its initial stages and its institutions and mechanisms are immature, we need to look at long-term trends as we plan for their sustainability: urbanization, an aging population, the need to balance social security expenses and financing.

c. A firm resolve to give priority to employment. Employment is the most important social security. Population and employment have always been the two most fundamental problems facing China's economic and social development. Whether for individuals or families, employment is the most reliable method of preventing poverty and eliminating dependency on the government. This is why it is included as a fundamental principle in our social welfare policies. We start with the intent to expand basic education and vocational training, particularly for the new generation of 'rural migrant workers'. We focus on efforts to improve their employability and entrepreneurship, to help them actively look for and create jobs and integrate with society. The government should significantly increase the number of available jobs, in part by encouraging workers to start their own businesses. In order to prevent benefits from becoming an excessive burden on enterprises, so that they have the counter-effect of reducing jobs, we should avoid 'excessive security'.

d. A firm resolve to have civil society complement government efforts, while the government takes the lead. Fundamentally, social welfare is the duty of the government. Therefore the government must actively pursue legislation, increase public finance capacity and provide public services. At the same time, the market should play a role too, bringing into play market-based incentives. The resources of social organizations [civil society organizations] and various initiatives should be mobilized and put to building the social welfare system. When designing the system, both contribution-based social insurance and free welfare items are important; the system should include mechanisms by which government, organizations and individuals all bear a degree of responsibility. The system should strengthen the direct links between benefits paid out and contributions paid in. Organizations and individuals should be encouraged to take part in social security programs in an uninterrupted fashion, so that the government and society at large do not have to assume the risk of unethical behavior, and step in and cover for them when they evade obligations. The system should also allow traditional modes of providing social security to continue to play a role, such as community-based mutual assistance, assistance from charitable organizations, and help from families.

3. Development phases and objectives

The building of a system of universal-access, developmental social welfare can be divided into the following two main stages. Stage One, from 2009 to 2012, sets up the institutional framework. Stage Two, from 2013 to 2020, gives shape to the entire system.

The objective for 2012 is to set up the beginnings of a welfare system that provides full coverage. Specifically, it aims at the following six considerations. First, gender-based discrimination of children at an age to enter school should essentially be eliminated. Tuition and fees of nine years of compulsory education in urban and rural schools should be completely waived, as well as tuition and fees for special education. Rural students should receive their textbooks for free, and free nutritious meals should be provided for boarding students in poor areas of central and western China. Pre-school education should be extended to cover all urban children and those in more developed rural areas. One year of free pre-school education should be made available to children from poor rural areas, as well as low-income families in urban and rural areas. In the case of children from poverty-stricken areas and those from low-income families, if they do not continue post-middle school studies, then one year of free vocational education should be made available. All students who are at a poverty level and still going to senior high school should pay reduced tuition. Second, by 2012, a basic system with full coverage for the elderly will be established. Called 'the elderly are provided for', it will be a universally accessible differentiated pension insurance system that covers farmers, migrant workers, and urban residents. At the same time, a pension insurance system for migrant workers will be established that is based on social pooling of funds at the national level. Basic pension insurance for agriculture workers will be subsidized by the Central government. Moreover, an 'insurance fund plan for the elderly' will be established for seniors who currently have no protection, and will be supported by State public funds. Third, the system will vigorously implement proactive policies with respect to employment, and will increase vocational training and job placement services. It will begin to explore ways in which the training of unemployed people can be organically linked to receipt of social welfare benefits. In this Stage One, unemployment insurance should cover all urban workers, and extension to full coverage of rural workers should begin. Fourth, Stage One will strive to have 90 percent of the population covered by basic medical insurance, including coverage for urban employees, the new rural cooperative medical system, and urban residents. It will basically resolve the problem of gaps in coverage of the floating [or transient] population, as different regions are linked together in social pooling systems. Fifth, the system will raise the minimum levels of coverage that guarantee a basic standard of living and will make all attempts to expand that level of coverage. It will increase the percentage of Central budgetary funds that are allocated for minimum living standards. Beneficiaries of the 'basic living allowances' will be provided with emergency assistance as required in terms of basic medical care, education and housing. Marginalized groups will be a focus of the system. Basic public services and social welfare will be delivered to such specific groups as children, seniors, those that are disabled and women. Sixth, with respect to the 'housing assurance system' for both urban and rural residents: the system will aim to increase the supply of low-rent housing, so that around 50 percent of urban low-income households and around 10 percent of the households of 'transient population' migrant workers have the assurance of low-rent housing. Construction subsidies will be provided for 2.6 million rural households that face difficulties in building a home.

The main objective for 2020 in the building of our system is to assure 'fairness' or 'equal access'—to rights and benefits, a decent and normal life, and to appropriate public services. By 2020, the system aims to provide similar benefits in both urban and rural areas. The following six aspects are included in this second stage of the plan. First, compulsory education will implement the '1+9+1' model, i.e. one year of free pre-school education for all school-age children prior to the nine-year compulsory education and one year of free vocational training for middle school graduates who will not continue their studies. In addition, children from rural and urban low-income families will enjoy free senior high-school education. Second, the basic 'elderly are provided for' will be further improved. By 2020, all urban and rural workers should be able to take part in social insurance plans, contributing at affordable rates and receiving proper social insurance benefits for situations that include old-age, illness, unemployment and work injuries. Seniors with no protection will have access to appropriate subsidies for the elderly. Third, basic medical insurance for urban workers, medical insurance for urban residents and the new rural cooperative medical system should be able to achieve full coverage of the population, while standards of medical protection [insurance] will be constantly improved. Fourth, allowances for basic living standards and medical services will be provided to non-workers and people with low-income or no income, and the standard will be substantially improved. Fifth, training and employment assistance will be provided to all unemployed people and those distressed groups that are unable to find jobs. Mechanisms for promoting employment over the long run will be set up. Sixth, basic housing guarantees will be provided to all urban low-income groups, as well as the 30 percent of the transient population of migrant workers who have lived in urban areas for a long time but been unable to afford any housing. 'Assisted housing guarantees' will be provided to those people in the middle- and low-income brackets with housing difficulties. In addition, another 5.2 million rural low-income households that have no funds to build their own dwellings will gain access to construction subsidies.

4. Major policy recommendations

a. 'The elderly are provided for.' We should establish a basic pension insurance system that covers both urban and rural areas and that combines social pooling with individual accounts. Old-age benefits for farmers in rural areas should be financed through public funding, while the individual accounts should be funded by individual contributions, collective subsidies and government grants. The employers' contribution for basic pension insurance of rural migrant workers should be set at 6 percent. The collecting of, management over, and delivery of these funds should be carried out at the national level, together with unified planning. Funds of individual accounts should be paid into by both employers and individuals; they should be managed as actual accounts and should follow the individual ['be portable'] as he changes jobs, and they should be 'owned by' the individual. The administrative level at which old-age pensions are managed in urban areas should upgraded as soon as possible, so that the pooling of individual accounts is handled at the provincial level and the pooling of basic pension insurance is handled at the national level. In order to expedite full coverage of basic pension insurance in both urban and rural areas, the first thing to do is substantially lower contribution rates so that more people can afford the coverage. Lowering contribution rates could start with the self-employed and 'flexibly employed' workers, and go from the current 20 percent to 14 percent; rates for other social groups can be lowered in due course. Second, the government should raise its public-finance contribution significantly, so that the participation rate of migrant workers can reach 50 percent or more by 2010 and then achieve full participation by 2012. As for urban and rural seniors over 65 who neither have a job nor any protection, we should set up a subsidy system for the elderly that is financed out of the State budget. Standards for subsidies should be slightly higher than the minimum living allowance. A long-term care guarantee for the elderly should be explored, and we should actively institute a socialized system of care for the elderly.

b. 'The sick are cared for.' We should vigorously expand coverage of the medical security system. By 2012, we should assure that coverage of the system incorporates 90 percent or more of the population and includes basic medical insurance for urban employees, basic medical insurance for urban residents, and the new rural coopera-tive medical system for rural inhabitants. We should basically have resolved the problem of making sure rural migrant workers are covered as they move from one pooling area to another—they should receive benefits since the pooling systems should be linked with each other, and they should have equal access to basic benefits as mandated by regulations. The government should increase its management of and investment into the health services system at the grassroots level, so as to attract more insured people seeking treatment at grassroots-level hospitals. In addition to attempting to improve medical-services delivery, the government should increase the actual amount as well as the percentage of its contribution, in order to lower the burden on individuals. An emergency assistance system should be set up on a comprehensive basis in both urban and rural areas, and its level of care should be improved. We should resolve the problem of managing socialized medical insur-ance for retirees. We should gradually advance three main overall plans: those for urban and rural areas, those for regional and municipal levels of government, and those at the level of clinics. We should explore setting up community clinics for first-time visits, and two-way referral for medical services. We should set up a system whereby medical insurance administrators are involved in the pricing process and we should explore consultation mechanisms between suppliers and consumers for establishing prices. We should explore different methods of payment that involve prepayment of the total amount, and payment depending on type of disease. We should facilitate the ability of the Central budget to make inter-regional transfer payments for healthcare purposes.

c. 'Those who would learn, [?] receive schooling.' The plan recommends extending basic education, so that the one year of preschool education and one year of free vocational training after completion of middle school are integrated into 'compulsory education'. We should gradually expand the objective so that '1+9+1' extended compulsory education is possible. Proactive measures that need to be taken include the following. Increasing public expenditures on education and raising the ratio of publicly-funded education budgets in total GDP to 4 percent by 2012 and to over 4.5 percent by 2020. Assure that budgetary ['public finance'] disbursals of funds for compulsory education account for around 95 percent of total compulsory education expenditures. In addition, ensure that regions receive equal treatment in allocation of funds. The plan recommends that free nutritious meals be provided to boarding students in poverty-stricken areas in central and western China. We should increase training for those rural migrant workers who are already employed, and improve its quality. In addition to increasing public investment in education, we should improve the quality of compulsory education, so as to reduce disparities in the education provided to rural and urban areas as soon as possible.

d. 'Those who work are paid.' We should increase the amount of public funding on policies to do with the active labor market. Proactive assistance should be extended to the most distressed groups, to encourage them to stay on in the labor market. We should avoid having them become dependent purely on welfare. We should vigorously expand full coverage for unemployment insurance. The delivery of unemployment benefits should be tied in more tightly to employment in public-service positions, to training programs, and to re-employment mechanisms. Our unemployment security system should actively explore ways to meet the needs of the flexibly employed, of migrant workers, and of employees from township enterprises in rural areas. Contribution and benefit levels for these sectors of the population should be correctly distinguished from those of overall unemployment insurance system. We should strengthen the building of labor markets, and break down the policy differentiation between urban labor and rural labor markets. We should improve all systems that enhance labor market services, including job placement, vocational training, occupational mobility and creation of jobs, in order to accelerate the overall integration of labor market.

e. 'Citizens [residents] are housed.' For low-income people in cities, low-rent housing should be considered the main solution to housing security. We will have to be more innovative in our approach to methods of providing low-rent housing. By 2020, we should have been able to provide housing security for all those low-income urban families, meeting the required conditions, who applied for housing subsidies. We should also explore other means of providing housing security, such as economically affordable housing, low-cost housing, relief of tax and fees and so on, so that those in the middle- and low-income brackets with housing difficulties will basically be covered.

Finding all ways and means to expand low-cost housing is the main concept behind 'providing housing for rural migrant workers'. This is particularly aimed at such people who have lived in cities for a long time already but are unable to afford housing. As for migrant workers with higher income, we should also consider subsidies on economically affordable housing. By 2020, we should basically have resolved the housing problems of migrant workers who are long-term urban residents. All levels of government should earmark more funds in their budgets for low-income housing. Every year from now until 2020, we should on average provide subsidies to assist in building homes for 650,000 rural low-income households. The government has the responsibility to moderate prices in the commercial housing market. Measures should be taken to bring real estate prices back to a level that ordinary wage-earners can afford.

f. 'The poor receive assistance.' The core philosophy aimed at improving the minimum-living standards for the poorest segments of our population is 'coverage for those in need'. Major policy recommendations include: allocating more of the fiscal budget and increasing financial support for minimum living-standard guarantees, to the extent that we double the figure provided in 2007, and redouble it again by 2020. We must improve social assistance for a number of targeted groups, including 80 million disabled, 100 million elderly, 240 million children and the half of the population that is represented by women. In particular, more funds should be spent on employment subsidies, children's nutrition, rehabilitation for the disabled, and protection of the rights and interests of women, children and the elderly. The positive role of social charitable donations, as well as revenue from social welfare lotteries and revenue from welfare enterprises should be brought into full play. We need constant improvement in a new social welfare system that 'exists through public participation and is enjoyed by all'.

5. The financial feasibility of creating a universal-access, developmental, social welfare system

Setting up the system envisioned in this document within the next 12 years will be an unprecedented accomplishment. Certainly, it will be a huge and historic change in the fabric of China's social and economic systems, and it may represent the first time such a thing has been done in the history of mankind as well. Structuring and improving upon this system will have the added benefits of improving our economic structure, which currently features high savings, strong exports, low consumption and weak domestic demand. However, 'there is no such thing as a free lunch'. Resolving so many issues in such a short time is going to require massive investments from the government as well as from society at large.

One of the most important contributions of this report is its systematic calculation of how much in the way of total government spending will be necessary to establish the envisioned system in the next 12 years. At the same time, this report undertakes a systematic analysis of how much money might be available. This report looks at the specific underlying economic conditions that will enable such a system to achieve full coverage. We have based our estimations on constant prices of the year 2007. To enable the accomplishment of all items in the new system, as proposed in this report, government spending will have to increase substantially every year, as follows. RMB 2.6 trillion will need to be earmarked in the fiscal budget of 2012, and RMB 5.7 trillion in the budget for 2020. Our calculations indicate that if GDP maintains an average annual increase of 8 percent, and the percentage of fiscal revenues to GDP remains at around 21 percent during the period in which we are adjusting to the financial crisis, i.e. from 2007 to 2011, and then gradually increases to about 26 percent in the years thereafter and continuing steady, if, at the same time, the percentage of fiscal revenues dedicated to welfare expenditures increases from the current 27 percent to 33 percent, at a pace of 1.2 percent annually from 2009 to 2012, then growing to 35 percent and remaining stable after that, we will indeed be able to afford the proposed system in terms of government outlays.

However, if government revenues do not increase, as described above, but stay at the level of 21 percent of GDP, and if the percentage of public monies devoted to welfare does not increase, as described above, but stays at a level of 27 percent, then we will not in fact be able to afford this program. Therefore, in the next 12 years, the percentage of GDP dedicated to welfare expenditures must go from the present 6 percent or so to over 9 percent, over the next 12 years. Lately, in response to the international financial turmoil, the government has introduced a series of policies intended to expand domestic demand. The economic stimulus plan of RMB 4 trillion focuses heavily on increasing investments in spheres related to people's livelihood. This greatly improves the feasibility of early implementation of many welfare measures. We should take advantage of this serendipitous 'eastern wind' and try to solve as many long-standing problems as we can with one fell swoop.

To a degree, our calculations have also revealed the necessity of maintaining an average economic growth rate of 8 percent. If the rate falls below 8 percent, then we will have to make fairly considerable adjustments in our estimates of the percentage of GDP that will have to be spent on this program. It will also require adjustments in the structure of our fiscal spending, and further reform of our system of public finance.

From another perspective, the calculations as put forth in this report sound a warning note, namely, that we should not place too high expectations on social welfare. Our national financial resources can only support a basic, low-level of welfare coverage. For quite some time, other than compulsory education, most welfare items that are provided without payment will focus on low-income sectors and certain specific groups. For people living in both urban and rural areas who earn an average income, and even more for those people who earn an above-average income, the main result of this program will be contribution-based social insurance. Therefore, contribution-based welfare arrangements of different types should still be considered the core of our welfare system.

1 Introduction

This report focuses on building a 'universal-access, developmental, social welfare system'. The term 'welfare' signifies the conditions conducive to improving quality of life and the feeling of happiness, including both material wealth that improves people's physical well-being, and factors affecting their free intellectual and mental development. The term 'social welfare' refers to the social institutions under which the government seeks to provide citizens with funds and services to ensure a certain standard of living and the best possible improvement in quality of life. The term 'social welfare' has a broadly defined and a narrowly defined meaning. In a broad sense it means the various policies and social services designed to provide a better life for all citizens. In a narrow sense it refers to provisions that the government makes for vulnerable groups. This book addresses social welfare in the broader sense. It treats 'social welfare systems' as a combination of all the institutional arrangements relating to social welfare policies and services that are available to members of a society.

The proposed new social welfare system is intended to serve each and every Chinese citizen, including inhabitants in rural areas and rural migrant workers. It is intended to cover pensions, medical care, education, employment, housing and the minimum living allowance. The system is termed 'developmental' since it is intended to move forward incrementally and be increasingly human-oriented. It brings 'upstream interventions' into the sphere of welfare, including expanding education, promoting good health, and assistance in finding employment. It calls for making greater use of public funds in the specific arena of human capital. In so doing it replaces the traditional compensation-oriented welfare system with one that benefits from, and in turn fuels, economic growth.

China has already entered a new stage of development. The 30-year period of 'reform and opening-up' has brought massive change to China's economy, the Chinese people and their way of life, and it has greatly strengthened the material basis for our strategic policy of harmonious development (Wang Mengkui, 2006[1]). Acknowledging the achievements, however, does not mean that we can neglect the acute social problems and challenges that exist. China has also entered a period of multiplying contradictions. How to address social conflicts in a proper manner and maintain the harmonious development of society has become a major concern of our social welfare system.

Four major challenges face our economic development. First, our demographic trends are going to have a severe impact upon the development of a harmonious society. The base quantity of our population is very large, we have a huge number of inadequately educated people, and an ageing society that is not yet well-off. All of these multiply social and economic problems and place enormous pressures on the social welfare system. The problems include how to handle employment, pensions and medical care. Second, with growing industrialization, urbanization and market-oriented trends, people's mobility has greatly increased, both in terms of moving between rural and urban areas and among various industries and occupations. The migration of rural workers into cities has brought severe challenges to our traditional social welfare system which continues to apply a 'dual treatment' to urban and rural people in terms of its distribution of public finance and public services. Third, in the course of transitioning from one system to another, our income distribution system is less than perfect and has resulted in widening income disparities. The rural poor are urgently in need of social welfare. Fourth, globalization has brought its own risks. China has become a major player in international trade and therefore is more and more reliant on global markets. Economic crises in other countries and turbulence in the global financial markets have both direct and indirect impacts on our domestic economic growth and the stability of our employment. They impose a very definite negative impact on the lives of Chinese people.

Traditionally, Chinese people believe that the respect one has for the elderly in one's own family should extend to respect for elderly in other people's families, and that love of one's own children should extend to love for children of others as well (*Mencius*). According to Confucius (*The Book of Rites – The Conveyance of Rites*), 'One does not love one's own parents only, nor only one's own sons. [We] enable the aged to age, the strong to use their strength, the youth to mature, and we provide for widows, orphans, those who are alone, and the crippled.' These beliefs are very close to the mission of today's social welfare system.[2]

Over the course of centuries, various social welfare systems have been developed in the western world, starting with the *Elizabethan Poor Law* in England. In recent decades, the interaction between systems has begun to result in certain convergences, while at the same time there are diverging trends. On the one hand such basic principles as universal coverage, equity [fairness] and sustainability are globally accepted. On the other hand, more and more people believe that the social welfare system in a country must be in alignment with its stage of social development and basic values.

The goal in building this 'universal-access developmental social welfare system' is to go further in improving the fair distribution of the outcomes of China's economic development, and to enhance the sustainability of that development. It is to build a 'moderately prosperous society' in a comprehensive sense. The requirements of our situation dictate that we adopt a system that can adapt to our fast-growing economy and its consequent social changes.

This report envisions that, with hard work over the next 12 years, by the year 2020 we will have built a welfare system that meets the needs of our country and serves its citizens. That system will include expanded free compulsory education, pensions and basic medical care programs for all citizens, affordable housing and minimum living allowances for all low-income families in urban and rural areas as well as certain rural migrant workers, and employment assistance and unemployment insurance for all workers. This social welfare system is an important institutional guarantee for the comprehensive and coordinated development of China's economy and society.

In view of the global financial crisis that has affected our country's economy, accelerating the improvement of the social welfare system is of particular significance. In order to deal with the consequences of the crisis, China's government has recently passed a series of policies to encourage domestic demand. We should recognize that these policies pave the way for starting many welfare measures in advance of their earlier timetables. Furthermore, the benefits these policies deliver will depend, to a large extent, on improving our social welfare system. Therefore, we are facing an opportune time to enhance our social welfare system. This will not only help ease people's worries about their jobs, and encourage greater consumption, but the process of implementing the system will in itself serve to stimulate domestic demand. It will bring about a great number of investment and employment opportunities. Priority should therefore be placed on this system as the best way to improve people's lives.

China's socioeconomic development: reflections on how things were

Profound changes in social and economic structures

Thirty years of economic reform in China have spurred rapid economic growth and brought about tremendous changes in the economic structure. The contribution of primary industries to GDP dropped sharply from 28 percent in 1978 to 11.3 percent in 2007, while the contribution of the tertiary industries gradually rose, from 23.9 percent to 40.1 percent during the same period.[3] Changes in industrial structure were mimicked by those in employment structure—the period saw a constant decline in the percentage of primary-industry employees and a steady increase in the percentage of tertiary-industry employees. Between 1978 and 2007, primary-industry employment as a percentage of the total declined by nearly 30 percent, while the secondary and tertiary industries both showed an increase. Tertiary industries in particular reported an increase of nearly 20 percent (see Figure 1.1). However, compared to industrial structure in GDP, the structure of employment still needs improvement, since the percentage of people working in the primary industry is still higher than that industry's contribution to GDP. This signifies that adjustments in employment structure will continue in coming years, and the number and percentage of people engaged in the primary industry will further decrease.

One effect of changes in employment structure is the migration of people and mobility of the labor force, moving from rural areas to urban areas and among different regions. The result has been a radical increase in the urban population in China. This population increase in cities is a positive part of the urbanization process, but it also places public services in cities under tremendous pressure.

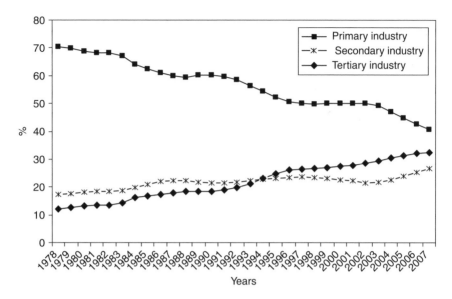

Figure 1.1 Percentages of people working in different industries in China, 1978–2007.

Source: National Bureau of Statistics of China (2008) *China Statistical Abstract 2008*. Beijing: China Statistics Press, p. 44.

Between 1985 and 2007 the number of Chinese living in urban areas increased by over 20 percent (see Figure 1.2). It should be noted that a large number of the urban population are rural migrants who have come to cities since the implementation of reform and opening-up policies, yet the large majority of these people have not received an urban 'residency card', i.e. officially become urban residents. We estimate that nearly 200 million rural laborers work in a place other than their hometown. This includes 130 million who are rural–urban migrants working in cities. Two trends have recently been observed with regard to rural migrant workers. One is that a large percentage of these people work all year round at a place other than their original home, and are thereby completely divorced from farming. The other is that a significant number of these people are moving to urban areas together with their families to engage in non-farming activities. More and more 'migrant' rural workers have changed from being peasant-workers who split their time between farming and non-farming jobs to full-time non-agricultural workers. Their employment versatility has weakened as a result. A *permanent* migration has gradually replaced a *seasonal* migration. The two-way flow between urban and urban areas has changed as more and more rural workers are integrating into urban environments by settling down in towns and cities.[4]

China's family structures are also undergoing enormous change, characterized most importantly by the decreasing size of the family in both urban and rural areas. In 2006 the average family size in China was 3.17 persons, down from

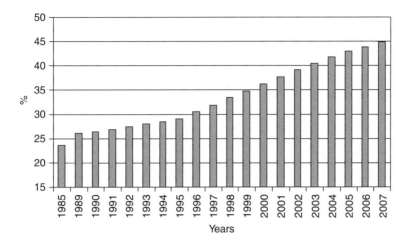

Figure 1.2 China's urbanization process (the urban population as a percentage of the national total).

Source: National Bureau of Statistics of China (2008) *China Statistical Abstract 2008*. Beijing: China Statistics Press, p. 39.

4.81 in 1973. In Beijing the number in 2006 was 2.64 and in Shanghai it was 2.65. The average family size in China comes close to that in developed countries such as the United States and Canada, where a family has around three members on average.[5] As family structure changes, more and more 'empty nests' appear in which elderly parents are living alone after their children leave home. When an older person is widowed the situation can be even worse. In rural areas the elderly were once supported by family members, while now they are not. Once the elderly are unable to work they face the very real risk of poverty, with absolutely no means to sustain their lives (Tang Can, 2006).

Success and lessons learned in China's social development

China is widely recognized for its successes in social development. One of its outstanding achievements is that, as a low-income country, it has realized the social development goals of many medium-income countries. With regard to some indexes of social development, China's performance has exceeded that of medium-income countries and is close to that of a developed country.

However, today's China also exhibits an increasing polarization of society, manifested particularly in continuously expanding income disparities. As shown in Figures 1.3 and 1.4 the Gini coefficient measuring rural residents' income disparity increased from 0.24 in 1979 to 0.38 in 2005. At the same time, urban residents' income gap increased as well. The Gini coefficient rose from 0.16 in 1979 to 0.35 in 2005. Long-term and continuous data about nationwide income disparities are not yet available, but based on the data of given years, a similar tendency is occurring

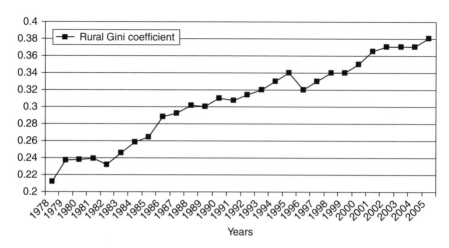

Figure 1.3 Chinese rural residents' income gap as measured in Gini coefficient, 1978–2005.
Source: Li Shi (2008).

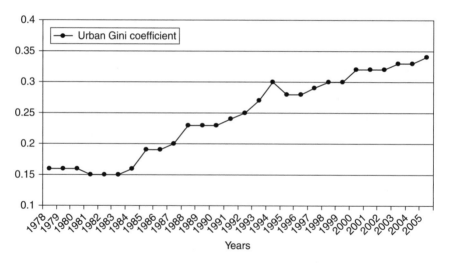

Figure 1.4 Chinese urban residents' income gap as measured in Gini coefficient, 1978–2005.
Source: Li Shi (2008).

nationwide. Still using Gini coefficient as the measurement, the national income gap was 0.3 in 1978 and rose to 0.45 in 2002. As shown by a recent survey, the national Gini coefficient reached 0.48 in 2007 (Li Shi, 2008). It is noteworthy that the planned economy and the egalitarian distribution system in the late 1970s kept the

Gini coefficient at a low level, which does not mean income distribution was rational or reasonable. One of the core tasks of our subsequent economic reform was to change this extreme egalitarian thinking, which has inevitably resulted in widened income gaps. It is now widely agreed that the current disparities are too large, to the extent that they are causing a whole host of social problems.

Social development in China lags somewhat behind economic growth. First, although China has made great achievements in eliminating absolute poverty, relative poverty in both rural and urban areas is yet to be fully addressed. The rural poor constitute a tremendous problem, according to all international measures of poverty. As estimated by the World Bank, about 80 million rural residents in China live below the one-dollar-a-day poverty line in 2006, three times the number of people in absolute poverty that are publicized by the government. Many wealthy countries apply the poverty line of 2 dollars per day. If we use this benchmark, the number of poor reaches 200 million in rural China, and 30 million in urban areas. Second, China has more disabled people than in any other country. In 2006 the number of disabled people reached 82.96 million—6.34 percent of the country's population.[6] People with disabilities lead better lives today and are better covered by social welfare provisions but, as a vulnerable group, they have their own physiological and psychological needs, many of which are still unmet. Third, the number of rural migrant workers and other migrant populations in cities is rising to unprecedented levels. These people live in cities and to some extent benefit from economic growth. However, the discriminatory 'resident registration system' prevents them from fully enjoying urban public services. Finally, although rural people as a whole have seen their income increase year by year, most are not included in the basic social security system, other than free compulsory education, inadequate rural cooperative medical care and the minimum living allowance. Due to the inadequate public services available to a rural situation that is relatively less advanced, farmers' requirements for social development are far from being met.

China's social welfare system: challenges and progress

The progress of the social welfare system in China

A social welfare system was introduced in China nearly 60 years ago, and has since gone through three main stages. The first started with the *Labor Assurance Regulation* issued by the government in the early 1950s; this ended only in the early 1990s. Under the planned-economy system the government took on 'unlimited responsibility' for all employees in the public sector. State-owned enterprise offered their employees low-level but complete benefits, for example, pensions, reimbursement of medical expenses, low-cost or free nurseries and kindergartens, cheap housing, winter heating allowance, family visit allowance, commuting allowance, and access to various culture and entertainment facilities, even sometimes sanatoriums. In addition the country provided low-cost and low-level medical care and education, and provided the elderly, young, sick and disabled with special assistance: for example, nursing homes, and orphanages. In contrast, the country offered very limited welfare to people in cities who had 'irregular' or non-state-owned-enterprise jobs, and either no or very limited welfare to people in the countryside. The elderly in rural areas were supported by family members and it was the responsibility of the rural collective to take care of five categories of 'protected people', called the *wu bao hu*.[7] To guarantee basic living standards in cities the government ensured that every urban household had the necessities of life by means of low and subsidized prices of goods and rationing systems. Given the prevailing socioeconomic conditions at the time, these welfare schemes helped stabilize society to some extent. However, the 'paternal' welfare system as adapted to the planned economy resulted in the dual problems of discrimination and egalitarianism. On the one hand, while the system benefited 'proper' employees, i.e. those employed in the public sector, a large number of informal or 'irregular' employees (particularly farmers, that is, rural residents) were discriminated against and denied equal benefits. On the other hand, this social welfare system applied an 'egalitarian' system to those it covered, the 'big pot of rice' system of distribution to all in equal measure, which easily led to the excessive reliance of individuals on the State. More importantly, this system was characterized by high costs and a low degree of coverage. Once the need for coverage expanded abruptly, the whole system ceased to be viable.

The second stage of our social welfare system started in the mid-1990s and lasted until 2003. As a response to the transition from a centrally planned economy to a market economy, and to the restructuring of state-owned enterprises, social welfare in this period was characterized by the reform known as 'One Center, Two Commitments, and Three Lines of Protection'. The so-called 'One Center' meant the service center for reemploying laid-off workers. In order to meet the policy of 'shucking off problems' in three years, and to implement strategic economic restructuring, the mid-sized and large state-owned enterprises began to streamline their workforces and 'reassign' redundant employees to increase efficiency. More than 30 million employees were laid off during this period as a result. The rational for the 'Center' was that, under a planned economy, a de facto *contractual* relationship existed among government, employers, and employees that ensured a lifelong job together with related pensions and medical benefits to employees. As part of its economic restructuring strategy, the government therefore set up the reemployment center to provide laid-off workers with the basic means of living, assist them with social security contributions and vocational training, and help match them to new jobs. The so-called 'Two Commitments' meant the government committed to pay basic subsistence allowances to laid-off workers and old-age pensions to retired workers. The 'Three Lines of Protection' were the basic subsistence allowance for laid-off workers, unemployment benefits, and the minimum living allowance for urban residents. Since 1998, reform of the social welfare system has picked up the pace, in order to meet the needs of a market economy. The priority in social development policy has become 'building a well-regulated social welfare system that is administered by specialized entities, independent from employers, and funded by diversified sources'. Through years of experimental efforts the basic framework for a social security system began to take shape that included pensions, medical care, unemployment, job-related injury and maternity insurance, and the minimum living allowance for urban residents. Its outstanding feature was that it transferred responsibility for welfare from the enterprise to society at large. It incorporated three main changes: enterprise-funded insurance now became social insurance; responsibilities previously shouldered by an enterprise alone now were shared among the government, the enterprise and employees; finally, employee retirement benefit programs were now administered by specialized agencies rather than the enterprise.

New problems cropped up during the transition period. Health care and educational institutions became market-oriented. Public services, particularly schooling and medical services, became more costly than ever before. Not surprisingly, with the market orientation of the real estate industry, the price of urban housing soared and became unaffordable for low-income households.

As a response to economic restructuring, the social welfare system during this period focused on reform, efficiency gains and individual responsibility. The system was redesigned to ease the burden on state-owned enterprise (through laying off redundant workers and streamlining the workforce), and to ease the burden on the government (by asking individual employees to contribute to their insurance plans as well). This conformed to international trends at the time in reforming social welfare systems. However, we must admit that the redesigned system put more priority on economic considerations than it put on social benefits. It attempted to reverse the excessive protectiveness of the old system, but failed to afford adequate protection to less advanced areas and to poor people. Three challenges arose in implementing the system. First of all, there was inadequate recognition of debts that had accumulated in enterprise budgets, and therefore 'individual accounts' in many insurance plans were often simply rendered empty. Second, institutional arrangements were not made to address the welfare needs of backward areas and poor people. Even as population rose, its coverage by social welfare shrank. Third, the Central government invested heavily in raising pensions with the intention of stimulating domestic demand. In some provinces, the pension replacement rate exceeded 100 percent with the average pension level becoming higher than the wage. This led to earlier retirement of employees, which placed more burdens on the social security fund. Most areas and cities began to face huge deficiencies in their pension funds.

The third stage started in 2003. The Chinese government announced what is known as 'people-oriented development', or taking the human being as the core focus in a more scientific approach to development. This signals a new era for China's social welfare system as we try to integrate it into all aspects of improving people's lives.

In 2003 the State Council issued a document entitled *Opinions on Setting Up a New Cooperative Healthcare System in Rural Areas,* to make health care services accessible and affordable for farmers. It specified that public finance was to pay four-fifths of the cost of rural medical insurance. In 2007, the State Council released *Guidelines on Experimenting with Urban Residents' Basic Medical*

Insurance, which planned to disseminate the new practices nationwide and cover any urban residents who were unemployed in three years. Departments under the State Council also released regulations on rural and urban medical assistance. In terms of the setup of the system, the 'Three Plus One' medical assurance programs[8] are now meant to cover both rural and urban inhabitants.

In 2007 pilot projects testing urban social security systems were expanded to 13 provinces and the practice of having provincial-level coordination of pension contributions was introduced in 17 provinces. It was successfully implemented in these 17 provinces in 2008. [Note: 'provinces' above includes those municipalities and districts that are designated as being at a provincial level of jurisdiction.] Social security is gradually being extended to rural migrant workers, and pension plans for rural inhabitants are being launched on a pilot basis in certain regions. In cities like Beijing or Shanghai a system of pension allowances is being implemented for older people without any income. In 2007 the State Council issued the *Minimum Living Allowance System in Rural Areas*, which expanded the coverage to farmers. In January 2009 pilot pension reform plans were formally announced for public institutions within the scope of five provinces and cities in the first phase.

In terms of compulsory education, in 2003, the State Council decided to accelerate the extension of compulsory education to the central and western rural regions. By this decision, school-age children in rural areas in poverty were entitled to a waiver on tuition fees and textbook expenses, and boarders were to receive an extra living subsidy. By 2007 this policy covered nearly all urban and rural students receiving compulsory education. All compulsory education costs are within various levels of governmental responsibility in terms of public funding.

In 2007 the State Council published a document entitled, *On Solving Housing Problems of Low-income Urban Families*. This proposes the creation of a low-rent housing system—it proposes improving the affordable housing system, improving the housing conditions of those in need, and building a multi-level housing support system. By the end of 2007 the Ministry of Construction, as well as eight other government departments, published *Rules on Guaranteeing Low-Rent Housing*. The Ministry of Finance issued *Regulations on Managing the Low-rent Housing Fund* which ensures stable funding sources and channels.

China's social welfare system has been built from scratch over the past 60 years and has experienced many ups and downs. It is now entering a new period of reform and development. More employees are now covered by improved social security plans as the urbanization has progressed. Pension insurance is one example. The number of insured urban employees (including rural migrant workers) increased from less than 49 million in 1989 to over 150 million in 2007 (see Figure 1.5), up an average of 6.6 percent per year. Over the same period unemployment insurance, basic health care programs and work-related injury insurance also made great progress as shown in Figure 1.6. In 1994 80 million employees participated in unemployment insurance. By 2007 this number had increased to nearly 120 million. In the same period the employees covered against work-related injuries increased

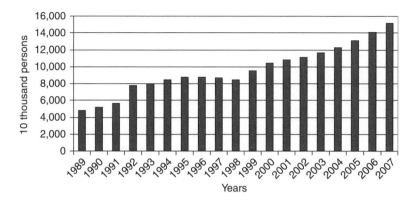

Figure 1.5 Number of Chinese urban employees participating in basic pension insurance program, 1989–2007.

Source: National Bureau of Statistics of China (2007) *China Statistical Yearbook 2007*. Beijing: China Statistics Press, p. 999.

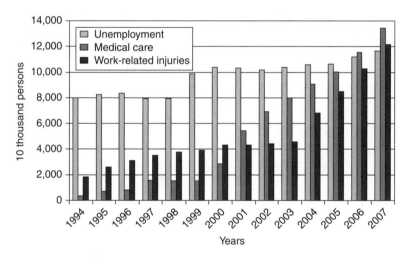

Figure 1.6 Number of urban employees participating in unemployment, medical care and work-related injury insurance programs, 1994–2007.

Source: National Bureau of Statistics of China (2007) *China Statistical Yearbook 2007*. Beijing: China Statistics Press, p. 999.

from less than 20 million to 120 million.[9] Note that the urban employees covered by social insurance programs also included a growing number of rural migrant workers. By 2007 18.46 million rural migrant workers participated in basic pension insurance, 31.31 million in medical insurance, 11.50 million in unemployment insurance, and 39.80 million in work-related injury insurance.[10]

The most noticeable advance in China's social welfare system is its new focus on universal coverage to benefit all citizens. From coverage of those officially employed in 'formal' work units, it is now being expanded to cover employees in informal sectors and those not working at all. The minimum living allowances in urban areas is one example. Beginning in 2001 the number of recipients of this allowance increased greatly. This was not because the numbers of poor increased dramatically but rather was due to increased government efforts to protect low-income people. By 2007 people benefiting from the allowance increased to 22.70 million, five times the figure in 2000 (see Figure 1.7). In recent years the speed at which coverage of rural residents has expanded in terms of minimum living allowances has far exceeded expectations. According to the latest statistics, as of May 2008 nearly 37 million rural residents were receiving the allowance,[11] well above the official figure for the number of rural residents living in absolute poverty.[12] Moreover, starting in 2008 basic medical insurance has expanded to cover those unemployed in urban areas, including school-age children, pre-school children, and older people with no official work experience. Meanwhile, all levels of government continued to expand their support for the new rural cooperative medical care program. It had been launched in 2,451 counties (districts and municipalities) by the end of 2007. A total of 730 million rural people, or 86.2 percent of the rural population, are covered.[13] Lastly, in some economically advanced regions (for example Beijing) pension insurance has been expanded to cover non-fee-paying urban residents. This means that older people who have no prior official working experience and have not contributed to pension funds are now entitled to basic pensions and benefits.

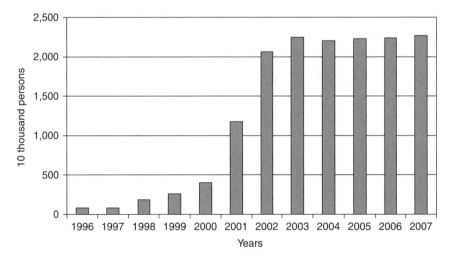

Figure 1.7 Number of urban residents receiving minimum living allowance, 1996–2007.

Source: Ministry of Civil Affairs *Statistical Communiqué of Civil Development* (for given years). Beijing: China Statistics Press.

Challenges facing the social welfare system

The social security system in China is not adequately developed to meet the demands of social and economic progress. First of all, coverage of social security is still extremely limited. As mentioned above eligibility for pension benefits was previously restricted to those urban residents employed in official sectors [recognized 'enterprises' or 'units'], while those working in informal sectors, rural migrant workers engaged in activities other than farming, and farmers themselves, were all excluded from the social security system. As shown in Figure 1.8, although the percentage of urban employees participating in basic endowment insurance is slowly increasing, it is still at a low level in absolute terms. In 2007 the percentage of participants was just over one half of all urban employees, which indicates that a large number of employees in informal sectors, including rural migrant workers, and the majority of rural laborers, are excluded.[14] As in the case of pension insurance, coverage of other social security programs is also quite limited. As shown in Figure 1.9, even in 2007 less than half of all urban employees participated in basic medical care (46 percent), unemployment (40 percent), and work-related injury (41 percent) insurance programs.

According to an urban residents' survey, taken in 2007, the percentage of urban employees enrolled in various social security programs varies greatly depending on the industry and the ownership of the employer. As shown in Table 1.1, a high percentage of employees of state-owned enterprise participated in social security programs, while a very low percentage of the self-employed and employees in private businesses. Pension insurance is one example. Nearly four times as many

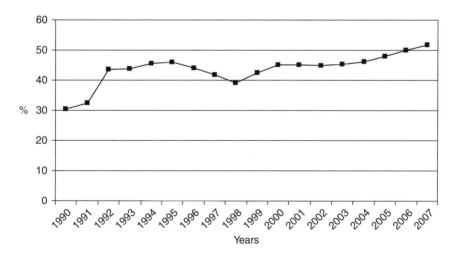

Figure 1.8 Percentage of urban employees covered by basic endowment insurance, 1990–2007.

Source: National Bureau of Statistics of China (2007) *China Statistical Yearbook 2007*; National Bureau of Statistics of China (2008) *China Statistical Abstract 2008*; and Ministry of Civil Affairs *Statistical Communiqué of Civil Development.* Beijing: China Statistics Press.

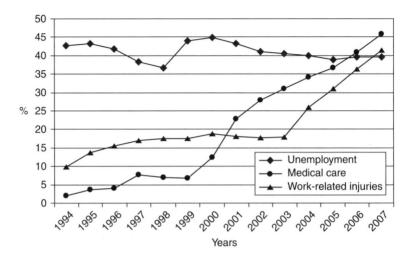

Figure 1.9 Percentage of Chinese urban employees covered by social insurance, 1994–2007.

Source: National Bureau of Statistics of China (2007) *China Statistical Yearbook 2007*; National Bureau of Statistics of China (2008) *China Statistical Abstract 2008*; and Ministry of Civil Affairs *Statistical Communiqué of Civil Development*. Beijing: China Statistics Press.

Table 1.1 Urban employees' social security program participation rate in 2007, by ownership of employer

Ownership of employer	Endowment insurance program participation rate	Medical insurance program participation rate	Unemployment insurance program participation rate
state-owned	83.8	79.7	72.9
Collectively-owned	65.0	53.1	42.6
Other types of economy	69.3	56.4	43.1
Self-employed or privately-owned	23.8	19.1	9.4
Other employees	40.3	36.9	24.0
Total	66.5	60.5	51.6

Source: A 2007 sample survey among urban households in 15 provinces.

state-owned enterprise employee participants have such insurance. With regard to unemployment insurance, the number could be up to eight times as many.

Table 1.2 lists by sector the percentage of urban employees participating in social security programs. It is easy to see that a high participation rate can be found in the government-agency and public institution sector. For example, a participation rate of over 90 percent is found in public administration and social organization, education

Table 1.2 Urban employees' social security program participation rate in 2007, by sector

Sector	Endowment insurance program participation rate	Medical insurance program participation rate	Unemployment insurance program participation rate
Agriculture, forestry, animal husbandry, fishing	37.4	59.9	37.4
Mining	70.7	60.4	54.9
Manufacturing	69.2	56.0	47.7
Production and supply of power, gas and water	76.4	62.6	42.9
Construction	53.2	41.4	34.6
Transportation, warehousing and postal service	63.0	56.1	42.1
Information transfer and computer service	55.5	46.4	33.4
Retail and wholesale	37.3	29.9	18.9
Lodging and catering	39.2	32.2	20.6
Financial	68.8	57.5	42.3
Real estate	55.8	49.7	31.3
Rental and business service	48.0	42.5	27.6
Scientific research, technological services and geological survey	93.8	95.5	93.5
Hydrology, environment and public facilities	54.0	61.4	46.6
Residential services and others	39.4	33.1	19.3
Education	94.5	95.0	93.6
Health, social security and social welfare	92.7	92.1	90.4
Culture, sports and entertainment	79.7	80.0	75.0
Public administration and social organization	96.0	96.4	95.0
Total	66.5	60.5	51.6

Source: A 2007 sample survey among urban households in 15 provinces.

and health as well as social security and social welfare sectors. In informal labor-intensive sectors, such as wholesale, retail, lodging and catering, a lower participation rate is found. This means that urban social security programs should expand their coverage to private sectors and informal sectors so as to benefit all employees.

Urban and rural residents all urgently hope for improved efforts in social security. As shown in Figure 1.10, according to the *2007 Report on Chinese citizens' Views about Government and Public Service*,[15] what Chinese citizens most want, among all social security programs, is for the government to improve pension insurance. Pension insurance is mentioned by 45 percent of the rural residents surveyed. This shows improved understanding of the functions of social security, as people start to realize that family provisions for old age are not sustainable in the long run, while a socialized pension plan is urgently needed. Medical insurance is also mentioned by over 20 percent of the urban and rural residents surveyed.

The roles of finance in social welfare systems

The building of a social welfare system is inextricably tied to support from public finance. Governmental financial support for social welfare has increased significantly in recent years. In 2005 the government spending in social welfare accounted for 27.08 percent of government expenditures (see Table 1.3).

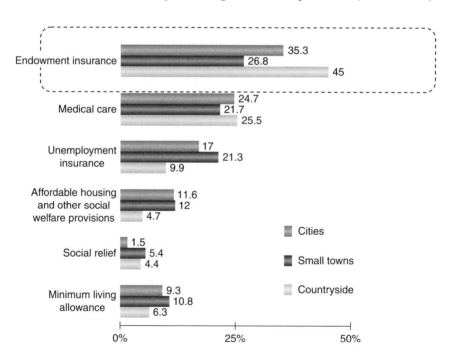

Figure 1.10 Social security programs deemed by residents as needing improvement.

Source: Horizon Research Consultancy Group, *2007 Report on Chinese Residents' Views about Government and Public Service.*

Table 1.3 The percentages of Chinese social welfare expenditures to GDP and government spending in 2005

	Urban			Rural			National		
	Government	Non-government	Total	Government	Non-government	Total	Government	Non-government	Total
Percentage in GDP									
Pension insurance	2.57	1.86	4.42	0.00	0.00	0.00	2.57	1.86	4.42
Medical insurance	0.38	0.63	1.01	0.04	0.00	0.04	0.42	0.63	1.05
Compulsory education	0.60	0.20	0.80	0.90	0.07	0.97	1.5	0.27	1.77
Minimum Living Allowance	0.10	0.00	0.10	0.03	0.00	0.03	0.13	0	0.13
Housing	0.39	1.01	1.40	0.00	0.00	0.00	0.39	1.01	1.4
Unemployment insurance	0.00	0.12	0.12	0.00	0.00	0.00	0	0.12	0.12
Maternity insurance	0.00	0.02	0.02	0.00	0.00	0.00	0	0.02	0.02
Total	4.04	3.84	7.88	0.97	0.07	1.04	5.01	3.91	8.92
Percentage in government spending									
Pension insurance	13.84	10.03	23.87	0.00	0.00	0.00	13.84	10.03	23.87
Medical insurance	2.05	3.38	5.43	0.20	0.00	0.20	2.25	3.38	5.63
Compulsory education	3.24	1.05	4.30	4.88	0.36	5.23	8.12	1.41	9.53
Minimum Living Allowance	0.57	0.00	0.57	0.18	0.00	0.18	0.75	0	0.75
Housing	2.11	5.45	7.56	0.00	0.00	0.00	2.11	5.45	7.56
Unemployment insurance	0.00	0.67	0.67	0.00	0.00	0.00	0	0.67	0.67
Maternity insurance	0.00	0.13	0.13	0.00	0.00	0.00	0	0.13	0.13
Total	21.82	20.71	42.53	5.26	0.36	5.61	27.08	21.07	48.14

Source: Luo Chuliang, Li Shi: *Analysis of Urban and Rural Welfare* (Background report, 2008).

Notes:
1 Some of the data on non-government spending for pension insurance includes contributions, and is from the table 5 in the original background report.
2 About the non-government spending on housing in the table,

The government mainly invests in low-rent housing and affordable housing. All subsidies to low-rent housing and affordable housing are deemed as the government's investment, while half of the revenue arising from affordable housing is regarded as the direct or indirect expenditure of the government, and the other half is considered as being paid by enterprises. The housing accumulation funds are equally paid by the employee and the enterprise.

And the part afforded by the enterprise is considered as non-governmental spending. It should be noted that the spending on economical housing is not the actual expenditures but calculated results. The total size is calculated by multiplying the sales area with the difference of the unit prices between middle- and high-grade apartments and economical housing. Although the calculation of housing might be doubtful, efforts have been made to the maximum extent that all available data allow.

3 The ratio of contribution to fiscal expenditure is calculated to figure out the proportion of the spending on social welfare, if all afforded by the government to the fiscal expenditure. Therefore, the author believes that the denominator should be the current fiscal expenditure. Moreover, in principle, the government spending should be a part of fiscal expenditure, while non-governmental spending is excluded in fiscal expenditure.

Specifically (see Table 1.3), governmental spending in urban social welfare accounted for 21.82 percent of fiscal expenditures in 2005—much higher than governmental expenditures in rural social welfare (5.26 percent) and demonstrating the great gap between the rural and the urban. Among funding sources of rural social welfare, government and non-government inputs accounted for 21.82 percent and 20.71 percent of the fiscal expenditures, respectively. In terms of social welfare in rural areas, government spending accounted for 5.26 percent of fiscal expenditures, while non-governmental spending was only 0.36 percent.

Nevertheless, financial input from Central finance in social welfare remains insufficient. Even after entering the twenty-first century, the publicly financed spending on social welfare can still only be considered very low. As shown in Table 1.3, the entire amount of social welfare expenses in 2005, including those paid by government as well as by enterprises and individuals, accounted for less than 9 percent of GDP. Of the total, government spending accounted for only 5 percent of GDP. Although social welfare costs paid for by the government accounted for 27 percent of fiscal expenditures, this was still much lower than in some other countries. Figure 1.11 shows the percentages of the public welfare component in GDP of some major OECD countries. It is not hard to see that not only have these countries increased expenditures since the 1980s, but the percentage of GDP that they have been spending exceeds 15 percent. Even the United States, with its strong advocacy of 'individual independence', spent more of its GDP on public spending than China did. Spending on social welfare by such developing countries as the Czech Republic and Hungary came to 19.6 percent and 16.4 percent of GDP, respectively.

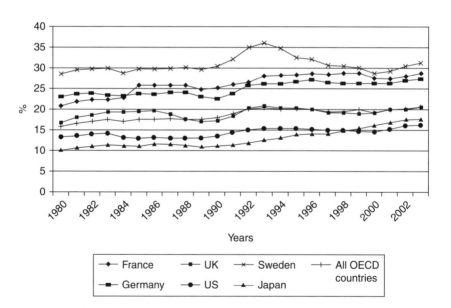

Figure 1.11 The percentages of OECD public spending to GDP, 1980–2003.

Source: Liu Minquan, Yu Jiantuo, *Comparison Research On Global Social Welfare Systems* (Background Report, 2008).

China's 'developmental social welfare system' in 2012 and 2020: ideas for the future

China currently faces an extremely opportune moment for setting up a developmental social welfare system. The government is promoting the idea of a 'scientific outlook on development' and the concept of 'building a harmonious society', which provide the ideological and political bases for establishing a universal-access welfare system. Meanwhile, rapid economic growth and the excellent state of national finances provide a solid foundation in terms of material and financial guarantees for such a system. Moreover, certain changes in our social situation urgently need attention in the form of social security and welfare systems. These include hyper-fast urbanization, population mobility and migrations, the aging population, increasing income disparities, heightened social conflicts due to the large numbers of low-income people, and the growing needs of people for better sanitation, education and housing once they have reached a level of sufficient food. None of these can be solved in a short period of time.

China's rapid growth over more than three decades of 'reform and opening up' has ensured the underlying conditions for the country to improve its social security system. In 2007 per capita GDP exceeded USD 2,500.[16] At this rate, per capita GDP is expected to reach USD 3,700 by 2012 and may exceed USD 10,000 in some developed regions. At the same time, fiscal revenues are expected to reach RMB 8 trillion.[17] The overall economic and financial resources of the country will be lifted to an even higher level, laying a very solid material foundation for building a healthy social security system.

To create such a system the government should build on relevant parts of the existing system, rather than totally throwing the old system out. Therefore, a certain period should be allowed for smooth transition between old and new, to ensure consistency, stability, and innovation in the course of transition.

We recommend that China build a developmental social welfare system that suits our specific national conditions, over the next 12 years. Such a process should consist of two stages: the period between 2009 and 2012 will constitute the initial stage, establishing the basic framework of the system; from 2013 to 2020 will constitute the second stage, in which the actual system will take shape.

Our goal for 2012 is mainly to start to establish the universal-coverage aspects of the welfare system. This consists of six aspects. The first is to basically eliminate gender discrimination in the enrollment of children in school. Nine-year compulsory education and special education in rural and urban areas should be provided for free, without any fees. Students from rural areas should also be given free textbooks, and students housed in communal facilities in western poverty-stricken regions should have nutritious food for free. Universal coverage for pre-school education should be provided for all urban children and those children in more developed rural areas. One year of free pre-school education should be provided to children from low-income households from depressed rural areas, and one year of free vocational training should be provided for middle-school graduates in poverty-stricken areas and those from low-income households who will not pursue further education. In addition, tuition fees for poor students in high school should be reduced or waived. The second aspect of a universal-coverage welfare system is to set up a basic system of 'caring for the elderly'. By 2012 an all-round pension system specifically targeted at farmers, rural migrant workers and urban residents should be created. A State-subsidized pension insurance system should be set up for farm workers that is nationally planned and coordinated. In addition, a system of providing benefits for the elderly who have no other means of support should be established with the government's financial support. The third aspect is to exercise proactive employment policies and spend more on vocational training and job agencies. The government should devise every possible means to link social welfare to training of the unemployed. Unemployment insurance should cover all urban workers and gradually be extended for rural laborers. The fourth aspect is to assure that medical coverage of people in cities reaches 90 percent of all urban residents, so that the migrant population can be covered by insurance programs and continue to receive benefits when they move to other places. The fifth is gradually to improve the coverage and the amounts of minimum living allowances. To that end, the government's Central financial authorities should contribute more. Recipients of minimum living allowances should also be provided with other assistance and social support, for example, basic health care, education and housing. Meanwhile, the marginalized people and more vulnerable groups must be better cared for, including children, old people, disabled people and women. Finally, we should improve the housing security system in urban and rural areas by increasing the supply of low-rent housing, to ensure that some 50 percent of urban low-income households and 10 percent of migrant rural laborers living under poor housing conditions can enjoy low-rent housing. Housing-construction subsidies should be provided for 2.6 million rural households who cannot afford to build their own houses.

The goal for 2020 is to further realize the equal access provisions of social welfare for all citizens, to ensure that they can afford a decent life and enjoy proper public services. The main goal, therefore, is to ensure a basic parity between urban and rural areas in terms of public services. Specifically, this goal incorporates six different aspects. The first is the adoption of '1+9+1' compulsory education. All school-age children will be entitled to one year of free pre-school education before their nine years of compulsory education. Middle school graduates who will not pursue further education can receive one year of free vocational training. Fees will be exempted for high school students from rural and low-income urban house-holds. The second is to improve the basic system of 'caring for the elderly'. All urban workers should be covered in social insurance programs by contributing an affordable amount in premiums. All workers should benefit from social insurance to varying degrees in the event of old age, illness, unemployment and work-related injuries. Older people without any means of support should receive a certain amount of pension benefits. The third is that the basic medical insurance for employees in urban areas, medical insurance for urban residents and new rural cooperative medical care system should be constantly improved to cover all citizens. The fourth aspect is to provide basic living allowances and medical insurance for the unemployed and people with low-income or no income, and to significantly improve their insurance. The fifth is to provide vocational training and assistance to the unemployed and those who have particular difficulties in finding jobs, and to form mechanisms with long-term effects to promote employment. Finally, basic housing support should be provided to low-income people in rural and urban areas as well as migrant rural laborers who are based in urban areas but occupying substandard housing. Low- and middle-income people in substandard housing should also receive housing assistance. In addition, 5.2 million rural households who face problems in building their own homes should receive construction subsidies.

Both Central finance and society need to put considerable investment into building this universal-access, developmental, welfare system over the next 12 years. Crafting such a system is time-consuming and complicated, and involves every aspect of society and economics. Therefore comprehensive planning is necessary, as well as systematic analysis of the total demands for social welfare and available finances to supply it, as well as the trends in these two parameters. Currently every different sector of our society is promoting its own welfare programs and crying out that its own problems are most important and urgently need resolution. This study is significant for its focus on an integrated approach. In looking at a combination of all relevant programs, it is attempting to quantify the extent to which Central finance can provide universal-access coverage, and under what conditions. By taking a comprehensive view of the general situation, we can make partial and local decisions with more concrete focus and more effective setting of priorities.

Using constant 2007 prices, all items in the new welfare system would cost RMB 2.6 trillion in Central finance expenditures in 2012 and RMB 5.7 trillion in 2020. We should be able to afford that, under the following conditions: if GDP growth is sustained at an average of 8 percent per year; if fiscal revenues remain 21 percent of GDP in this current 'adjustment period' as we accommodate the financial crisis (between 2007 and 2011), while growing to 26 percent after that; if the percentage of government spending on welfare relative to total spending increases 1.2 percent annually to 33 percent between 2007 and 2012, and then goes up to and remains stable at 35 percent.

If we do not maintain a growth rate of 8 percent, then the percentage of government expenditures dedicated to social welfare will have to increase if we want to realize the goals in this proposal. This proposal therefore also calls for restructuring government spending and further reforming the fiscal system.

It should be noted that increased operating costs are not included in this calculation, costs that undoubtedly will go up as a result of expanded coverage. If we assume that such operational costs will be borne by Central finance and incorporate them into our calculations, the government will not be able to afford the proposed system even if operating costs account for only 10 percent of total expenditures on the system. Either our assumption about the percentage of government expenditures to GDP will have to change, or our assumption about the percentage of welfare spending in total government spending will have to change.

Our calculations also show that we should not expect too much of social welfare. The financial capacity of the government is only sufficient to maintain a basic system with a low level of coverage for many components. For a long time to come, free welfare programs (excluding compulsory education) will need to focus on low-income populations and special groups. Most middle- and above-middle-income people in urban and rural areas will have to pay for their social security programs. Paid-for welfare services are therefore going to continue to be primary in our social welfare system.

Notes

1 Wang Mengkui (2006), *China: Economic Development and Social Harmony,* People's Publishing House.
2 *The Book of Rites—The Conveyance of Rites* expresses the eagerness to a grand union by

> When the Grand course was pursued, a public and common spirit ruled all under the sky; they chose men of talents, virtue, and ability; their words are sincere, and what they cultivated was harmony. Thus men did not love their parents only, not treat as children only their own sons. A competent provision was secured for the aged until their death, employment for the able-bodied, and the means of growing up to the young. They showed kindness and compassion to widows, orphans, childless men, and those who were disabled by disease, so that they were all sufficiently maintained. Males had their proper work, and females had their homes. They accumulated articles of value, disliking that they should be thrown away upon the ground, but not wishing to keep them for their own gratification. They labored with their strength, disliking that it should not be exerted, but not exerting it only with a view to their own advantage. In this way, selfish schemes were repressed and found no development. Robbers, filchers, and rebellious traitors did not show themselves, and hence the outer doors remained open, and were not shut. This was the period of what we call the Grand Union.

3 See *China Statistical Abstract 2008*, p. 21.
4 See *The Research on Transition of Chinese Rural Economy and Society Since Reform and Opening-up* by Hanjun, 2008 (http://edu.drcnet.com.cn/DRCNet.Channel.Web/expert/showdoc.asp?doc_id=199631).
5 Sources: *China Statistical Yearbook 2007,* compiled by the National Bureau of Statistics of China and published by China Statistics Yearbook Press.
6 See *Notes on the Major Statistics Of the Second National Sample Survey on Disability* (http://202.123.110.5/ztzl/gacjr/content_459223.htm).
7 'Five Guarantee' households refer to the elderly, disabled or children under 16 who have no ability to work and are deprived of livelihood. Besides, there are no legally obliged people to support them, or these legally obliged people have no ability to do so. These vulnerable people can enjoy service and material assistance in food, clothing, medical care, housing and burial expenses.
8 'Three Plus One' medical insurance program includes daily medical assistance, medical assistance for major diseases, temporary medical assistance, and charity medical aid.
9 Figures about employees covered by the basic medical insurance in Figure 1.6 may be misleading. The data do not simply indicate that few employees enjoyed medical insurance in early 1990s, because the employees in state-owned enterprise and collectively-owned enterprises were covered to different extents by public-funded medical insurance before the basic medical insurance was launched.
10 *Statistical Communiqué of Labor and Social Security Development 2007* (http://www.molss.gov.cn/gb/zwxx/2008-06/05/content_240415.htm).
11 See *Monthly Statistical Report on Civil Affairs Development of 2008 May* (http://cws.mca.gov.cn/accessory/200806/1213777613733.htm).

12 According to the National Bureau of Statistics, the number of people in absolute poverty in rural areas in 2007 was 14.79 million (see *China Statistical Abstract 2008*, p. 103), accounting for only 40 percent of the rural population who received the meager minimum livelihood allowances.

13 See *Statistical Communiqué of the People's Republic of China on National Health Development 2007* (http://202.96.155.169/publicfiles/business/htmlfiles/mohbgt/s6689/200804/33525.htm).

14 In 2007, 18.46 million rural laborers were covered by the endowment insurance system, while 0.13 billion rural laborers worked in urban areas—indicating a 13 percent coverage.

15 Horizon Research Consultancy Group, *2007 Report on Chinese Residents' Views about Government and Public Service*, internal circulation, 2008.

16 According to the adjustment data newly issued by the National Statistics Bureau in January 2009, the GDP in 2007 is RMB 25,730.6 billion, and the per capita GDP has been adjusted accordingly.

17 For the related calculation details, see *The Minimum Living Allowance System* (Background report, 2008).

References

Li Shi, *The Change of Income Distribution in China over the Past 30 Years of Reform and Opening: A Paper for the Forum on Economic Theories over the Past 30 Years of Reform and Opening and for the Centennial of the Birth of Sun Yefang.* Hong Kong: October 21–22, 2008.

Wang Mengkui, China: Economic Development and Social Harmony. People's Publishing House, 2006.

2   Basic principles and overall framework for a 'developmental social welfare system'

Social welfare systems in the modern sense have existed for over 120 years. Currently, nearly 200 countries and regions around the world have established diverse social welfare systems. Although different countries have differing systems and practices, they all have selected and adjusted their models and policy frameworks in light of their own conditions: economic and social development, social and political systems, and historical and cultural backgrounds. China's current welfare system must conform to the unique features of rapid economic growth and constant social change.

Basic principles for building a 'developmental social welfare system'

(1) The main principle embodied in our recommendations is 'combining fairness [or equity] with efficiency while giving priority to equity'. In building a social welfare system, our primary objectives should be to ensure universal coverage, reduce social polarization in the process of industrialization, and promote social equity and stability. At the same time our system should aim to eliminate inequalities arising from differences in household registration [urban, rural], sex, occupation, status and other identity markers. In particular, the system should provide equal education and other development opportunities for the children of poor families, so as to prevent poverty from becoming a generational inheritance. While emphasizing the equity principle the system should give due consideration to efficiency and protect developmental vitality, so that it can effectively promote long-term and sustainable economic growth.

(2) Our recommendations adhere to the principle that the level of social welfare should match the level of economic development and the capacity of all sectors to carry the costs of the system, so that social welfare can develop in a sustainable way. In building a complete national welfare system our first tasks relate to the problems of starting the process from scratch; our next tasks can then focus on gradually 'improving' the benefits. While security issues badly needed by the public should receive priority consideration, levels of security should be established in light of fiscal and economic

capacities so as to build long-standing mechanisms that can develop in a sustainable way. Since China is still in the initial stages of building its social welfare system and relevant systems, and since the mechanisms are still unsound, the country has to proceed with two things in mind: resolving the absence of systems and striking a long-term balance between the need for and the availability of funds. Given the intractable trends of urbanization and ageing, we need to make sure we are incorporating sustainability into a growing system.

(3) The principle of 'employment first'. 'Population' and 'employment' are the two fundamental problems that have long plagued China's economic and social development. Whether in terms of individuals or families, employment is the most reliable way to avoid poverty and reduce personal dependence on government. It provides the greatest social security. Therefore, 'employment first' must be one of the basic principles of our social welfare policies. In this respect, the first step is to offer occupational training to able-bodied youth and especially the new-generation farmer-workers, to enhance their ability to get jobs and create businesses so that they can integrate with society. The government should do its best to create jobs and encourage laborers to create businesses on their own. If the level of security is too high, however, and the rate of corporate contributions is too high, the unintended consequence will be that overly heavy burdens will force enterprises to cut jobs. For those workers who have been without jobs for an extended period and who cannot be re-employed under normal conditions, the government should reduce or subsidize their social insurance premiums in order to encourage employers to hire them.

(4) In creating a social security system the role of the government should be combined with the role of society at large, but the government should play the leading role. Building a social welfare system is fundamentally the undertaking of government. Therefore, the government must play the leading role by actively promoting legislation, increasing fiscal revenues and providing more public services. In the meantime, markets and families should also play their roles and social organizations [or civic organizations] and various other sectors should mobilize their resources as well. Joint initiatives are required to enable the building of the system. In selecting social welfare models, both contribution-based social insurance and free welfare items are of equal importance. Both can help form the mechanisms in which government, units and individuals jointly bear responsibility. In designing and operating a social welfare system it is necessary to emphasize the correlation between premium payment and benefit entitlement, encourage units and individuals to participate in social insurance and continue to pay premiums so as to minimize the moral risk involved when individuals evade their premium-payment obligation and begin over-reliance on government and society.

Framework for a 'developmental social welfare system'

Overall framework

The framework for China's developmental social welfare system mainly consists of the following major components: education security, employment security, basic living security, pension security, health security, housing security, and miscellaneous other securities. In all it has seven parts, dozens of items and numerous sub-items (see Figure 2.1). First, the new system moves from the more passive 'ensuring security and providing relief' to a more proactive direction that includes 'being human-oriented and caring for and promoting all-round human development'. It is more systematic, balanced and innovative. The diagram indicates that a developmental social welfare system has broad coverage in terms of things it addresses. It not only covers all the provisions of the existing social security, such as pension security, medical security, unemployment insurance and work injury insurance, but also many more things related to 'well-being', such as education security, housing security, employment assistance, and protection of special groups. Further, a developmental social welfare system offers full coverage for all urban and rural populations. The most typical example is pension security. In addition to the existing pension insurance for urban workers, for employees of public institutions and for civil servants of government organizations, the system will also establish pension insurance for rural workers in cities, for rural residents, and for seniors. Third, a developmental social welfare system takes diverse forms, has low starting points, and makes transitions gradually. For example, education security starts from elementary education for school-age children. On the basis of nine-year compulsory education, it moves further to offer one year of free pre-school education for infants, then to offer one year of compulsory vocational education for junior high school graduates, and eventually to provide equal education opportunities for all. Housing security is another example—systems such as housing reserve funds, affordable housing, low-rent housing and housing price stabilization are used to meet the housing demands of the low-income groups, migrant workers in urban areas and middle-income groups, respectively.

Welfare items corresponding to the demands of different social groups

The programs, or 'items' in China's developmental social welfare system have been set up in light of the unique features of China's economy and society. Within a unified framework the system employs diverse approaches to meet the demands of different social groups. In designing the items of the new social welfare system, payable social insurance and free welfare items play similarly important roles. Able-bodied groups of people with incomes must participate in social insurance, pay premiums according to the standards affordable to them, and receive insurance benefits during child birth, old age, sickness and death. Security problems of low-income groups—those without stable jobs or some seniors and children—must be solved through welfare systems since they have no money to pay premiums. A social welfare system for all involves both the establishment of new systems and

Education security

Free compulsory education

Senior high and middle-level vocational education

Employment security

Two exemptions and one subsidy

Literacy

Student grants

Work-study programs

Scholarships

Employment service

Employment training

Employment assistance

Unemployment insurance

Human resources market

Public employment service institutions

Intermediary institutions

Re-employment training for jobless people

Training for peasant workers

Pre-employment training

Government public-interest posts

Zero-employment families

Social insurance exemption subsidies

Discount loans

Basic living security

Minimum living allowances for urban residents

Minimum living allowances for rural residents

Disaster relief

Rural 'five-guarantee' household system

Relief for people with no successors, handicapped and vagrant persons

Pension security

Basic pension insurance

Additional pension insurance

Old-age subsidy

Old-age subsidy for family-planning households

Old-age daily nursery

Pension insurance for urban workers

Pension insurance for employees of public institutions

Pension insurance for civil servants of government organizations

Pension insurance for peasant workers

Rural pension insurance

Corporate annuities

Occupational annuities

Urban residents

Rural residents

Community homes for the elderly

Nursing homes

Seniors apartments

Health security

Basic medical insurance

Additional medical insurance

Medical relief

Public health

Housing security

Medical insurance for urban employees

Medical insurance for urban residents

New rural cooperative medical system

Additional medical insurance for corporate employees

Medical subsidies for civil servants

Medical relief for poor families

Medical relief for emergency and unexpected incidents

Key disease prevention and control

Community medical services

Rural three-level health service institutions

Housing reserve subsidies

Affordable housing

Low-rent housing

Housing subsidies for poor rural households

Other securities

Work injury insurance

Child-birth insurance

Disability insurance

Social insurance for servicemen

Social mutual help

Charity

Figure 2.1 Framework of China's developmental social welfare system.

their integration with existing systems. Table 2.1 shows the correlations between different welfare items and different groups. The items include pension security, health security, basic living security, housing security, employment assistance and security, education security and other securities. The recipients include corporate employees, employees of government organizations and public institutions, self-employed professionals, urban residents, peasant workers and rural residents. In addition, we classify urban residents without incomes, the urban poor and rural families as separate groups. In our welfare system each group has a corresponding item arrangement. See Figure 2.1 for detailed information.

Table 2.1 indicates that different social groups are entitled to different social welfare benefits. For example, urban poor families are entitled not only to minimum living allowances but also medical relief, low-rent housing, employment training and employment assistance. As citizens they are naturally entitled to free compulsory education and pension insurance.

Multi-level social welfare structure

A multi-level social welfare structure is designed to ensure that public finance benefits vulnerable social groups first. A payable social insurance security model is applied to most working groups with incomes, while at the same time the State encourages units and individuals to establish additional insurance to meet the higher demands of groups that can afford higher benefits. Figure 2.2 shows the structure.

Management system for a 'developmental social welfare system'

Raise the governmental level at which social insurance is planned, managed and pooled in order to increase capacity

At present China's social insurance is notable for its decentralized management, limited number of functions, and the low governmental level at which decisions

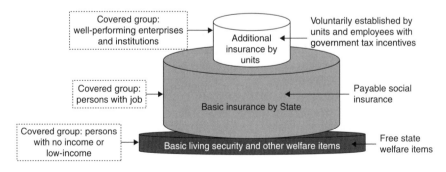

Figure 2.2 Multi-level social welfare structure.

Table 2.1 Item-group correlations of China's developmental social welfare system

Item	Group		Urban corporate employees	Employees of government organizations and public institutions	Self-employed professionals	Peasant workers	Jobless persons	Urban residents	Rural residents	Urban seniors without incomes	Urban and rural poor families
Pension security	Basic pension	Basic pension	■	■	■	■	■	■	■		
		Individual account	■	■	■	■		■	■		
		Transitional pension	■	■							
		Others	■	■							
	Additional pension	Corporate annuity	■								
		Occupational annuity		■							
	Old-age subsidy										
Health security	Basic medical insurance	Insurance for urban employees	■	■	■	■	■				
		Insurance for urban residents						■			
		New rural cooperative medical system				■			■		
	Additional medical insurance	Corporate subsidy	■								
		Medical subsidy for civil servants		■							
	Medical relief	Medical relief for poverty								■	■
		Medical relief for unexpected incidents						■	■		
Public health		Prevention and control	■	■	■	■	■	■	■		
		Community medical service						■	■		
		Rural three-level health service							■		■

(Continued overleaf)

Table 2.1 (continued)

Item	Group	Urban corporate employees	Employees of government organizations and public institutions	Self-employed professionals	Peasant workers	Jobless persons	Urban residents	Rural residents	Urban seniors without incomes	Urban and rural poor families
Basic living security	Urban minimum living allowance									■
	Rural minimum living allowance									■
	Disaster relief						■	■		
Housing security	Housing reserve fund	■	■							
	Affordable housing	■	■	■			■			
	Low-rent housing					■	■			■
	Peasant housing relief				■					■
Employment assistance and security	Employment service				■	■	■	■		■
	Employment training				■	■	■	■		■
	Employment assistance				■	■	■	■		
	Unemployment insurance					■				
Education security	Free compulsory education		■				■	■		
	Middle-level vocational education						■	■		
Other securities	Work injury insurance	■	■		■			■		
	Child-birth insurance	■								

Note: ■ indicates the corresponding group covered by a specific welfare arrangement.

are made. Social insurance now has three 'pooling' levels, or levels at which funds are managed: provincial, prefectural and county. [Note that some municipalities are classified as prefectures.] Pension insurance is a good example. While 13 provinces have realized provincial pooling, more than 100 places resort to prefectural pooling and more than 1,000 places resort to county pooling. The low administrative levels at which funds are managed does not conform to the majority rule requirement of pension insurance and has caused many prominent problems. One, policy inconsistencies between different provinces and even between different cities or within a province have made it hard for migrant workers to have 'portable insurance', i.e. to carry along their insurance with them. Two, it makes management of benefits more difficult. When developed coastal regions decide to adjust pension benefits other regions are forced to follow suit and keep up, but their funding shortages then have to be covered by Central finance. Three, fund use is inefficient. Nationwide, the regional distribution of fund surpluses is inconsistent with the regional distribution of retirees. As much as 60 percent of the funds surplus is in the seven provinces and municipalities on the eastern seaboard, whose insured retirees account for only 34 percent of the national total of insured retirees. Even within a province, funds cannot be redistributed between different cities. The result is that some cities have fund shortages and others have fund surpluses. [Note that some regions and municipalities are classified as provinces, and that some counties are classified as cities.]

The key to raising the administrative levels at which pooling management occurs is to clearly define the responsibilities of government at each level and mobilize its initiative to expand collections and ensure release. In view of China's practical conditions, it is impossible to move from county pooling straight to national pooling. A more practical approach is to realize provincial pooling first and then move to national pooling. Provincial pooling means that the whole province observes a uniform pension insurance system, and uses the uniform base figure and ratio for premium payments, as well as uniform methods for the calculation and release of benefits and for the adjustment of planned items and benefits. The pension insurance fund is then redistributed and used in a unified way across the province, the budget for basic pension insurance funds is compiled and implemented in a unified way, and the operational procedures for basic pension insurance are unified. The core concept of provincial pooling is unified fund redistribution and use.

More effort should be made to realize provincial pooling. At the same time, the building of a 'national uniform social security information network' should proceed at a faster pace. On the basis of a national information network the pension insurance liability of the Central government and local governments should be divided reasonably to promote national pooling of basic pension insurance. The main concept is: adhere to a combination mode of social pooling and individual accounts, under which a basic pension still consists of the basic pension and the individual account pension. In time the basic pension, which was previously under the administration of local governments, will be distributed by the Central government, and the Central government will collect premium payments from participating organizations at a certain percentage of total salaries. It will resolve any gap in funds by adjusting the structure of expenditures and by opening up new financing channels. The provincial government will mainly be responsible for distributing that portion of pensions for the elderly, transitional pensions for the 'middle people', individual-account pensions for 'new people', and local subsidies.[1] It will collect premium payments from participating organizations at a certain percentage of total salaries; any deficiencies in provincially pooled funds of individual payments will be resolved by local finance. Any provinces with financial difficulties may only borrow the funds from individual accounts to distribute pensions that are due after abiding by very strict procedures. The Central government will provide special transfer payments for those provinces under-going special financial difficulties. As the 'middle people' and 'old people' decline in number and disappear, the provincial government may reduce the proportion of premium payments from organizations. A national pooling pattern will eventually emerge in which the Central government is responsible for the basic pension, while local governments are responsible for individual-account pensions.

Services guided by the government and participated in by society, in order to use market forces in reasonable fashion

The building of the social welfare system should be guided by and handled by the government. Non-governmental public organizations, urban communities and rural collectivities will constitute an invaluable medium for the dispensing of public services during the actual implementation and operation of the social welfare program. The government should encourage and guide their efforts and resources. In reality these non-governmental organizations and communities have already been playing an important role in disaster relief, rehabilitation of orphans and disabled children, assistance to the poor, education of dropout children, care of childless seniors and the nursing of the elderly.

Reasonable use of market methods for public services is also an area that is worth exploring. Social policy does not exclude market mechanisms. To develop effective social policies, the first priority must be those public welfare areas about which the government is most concerned; second, social policies should be liber-ated from the traditional modes of social administration, in order to tap the spontaneous functions of market mechanisms; third, demand-oriented social cooperation mechanisms should be encouraged, that is, benign cooperation and interaction should be fostered among government, enterprises and social sectors, to mitigate social conflicts and serve increasingly diverse social needs. To use public resources more efficiently, certain market means may be introduced into the social management field. Social corporate organizations cover a broad range and operate under a multitude of descriptions, including cooperative organiza-tions, fund organizations, charitable organizations, community development companies, volunteer organizations, social companies and development credit unions. Entrusting part of the management and operation of social welfare programs to such organizations has been proven effective. Employment training services is an example. The government may purchase the training results of market-based training institutions, introduce private employment agency institutions into the employment service, and entrust the investment and operations of social security funds to reliable financial institutions for authorized investment. All these methods can be effective. Using market mechanisms in the provision of social services is largely unexplored, so requires further attention.

Risk prevention mechanisms based on internal controls and social supervision

Building the social welfare system is a government intervention in the failure of the market to provide the service. Government behavior must therefore serve public interests, and be based on the prerequisite that it is being done to maximize public interest. Implementation and operation of social welfare programs must have only one purpose, which is maintaining social fairness and equity as well as the rights of citizens. However, just like the market, the government may also fail. Many incidents show that the government too has problems of low efficiency, gross negligence, and even corruption in the areas of social welfare as well as public management and public service. To mitigate the risk of government failure it is of great importance to build strict internal control systems and effective external social supervision mechanisms. Generally, the public affairs management structures of the government have established relatively strict systems and measures. In addition to the service codes and disciplines of operating departments all bodies have set up professional disciplinary inspection and supervision institutions. Nonetheless, there are still frequent cases of noncompliance and violating the law, showing that internal controls have limited effect. This is because internal control institutions and those who are being supervised always share common interests. Therefore, an external social governance supervision mechanism should be built that is robust. The social welfare system must assure that administrative management is separated from business management, and that business management is strictly separate from oversight and regulation. The system must be set up as a democratic management system that is jointly participated in by the State, society, organizations and individuals. Decision-making, execution, and supervision are separate functions and should be undertaken by three separate institutions. Each should have clearly-defined responsibilities to forge a management system featuring clear division of work, mutual coordination and mutual constraint. The setup should assure institutional support, efficient management, advanced means, quality service and effective supervision for the operations of China's social welfare system.

Implement a mega-ministry unified administration

Administration of the social welfare system mainly involves such functions as the researching, formulation, and implementation of policies, laws and regulations; law enforcement supervision, punishments and arbitration of disputes; and selection, accreditation and supervision of social welfare management and service institutions. As a security network consisting of multiple interrelated items, the developmental social welfare system should be unified, coordinated and complementary. Its administration should be unified wherever possible. At present employment, social insurance and part of relevant social security affairs are handled by the Ministry of Human Resources and Social Security. The new rural cooperative medical system is under the jurisdiction of the Ministry of Health. The minimum living allowance for urban and rural residents is in the hands of the Ministry of Civil Affairs, and pension subsidies for rural households with only one daughter or two daughters fall under the scope of the National Population and Family Planning Commission. As to social insurance premiums, these are collected by local tax authorities in some regions, and by human resources institutions and social security institutions in others. Such a fragmented management system is not conducive to uniform planning nor to coordination and linkage between different items and policies. To meet the needs of building a developmental social welfare system that covers all of our 1.3 billion people, we recommend the establishment of a unified administration under a form of mega-ministry. Given that restructuring of the institutions under the State Council has just been completed, we recommend first setting up a National Leading Group for Building a Social Welfare System, to be headed by the sponsoring Vice Premier and composed of members from the General Office of the State Council, the National Development and Reform Commission, the Ministry of Civil Affairs, the Ministry of Finance, the Ministry of Hunan Resources and Social Security, the Ministry of Health, the National Population and Family Planning Commission, the General Administration of Taxation, the National Audit Office, the All China Federation of Trade Unions and the National Council for Social Security Fund. This Group will be responsible for organizing and leading the work of building the system, researching significant issues related to its reform and development, coordinating important policies and affairs that concern other bodies, and building work coordination mechanisms. Each provincial government will also establish a comparable leading group. When it is appropriate the plan to establish a formal 'mega-ministry unified administration' will be implemented.

Legal environment for a 'developmental social welfare system'

Legal background of social welfare programs

The social welfare program is a fundamental system that is established and enforced by the State through legislation, and that must be guaranteed by sound laws and regulations. Since the 1990s China has successively adopted a host of laws concerning social welfare, including *Law of the People's Republic of China on the Protection of Disabled Persons*, *Law of the People's Republic of China on the Protection of Minors*, *Law of the People's Republic of China on the Protection of Rights and Interests of Women*, *Adoption Law of the People's Republic of China*, *Labor Law of the People's Republic of China*, *Law of the People's Republic of China on Maternal and Infant Health Care*, *Law of the People's Republic of China on Protection of Rights and Interests of the Elderly*, *Labor Contract Law of the People's Republic of China* and *Employment Promotion Law of the People's Republic of China*. The State Council has also promulgated a series of administrative regulations and policy documents concerning social welfare. In 1997 the State Council issued the *Decision of the State Council on Establishing a Unified Basic Pension Insurance System for Enterprise Employees*, which unified the basic pension insurance system for enterprise employees. In 1998, the State Council promulgated the *Decision on Establishing the Urban Employees' Basic Medical Insurance System*, which defined the major policies and reform direction for the system covering urban employees' basic medical insurance. In 1999 the State Council published the *Regulations on Unemployment Insurance*, further elaborating the coverage, financing methods, payment proportions, access conditions, and benefits levels for unemployment insurance. In the same year the State Council released the *Regulations on Minimum Living Allowances for Urban Residents* and *Interim Regulations on the Collection and Payment of Social Insurance Premiums*, further regularizing the social assistance for urban needy residents, and providing the legal basis for reinforcing the collection of social insurance premiums. In 2003 the State Council released the *Regulation on Work-Related Injury Insurance*, indicating that our work-related injury insurance system has entered a new era. In 2005 the State Council announced the *Decision on Improving the Basic Pension Insurance System for Enterprise Employees*, specifying the long-term mechanisms for building the basic pension insurance system for enterprise employees. In early 2006 the State Council published *Several Opinions on Solving the Issues of Rural Migrant Workers*, formulating a series of policies and measures to protect the rights and interests of rural migrant workers.

Although China has made significant progress in establishing the legal framework for a social welfare system, the administrative levels at which the legislation is aimed are too low and constraining mechanisms are too weak. In actual practice, many problems are related to unsound laws and insufficient supervision. In order to form a sound legal basis for the cause of social welfare, we greatly need both a legal and regulatory system that combines basic laws with implementing regulations and rules. While strengthening supervision and legal enforcement, at the same time we need to urge social welfare institutions of the government, employers and employees to abide by laws spontaneously. Legal compliance, strict law enforcement, and accountability for violations constitute the basic foundation for safeguarding the social welfare rights and interests of each citizen.

Main aspects of a legal structure for social welfare that is in urgent need of standardizing

The first task is to make adjustments in and standardize the relations among the various parties involved in the social welfare legal system. These include the relationship between the State, or government, and social members, the relationship between the institutions implementing social welfare and members of society, the relationship between employers and employees, and various specific relations of social members in the social welfare system. The social welfare legal system should clearly identify the rights, responsibilities and obligations of all the above parties with respect to social welfare, and regulate and govern various relations that exist in the practical life. The following lists some aspects of this process.

Make adjustments in and standardize the social welfare management system. Regularize the setup and functions of social welfare institutions; adjust the internal and external relations of social welfare management institutions; and adjust the management and operating mechanisms of social welfare programs, in particular items relating to division of responsibilities, financial management, and fund use and allocation.

Make adjustments in and standardize the various relationships that exist in the management of social welfare funds, including the tasks and responsibilities of various parties in fund collections, operations and payment.

Make adjustments in and standardize the qualifications for coverage and standardize the treatment of all parties. Adjust the settlement of disputes arising out of the performance of social welfare program laws and regulations as well as supervision of the operating of the system.

Legal aid in the functioning of the social welfare system

Legal aid is a judicial remedy practice in many countries. In practical life most vulnerable groups in society usually resort to petitioning or rioting when they suffer unfair treatment under a social welfare program. This results in extreme conflict events and seriously affects social stability. The social welfare program, in essence, aims to help the vulnerable groups who are confronted with various risks and problems. To ensure that they truly do have access to effective social security it is necessary and urgent to establish effective legal aid. The State should establish uniform laws concerning the legal aid system, and the legal costs reduction and exemption system. It should stipulate the basic contents, principles, funding sources and procedures with respect to legal aid.

Notes

1 'Old people', 'middle people' and 'new people' are the new concepts that have come out in recent years after the introduction of individual accounts into the reform of the pension insurance system. To implement the 'combination of social pooling and individual account' system, it's necessary to open an individual account that remains unchanged for every incumbent enterprise employee. New employees will have an individual account once they start working, and the individual account fund will be recorded. Therefore, the individual account pension for the employee will be the accumulative individual account fund divided by 120 after his retirement. All the pensions for the employee at his retirement will consist of the individual account fund and the basic pension. In other words, the pension for employees who start work after the implementation of the 'combination of social pooling and individual account' system can be directly calculated with the unified pension calculation and payment method, without considering other factors, so these employees are called 'new people'. Employees who start work prior to, and retire after, the implementation of the 'combination of social pooling and individual account' system, have no individual accounts for their working years prior to the implementation of the system, and the cumulative indi-

vidual account fund in their accounts does not reflect the contribution they have made prior to the implementation of the system. Therefore, a transitional method must be used to calculate and pay the pension for these employees at retirement, rather than simply using the unified system. 'Old people' means those employees who start work prior to, and retire within three years after, the implementation of the 'combination of social pooling and individual account' system, and comparably, 'middle people' means those employees who start work prior to, and retire three years after, the implementation of the 'combination of social pooling and individual account' system.

3 The course of development and reforms made in other social welfare systems in the world

Social welfare has undergone a long developmental process in different countries in the world, and has seen continuous reform and adjustment. It was originally designed to reduce the personal income risk caused by marketization and industrialization, to maintain social stability and protect the rights of citizens. Countries are now increasingly concerned about the financial affordability and sustainability of their systems. More importantly, many people are now viewing welfare systems in a proactive light, as a way to increase social investment in human resources, improve economic competitiveness, and boost economic development. Welfare systems are regarded less and less as passive measures, set up mainly to deal with the negative effects of economic cycles.

History of social welfare systems

The concept and practice of social welfare has a long history. In the ancient Egyptian, Mesopotamian and Greek civilizations, people had already formulated and practiced some basic welfare systems to help the poor and the weak and reduce social contradictions. In China, during the Xia, Shang and Zhou dynasties, State expenditures included spending on famine relief. Modern social welfare systems emerged in tandem with industrialization and the rise of market-oriented economies. Industrialization caused large-scale mobility of people, unemployment in urban areas, and severe poverty, which impacted social stability and forced early industrialized countries to begin social interventions. In 1601 Britain promulgated the first *Poor Law*. According to that law, each parish was responsible for levying a 'poor tax' on residents and real estate owners in order to give relief to those who were unable to make a living. This was the earliest legislation that dealt with formal intervention by a government in social welfare via basic living allowances. In 1834 Britain adopted *The Poor Law Amendment Act*, changing decentralized management to centralized management of a system of social relief—the law defined the safeguarding of people's basic livelihood as a fundamental obligation of the government.

In Germany, labor movements sprang up in the middle and late nineteenth century and the government, even as it suppressed these movements, passed social welfare measures that were intended to reduce conflicts between different classes, lessen workers' resistance, and maintain social stability. On November 11, 1881, the German emperor Wilhelm I, at the suggestion of Bismarck, issued an imperial edict establishing a complete social insurance system. By this edict, workers were to be protected when ill, injured, disabled and old, and had the right to demand social relief. Employee security was to be managed by the employees themselves. The edict also created a social insurance development program and established occupational medical insurance, a pension plan, unemployment relief and so on. Later, Germany issued in succession the *Illness Insurance Act, Work-related Injury Insurance Act,* and *Pension System as well as Disability and Death Insurance Act.* In 1911 these three acts were integrated into the *Social Insurance Code.* This was pioneering work in social insurance legislation, and helped bring about an important transformation from simply 'helping the poor' to 'securing workers' livelihoods'.

The establishment of social security systems eased the tension between different classes in Germany. Social stability played an important role in economic development. The late nineteenth century witnessed rapid industrial development in Germany, contributing to a growth rate that was higher than that of Britain or France. Later, other European countries also established their own social security systems.

In the United States the Great Depression (1929–1933) was the source of severe unemployment and poverty. Once President Roosevelt took office he began to implement the New Deal, taking comprehensive interventionist action to spur economic development, including measures to help the poor and the unemployed, and to improve the relationship between employees and employers. In 1935 America passed the *Social Security Act* and established its unemployment and pension plans. With respect to this Act, President Roosevelt noted:

> In the past, security depended on families and neighbors. Now, large-scale production has limited the usefulness of those simple measures. We are forced to advance the social security of all by having the government mobilize the active concern of everyone in the population. The universal implementation of welfare policy can eradicate people's fear of unexpected misfortunes or vicissitudes of life.[1]

These policies greatly helped the recovery and growth of the American economy.

After World War II, social welfare systems developed quickly in various countries. The State not only began to provide universal welfare benefits for its citizens, but social security programs were being improved upon. In December 1942 the British economist William Beveridge published a report entitled *Social Insurance and Related Services*—the famous 'Beveridge Plan'. He proposed a comprehensive social security plan based on social insurance and a series of welfare concepts and principles: social security must be compulsory and must provide universal access; social security programs should be managed in a unified way; the government has the obligation to prevent poverty and misfortune; social welfare is a social responsibility; full employment should be realized; all citizens are entitled to get relief from society, so as to meet national minimum living standards. After the war, based on Beveridge's design, the British government passed and implemented a series of social security acts between 1946 and 1948, including the *Family Assistance Act*, *National Health Service Act Industrial Injury Insurance Act*, *National Assistance Act* and *Social Insurance Act*.

In 1948 Britain was declared the first welfare state in the world. It had established a comprehensive system that included assistance in social insurance, housing, matters to do with children, food, and senior citizens, social relief for low-income families, poor senior citizens and the unemployed, as well as health care services and social services. Northern and western European countries, Latin American countries and Japan and South Korea followed suit and established their own welfare systems.

Different forms and classifications of social welfare systems

Since each country differs in its social systems, economic strength and cultural background, its welfare systems, despite some common features, vary in such respects as systems design, policy orientation, welfare programs, specific standards, and implementation measures. Based on the sources and composition of welfare funds, distribution methods of revenues, benefit measures and levels for citizens, and the method and degree of balancing interests of citizens and social resources, social welfare systems can be mainly classified into the three categories shown in Box 3.1.

Box 3.1   Classification of welfare modes and their institutional features

Back in 1958, several scholars began related studies on welfare modes and systems at virtually the same time.[2] They proposed several important concepts that are still in use today. Two of these are the 'residual welfare model' and the 'institutional redistributive model'. To simplify, the residual model is designed to provide assistance for restoring the normal functions of the market and the family; while the institutional model implies a welfare system that can play a preventative role in modern industrial society. In the several decades since then, more and more research has been conducted on these two models. Among the studies, a book[3] written in 1990 was the most famous and most frequently cited. This book was the first to use the concept of a 'welfare regime'. It proposed a division of welfare systems into three categories: the social democratic model represented by Sweden and some other Nordic countries, the conservative model represented by Germany on the European continent, and the liberal model as represented by the US. The features of the three models are listed in Table 3.1.

Table 3.1 Three typologies of welfare regimes and their institutional features

Titmuss' approach to classification	The industrial achievement performance model	The residual welfare model	The institutional redistributive model
Esping Andersen's way of classification	The conservative corporatist model	The liberalism model	The social democratic model
Geographic location	European continent	Anglo-Saxon	Scandinavia
Originated by	Bismarck	Beveridge	Beveridge
Objective	Supporting policies for workers' income	Assistance to the poor and the unemployed	An equal and fair redistribution of social wealth
Basic principles for payment	Contribution-based	Selective	Universal
Technical principles for payment	Social insurance principle	Target oriented	Redistributive principle
Payment structure	Partial payment model (related to contributions and incomes)	Family income investigation model	Unified rate
Accesses	Social status and work environment	Needs and poverty level	Citizenship and residential qualifications
Financing mechanism	Job-related contribution	Tax	Tax
Regulation and decision making	Social partnership	Controlled by the Central government	Controlled by Central and local governments

Source: Zheng Bingwen, *Welfare Systems and Practices in Foreign Countries* (Background Report, 2008).

1. Welfare State

The term 'welfare state' refers to a country in which the government is responsible for safeguarding citizens' welfare and trying to provide universal access to social welfare for all citizens. The welfare state in Britain contains a great variety of programs, such as medical service for all, social insurance and social services. The medical service for farmers and foreigners who have lived in Britain for more than one year are basically to be covered by the government. Social insurance and social services mainly include providing pensions, unemployment relief and family subsidies. Pension coverage consists of three parts: basic pension, contribution-related pension and occupational pension. Unemployment relief includes unemployment benefits, as well as extra allowances and subsidies for the unemployed. Family subsidies include subsidies for pregnant women, children, low-income families, widows and housing, as well as Christmas bonuses. In order to carry out its welfare state policies Britain has established huge managerial institutions.

Northern European countries like Sweden and Denmark started to build 'welfare states' in 1948. Under the principles of universality and unified approach, all citizens are entitled to a basic living allowance, and the government takes on various risks on their behalf. The government not only provides security programs to do with birth, disease, injury and disability, unemployment and pensions, but also subsidies for children, relatives of the deceased, single parent families, housing, education and training. Besides cash allowances, the government also provides services like medical treatment and care. This welfare system with universal access and wide coverage has rightfully allowed Sweden to be described as 'the showcase of welfare states'.

The welfare model in northern European countries can be summed up as featuring generous transfer payments, high substitution rates, well developed public services, limited market supply in public services and strong family policies, etc. The major problem with this system is its high unemployment rate and the rigidity of the labor market.

2. Social security that is 'mutually supported by three different elements'

This is the earliest social security model. It is regarded as the 'traditional model', and it has been adopted by many developed countries including Germany, America and Japan. Different from the welfare state model, this model puts a social insurance system at its core, and is therefore called a social insurance model.

Through relief measures and welfare policies that meet the needs of an industrialized society, this model is able to form a fairly complete social safety network. As opposed to the welfare state model, it has the following features: first, it has established a mechanism of sharing responsibilities among the government, society and individuals to ensure mutual aid when dealing with risks; second, it stresses that people covered by the welfare system should enjoy rights and fulfill their obligations as well, that the two are linked; third, the principal aim of social security system is to free laborers from worrying about what is going to happen to them; fourth, it is able to balance market efficiency and social justice.

Germany, the first country to establish a social insurance system in the world has, since World War II, pursued a social market economy that includes two inseparable areas: a market that allows free competition and can promote economic efficiency; and a social security system that can create and provide social justice. Perfecting its social security system has been regarded as a necessary and important part of Germany's social market economy. The country's social insurance model was already fairly mature in the 1970s. Its core parts include social insurance programs for pensions, medical service, industrial injury, and unemployment insurance, supplemented with social relief and social care. The system can be summed up as follows: first, it provides universal access to social insurance. Its coverage has been expanded from industry workers to office workers and farmers—to include essentially all working people. Social insurance has therefore become the main component of the social security system. Second, social insurance fees are paid by individuals, employers and the government. Third, social insurance is autonomously managed, namely, each institution undertaking social insurance programs must set up a board of directors and a representative conference to handle social insurance business. The board and the conference are composed of representatives of the participants in various programs as well as the employers.

3. Compulsory Savings Security Model

This is a social insurance system that centers on savings accumulated in individual accounts. The 'Central accumulation fund system' in Singapore is a prime example. This security model is also employed by some South American countries like Chile and Argentina, as well as the Hong Kong specially administered region [SAR] of China.

In the 1950s, Singapore started to consider building its own social security system after it won independence. After studying and evaluating the security systems in industrialized countries, Singapore abandoned the idea of simply imitating other countries and decided to establish its own accumulation fund system. This system has the following features: first, both employers and employees are legally subject to certain responsibilities, they are obliged by law to participate in the accumulation fund system and to contribute fees accordingly; second, a government entity called the 'Central accumulation fund bureau' is responsible for supervising and managing the fund; third, the total amount of accumulated funds is applied, namely, both funds contributed by both the employer and the employee are deposited into the individual account of the insured, and will be paid to the insured as his pension after he retires; fourth, unlike the social insurance system, there is no mutual aid or shared sum of funds that operates among the insured, employers, government and citizens. All workers have their own dedicated accumulation fund accounts that are exclusively used by themselves. In time, the uses to which Singapore's accumulation funds were put expanded from social security to medical services, housing, and so on. Indeed, the system has become the core of Singapore's entire social security system.

Chile and Hong Kong SAR also adopted this model, although Chile's system differs from that of Singapore. First, the accumulation fund is paid into solely by the employees; second, a private institution is in charge of operating pension funds. Third, the compulsory savings in the individual accounts can only be used for pensions, instead of such other purposes as housing and medical care—therefore, Chile has other supporting social security policies. The compulsory savings model is also applied in Hong Kong but, in Hong Kong, accumulation funds are jointly contributed by employers and employees; while different from those in Singapore, private agencies manage the accumulation fund. In addition, the compulsory accumulation fund system is only a part of the social security system in Hong Kong. Hong Kong also has a sound comprehensive aid network and well developed social service undertakings. Strictly speaking, Chile and Hong Kong utilize this model only for their pension systems; the model is not the principal component of all their social security systems.

Each of the three models has strengths and weaknesses. The dividing line between them has also become less clear due to prevailing trends in social welfare system reform and the way different systems have begun to influence each other. Unlike economic systems, social welfare systems can hardly be transplanted from one country to another. There is no one model that China can copy, though it can learn from other countries as it sets up a system that is suitable to its own conditions and can satisfy its own needs.

Reforms of social welfare systems in different countries

As the economies of various countries grow and their social structures change, each is having to undertake a relatively substantial degree of reform and adjustment in welfare systems.

Welfare reforms in developed countries in Europe and North America

Since the 1980s the two key issues of an aging population and globalization have put pressure to reform on welfare systems. Due to tight budgets and high unemployment rates, welfare reform is heading in the direction of marketization and privatization in all countries. 'Parameter reform' and 'structure reform' are the main methods being used to reduce costs and lower welfare standards. The politics of 'Thatcherism' in the UK, and 'Reagonimics' in America, accelerated welfare reform in Europe and North America and generated new policies.

The focus of welfare reform in northern European countries is to increase employment

The unemployment rate has remained high in these countries for quite some time and is seen by some as being related to the high degree of unemployment benefits. Unemployment benefits not only affect the supply of labor and the cost of products, but make the labor market less elastic and limit the competitiveness of enterprises. In the 1990s Sweden suffered from its most serious economic recession since the 1930s: between 1992 and 1996 the unemployment rate of young people aged 18 to 24 was nearly 20 percent and welfare state policies faced unprecedented challenges. In Denmark the number of people relying on unemployment benefits soared. Paying unemployment benefits had not only become an uncontrollable burden on government expenditures, but had helped to form a dependency culture which further burdened the government.

To address this problem northern European countries have put forward such initiatives as 'a proactive labor market policy', 'from welfare to working welfare', 'replacing passive payment with proactive measures', and 'changing rights into duties or responsibilities'. Since the 1990s the core aspects of reform measures relating to unemployment security include: reducing payment levels; shortening payment duration, and setting stricter payment requirements.

Denmark issued three acts to shift the definition of its 'welfare path' from 'opportunities and rights' to 'obligations and rights'. In 1998 it began to emphasize the obligation aspect. This year also witnessed the release of the *Social Service Act,* in which 'self-independence' was defined as a personal responsibility, and local governments were given the right to demand that anyone applying for social relief must receive training. Like Denmark and Norway, Sweden introduced 'working benefits' into social relief plans for the first time. Two measures were adopted in Sweden: first, authority was decentralized, and the range and decision-making mechanisms of decentralization were expanded, so that local governments could be more flexible in coping with a growing number of people in need of social relief. In doing this responsibility was shifted from the State to local governments in terms of who served as agent for workers employment compensation. Second, private sectors replaced public sectors in carrying out the implementation of social relief plans. From 1995 local governments started to be responsible for the employment of 20-year-olds and under, and by 1998, the age group included 20 to 25.

In 1998 Sweden passed an act that made local governments responsible for young people aged 20 to 24. By this act local governments must arrange employment for 12 months for any young person who has not found a job or been in educational or training positions for the previous 90 days. Another three months is then allowed for 'job hunting' if the young person fails to find a job in 12 months. Then the 'flexible' plan goes into effect, whereby a young person either takes a job as presented, or loses any welfare subsidies. Another measure Sweden took was to reduce payment standards and set stricter payment requirements, so as to increase the motivation of workers to find jobs and to reduce financial pressures on the government. In 1993 Sweden reduced unemployment benefits by 1 percent and 3 percent respectively for the unemployed with and without children. The duration of unemployment benefits for those who did not contribute fees was also shortened to one year. In 1995 the government again reduced unemployment benefits from 90 percent to 75 percent. Other subsidies, such as illness subsidy, injuries subsidy, and disability subsidy, were also reduced. Any new applicants had to wait six days before receiving their first subsidies, and so on.

After such reforms as described above, northern European countries have not only continued to guarantee the basic welfare level of their citizens, but they have improved their economic competitiveness and growth rates. Welfare has thus become a new incentive for economic growth and for improving the competitiveness of enterprises.

The focus of welfare reform in western European countries is to
assure the financial sustainability of pension security

Pension security is by far the largest and most complicated part of welfare systems in western European countries. Since pensions take the form of 'delayed payments' they are vulnerable to the phenomenon of aging populations. They involve large amounts of money and cast far-reaching influence, so are a particularly hard nut to crack in terms of overall reform of a social security system. Traditional pay-as-you-go systems had already existed for over a century when they faced severe challenges after the oil crisis of the 1970s. Almost all developed countries faced the harsh reality that their revenues were not going to be able to afford their required expenditures. As burdens on the government became heavier, demands for reform grew.

Since the middle and late 1980s the governments of many countries have begun exploring various kinds of reform. Most countries adjusted or improved existing welfare systems. Only a few countries completely abandoned their old system and built a new one. The general goal of reform was to increase individual responsibilities, let the market play its role, and reduce government burdens.

The basic principle in this process was that specific measures should be changed without changing the overall system. Such measures aimed to increase government revenues, reduce expenditures and ease financial pressures. Measures included: resetting the retirement age for receiving pensions, increasing the fee-paying duration and years of service required for a full pension, increasing contribution rates, and adjusting calculation and payment methods and lowering substitution rates.

Governments also reformed the structures of their systems. This included transforming a single structure into a new pension insurance system that incorporated the government, enterprises and individuals, reforming the systems operating mechanisms, reforming the management of funds, and introducing individual accounts into the pension system.

Introducing individual accounts into pension systems constituted a major reform of traditional systems. It was significant for two reasons. First, through establishing accumulated funds for pensions and connecting them with the capital markets, it explored ways to increase the value of funds in pension plans. Second, it served to motivate individual initiative and to overcome problems of low efficiencies and the moral hazard caused by traditional systems. Though there is still debate about whether individual accounts should be introduced into the pension system, the method is increasingly used. In some countries, this is the only method used in pension systems. In other countries, governments have gradually introduced individual accounts while reducing the scale of pay-as-you-go systems at the same time, hoping to combine the two.

Welfare reforms in the United States and Canada

America's traditional social welfare system, and its reform

The 'Bismarck welfare model', born in Germany in the 1880s, not only influenced Europe, but has had a profound influence on North America as well. This influence began with the *Social Security Act* in 1935, after which America expanded welfare coverage over the next half century and made the model the basis for a unified US system. It became one of the key aspects of the 'American model'. A second aspect of the American model is that the universal-access coverage of its welfare system is less developed than that of European countries. For example, there is no medical and health-care security system that covers all Americans. There is only a 'Medicare' system that covers senior citizens over the age of 65, which is contribution-based, as well as a non-contribution-based Medicare system for the poor. A third aspect is that the percentage of the system spent on social projects that require investigation of one's assets is rather large. These mainly include the system of food stamps and *Aid to Families with Dependent Children*. Welfare programs for illness, maternity (temporary loss of work capability), and family subsidies as well as other issues have not been established in the US, while they are prevalent in European countries. Fourth, America has never regarded full employment as being a government responsibility, and as a result proactive labor policies have not been enacted. Responsibility for unemployment insurance mainly goes to local governments. Tolerance of high unemployment rates is far greater than it is in Europe.

The period between the end of World War II and 1981 was a golden age for the welfare system in the US. It saw steady increases in welfare spending and an unemployment rate that stayed below 5 percent. When the oil crisis broke out in 1973, however, the unemployment rate increased dramatically, and by the time Reagan took office in 1981 it had climbed to 7 percent. The biggest difference between America and Europe, in dealing with unemployment, was that European countries created new jobs by increasing social spending on the labor market, while America reduced taxes and increased deficit spending in order to stimulate investment. America's first welfare reforms after World War II started with what was known as the 'Reagan Revolution'. Reagan's tax-cutting policies led to a great reduction in the country's revenue, equal to almost 4 percent of America's GDP. Meanwhile, the country's budget deficit quadrupled (to more than 200 billion US dollars), an increase in the deficit of around 4 percent of America's GDP. Yet from an overall perspective Reagan's reforms were successful. The American economy recovered from 1983 to 1984, and the unemployment rate decreased to the level of the late 1970s.

America's second welfare reform was conducted in 1996 by President Clinton, and it focused on *Aid to Families with Dependent Children* (AFDC). AFDC had been a law enacted in 1936, with the aim of helping vulnerable households by providing non-contribution-based social relief. Since being put into practice, however, due to the number of applicants, it placed an increasingly heavy burden on the government. During the late 1980s and early 1990s the number of benefi- ciary families increased by 30 percent due to economic depression. Based on an extensive study the Clinton Administration issued the *Coordination Act of Indi- vidual Responsibilities and Job Opportunities* in 1996, fundamentally changing the original social aid method and replacing it with the *Temporary Assistant to Needy Families* (TANF). The most remarkable differences were as follows: first, the Federal government stopped providing all-covering financial support to vulnerable families in each state, and replaced it with a fixed allocation; second, the government limited the beneficiary period for vulnerable families; third, the government determined the amount of benefits by evaluating the qualifications of vulnerable families and setting strict requirements on extension of benefits.

The third reform was conducted by the Bush Administration between 2001 and 2005. During his term President Bush vigorously promoted reforms to do with vocational training, and allocated several hundred million dollars for such training to increase employment and boost the economic competitiveness of the US. Bush also tried to reform the Old-Age Survivors and Disability Insurance (OASDI) system, with the aim of changing the contribution-based pay-as-you-go system into a partial accumulative system. He set up a committee to reconfigure the social security system which spent six months designing a new system with three imple- mentation methods. The main concept was to introduce individual accounts and allot a small portion of personal contributions to individual accounts, while the rest would be allocated to the ongoing pay-as-you-go system. The new model was rejected by the American society at large and Bush's efforts essentially failed.

Welfare reform in Canada

The welfare system in Canada was greatly influenced by post-war Britain. After Britain published the *Beveridge Plan* in 1942 Canada also published a similar *Marsh Plan*, which became the blueprint for the welfare system in Canada.

During the 1960s the unemployment rate in Canada remained at 5 percent. The golden age of welfare ended when the oil crisis broke out in 1973. From the mid- 1970s onward, full employment was replaced by a high unemployment rate and the government began to bear a heavy burden in terms of welfare expenditures. When the Conservative Party came to power in 1984 Canada was experiencing its worst economic crisis after the war, with the unemployment rate as high as 10.5 percent and the inflation rate at 4.5 percent.

The new administration proposed a welfare reform in 1984, advocating the 'use of scarce resources where they are most needed'. This was interpreted as a shift from universality to selectivity. Indeed the new administration proposed decreasing welfare spending and abandoning the principle of universality. It promised to further reduce the deficit, but by 1986 the reform had come to an end. Compared with the US, welfare reformed to a lesser degree in Canada and was called 'stable transition reform'.

Welfare reforms in transitional countries in eastern Europe

Eastern European countries have also reformed and adjusted their original social security systems while undergoing economic and political transition. Due to ongoing economic recession, inflation, severe unemployment, and an aging population, these countries were unable to afford welfare projects. Hungary is one example: in 1990 the country's welfare expenditures accounted for 28.4 percent of its GDP, 46.3 percent of the State budget. When coupled with various economic subsidies like price subsidies, welfare expenditures actually constituted 38.4 percent of the country's GDP and 56.8 percent of the State budget—unsustainable in terms of the country's finances. Like Hungary, other Eastern European countries had to rebuild their social welfare systems, and replace an egalitarian system with social security funds that were independent of the State budget.

The new welfare system in Eastern European countries is based on social insurance, which consists of pension plans, medical insurance, unemployment insurance, industrial injury insurance, illness and maternity insurance and family subsidies. Among these, the policies relating to pensions, medical insurance and unemployment insurance refer to the model of 'EC' countries, and are implemented in the form of social insurance funds. These funds are paid by enterprises and employees. Maternity insurance and family subsidies are paid by the national welfare funds.

In order to expand the sources of funds and reflect the unification of rights and duties under market-oriented economies, Eastern European countries have been setting up social security tax systems. According to the *Government Finance Statistics Yearbook 1995* of the International Monetary Fund (IMF), the proportion of social security tax to total tax revenue is as follows: Bulgaria 21.7 percent, Croatia 31.74 percent, the Czech Republic 38.75 percent, Estonia 32.24 percent, Hungary 29.23 percent, Latvia 34.49 percent, Lithuania 32.26 percent, Poland 24.31 percent and Romania 28.7 percent.

Most Eastern European countries have adopted a 'three-pillars' plan as recommended by the World Bank. At the beginning of their transition, expenditures on pensions constituted the largest part of Eastern European country budgets, accounting for 10 to 15 percent of their GDP. In 1994, in the report called *Avoiding the Crisis of Aging*, the World Bank proposed a 'three pillar' pension system, which consisted of compulsory public pensions, compulsory individual account funds, and elective occupational pensions. Between 1995 and 2000 Latvia, Poland, Hungary and Bulgaria all adopted this model. The Czech Republic is one example where pensions provided by the government include two parts: first, all retirees receive the same amount of money to ensure a basic living, which is decided by various factors such as the country's economic development and cost considerations. Second, they receive a fluctuating amount of pension that depends on their seniority, salary, and so on. In order to solve the problem of invisible pension debts during the process of transforming a pay-as-you-go system to an accumulation system, countries like Poland practiced 'nominal accounts' as a transitional method. This method reduced not only debts, but also difficulties for pension reform that were caused by immature financing markets and capital markets.

Eastern European countries have also made changes in the area of medical security. In the past the government paid all medical spending in full—now, that spending is shared by the insured, the employers and the government. The government is responsible for building health care facilities, cultivating medical workers, implementing nation-wide health plans and providing funds for the daily operation of health supervision institutions. When medical insurance funds are insufficient, due to various objective reasons, the government offers necessary financial support to maintain the regular operation of medical security undertakings. Beneficiaries of free medical care must participate in the medical security program, and pay fees as required. The fees of incumbent employees (including army personnel, policemen and firefighters, etc) are to be equally shared by employees and employers. Fees for pensioners are determined by their actual income. In some cases such fees are covered by insurance companies, whereas in other cases they are shared by the insurers and insurance companies. Medical premiums of the unemployed are paid by labor management departments, and will be paid by the unemployment security fund after the implementation of an unemployment security system. Self-employed farmers and private enterprise owners pay fees by themselves on a regular basis as required.

Eastern European countries have also adopted other measures to deal with unemployment. On the one hand they have accelerated the building of employment insurance systems to ease social pressures; on the other, they have adopted various measures to increase employment channels, so as to promote re-employment and reduce the unemployment rate. For example, Hungary set up a commission to coordinate national and local employment policies (namely the 'labor market committee'), to deal with problems related to unemployment, and to balance the labor distribution within and among regions. Meanwhile the government established special unemployment funds such as 'mutual aid funds', 'employment funds' and 'unity funds', to provide material help and vocational training for the unemployed.

Welfare reform in Latin American countries

Most of the 33 countries in Latin America have practiced a typical European continental model of welfare reform. Their welfare systems present almost all features of the European model. First, they are based on the division of industries and social groups. People's social welfare is characterized by vocational welfare. There is a great disparity between different vocations and industries in terms of welfare levels, since great differences exist between good jobs and bad jobs. Second, government finances are heavily burdened by the systems. The beginning of the twentieth century saw rapid economic development and low unemployment rates in Latin America. In addition, due to the dominating influence of Populism, their welfare systems were established to catch up with Europe. Several decades later these systems have become a heavy financial burden on the governments.

One key feature of welfare reform in Latin America is that it has pioneered the privatization of welfare systems, guided in this direction by the 'new liberalism' of the 1980s and the Washington Consensus of the 1990s. Latin America has created the world-famous 'Chile model' in the global wave of welfare reform.

Chile's reform is mainly characterized by the privatization of its pension fund. In the early 1980s the military government, which took office by a military coup, impaired government functions institutionally and then transferred these functions to private sectors by changing the Constitution. Beginning in 1981, Chile began to implement a new pension system based on individual accounts, which consist of a basic account (individuals put 10 percent of their taxable income aside as input into their pension) and a supplementary account (the account is set up for individuals to put more money into pension reserves so as to get more when they are older). The system is run by private pension fund management companies. Under this system all fees are paid by individuals and employers bear no responsibility. Through this reform the government lightened its financial burden and the operational efficiencies also increased notably. Watching Chile's success more than 10 countries, including Peru, Columbia, Argentina, Uruguay and Mexico, have followed suit. This kind of reform is therefore called the Latin American privatization model.

After reforms, Latin American countries showed a notable increase in financial sustainability and their financial burdens decreased. Due to the very narrow coverage of the social welfare system, however, the reform contributed little to reducing poverty and to redressing unfair distribution of wealth. Therefore, poverty rates that climb along with economic growth have become a special Latin American phenomenon.

Welfare reforms in East Asia

Welfare reform in Japan in the course of its 'lost ten years'

In the 1990s Japan faced a stagnant economy and rising unemployment rates. The welfare system, which had worked well under a booming economy, began to exhibit 'systemic failure'. Economic stagnation caused continuous job cuts in enterprises, which in turn brought on a continuous decrease in welfare benefits. The living standards of the working population were greatly affected. Expenditures on public welfare had to be increased year by year until the speed of their increase surpassed the growth rate of the country's GDP. Welfare expenditure climbed from 11 percent of the country's GDP in 1990 to 17.7 percent in 2003. During the 'lost ten years', Japan's welfare expenditures grew faster than those of any European or North American country.

Since the 1990s Japan's welfare reform has mainly focused on cutting the payment standards for beneficiaries to reduce the government's burden, and increasing rates to improve budget levels. Meanwhile the government has encouraged the private welfare market to play a stronger role, strengthened the financial responsibilities of local governments and increased their authority. In order to compensate for the reduced welfare benefits the Japanese government has increased social insurance projects. For example, the *Long Term Care Insurance Act*— established for Japanese seniors—was finally put into practice in the late 1990s. This was a typical contribution-based project, rather than a relief for the poor based on investigation of livelihood. It replaced free medical care for low-income seniors. Subsidies to children from low-income households also underwent similar changes.

Japan's welfare reform is quite opposite to that of European and North American countries. Japan reduced the role of selectivity and emphasized the role of universality, especially during the 'lost ten years'. Such reform was moving in a direction that was further and further from the former relief system and the European model. Japan's welfare system is now facing a dilemma: on the one hand, the mechanisms that substitute for family welfare are growing ever weaker; on the other hand, the level of benefits that enterprises pay is declining. Welfare expenditures are increasing while payment levels are decreasing. This may exclude needy low income families from the welfare system.

Welfare development and reform in South Korea, Singapore, Taiwan and Hong Kong

South Korea's postwar welfare development went through four stages: the first was a postwar recovery stage (1945–1959), during which the country's welfare mainly relied on economic assistance from the United States. The welfare system basically continued to use an 'order' that Japan had issued in Korea in 1944 entitled 'Rescue Korea'. The second was the stage of preliminary establishment of welfare (1960–1979). During this period, guided by the principle of 'first increase, then think of distributing', the government issued some social-benefit steps in order to consolidate power, ensure supply and lessen extreme poverty. This was an important stage in South Korea's economic takeoff and a considerable amount of welfare legislation was established during this period. On the whole, however, the country's main concern remained economic growth as opposed to social welfare. The third stage could be described as 'coverage expansion' (1980–1997). After 20 years of rapid economic growth South Korea had strengthened its financial capabilities and set new targets on that new financial foundation. These included building a welfare society, building a just society and reforming education. The country aimed to gradually eradicate the discontent and protests that had accumulated over 20 years' practice of 'first increase, then distribute'. During this period workers went on nationwide strikes, demanding higher pay and benefits. Even as this was occurring welfare policies like national medical insurance programs, national annuity programs, minimum wage programs, and employment insurance programs were being put into place, as social welfare developed to a higher stage. The fourth stage started in 1977 and extends up to today. Social welfare is maturing in South Korea. A series of acts such as the *National Health Insurance Act* and the *National Basic Livelihood Security Act* have been issued. Among these measures, the annuity reform launched in 2007 is still under way.

Much of the South Korean literature demonstrates that the country has had a very clear idea about the role of a welfare system over the 50 years during which their system was being constructed. On the one hand, Koreans understood that increasing welfare levels and expanding social expenditures could protect vulnerable groups and be conducive to the stable and sustainable development of their national economy. On the other hand, they recognized that one could not ignore too rapid increases in social costs and their negative influence on economic development and the country's finances. The fact that Western European countries have reformed their traditional welfare models precisely in order to restore economic growth fully demonstrates that high welfare levels have the potential to cause great problems in social development. South Korea's welfare expenditures have remained low, accounting for 6.87 percent of the country's GDP in 2005, excluding education spending, far lower than the average 20.7 percent of OECD countries. Some scholars in South Korea believe that the government is afraid of the 'welfare disease' appearing in developed countries. South Korea is now facing multiple challenges, including low economic growth, low birth rates and an aging population. If it were to set up a welfare system similar to that in developed countries, it would definitely face the harsh reality that high welfare leads to high taxes. This in turn affects any enthusiasm for investment, as well as work, which further diminishes the vigor of any economy. South Korea's national debt has increased rapidly, particularly as a result of the Asian financial crisis of 1997, and its welfare costs have also increased. These factors have further confirmed South Korea's belief that it must follow its own 'Korean model'.

There are two major lessons we can learn from South Korea. The first is that a law passed long ago could not be implemented until much later due to inadequate underlying conditions. The *Medical Insurance Law* was passed back in 1963 but, due to lack of consensus as well as insufficient finances, its partial implementation began only in 1977 and it was only put fully into effect in 1989. The second lesson relates to misjudgments in setting annuity rates: when the national annuity system was implemented in 1988 it followed a principle of 'low premiums and high benefits' which has put burdens on State finances as a result of insufficient revenue. Calculations determined that. if the situation remained unchanged, the system would have a deficit in 2036 and run out of money by 2047. To deal with this problem South Korea conducted two annuity reforms in 1998 and 2007, first to adjust the rate (1998) and then the payment level (2007).

Singapore set up a centralized public-fund welfare system in 1955 which, after half a century and various evolutions, has grown into a comprehensive social insurance system that integrates such multiple functions as pensions, housing and medical care. In addition, the government has also established a series of other welfare systems to improve low-income people's livelihood. Major components of other systems include housing subsidies, livelihood subsidies, education subsidies, medical subsidies, employment services, child benefits and transportation subsidies.

Social welfare in Taiwan was first established in the 1950s and at its inception only covered such groups as soldiers, civil servants and teachers. Since the 1980s, with economic growth and the worsening of social contradictions, a welfare assurance system has gradually taken shape. It developed quickly in the 1990s, but was still divided into four separate plans for workers, army personnel, civil servants (government officers, and teachers in public and private schools) and farmers. Establishing a unified system has become the inevitable trend. In 1995 Taiwan promulgated a national health insurance act, which covered the entire population. This is a compulsory insurance system that requires the insured to pay a portion of the premiums. Taiwan has also established other welfare projects such as social relief, social welfare, employment training and vocational training to provide subsistence relief, medical benefits, emergency help, disaster relief, and aid facilities to low income populations and people requiring emergency assistance. Social welfare mainly includes programs targeted at children, teenagers, the disabled, and senior citizens.

Social welfare in Hong Kong is composed of three main parts. The first includes various welfare benefits from national taxes. This is an 'income security system' and is called 'social security'. It includes the following programs: comprehensive social security assistance program which targets elderly populations, those that are disabled, those that are in ill-health, the unemployed, single parent families and low-income families; the public security fund program which provides subsidies to elderly people and the severely disabled; compensation program which provides cash for victims of violent crimes and those who are injured in the course of enforcing laws; the emergency relief program which offers emergency aid to victims of natural disasters, fires and other disasters (the relief covers funeral aid, aid in rebuilding houses, aid for repairing and replacing boats, aid for agricultural losses and special subsidies). The second part of Hong Kong's system is 'elective vocational welfare' for employees as provided by the employers. Since, prior to 2000, Hong Kong had no social insurance system that covered the whole population; employers provided security for employees by way of vocational welfare. The welfare programs included security for old age, disability, death, illness, maternity, industrial injuries and unemployment. The third part of Hong Kong's system includes social welfare facilities and services provided by public sectors and civil societies. The fourth part is the basic pension scheme established in 2000. The establishment of this compulsory accumulation fund ended the historical period during which retirees relied upon vocational welfare for their living. By the end of June, 2008, 68 percent of Hong Kong's 3.53 million employees have participated in this program, 17 percent in other retirement programs (e.g. civil servant), while 11 percent needed no programs. Only 4 percent did not join any programs. As a result, 96 percent of the working population in Hong Kong is currently covered by retirement programs.

Analysis of the Confucian welfare model in East Asian countries

Generally speaking, welfare development in East Asian countries can be classified according to two main characteristics. The first relates to the general cultural background of these countries; the second relates to the fact that their provision of welfare benefits is far lower than that of European and North American countries. Welfare development trends in South Korea, Singapore and Hong Kong are particularly different from European models and indeed are growing further and further apart. The structures of their expenditures are different, though it cannot be said that they resemble those of Britain and America either. Such models have been called the 'East Asian Confucian model'. It provides low benefits in the face of high economic growth and high employment. In this East Asian context the 'family centralism' of traditional culture co-exists with the 'centralism' of the modern state.

The basic reason this 'East Asian Confucian model of welfare' came into being can be attributed to the unique half-century of economic development in the region, and can be best exemplified by systems adopted in Japan and South Korea. Just as with their intent to 'catch up with and surpass' in the arenas of industrialization and modernization, these countries intended to do the same in the arena of welfare development The process included learning from the west—drinking in western knowledge, technology and civilization. The specific models to follow in this 'catching up with and surpassing' were, most importantly, American and European. Welfare development in Japan played an extremely important role in paving the way for the rest of East Asia—South Korea soon followed suit and, learning from Japan, South Korea became hyper-alert to any drawbacks of 'westernizing' during the 'lost ten years'. The outbreak of the Asian financial crisis in 1997 made South Korea even more cautious. In 1973, after being hit by the oil crisis, Japan began a deep reconsideration of its system (between 1975 and 1985 unemployment tripled, greatly increasing welfare expenditures). When Thatcherism and Reagonomics were starting a 'revolutionary movement' in welfare in the capitalist world, Japan was experiencing its 'lost ten years', further putting that country in a quandary.

Given this ambivalent attitude, East Asian countries began to set up and evolve their own welfare systems. The most outstanding in this regard turned out to be Japan. As a developed country, Japan had to institute social welfare systems both to satisfy domestic needs and to deal with foreign pressures. On the other hand, Japan had no alternative but to take measures to maintain the 'family centralism' of traditional Confucian culture, due to great concerns about the westernization of its welfare system. Therefore it implemented the policy of constantly increasing welfare expenditures, even as it espoused reducing benefits in favor of the use of substitution.

Debates on social welfare reform, and the risks involved

The international community constantly debates welfare reform and, particularly, the issue of privatization. Privatization started with pensions and is now spreading to medical insurance, unemployment insurance and industrial injury insurance. It touches on investment, operations and management, and its role appears to be expanding. The most representative arguments for pro and con have been put forward by the International Labor Organization and the World Bank.

Box 3.2   Three groups of countries in world welfare reform

The countries reforming their welfare systems from the 1980s up to now can be divided into three groups according to their level of privatization: radically privatizing countries, mildly privatizing countries and countries that are basically not reforming at all.

Radical privatization reform refers to reform in the whole system; it implies major changes in the nature of the welfare system. The purpose is to increase and strengthen the financial sustainability of the social welfare system and partially transfer the responsibility of caring for senior citizens to markets, families or individuals, supplemented by other measures such as lowering welfare payments. Radical privatization countries include Britain, America, Italy, Switzerland and Holland.

Britain made fundamental changes to its welfare system in 1986, 1992 and 1996 respectively. These included reducing the government's percentage in State Earnings Related Pension Scheme (SERPS), changing payment levels from 25 percent of the total sum earned over the 20 years with highest income, to 20 percent of the income earned during one's whole lifetime. Meanwhile, the employees are allowed to quit SERPS by agreement. The government will offer them preferential policies to participate in welfare programs provided by the market. The reform has cut the government's expenditures on pensions as a whole.

Pension reform throughout the world, including that in Britain, by nature is increasing the role of individuals and the market and decreasing the responsibilities of the government. Except for Britain, countries (including Italy) have, through unwritten agreement, begun to introduce 'nominal account' systems since the 1990s.

The second group could be termed 'mildly privatizing' countries. They include Germany, Hungary, Ireland, Canada and Australia, etc. In order to ease the pressure of high welfare expenditures these countries have carried out reforms to lower payment standards, delayed retirement age, and set stricter requirements for payment. Reform of this kind can be called single-program reform or marginal reform.

Germany conducted two pension reforms in the 1990s. The first was conducted in 1992 with two major measures: first, the government changed the payment-related index from gross income to net income, which reduced payment levels to a degree, and the pension costs were redistributed between retirees and the employed. Second, the government raised the cost of early retirement. The mandatory retirement age was set at 65 for both men and women. This measure will require a relatively long transition, and will be put into full practice in 2012.

Due to rising unemployment rates Germany conducted another reform in 1996. The government reduced social insurance fees and advanced the transitional period as stipulated in the 1992 reform to the year 2004. The most notable and controversial reform was passed in 1997 and implemented in 1999. It introduced a weighting scheme into the calculations. If life expectancy increased, the government would change calculation formulas to reduce pension payment standards, namely, lowering payment standards by changing the indexes. It is estimated that, on the basis of demographic data, the payment standards would thereby be decreased from 70 percent to 64 percent of average income.

In sum, some countries have adjusted their pension systems in a mild manner, without changes in their basic nature. These countries adjusted almost all indexes related to payment levels and set forth a long transitional period—as long as 20 years in some countries. This means that reform will be completed by the 2020s. To some countries, mild reform has changed the government's role of 'national protector' in pension policies. The pension risk is gradually being transferred to individuals in the reform and recommercialization process.

The third group is countries who are not reforming at all. They include France, Austria, Spain, and Belgium. These countries have failed to conduct reforms mainly because their reform measures were not effective. Even reforms addressed at single programs were the object of great controversy and thereby suspended. Due to the rigidities of their systems, welfare in these countries is headed in precisely the opposite direction to those noted above, namely towards an expanding welfare system.

Source: Zheng Bingwen, *Welfare Systems and Practices in Foreign Countries* (Background Report, 2008).

The debate on social security objectives

The World Bank believes that social security is not simply a system for stabilizing society, but should also contribute to efficiencies and promote economic growth. Therefore, it espouses 'protecting the elderly even as it promotes economic development'. On the other side of the equation the International Labor Organization holds that it is the government's unavoidable responsibility to secure the livelihood of the elderly and maintain social stability.

Over time the World Bank's ideas have had great influence on the reform of pension schemes around the world, but in recent years the setbacks hitting the world—including economic recession and financial crisis—have greatly increased economic uncertainties and disturbed financial markets. These have intensified people's worries about the risk of individual accounts and the entire accumulative welfare system. The fact that the Enron bankruptcy in America exposed its pension to massive shrinkage has further increased people's doubts about individual account systems.

Payment pressures caused by pay-as-you-go systems, and the financial risks facing full accumulative systems, are at the core of national quandaries about how to run their respective systems

The debate about social security privatization

The World Bank advocates a market-oriented, privatized, management system, while the International Social Security Association (ISSA) holds the opposite view. In 2001, at the 27th world conference of the ISSA held in Stockholm, some delegates expressed the belief that privatization is not a solution to every problem of social security, and that unsuccessful privatization will in the end only bring more problems for the government.

The political and social risks of welfare reform

As theories, strategies and concepts in the international community are changing with regard to modes of governance, each country is paying more attention to the actual application of social policies in order to solve social, economic and political problems. From this perspective social security is not only an important public policy, but it also directly affects the authority and popularity rating of the ruling party in any given country. In 1935 Roosevelt started the New Deal, with social security as its core—this alleviated social contradictions such as unemployment and economic depression, and helped America get through the economic crisis of the 1930s. The fact that, after World War II, social democratic parties won elections in 29 countries by relying on social welfare proposals also fully demonstrates this point.

Social security, especially pension plan reform, is facing considerable political and social risks. It is hard to persuade people to give up welfare benefits they already have. The former US President Reagan and the former British Prime Minister Thatcher conducted radical social welfare reforms. Since they were seen as being 'heartless acts of a market economy', they provoked sufficient opposition that both of these parties lost the support of lower social levels and eventually lost power altogether. In 1991 the Juppe government in France, in order to be able to participate in deciding on the 'Euro', tried to reduce financial deficits by cutting social security expenditures, thereby causing a massive strike and bringing about the replacement of government leaders.

All these examples indicate that welfare reform faces considerable obstacles, which is why many countries are quite cautious when issuing policies concerning the majority's interests. Even when dealing with problems like delaying retirement age, many countries try to make this a gradual process to avoid hurting people's vested interests. South Korea plans to raise the retirement age from the current 60 to 61 in 2013, and then one year more after every five years, until the country finally reaches the objective of 65 in 2033. Many countries, among them America and Japan, have adopted similar methods. Such practices will not overly impinge upon people's present interests and can ensure a stable reform.

On the whole, each country's welfare reform is targeted at providing necessary securities for citizens, reducing financial burdens, and improving economic competitiveness and growth at the same time. However, once welfare has been established in a certain country, it takes on a certain degree of rigidity, making any reform more difficult. Though welfare reform is much discussed in the international community, implementation of reform remains a hard and long process. For China, it has become particularly urgent to establish reasonable guiding principles and the overall framework of the system at the outset, so that it can satisfy not only immediate practical needs but also the demands of ongoing sustainable development.

Notes

1 *Collection of Roosevelt*, Chinese version, published by The Commercial Press in 1982, pp. 58, 60, 77–81.
2 Harold L. Wilensky and Charles N. Lebeaux, *Industrial Society and Social Welfare: The impact of industrialization on the supply and organization of social welfare services in the United States* (New York: Russell Sage Foundation, 1958), R. Titmuss *Essays on the Welfare State* (London: Allen and Unwin, 1958).
3 Esping Anderson (Denmark), *The Three Worlds of Welfare Capitalism*, trans. by Zheng Bingwen (Law Press China, 2003).

4 A welfare system with coverage for all rural migrant workers

To ensure equity, China's new social welfare system must, first of all, benefit all of China's 1.3 billion citizens. Within that responsibility, the most urgent priority is to establish pension plans and various other security programs for rural migrant workers. The term 'rural migrant workers' refers to a specific group of people who have formed as a result of specific factors in our socioeconomic transition. The concept is uniquely Chinese, because of the way China's system defines the rights of countryside people differently from the rights of people living in cities. 'Rural migrant workers' are people who are still identified as 'farmers' in terms of their official 'household registration', since they are still formally registered in rural areas. They have contracted farmland that was allocated to them, but their primary earnings come from non-agricultural activities. There are currently 200 million such rural migrant workers in China. Of this total, 130 million are transient, moving from one region to another (see Table 4.1). Rural migrant workers work for a broad range of industries and have become a key component in China's labor force. They occupy 68 percent of all jobs in the processing and manufacturing industries, almost 80 percent in the construction and mining industries, and more than 50 percent in the industries of environmental waste management, domestic service and the food and beverage industries. Their huge contribution to socioeconomic development, as well as urban construction and general urban prosperity, presents a sharp contrast to the unequal treatment they receive when it comes to accessing public services and social welfare programs. ['Rural' registration entitles a person to fewer rights and privileges than a person registered under 'urban' status enjoys, even if that 'rural' person is living in an urban setting.] The issue is causing broad social concern.

Inadequate social welfare programs for rural migrant workers

The inadequacy of social welfare programs for rural migrant workers is most evident in the pension system. At present there are three experimental models for the rural migrant workers' pension scheme. The first is the Guangdong model, an exact replica of the urban arrangements. The second is the Zhejiang model, which also copies the urban basic pension plan except for lower premiums and lower criteria for enrollment. The third is the Shanghai model, a comprehensive

Table 4.1 Number of migrant workers moving between regions, 2000–2006

Year	Number of migrant rural workers (10,000 people)	Proportion in urban employment (percent)	Proportion in employment in secondary and tertiary industries (percent)	Proportion in urban and rural employment (percent)
2000	7,849	36.9	21.8	10.9
2001	8,399	35.1	23.0	11.5
2002	10,470	42.3	28.4	14.2
2003	11,390	44.4	30.1	15.3
2004	11,823	44.7	29.6	15.7
2005	12,578	46.0	30.1	16.6
2006	13,212	46.7	30.1	17.3

Source: The statistics under 'Number of migrant rural workers' come from *The China Rural Household Survey Yearbook* compiled by the Rural Socioeconomic Survey Department of the National Bureau of Statistics; and the percentage figures are calculated based on *China Statistical Abstract 2007*.

insurance plan specifically designed for rural migrant workers with a relatively low premium. In spite of many advantages each of the three models has its own disadvantages as well: the biggest problem with the Guangdong model is that the personal contributions may be withdrawn, but not the pooling part, if migrant rural workers leave the province and exit the insurance plan; in the Zhejiang model, the insurance premium is far lower than the requirements for urban workers, but the benefits are only slightly lower, which will place subsequent governments under increasing budgetary pressures As for the Shanghai model, the benefits are on the low side, and more centralized pooling will be hard to achieve in the future. Overall, the insurance coverage of rural migrant workers remains at a very low level. According to the data, by 2007 less than 50 percent of the nearly 200 million rural migrant workers were employed in formal sectors and participated in social insurance. Only 18.46 million participated in any basic pension plan.

Housing represents another welfare issue for rural migrant workers. Studies show that in 2006, 29.19 percent of them lived in dormitories, 20.14 percent in housing that lacked kitchen and toilet facilities, 7.88 percent lived right there on their work site, and 6.45 percent lived in makeshift sheds.[1] The average per capita living space of these people is less than seven square meters, while rent accounts for 30 percent of their income. The urban planning of most cities fails to consider the housing needs of rural migrant workers.

Medical insurance, education and training constitute the third welfare issue for rural migrant workers. In 2007 only 31.31 million [out of 200 million] were covered by any medical insurance. The health of this segment of the population is of considerable concern. The rate at which 'notifications' are made of infectious diseases among this population is rising at an extremely fast 15 percent per year. Such diseases include HIV/AIDS. Basic services related to such things as family planning and reproductive health are not universally accessible. The self-education and re-education of rural migrant workers, as well as the education of their children, remains largely unaddressed.

In recent years the State Council has adopted a series of policies to safeguard the rights and interests of rural migrant workers and to improve their employment opportunities. It has formulated guidelines that call for 'equitable treatment, reasonable guidance, improved management and service' for these people. It has taken actions to eliminate discrimination against them, protect their legitimate rights and interests, help them build skills and provide educational services for their children. The most practical and immediate issues have been improved to some extent. However, in general, the conflicts have only been alleviated partly, while the fundamental problems have yet to be resolved. The problems faced by rural migrant workers are transitional ones, stemming from the economic and social transition, but it will take a long time to address them fully. Much needs to be done in aspects such as social policy, public services and social welfare, to properly solve the problems and provide them with a fair and decent working and living environment.

Establish and improve the pension system for rural migrant workers

The wage level of rural migrant workers is generally quite low (in 2007 the average monthly salary was about RMB 1,100). They are highly transient, not only moving between cities but also frequently changing jobs with any one employer. According to a survey, less than 15 percent work for an employer for more than three consecutive years. This situation poses a host of difficulties if workers participate in pension schemes that are devised for urban employees. The high entry threshold and poor portability of urban-employee arrangements makes these urban plans inappropriate for protecting their interests and benefits (see Box 4.1). A pension arrangement suitable for them should consider low premiums, universal coverage, and excellent portability.

Box 4.1 A migrant worker's recommendation on the portability of social insurance schemes

I am a rural migrant worker, and I pay close attention to how well social insurance plans for tens of millions of people like me can be carried along with us. China saw its fastest growth ever in the year 2007. That same year, many of us suffered the greatest losses. Due to the shutting down of factories and relocation of enterprises in Guangdong, a wave of people had to exit social insurance. We were only able to get back our personal payments, however we got nothing out of the premiums previously paid by employers. In Shenzhen, 4.3997 million migrant rural workers participated in social insurance. Last year, 830,000 of them had to exit their systems, meaning they had to leave behind RMB 800 million that could not be withdrawn from the local social insurance fund. This was money we were going to rely on when

---

we got old. We left our hometowns to contribute to the economic development of this city, yet we cannot keep the social insurance we've paid into for years. Is that fair? Many friends around me don't participate in the social insurance because of the poor portability between provinces. Everybody knows it is good to purchase social insurance. But if the Ministry of Human Resources and Social Security doesn't fix this issue together with the other parts of the government that are involved, it will never get resolved. The reason is that the more developed a city is, the more reluctant the local social security bureau is to allow the portability of a social insurance scheme. If a migrant rural worker fails to stay in a city for 15 years, he has to give up the pooled funds when he leaves. Because it is in their local interests, social security bureaus in these cities hate to make a social security plans portable—the social insurance fund is regarded as their own financial bonanza. Why is it our government departments have failed to work out a solution? Large banks in our country allow global transfer of deposits, why is it so difficult to make the same happen for the social insurance scheme? Here, I would like to make a proposal: large banks may launch bank cards or bankbooks exclusively for social insurance, and individuals may open bank accounts with their ID cards, so that their employers may pay the social insurance premium into the accounts. Both the payments made by individuals and enterprises are deposited into individual accounts. Enterprises submit the cards to the social security bureaus for registration, so that the bureaus can supervise the premium payments, and migrant rural workers can also trace the payment status. If a rural migrant worker works in city A for a few years, and then moves to city B, he can still have right to the premiums he and the employer have already paid, and he may also continue to pay for his social insurance so long as he carries his social security card or bankbook. The social security fund must be operated by the National Council for Social Security Fund, while each special account for social security must contain specific information on the participant. The participant cannot withdraw funds from the account until he reaches legal retirement age. If a participant has a good income in a certain period, he may deposit more in his account to better provide for his old age. If we set up such a system, all citizens will have the confidence to participate in social insurance. I believe this issue should be addressed at the earliest possible time, ideally before the end of 2008. 2008 is the year of the Olympics and a good year for China. Eighty million rural migrant workers are counting on you to set up a better pension plan for us. It will be the largest program for people's well-being ever accomplished, and the largest social security project. On behalf of all the rural migrant workers in the country, I extend my sincere gratitude to you.

Source: A letter written by a rural migrant worker in Shenzhen to Zheng Bingwen, Director of the Latin America Research Institute of the Chinese Academy of Social Sciences.

It should be possible to set up a pension system for rural migrant workers that is innovative—lower premiums, higher administrative levels at which pooling is managed, improved financial viability of individual accounts, and implementation in one step. The pension system of rural migrant workers may consist of both the basic pension account and the individual account. The basic pension account should be pooled at the national level, while the financial viability of the individual account should be improved. A lower premium rate should be applied to rural migrant workers, while the insurance premium should be paid by both employers and employees. An enterprise should pay the premium at 12 percent of the total wages of rural migrant workers, where 6 percent will go to the pooled fund and be managed under uniform national management, and the other 6 percent will to the individual account. A rural migrant worker will pay the premium at 4 percent of his wages, to bolster the individual account, and he will receive an account card. The card will record the status of premium payments, and allow for inquiries, but will not support premature withdrawal. At the same time a national pension settlement system should be established to pay rural migrant workers upon retirement, as per national pooling regulations. The responsibility for the insurance procedures and the account management in principle rests with the Labor Welfare Security Department, from top to bottom.

In terms of managing the funds, both maintaining and appreciating their value, funds in the individual accounts of rural migrant workers may be separated out and handled differently from the overall urban [social] insurance fund. Policies should be formulated that allow a certain percentage of the fund to be used for indirect investments in national infrastructure projects and other key projects as well as other market-oriented investment initiatives. Meanwhile, special government bonds may be issued to ensure the appreciation of the fund. The objective is to have more than 50 percent of rural migrant workers covered by pension plans by 2010, and to have all of them covered by 2012.

Rural migrant workers that have worked in the 'formal sector' [proper or official, meaning State-sector or State-recognized] and participated in the urban workers' social insurance plans should be encouraged to maintain the insurance, and at the same time be guaranteed the equal benefit of it. The employers should pay social insurance premiums for these workers as required by law. Rural migrant workers in the informal sector, especially in the cities' service industries where businesses are small and jobs are unstable, may be included in the urban pension system as the economy develops, in the same way as informally employed urban residents.

Reform of the pension scheme will reduce the loss of income risks faced by rural migrant workers, encourage them to build skills and take jobs in a stable manner, and finally to settle down in cities.

Housing security for rural migrant workers

Housing is one of the most fundamental problems rural migrant workers encounter in their urban life. A survey done by the Construction Ministry shows that most rural migrant workers live in rented housing (about 60 percent of them) or dormitories provided by employers (about 30 percent of them). Only a very small percentage lives in housing that they have purchased.[2] The conditions in dormitories provided by employers vary considerably, depending on the job. For example, in big manufacturing and mining businesses in the formal sector, rural migrant workers may live in better equipped dormitories by paying a housing fee, while those in the construction industry have to be accommodated in makeshift sheds or the unfinished housing that they are working on at the time.

The main housing problems faced by rural migrant workers are twofold: the first is affordability. Both housing rents and purchase prices in cities are prohibitively expensive, preventing the majority of these people from living in a decent place. The second challenge is substandard housing. Even when the migrant workers can manage to rent housing or live in the dormitory provided by the employer, the housing conditions are usually extremely poor. The housing is usually located on the outskirts of cities; it is often crowded, poorly equipped and has no access to essential sanitary and firefighting facilities.

China's 200 million rural migrant workers have contributed enormously to the country's economic progress and to its urban development. In the interests of both social equity and social security [harmonization] it is essential to address their housing needs and enable them to have a share in the fruits of economic growth and urbanization. Improving housing conditions in cities where rural migrant workers both live and work will not only reward the people who have contributed to local development and prosperity, but will also facilitate the further development of the cities themselves. Currently, the underdeveloped city outskirts and the 'villages within cities' are densely inhabited by rural migrant workers who cannot find housing elsewhere. These areas are usually poorly supported by public utilities. They contain a great many unauthorized structures, thus presenting a great challenge for city management and social stability and restricting the further development of urbanization. Addressing the housing problems of rural migrant workers is a bounden responsibility of municipal governments.

In view of the country's current status of economic and social development, we propose the following approaches to address the problem: in the process of urban development, the housing problems of rural migrant workers should be incorporated into urban planning. Their housing systems should be planned out from an overall perspective, based on local economic structures, industrial patterns and infrastructure, the financial resources available to the local government, demographic structures and other considerations.

Market mechanisms should be brought into full play in addressing the housing needs of rural migrant workers, and the issues should be attacked through various channels. The government needs to take responsibility for their housing security, but that does not mean it is the sole provider of housing. Instead, the government should promulgate policies and mobilize all the stakeholders, in particular, employers. Financially strong businesses should be encouraged to build dormitories for their employees. This should not only relieve the housing problems of rural migrant workers and attract more of them to a given business, but should also enable the business to play an important role in the management of and services for these workers, thus lessening the pressures on society. The government may formulate preferential policies to do with land-use approvals and taxation when considering such dormitories.

Multi-layered solutions should be worked out to address housing issues. The region from which rural migrant workers originate, their general occupations, income levels and family backgrounds usually vary greatly—which accounts for a huge difference in their needs for housing. Therefore, a multi-layered housing security system should be in place which is capable of delivering diversified solutions for differentiated needs. For example, for a low-income rural migrant worker who has stayed in cities for a long time and who is in great need of housing, a low-rent option (through a relief system where eligible applicants are allowed to rent the designated housing, or through a rent subsidy) may be made available. By referring to preferential policies on low-rent housing, local governments may build housing that caters to the needs of these workers and can be offered to them at a low rent. On the other hand, higher earners can be encouraged to purchase affordable housing, i.e. another housing relief program. Local governments should refer to policies concerning urban low-rent housing and affordable housing to provide preferential treatment in land-use and taxation.

A legal framework should be formulated to address the rural migrant workers' housing needs. Addressing housing needs is a long process, thus a legal framework at a high level is essential to ensure the stability and continuity of housing security policies.

This book recommends that direct or indirect subsidies (up to RMB 100 per capita per month) be provided, by 2010, to 10 percent of the low-income rural migrant workers in need of housing, so as to ensure a minimum housing security level equivalent to that for urban residents. The percentage of beneficiaries should rise to 30 percent with the subsidy doubling to RMB 200 by 2020. This will address the housing problems of those rural workers who have already settled in cities for a long time.

Employment training and services for rural migrant workers

According to a sample survey conducted by the former Ministry of Labor and Social Security, most rural migrant workers are young and middle-aged adults between the ages of 20 and 40. They are notable for their poor education, with 55.7 percent of them having received junior high school education or below. Junior and middle-school graduates in rural areas currently total some 10 million people, most of whom are unable or unwilling to proceed with their study. To improve their employability, the '9+1' compulsory education designed for junior high school graduates in rural areas should be promoted incrementally so that most of them will be able to receive one free year of additional vocational education. Efforts should be made to ensure that the free year is accessible to 80 percent of graduates by 2012, and to all of them by 2020. After obtaining the corresponding vocational qualifications, these young junior high school graduates may have more opportunities for better-paid jobs.

Rural migrant workers mainly find work through the recommendations of people in their own local community or through relatives—some 56.8 percent find work in this way. To reduce the 'blind' nature of how people look for jobs the public employment service systems in their hometowns, or the cities they work in, should provide free services and help them find suitable jobs as soon as they arrive. New rural migrant workers should receive free pre-service training, including training to do with labor rights and interests, occupational safety and hygiene, and minimum salary security, so that the rural migrant workers will clearly know their rights and interests and how to protect themselves when such rights and interests are transgressed. The government may sponsor the training of rural migrant workers by offering them training coupons or through contracted training organizations.

Such training has already become a priority for the governments at all levels. For example, almost 10 million rural migrant workers have been trained since the implementation of the Sunshine Project in 2003. Now the training is more institutionalized and systematic. However, the current training is mostly 'orientation training' designed for those farmers moving to cities for the first time, to better prepare them for future jobs. The training programs are vastly inadequate for those people who have already worked in cities for some time.

The fact that farmers are working in non-agricultural sectors has evolved to a new stage, which requires that we be more innovative in our training of rural migrant workers. More attention should be paid to continuous training of such people who have already landed a job in cities. Continuous training will enable them to improve their skills, and the opportunity to find a well-paid job. With ongoing training, and improved employment opportunities and consequently rising income, they are more likely to remain in cities and truly become urban residents. Market forces should be encouraged. Private vocational training providers should play a leading role in this regard. The government may further lower the entry threshold for the training schools for rural migrant workers. Relevant government entities may also provide tax preferences for new schools (see Box 4.2). The government may introduce a bidding process to support certain private schools that may serve as 'centers of excellence', and help them work out continuous training programs best suited to rural migrant workers.

Box 4.2   Training of rural migrant workers in Zhongshan, Guangdong Province

A large number of rural migrant workers have swarmed to Zhongshan, Guangdong Province, attracted by its ongoing rapid economic growth. By the end of 2006, the number of such rural workers in the city had hit 1.3 million. They are now an important component of the city's population, and make an active contribution to its economic and social progress. In this context, vocational training for these rural migrant workers has become an important task of the local government.

To better implement training programs for rural migrant workers, the government has formulated *Measures of Zhongshan City on Subsidizing Training of Migrant rural workers* (The Measures). The Measures specify that trained rural migrant workers may register as permanent urban residents of the city, if they obtain the 'vocational qualifications for senior technicians' as reviewed by and registered with the Labor and Social Security Bureau. Rural migrant workers who are willing to participate in various upgrading of skills programs may receive free Training Discount Coupons, choose from training programs within the specified scope of disciplines (work types) that they like and may suit them most, and receive training from designated institutions. In addition, if they are accredited as qualified and employed after the training, and participate in the social insurance and pay the premium, they will receive a subsidy equivalent to 50 percent of the total expenses of the corresponding vocational qualification training and skills accreditation.

Zhongshan has built vocational training schools in four of its subdivisions: Sanxiang, Dongsheng, Nantou and the Torch Development Zone, to explore the development of public vocational training bases. The city has also adopted measures to encourage rural migrant workers' participation in vocational training. It offers training subsidies to those eligible rural migrant worker-trainees. Highly skilled workers will be entitled to the same benefits as other high-skilled members of the population. Since 2006, 10 Excellent Tutors for Technical Professional Training, 10 Excellent Skilled Workers, 20 Talented Craftsmen and 60 Technical Experts have been cited among the city's employees every two years. The city government grants honorary titles and certificates as well as a prize of RMB 10,000, RMB 5,000, RMB 2,000 and RMB 1,000 to these people respectively. Enterprises are encouraged to train rural migrant workers. A specified percentage of staff-education expenses that has been accrued by enterprises may be included in pre-tax costs. At the same time, an 'employment qualification system' has been introduced to promote training. If enterprises recruit rural migrant workers for technical jobs, they should train the workers in line with relevant vocational standards of the State, and the rural migrant workers should secure the vocational qualifications before taking up jobs. Moreover, employers are required to train existing employees within five years, with a minimum of 20 percent of them trained each year.

To reinforce the vocational training and job seeking registration and management, Zhongshan has also developed a Training Discount Coupon and Job Seeking Discount Coupon system for rural migrant workers, including such functions as basic information management and Training Discount Coupon management. Regarding basic information management, the labor and security office of each town or district can enter the name, gender, ID card number, native place [home town], family address, contact phone, serial number, identity type, diploma and skills of a rural migrant worker into the management system. Meanwhile, the office will print the

Job Application Discount Coupon or Training Discount Coupon as requested by migrant rural workers, and distribute them free of charge. As for Training Discount Coupon management, within one week after the start of training with a designated vocational school, the level and name of the school, type, area of specialty, categories, classifications and the starting and ending times of the training will be reported to the local Labor and Social Security Sub-bureau or Training and Employment Section, which will confirm such information. After training, the Vocational Skill Accreditation & Guidance Center of Zhongshan City will organize a 'uniform skills accreditation and evaluation', and enter the trainee's score for theory and practice as well as the time of confirmation.

Source: China Labor Market Net (http://www.lm.gov.cn/).

Other social security programs for rural migrant workers

Occupational injury insurance

All employers should provide occupational injury insurance coverage for rural migrant workers in line with *the Regulations for Occupational Injury Insurance*, including those industrial sectors where commercial insurance is already purchased. To further safeguard the rights and interests of rural migrant workers, much more needs to be done to expand insurance coverage, especially in such high-risk industries such as mining and construction, which employ a huge number of migrant rural workers. Policies requiring the participation of high-risk industries and enterprises in occupational injury insurance should be improved. Prevention of occupational injuries must be reinforced in order to minimize occupational injury accidents and occupational diseases at the source.

Medical insurance

Rural migrant workers should be included within the existing medical security framework that covers urban staff. However, their great mobility and low income should be fully taken into account in formulating certain tailor-made measures. The current arrangement should be maintained if migrant rural workers work in formal sectors and have participated in the medical insurance for urban staff previously. Rural migrant workers in informal sectors may participate in the medical insurance system for urban residents, which requires a relatively low level of contribution. After rural migrant workers return to their villages their medical insurance files and funds should be transferred into the new 'rural cooperative medical system'. In addition, a special assistance system that is oriented to the floating population should be established, to effectively prevent and reduce the basic medical risks that this population faces. A flexible mechanism should be built in to allow the switch between different security systems, and to realize the portability of the medical security plans and benefits between different regions and sectors.

Emergency relief mechanism

Rural migrant workers, who generally do not settle for long in a city, are one of the vulnerable groups in cities. To safeguard their basic livelihood, rights and interests, an emergency relief mechanism should be established specifically for them. The government and relevant NGOs should safeguard their rights and interests, and provide them with legal assistance and the local civil affairs department should offer temporary emergency relief for those migrant rural workers that are caught in emergencies due to accidental injuries or serious diseases.

Notes

1 National Bureau of Statistics: *Living Quality of Migrant Rural Worker, Survey 2: Life & Education Status* (http://www.stats.gov.cn).
2 Li Chunguang, *Q & A on Labor and Housing Security Policies for Migrant Rural Workers* (China Agricultural Science and Technology Press, 2006).

5   Old-age security

Security in old age, or 'old-age security', is at the core of the social welfare system. The institutional arrangements for pension systems directly affect the functioning of the entire social welfare system and even of the national economy. As old-age security gradually becomes a social system, the government plays an increasingly important role. To achieve our stated objective that 'the elderly are cared for', we must, as soon as possible, set up an old-age insurance system for migrant workers, a new one for farmers, an allowance system for those elderly who would otherwise be left unsupported, and a national 'basic pension' operating mechanism.

The current status of the old-age security system

Throughout its industrialization process, but especially in the 30 years following the introduction of reform and opening up policies, China has established various types of old-age social security systems. A basic pension insurance system for workers and a pension system for employees of public institutions are in place in urban areas. Their rural counterparts include the pension insurance system introduced in 1992 by the Ministry of Civil Affairs, as well as another system introduced in certain areas in the current decade. In addition, pension insurance systems have been established independently in some areas for workers coming from other areas, i.e. mainly migrant workers. More and more people are covered by these systems. By the end of 2007, the number of workers enrolled in a pension social insurance plan or who were still working but qualified for retirement benefits stood at about 200 million. This was on top of the 60 million recipients of 'basic' pension insurance benefits (49.54 million), retirement pensions (about 8 million)[1] and pensions paid by rural social insurance plans (3.92 million).

The urban 'basic' old-age insurance system

The 'basic' old-age insurance system for workers in urban areas is the primary social security system for the elderly. Throughout the planned economy period, urban retirees generally received pensions from the organizations for which they had worked. To facilitate reform of state-owned enterprises, from 1984 onwards, experiments with the 'socially pooled fund' for workers' pensions were conducted in certain areas. In 1993 the Third Plenary Session of the 14th CPC Central Committee passed the *Decision on Several Issues regarding the Establishment of the Socialist Market Economy*. In July of 1997 the State Council promulgated the *Decision to Establish a Unified Basic Old-age Insurance System for Enterprise Workers*, which was to be applied to enterprise workers across the nation. To address problems in collecting basic old-age insurance premiums, as well as financial deficits in the social accumulation fund and the absence of well-informed investment plans for the accumulated funds of personal accounts, in 2000 the State Council decided to reform the urban social security system in Liaoning Province[2] on a trial basis. By 2005 unified insurance enrollment and premium payment policies were implemented for the self-employed and flexible workers in urban areas. Methods of basic pension calculation and payment were reformed, and personal account experiments, starting with Liaoning in 2001, were expanded in order to decrease defaults on payment.[3] In 2008 the State Council chose Guangdong, Shanxi, Zhejiang, Shanghai and Chongqing for further experiments with the basic old-age insurance plan for employees of public institutions.

Box 5.1   China's three-pillar pension model

The three-pillar approach to pensions was first proposed and recommended to national governments by the 1994 World Bank report, *Averting the Aging Crisis*. It was widely adopted in many countries.

China's pension reform also reflected the three-pillar approach to a large degree. The State Council issued the *Notice Regarding Deepening the Reform of the Old-age Insurance System for Enterprise Workers* in 1995 and the *Decision to Establish a Unified Basic Old-age Insurance System for Enterprise Workers* in 1997. Both specified a three-level old-age insurance system, i.e. basic old-age insurance, supplementary old-age insurance plan of enterprises and old-age insurance through personal savings.

In the three-pillar approach, the first level of a pension system is government-sponsored basic old-age insurance. Managed directly by the government, it provides a minimum pension to guarantee the livelihood of all retirees through society-wide income redistribution. It is funded through a pay-as-you-go system. A certain level of benefits is pre-defined, and the government promises its payment to workers entitled to old-age pensions after their retirement, and bears the risk of any deficit in pension fund. The second level is the supplementary old-age insurance plan of enterprises, a statutory form of pension provision that is enforced through tax differentials and penalties, as well as legal means. A fully-funded system is adopted for the second level, with contributions defined and managed in a decentralized manner. The third level is voluntary personal savings; the government only needs to offer incentives in insurance and savings policies and these savings may be invested and managed by banks, insurance companies or other investment companies. Individuals may deposit their savings, purchase insurance, make other investments or liquidate them when necessary.

Table 5.1 China's three-pillar pension model

	1st Pillar Basic old-age insurance	2nd Pillar Supplementary old-age insurance plan of enterprise	3rd Pillar Old-age insurance through personal savings
Funding	Tax	Contribution	Personal savings/insurance/other
Category of insurance plans	DB (defined benefit)	DC (defined contribution)	DC (defined contribution)
Contributed by	Enterprise and individual	Enterprise and individual	Individual
Enforceability	Legislatively regulated	Legislatively regulated	Voluntary
Management	Publicly managed	Publicly/privately managed	Financial institution/insurance company
Contribution rate	Tax rate	Fixed	Voluntary
Pension replacement rate	Promised	Determined based on fund accumulation	

Source: Zhang Jun. 'Design and Assessment of Target Model for China's Pension System Reform', *Theory Horizon*, Issue 1, 2005, p. 158.

Coverage of basic old-age insurance for urban workers has been increasing over the course of more than 20 years of reform (see Table 5.2).

Table 5.2 shows that in 2007 the total number of workers covered by basic old-age insurance stood at 151.38 million, accounting for 51.6 percent of urban employment; the number of retirees covered was 49.54 million, accounting for over 80 percent of the people receiving social pensions, and 49 percent of the 100.94 million urban people aged 55 and above.[4] The basic old-age insurance system for urban workers and the retirement pension system for employees of government departments and public institutions cover nearly all regular workers in urban areas. Nevertheless, a considerable number of urban workers, mainly 'flexible' workers [people who work at odd jobs], large numbers of migrant workers, and the farmers whose land has been requisitioned in the process of urbanization, have not yet been included in the systems.

Rural old-age insurance system

Having the family provide for the elderly has long been the primary form of old-age security in rural China. Although this still holds true today, supporting the elderly

Table 5.2 Participants in and coverage of basic old-age insurance for urban workers

Years	Participating workers (10,000)		% of urban employment
	Total	Incl.: enterprise workers	
1990	5200.7	5200.7	30.5
1995	8737.8	8737.8	45.9
1996	8758.4	8758.4	44.0
1997	8671.0	8671.0	41.7
1998	8475.8	8475.8	39.2
1999	9501.8	8859.1	42.4
2000	10447.5	9496.9	45.1
2001	10801.9	9733.0	45.1
2002	11128.8	9929.4	44.9
2003	11646.5	10324.5	45.4
2004	12250.3	10903.9	46.3
2005	13120.4	11710.5	48.0
2006	14130.9	12618	49.0
2007	15138.0	13691	51.6

Source: National Bureau of Statistics of China: *China Statistical Yearbooks* (1991, 1996, 2001 and 2006) and *China Statistical Abstract* (2008); Ministry of Human Resources and Social Security and National Bureau of Statistics of China: *Statistical Communiqué on Labor and Social Security Development in 2008.* The data percentages in the table were calculated by the author.

through extended family relationships is facing increasing challenges given rapid industrialization and urbanization and the dramatic changes in socioeconomic structure.[5] The massive transfer of labor forces and numbers of people moving away from their original homes make it difficult for the old to live with children. The earnings derived from land and the financial security it used to signify are constantly diminishing and rural social networks are losing their former function.

In the mid-1980s, in order to address the growing inadequacy of the traditional means of providing for the elderly, the Chinese government carried out experiments in building a formal old-age security system for rural areas. In 1986 the Ministry of Civil Affairs carried out pilot projects in certain rich townships including those in Shanghai's suburbs and in southern Jiangsu. In 1992 the ministry developed the *Guidelines on Public Pension Plans for Rural Areas*, which, as an important framework, guided and accelerated the establishment of an old-age insurance system in rural areas. However, the system's inherent defects and management problems, coupled with such factors as the 1997 Asian financial crisis and the shift of responsibilities for the system from the Ministry of Civil Affairs to the Ministry of Labor and Social Security in 1998, put the system at a standstill for the next few years. The number of rural participants declined greatly, from more than 80 million to 50 million (see Figure 5.1).[6]

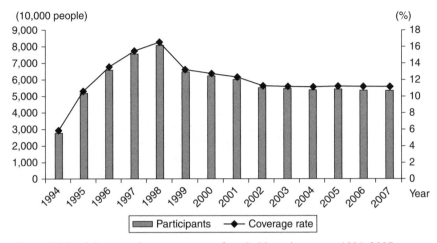

Figure 5.1 Participants and coverage rates of rural old-age insurance, 1994–2007.

Source: China Labor Statistical Yearbook and *China Statistical Abstract* (2008), National Bureau of Statistics of China.

With the old-age insurance system at a standstill some local governments, starting from their own conditions, experimented with a new alternative for rural areas (see Box 5.2). Countrywide, however, the number of farmers enrolled in old-age insurance remains low and family-based support for the elderly is primary. As for the great number of laborers who remain in rural areas, the rural old-age insurance system covers only slightly more than 10 percent and leaves more than 400 million people uninsured. Of the 476.4 million rural workers in 2007, 310 million were engaged in agriculture in the traditional sense, in the primary industry, while 160 million or so worked in secondary and tertiary industries. How to devise a basic old-age insurance system for these rural laborers has become the most outstanding issue for China's old-age security system. A rapidly aging population has made this issue the number-one priority on the agenda.

Box 5.2 Types of new rural old-age insurance plans	
Area/Type	Content
Beijing: dual security	The People's Government of Beijing promulgated in December 29, 2007 the Interim Measures of Beijing for New Rural Old Age Insurance. The new security system establishes a model of linking up personal accounts and basic pension. Basic pension will directly benefit participating farmers when receiving

benefits and are funded by both municipal and district governments. Contributions to the new insurance plan are flexible, starting from a minimum 10 percent of the previous year's net income per capita of farmers of each district or county. By the end of May 2008, the number of people enrolled in the insurance had increased dramatically to over 700,000, up 64.9 percent. In 2008, the monthly pension collected by an average farmer stood at about RMB 400, and the financial subsidies from the government accounted for 70 percent of per capita benefits received.

Currently the number of old people aged above 60 in the urban and rural areas of Beijing totals 2,360,000; 700,000 of them are not supported by old-age security benefits, including 510,000 old people living in the rural areas. The People's Government of Beijing promulgated in December 207 the Old Age Security Measures for Beijing's Old Urban and Rural Citizens Not Yet Covered by Social Security Schemes, specifying that each permanent resident of Beijing, aged 60 years or above and not yet supported by social security schemes, may receive a pension of RMB 200. The financial departments at municipal and district levels will use RMB 1,680 million as pension benefits in 2008. This policy benefits both urban and rural residents in the same way. And Beijing thus became the first in the country to apply a government-backed pension plan equally to both urban and rural residents. These measures have helped Beijing achieve the objective of 'all old people are provided for'.[7]

Zhengzhou: old-age security covering all people

In June 2008, Zhengzhou passed the Measures of Basic Old Age Insurance for Urban and Rural Residents of Zhengzhou (Trial), with the objective of covering the 4.35 million uninsured residents aged above 16 (including 1 million in urban areas and 3.35 million in rural areas). It is required to set up personal accounts for participants and to include all personal contributions to their personal accounts. The contribution rates, a certain percentage of the average income of residents, are divided at 7 levels (6 percent, 7.5 percent, 10 percent, 20 percent, 30 percent, 50 percent and 85 percent). The governments at municipal and county levels provide subsidies equal to 1.5 percent of the contribution base (1 percent going to personal accounts and 0.5 percent to pooled funds). The subsidy ratio is independent of specific contributions. An insured urban or rural resident may receive pension ever since he/she reaches 60, which consists of personal account benefits received on a monthly basis and a government allowance equal to 4.5 percent of the monthly income of an average resident.[8]

Shanghai: old-age allowance | Shanghai adopted its first minimum pension subsidy policy for old farmers in 2004, ensuring a monthly pension of RMB 75 received by each rural resident aged 65 or above. Through government subsidies at municipal, district (county) and township levels, this policy would include uninsured old farmers in the social security system and raise the benefits paid to those previously insured who used to receive less than RMB 75 per month. It benefited 300,000, 260,000 and 240,000 people in 2004, 2005 and 2006, respectively. Among those entitled to the minimum old-age pensions, *wubaohu* (childless and infirm old persons who are guaranteed food, clothing, medical care, housing and burial expenses) took a big share. From 2007 the minimum pension subsidies to each farmer aged 65 or above in Shanghai was increased to RMB 85 each month.[9]

Main problems in the old-age social security system

Inadequate coverage

A very large number of China's elderly, especially those in rural areas, are left unsupported by the old-age security system. Among people over the age of 55, fewer than 30 percent are entitled to pensions. That means that more than two-thirds of the elderly, nationwide, receive no pension, while the percentage approaches 90 percent in rural areas. The elderly in rural areas depend mainly on their families, while a portion of poverty-stricken old people are included in the minimum subsistence security called the 'five guarantees system', or the *wubaohu*. Family support for the elderly is a Chinese tradition that deserves acclaim, but relying solely on it will result in many problems. Meanwhile, benefits provided under the minimum subsistence security system are quite low.

Second, coverage of the basic old-age insurance system does not reach many urban, not to mention rural, workers. Nearly 40 percent of workers in urban areas have not yet enrolled (approx. 120 million, mainly flexible workers and migrant

Table 5.3 Pensionless people as a percentage of the urban (unemployed) elderly

Age	Male	Female	Total
55–59	0.0[1]	15.5	15.5
60–64	6.9	17.6	12.7
65–69	5.0	18.6	11.6
70–74	3.9	21.9	12.1
75–79	1.9	28.7	14.1
80–84	5.6	41.6	24.6
85–	13.2	61.8	47.2
Total	5.2	20.5	14.4

Note:
1 The figure here actually is not 0 but not applicable. This table discusses the pension coverage of the old who have already retired, and the retirement age is 60 for men and 55 for women. So for males aged 55–59, there is no data on percentage of pensioners.

Source: A 2007 sampling survey of urban residents in 15 provinces.

workers). Once these uninsured people reach retirement age China's old-age security system will be strained even further.

High contribution rates

Excessively high contribution rates have crippled the enthusiasm of enterprises, especially those in the private sector, to participate in old-age insurance. These contribution rates remain high mainly because the present system was originally designed for state-owned enterprises, and thus had to give consideration to the pension levels to which their retirees were formerly entitled. Old-age dependency ratios and excessively high contribution rates usually make the self-employed, private business owners, foreign-funded enterprises, and even workers themselves unwilling or unable to get enrolled in insurance.

Personal accounts running on 'empty'

In terms of actual implementation, the objectives of the 'social pooling + personal account' system for basic old-age insurance have not been met due to various constraining factors. The co-existence of the two funding mechanisms, i.e. the pay-as-you-go approach for socially pooled funds and the fully funded approach for personal account funds, led to excessively high nominal contribution rates for individuals. This made it hard for low-income and flexible workers to get enrolled. In addition, the lack of regulation over investment of the funds, and the lack of a market-based system for investing the funds, meant that the personal account funds were not 'accumulating' as expected. The 'personal account system' has therefore simply not worked.

Low pooling levels and severe regional segmentation

In theory there are currently more than 600 pooling jurisdictions at the 'local city or above' level throughout the country, but in fact over 90 percent of the pooling is carried out at county level. Each 'pooling jurisdiction' has different contribution rates. Benefit standards and management methods also vary, making it hard for labor to be mobile. When people move from jobs in one place to jobs in another, they can only carry with them the contributions to their personal accounts, whereas the socially pooled funds account for the larger percentage stays behind. This causes inequalities between places that have a net inflow of labor and those that have a net outflow. It is precisely those economically underdeveloped regions, with a net outflow, that suffer more.

In addition, the excessively fragmented pooling jurisdictions under the present system prevent the 'mutual-aid' function of social insurance from taking effect. Due to different age structures, pooling jurisdictions have vastly different burdens in terms of old-age security. There are more retirees in older industrial regions, and those regions in which state-owned enterprise predominated. Old-age dependency ratios are higher in these areas and contribution rates are also higher, while contribution burdens are lighter in emerging cities and regions that have attracted in more young laborers from 'outside'. The striking imbalance of old-age security burdens among regions has severely weakened the mutual-aid function of social insurance; those regions with heavy old-age security burdens are usually unable to make ends meet.

Difficulties in transferring and renewing old-age insurance

Due to such factors as overly local levels of pooling jurisdiction, local management of funds and public finance systems that oblige each place to 'eat at its own hearth', some local areas impose 'additional conditions' on insurance plans, making it hard for migrant workers to renew their old-age insurance, and for eligible workers to handle retirement formalities and receive pensions. Many people therefore withdraw from insurance.

Development objectives of the old-age security system

Principles and objectives relating to the old-age social security system

The overall objective of any modern old-age security system is to eliminate poverty among the elderly and make sure there are provisions for all people when they get old, by means of society-wide financial and service security. The efforts of all participants are mobilized to achieve this objective, including government, society, community, families and individuals. A combination of governmental organization and market operations is necessary to assure the financial and service security required for all citizens in their older years. Ultimately, the goal is to allow the elderly to live a life with dignity that is appropriate to the socioeconomic development level of the country.

In China, in order to build an old-age security system that follows our abiding tradition that 'the elderly are cared for', within the context of a 'moderately prosperous society', we further specify the following important principles:

- Full coverage. In building the system, coverage should be expanded from the rather elastic 'broad coverage' of basic old-age insurance for workers to 'full coverage'.
- Connected pooling. We acknowledge the reality of the urban–rural divide, as well as regional imbalances, but don't perpetuate those differences by embodying them in our policy guidelines. We aim to remove all tangible and intangible barriers that obstruct the flow of labor and the realization of citizen's rights and interests, including regional, and including restrictions of a person's 'status' or identity [*shen-fen*] and a person's registered place of residence [*hu-ji*]. Each citizen should have equal access to the security that the country provides.
- Assurance of security to an appropriate degree. A moderate level of security does not mean 'the higher the better' and it certainly does not mean 'the lower the better'. The level of security should be improved as feasible, as socioeconomic development proceeds. Given the need to ensure 'essential subsistence', 'moderate security' can be defined as 'allowing the old to share in the results of economic development, and ensuring that they live with dignity, in a decent fashion, and in relative comfort.
- Socialization. We confirm that old-age security should cover all citizens, that each citizen should have access to socialized security. Our old-age social service system, as appropriate to conditions in China, should provide socialized care or nursing services to all elderly that are in need.
- Primary role of the government. The government must play the leading role in our old-age security system, promoting legislation, increasing financial inputs, and providing more public services.
- Robust management. We should establish and improve upon management systems and services that are appropriate to old-age security systems that provide coverage for all urban and rural citizens. We should build an information network that is unified nationwide, so that various old-age security systems can be connected in an organic way and labor can flow freely among cities. In doing this, we should change from extensive to intensive management, and ensure that management and services are provided to people throughout their lives.

Incremental steps in building an old-age security system

Building an effective old-age security system is a long-term and formidable task. We recognize the challenge and therefore divide the process into incremental steps. Our goal is to assure that all citizens enjoy old-age security by the year 2020. The period from 2009 to 2012 can be regarded as the first step, aimed at establishing systems for social groups who enjoy no institutional security, building old-age insurance systems with lower contribution rates for farmers and migrant workers, providing old-age security for elderly in both urban and rural areas who have no income, and forming old-age security systems that match the basic old-age insurance system for urban workers and the retirement pension system for government officials (public servants). Emphasis should be placed on solving old-age security problems for people who have no security at all, building a baseline system that supports the objective of 'the elderly shall be cared for', namely, an old-age allowance system, and striving to ensure that by 2012 all urban and rural old people who are without old-age security are covered by allowances. By that time, average monthly subsidies to people above the age of 65, who have no old-age security, should reach RMB 300 for urban residents and RMB 100 for rural residents. While expanding the coverage of old-age insurance for workers, efforts should be made to establish basic old-age insurance systems in which various urban workers can participate. By referring to the old-age insurance for migrant workers, lower old-age insurance contribution rates for urban self-employed and flexible workers should be adjusted to around 14 percent from the present 20 percent, so as to expand the old-age security coverage of these people.

The period from 2013 to 2020 marks the stage in which our old-age security system will develop on all fronts. This will be a critical period in China's socio-economic development. Most regions will basically achieve industrialization. The percentage of people working in agriculture will further decline (it went down by 1 percentage point on average each year from 1978 to 2007, and is expected to go below 30 percent by 2020). The rate of urbanization will continue to increase (it increased by 0.9 percentage points on average each year in the 30 years since China's reform and opening up and is expected to increase to around 55 percent by 2020). By 2020 the aim is to build an old-age security system that is appropriate to a 'moderately prosperous' society. During this period the actions undertaken will be clustered around the following three objectives: first, we will gradually improve the level of benefits that elderly receive, to achieve the realization of 'the elderly are cared for'. The old-age allowance system will be extended to provide full coverage to those currently without any old-age security. Second, we will reduce contribution rates for migrant workers and urban flexible workers, to further expand the coverage of various basic old-age insurance in urban and rural areas. By 2020 we will ensure that enrollment in old-age insurance reaches 100 percent for both urban and rural workers. (Enrollment of urban workers increased by 1.2 percentage points on average each year from 1990 to 2007.) Third, we will establish proper mechanisms for managing basic old-age pensions and security pensions and we will create nursing-insurance systems, to increase the level of security of the old-age security systems. We will rationalize the relationships between basic old-age insurance and other forms of old-age security, and vigorously develop various non-basic old-age insurance as guided by policies, to create a 'multi-pillar', 'multi-level' old-age security system. We will resolve unfortunate issues relating to management of the funds in the non-basic old-age insurance arena, and realize both value preservation and value increase in those funds. We will achieve the pooling of basic old-age insurance funds at a provincial level, and assure their regulation at a national level. We will resolve the problem of transfer of, and continuity of, social-security plans among different jurisdictions.

Policy recommendations

Accelerate the building of basic pension systems for those elderly who currently have no old-age security

The reality is that more than 100 million old people currently have no old-age insurance, and a considerable number of people will become 'insecure elderly' in the future as well. In the face of this reality, it is not enough to rely merely on the 'two pillars', the social old-age security system and the traditional family-based system of old-age security. An old-age subsidy system that is supported by State-provided public finance must be created as the 'fundamental pillar' for old-age security in China. Those covered by this system should enjoy basic security subsidies that are calculated according to their age rather than contributions. Security benefits should be lower than basic old-age insurance benefits but should not be lower than the minimum subsistence standards. If they are, it will be very hard to alleviate poverty among the elderly. The specific form of basic old-age security systems may refer to the practices in such places as Beijing and Shanghai, and may then be improved gradually. We aim to ensure that by 2012 the elderly who are currently unprotected will each receive a monthly subsidy of RMB 300 in cities and RMB 100 in rural areas, and that by 2020 they will receive RMB 550 in cities and RMB 285 in rural areas (see Table 12.6 in Chapter 12 for detailed calculations).

Central financial authorities should provide adequate financial support to economically less developed areas, so that this system meets the needs of all elderly throughout the country. Different regions may provide additional financial support according to local living standards.

Build a new form of old-age insurance system for farmers

We recommend that the principles of the 'new rural cooperative medical system' serve as a model for a new form of old-age insurance for farmers. Farmers have particular disadvantages—they are not affiliated with any 'units' through whom they can make contributions, they have low incomes and inadequate ability to pay. Given these circumstances, the system for their coverage uses the model of 'basic old-age pension + personal account'. It features co-contributions by the State, collectives and individuals, with the government providing greater inputs. A detailed description follows.

Both Central and local financial authorities co-fund the non-contribution based 'basic old-age pensions'. Since there are no individual contributions and all funds are paid in by the 'country', by 2012 we aim to have basic old-age pensions for each eligible person of RMB 50 per month, and RMB 100 per month by 2020.

Farmers' personal accounts consist of personal contributions, collective subsidies and investment returns, and are subsidized by local governments. Personal contributions may, at personal discretion, be 5–10 percent of the local net income per capita per year. Local governments may provide subsidies to personal accounts. Rural collectives and Township-and-Village Enterprises may also do so.

The eligible age for the new old-age security for farmers is set at 65, before which farmers who lost the ability to work may also receive minimum security benefits. In addition to basic old-age pensions, rural residents with personal accounts may also receive old-age pensions from their personal accounts. It is generally desirable to ensure that basic old-age pensions for the rural elderly be about 30 percent of the net per capita income of the local farmers. That, added to personal account benefits, should mean that basic subsistence can be maintained.

For rural elderly who are above the eligible age for the insurance, the State should provide old-age subsidies at a level not lower than 20 percent of the net per capita income of local farmers and higher than the local rural minimum-security level. For those elderly who have contributed for less than 15 years, in addition to personal account benefits, a certain percentage should be added to rural old-age subsidies, depending on the length of time they have made contributions. At the same time this system should be linked to the minimum-subsistence security system and the social-aid system. Economic support and care for the extremely elderly should be established, such as 'older age welfare benefits' and 'nursing security systems'. The aim is to allow people not to have to rely on the traditional system of family-based old-age security, to allow them to enjoy socialized old-age security benefits.

Given the good news that the State recently announced about investing RMB 4 trillion on programs related to 'people's livelihood', we should accelerate the process of increasing coverage of rural old-age insurance. In terms of our technical capability, we have already had years of experience in social insurance for urban areas, and have done pilot-project experiments regarding social insurance for rural areas. Since the State is covering the majority of funds, it will be less difficult to extend this system, given the results of the new rural cooperation medical insurance. Therefore this system should be introduced and extended as soon as possible. We recommend that test projects be carried out in two or three counties in each province in 2009, and that that number be expanded to cover an additional one-third of counties in each following year. By the end of 2012 we should have covered all rural areas in the country. [Note: certain regions and municipalities are included in the designation 'province' above.]

Establish a unified operational mechanism for basic old-age pensions

Option 1

National pooling of basic old-age pensions. Promote provincial pooling first; achieve pooling at a provincial level countrywide by the end of 2009 and, on the basis of this, realize the provincial pooling of basic old-age pensions throughout the country by 2012. Establish a pooled fund that is under Central authority;

put basic old-age pensions that were formally under local authority under Central management. Objectively speaking, the national pooling of old-age pensions is required in order to unify and standardize the system; it helps the country in managing ongoing development of the old-age insurance mission. It helps avoid risks related to nonpayment, and it is conducive to further separating out Central and local responsibilities and mobilizing the initiative of all parties concerned.

Option 2

On a nationwide uniform basis, collect social security tax for basic old-age pensions. Take the part of basic old-age pensions that are supported by socially pooled funds out of the existing system and begin pooling that comes from a nationwide tax. Employers are responsible for paying the tax, and national tax authorities are responsible for collecting them, nationwide, on a uniform basis. The basis on which the tax is calculated is the total or gross income of wage earners, and all urban workers including those working for township enterprises are to pay the tax. Eliminate previous differences that were applied to the 'status' of any person, including whether that person worked for an 'enterprise', a 'government body', or an 'institution', and assure that all pension benefits are applied equally to all people.

Setting up national pooling of funds for urban basic old-age pensions assures the following considerations. It reflects the principle of ensuring basic subsistence benefits while decreasing insurance costs, and serves as a stimulus for units and individuals to participate, thereby maintaining the market competitiveness of enterprises. It is sustainable and has reliable sources of funding, as a result of the mandatory taxation and institutional security in the manner of collections. It enables 'mutual aid' across society to the maximum extent, reflects the impartiality of the redistribution system, the equality of basic security rights of citizens, and it establishes the principle of 'no discrimination' in terms of a citizen's status [*shen-fen*]. It meets the needs of various forms of employment to the maximum extent, encourages the broad involvement of various laborers, and serves the needs of laborers for rational movement between units, regions, urban and rural areas, as well as for flexible employment during economic and social transition. It differentiates between the responsibilities of Central and local governments, and between social pooling and personal accounts, and delineates the nature and scope of authorities and responsibilities of both, as well as providing appropriate incentives and constraints.

Realize personal accounts

Funds in personal accounts are to be accumulated in actual accounts and invested. After a participant retires, they are to be used as old-age pensions, depending on how much has been accumulated and what the life expectancy of the participant is.

The plan for realizing personal accounts is based on experience garnered from the initial practice in 13 provinces. That will be broadened to a nationwide program: the program will start in 2010 with no less than 3 percent of personal accounts being 'realized', and the number of accounts will grow annually at a rate of 1 percent every two years, so that it achieves 8 percent coverage by 2020. Gaps in funding the pay-outs in each province will mainly be handled by growing the system so that new-account additions are sufficient to pay for the necessary benefits due on the old accounts. Central finance will continue to provide certain subsidies to the central and western regions as well as the old industrial bases. All 'empty accounts' that existed before 2010 must be 'realized', in the sense that they are funded; funds required may be raised through multiple channels, such as liquidating certain state-owned assets, fees earned on assignment [transfer of land-use rights] of State land, excess profits of monopoly industries, income from use of concessions granted for resource extraction, transfers of special items in personal income tax, and the issuance of special bonds.

Personal account funds are to be managed by local governments. When participants move, funds are to be transferred along with the participant, and the transfer and redesignation is the responsibility of the local social insurance governing bodies. Accumulated personal account funds are to be invested by financial institutions on a commission basis. Authorized government departments, financial regulatory agencies and organizations are responsible for regulating the process subject to their respective jurisdictions.

Build and improve the old-age insurance system for migrant workers

Completely new concepts must accompany the building of an old-age insurance system for migrant workers. Local contribution rates, the higher administrative levels at which pooling of funds is handled and improved personal accounts, will all have to be addressed in one fell swoop. Old-age insurance for migrant workers should consist of basic old-age pensions, nationally pooled funds, and personal accounts, managed on an actual basis. At the same time the system must establish a nationally unified benefits payout process to pay old-age pensions according to national pooling regulations. In principle, the handling of migrant-worker insurance and accounts should be a top-down process, organized by labor security departments.

Funds in the personal accounts of migrant workers may be managed separately from urban insurance funds. Policies and measures should be formulated that allow funds to be invested indirectly in State infrastructure and key projects, and to be operated through market-oriented investments. Special bonds may be issued to ensure the appreciation of funds. Efforts should be made to ensure that the enrollment ratio of migrant workers reaches 50 percent by 2010 and, ideally, 100 percent by 2012.

Rural migrant workers who have been working for official [proper or publicly recognized] entities and who are therefore enrolled in social insurance plans for urban workers are not allowed to withdraw from such insurance, and they are entitled to equal benefits. Employers should pay social insurance premiums for these migrant workers. Rural migrant workers who are employed by 'unofficial entities', especially in the huge number of urban services industries, may be included in the category of 'urban old-age insurance systems for workers in unofficial entities'. The consideration here is that their employment is unstable and the size of enterprise for which they generally work is very small. As the economy develops, these rural migrant workers can gradually be incorporated into the category 'urban old-age insurance systems'.

The reform of old-age insurance will reduce the income risk of rural migrant workers and encourage them to improve skills, enjoy stable employment and ultimately settle down in cities.

The old-age security system for other urban residents such as 'flexible workers' and individuals running small businesses

The present old-age security measures are directed mainly at workers in official entities in cities. Those working in unofficial entities usually are not fortunate enough to be enrolled. Although percentages of urban workers enrolled in old-age insurance are increasing, in absolute terms the number still represents a very low degree of coverage. In 2007 the number of 'urban workers enrolled in the basic old-age insurance' as a percentage of 'all urban workers' was slightly higher than 50 percent. This means that a large number of urban workers in unofficial entities, including employees in medium and small-sized enterprises, flexible workers, township enterprise employees and individuals running small businesses, enjoy no old-age insurance.

There are currently 60 million urban self-employed workers and flexible workers. Only 35 million of them are enrolled in insurance, for many cannot afford old-age insurance premiums at their sole expense. The situation regarding workers in small enterprises and unofficial entities in cities is the same. We can consider using the same methods as for rural migrant workers in order to get them covered: lowering the contribution rate from the present 20 percent to 14 percent (8 percent into personal account and 6 percent into pooling). Because self-employed and flexible workers differ greatly in income and their income is unstable, the contribution base should be calculated on a unified basis according to the average wage of local workers. The granting of old-age pensions should be calculated as per the practice of the enterprise insurance for the elderly, i.e. taking the local monthly average wage of the previous year and the average of one's indexed monthly contributing wage as the basis for basic old-age pensions, and granting 1 percent for every year contributed. The personal account's old-age pension standard is calculated by dividing the balance of personal account savings by the calculated number of months for pension granting, and this calculated number of months is determined by considering such factors as the life expectancy of urban populations when the contributor retired, his or her retirement age, and investment income.

Take proactive measures in promoting the occupational annuity system

Under conditions of a market economy, personal income often differs greatly due to differences in enterprise profitability and occupation. People's needs for old-age security are also different. Therefore, in addition to the social old-age insurance, the government should also provide related policies in support of accelerating the development of an occupational annuity system. The idea is to achieve a balance between impartiality and efficiency. Setting up such an annuity system will embody the 'impartiality principle' of old-age benefits when it comes to basic insurance, and it will balance the varying interests among regions, departments, industries and occupations. It will reflect differences in the actual levels of 'security'. It will realize the principle of achieving market efficiencies based on level of income, and thereby motivate people to create social wealth with an enterprising attitude.

Establish a social security budgeting system and a unified transfer-payments system

Establish a dedicated budget for social security. Fund revenues and expenditures should be under the management of this dedicated budget. Basic pensions should be administered on a nationwide basis. Specific functions should be performed by the social security departments. Depending on the old-age insurance burdens of various regions, Central finance should establish a unified, standard, transfer payment system so that the socially mutual aid is maximized within the scope of basic old-age pensions.

Push back the mandatory retirement age as appropriate and establish a long-range mechanism in response to the issue of an aging population

Pushing back the mandatory age for retirement, i.e. having people defer retirement, is an important policy measure for changing the ratio of the number of people dependent on old-age insurance. It is important for balancing the intergenerational rights and interests, and important in responding to the whole issue of an aging society. The mandatory age for retirement may be pushed back gradually, as per the extent of aging, by giving consideration to changes in labor structure and by referring to international experience. For the time being the first thing to do is to strictly enforce the retirement age policy so as to control early retirement. The second is to annul any early retirement policies regarding special types of work. Several areas (such as Shanghai and Guangzhou) may be selected for pilot projects in carrying out the policy of deferred retirement directed at high-ranking, knowledge-intensive or technically-intensive employment groups as well as human resources that are in short supply. This should be done on a voluntary basis and in a flexible way. In addition, we should gradually increase the mandatory retirement age to 65 gradually, as changes in demographic structure require. In concert with pushing back the mandatory retirement age, we should further strengthen benefit-based incentive mechanisms by lowering pensions for workers who retire early, and increasing benefits for people who defer their retirement.

Explore the possibility of establishing long-term nursing care for the extremely elderly, and be proactive in developing socialized services for the elderly

Old-age security refers not only to the economic independence of someone after he or she is older, but also to the availability of essential services when needed. The experience of developed countries (such as Germany and Japan) in establishing long-term nursing care insurance and of welfare countries (such as Denmark and Sweden) in providing the old with social care services may be used as reference in this regard. In these countries, decentralized family-based old-age security (for the old who are able to take care of themselves), and centralized social-care locations (for a portion of the elderly) are combined to provide social services for old-age security. In Copenhagen, as much as 22 percent of the population is over the age of 65, but less than one-tenth require centralized care. Over one-third are provided for within families and require certain social services provided by social workers.

Box 5.3 Socialized old-age security in Copenhagen, Denmark

In July 2008, our work team visited Denmark, including its capital, Copenhagen, a city with a population of 500,000, 22 percent of whom are aged 65–79. In one of the city's districts, there are 55,000 people above the age of 65. Of these, 30,000 require no assistance at all, 20,000 receive family assistance (as in cleaning, bathing, laundering, etc.) and 5,000 live in homes provided for the elderly. The city has 55 homes for the elderly in all; the main financial source for these homes is the old-age pensions of the old people admitted, with any shortfall being subsidized by government finance. Expenditures go mainly on wages for doctors and nurses, subsistence and nursing care of the old, and a portion for overhead expenses. All these homes are public facilities, but there are also a few market-oriented services that are paid for directly by the elderly and their children.

Source: The Work Team's Report on Study Tour to Denmark (2008).

China has a strong tradition of family-based old-age security. It is no longer sufficient to rely on families for all care of the elderly, however. We must develop a mode in which communities take the lead in providing family-based old-age security services. For example, community-based temporary families for taking care of the elderly may be considered for those people who cannot receive in-time care from their children, and locations may be set up that provide recreational activities for the old. We may also consider homes for the elderly where care is provided in a centralized way and services provided by an expanding team of social workers. To resolve the shortage of money needed for the care of the elderly, market mechanisms can be used to develop old-age industries, produce products used for the elderly and attract social employment. Strict admittance procedures and financial security systems should be established for public homes for the elderly, to enable them to focus on their core role of providing care to the old in a centralized way. In recent years the country has been promoting the vigorous development of social workers. It is therefore an opportune time to explore the development of long-term nursing care insurance for the elderly. This should be linked to reforms of our social old-age security system, to promote the healthy development of the socialized old-age services system.

A complete old-age services system should be established, that provides diverse services for groups with different levels of income. We should authorize communities to set up in-house old-age service systems, to provide rehabilitation nursing services in institutions that are diversified according to need, and to build a complete old-age service network that relies on comprehensive social welfare centers at various levels.

Currently, nearly 30 million old people need different degrees of service throughout the country, and more than 10 million of them require professional nursing help. China has a total of only 20,000 certified nurses, a number far below what is required. Comprehensive plans should address the whole sector of nursing care for the elderly. We should develop training systems, begin to create employment positions and promote employment in this sector.

The experience of such places as Beijing is worthy of special note. Beijing grants a welfare pension of RMB 200 per month to each person over the age of 65 who has no old-age insurance. In places that don't have the financial wherewithal to do this an allowance system could be established for people over the age of 80 who have no pensions, subsidizing them with RMB 200 per person per month. At present over 15 million people in China are over the age of 80, most of whom have no old-age insurance. Spending RMB 30 billion in public funds each year on supporting these people would be a very worthwhile form of welfare.

Increase expenditures on infrastructure that provides old-age services. Each county or district should set up at least one public facility that serves as a nursing home for the elderly; these facilities should be used to demonstrate what is possible. At the same time we should encourage society at large to build nursing homes by providing every conceivable preferential policy as an inducement.

Increase support to the artificial limb industry, spur development of industries that provide products or services for the elderly, and promote the development of various rehabilitation hospitals.

Accelerate legislation that deals with old-age security, and improve
management standards in the old-age security system

In order to standardize operations within legal boundaries, strengthen constraints on the behavior of government, and reduce the randomness of decision-making, improve scientific management according to laws and enhance people's confidence in social security and their enthusiasm to participate, the process of enacting social security legislation must be accelerated. We must actually implement the *Social Assistance Law*, *Social Insurance Law* and *Social Welfare Law* as soon as possible. Established contents should be standardized to make them basic rules that people abide by. At the same time we must clearly delineate managerial responsibilities for social-security pooling of funds among regions and define rights and responsibilities between Central and local governments. We must remove barriers to the transfer and re-registration of social security among various entities and in the investment of personal account pensions. We must build an institutional basis for the smooth functioning of the old-age security system. We should make full use of the favorable conditions that information technology has created for China's social security reform. We should accelerate the building of information-based social security and old-age security, establish records on contributions and benefits on a nationally networked basis, and establish personal accounts as an important medium for holding information. Personal accounts will serve as the information platform for records, transfer, investment and benefit distributions, making them an important technical guarantee for China's old-age security, as well as social management systems. We must accelerate the training of professionals in the field of old-age security, providing an intellectual guarantee for the development of the country's old-age security system. Efforts should be made to solve in an expedited way the policy barriers that make it difficult to transfer and renew social security relations, formulate administrative measures regarding transfer and renewal of social security relations within the range of the country, so as to promote the rational flow of labor forces. We should be adept at borrowing international experience, but we must formulate policies according to the current conditions of our country. We must start from China's realities in establishing China's old-age security system—on the basis of practice and actual experience we can then improve the system and take it in the direction of a more advanced reality.

Notes

1 Statistics on annual retirees from government departments and public institutions are not available. In 2005 the total number of urban retirees throughout the country was 50,882,000, of which 43,675,000 were enrolled in old-age insurance. It can be calculated from the figures that 7,207,000 people received pensions from government departments, public institutions and civil affairs departments in the year; with new retirees in 2006 and 2007, the total number is estimated to approximate 8 million. See *China Statistical Yearbook 2006* (National Bureau of Statistics of China: China Statistics Press, 2006), p. 908.

2 A rather comprehensive social security reform package was put together for Liaoning. As far as the basic old-age insurance system is concerned, the proportion of contribution to personal accounts was lowered from 11 percent (jointly paid by enter-

prises and workers) to 8 percent (paid by workers only). In this way, the default rate was decreased. Any deficits in the socially pooled fund and the personal account funds already diverted for other purposes were made up by the Central and local governments on a percentage basis. In this way tens of billions of personal account funds were collected, but these funds were still kept in the custody of financial departments rather than used for market investment.

3 From 2001 through 2006, personal account experiments to decrease default rate had been made in 11 provinces or regions, with RMB 48.5 billion paid to personal accounts. See 'China Social Insurance Facts in Recent Years', *China Labor and Social Security News,* November 30, 2007.

4 According to a demographic sample survey, the proportion of urban people throughout the country aged over 55, i.e. the official retirement age of enterprise employees, stood at 17 percent in 2005. We will get the total number of the urban people aged above 55 – 100.94 million – if we multiply the 2005 proportion by the total urban population in 2007. The 2005 proportion was quoted from Almanac of China's Population 2006 which was written by the Institute of Population and Labor Economics under the Chinese Academy of Social Sciences (CASS) and published in 2006 by *Almanac of China's Population* magazine, p. 429.

5 Dewen Wang, 'China's Urban and Rural Old Age Security System: Challenges and Options', *China & World Economy*, 2006, vol. 14, issue 1, pp. 102–116.

6 Zhao Dianguo, 'Build a New Rural Old Age Insurance System', *China Finance,* Issue 6, 2007, pp. 34–36.

7 Tao Ying, 'Beijing Introduces *Implementation Rules for New Rural Old Age Insurance,* Ensuring for the First Time the Consistence between Rural to Urban Old Age Insurance Plans', *Legal Evening News*, January 15, 2008.

8 Chang Hongxiao, 'Old Age Security Covering All People: Easy to Understand yet Difficult to Run', *Finance*, Issue 14, 2008.

9 http://news.sohu.com.

6　Health security

Health serves as the foundation for the overall development of individuals and relates to the well-being of every person. One of the goals of the Chinese government in 'building a moderately prosperous society' in an all-round way is 'to enable each person to have basic medical and health services' and 'to have medical treatment when he or she is ill'. This is an important part of China's social welfare system. Health security, a much broader concept than just medical security, is the social welfare that all citizens should be entitled to in terms of public health, disease prevention and control, health protection, health promotion and so on.[1] Although encompassing a much broader scope, health security also covers medical security, medical services and public health. In addition to disease treatment it focuses more on disease prevention, health care, nursing and rehabilitation. The recipients of these services include not only sick people but also the great majority of healthy people, and indeed the entire population. Health security concerns itself primarily with building grass-roots health service systems and basic medical security systems, and it aims to improve the impartiality and efficiency of health services and funding. Health security is implemented mainly through the health service system and the medical security system. The following analyzes the present situation from these two perspectives. It discusses the problems of China's health security system and proposes the objectives and measures for the development of a health security system in a moderately prosperous society.

Development of China's healthcare services system

A healthcare services system is the foundation of health security. Under the planned-economy system the Chinese government tried hard to provide the entire population with the most essential health services. At that time the government placed the emphasis of its medical and health work on the prevention and elimination of infectious diseases. In particular, it strengthened health work in rural areas, and established 'medical service teams' for the most essential healthcare, and a unique 'cooperative medical system' that allowed urban and rural residents, especially farmers, to receive basic healthcare services without paying high costs. That was a so-called 'Chinese Revolution'[2] in public health security.

In disease treatment the provision of services for disease prevention and control was twofold: medical institutions owned by the whole people and built with State investment, medical institutions under collective ownership and co-built by government and collective investment. These distributed healthcare more broadly and improved equality of access. They basically controlled the massive prevalence of infectious diseases, parasites, endemic disease and other diseases severely harmful to people's health.

In the 1980s, as reform of the economic system proceeded, new problems arose in the provision of medical and health services. The main one was the contradiction between the amount of medical resources available and the sharply increasing need for medical treatment, a need that soared in a very short period of time. It was exemplified by the numbers of people seeking medical assistance, hospitalization and operations.

To relieve the contradiction, relevant government departments introduced a series of policies to encourage 'social forces' to enter the field of medical services. Subsequently, private clinics, privately-run hospitals, joint-stock hospitals, joint-stock cooperative hospitals, joint-venture hospitals, hospital groups, etc appeared one after another. Driven by the supply-expanding policies, a pattern began taking shape nationwide, especially in cities in which health resources were gathered through multiple channels and at multiple levels and hospitals were established through multiple channels and in various forms.[3] At the same time, medical and health institutions initiated reform of micro-management mechanisms and introduced some practices that were being used in the reform of state-owned Enterprises, with the basic idea of 'decentralizing authority and allowing hospitals to retain a higher percentage of profits, expanding their decision-making power, revitalizing with an open mind, and improving their efficiency and results'.[4] By the 1990s the reform began to be thoroughly 'market-oriented', and some local governments even hoped to raise funds and operate purely through market-based channels and completely disengage from any public finance.[5]

It should be acknowledged that the reforms in the direction of diversified investment and market-based operational mechanisms to a certain degree improved the availability of medical services. After reforms began the number of medical institutions, sickbeds and health personnel increased considerably, and the problem of 'shortage of medical services and medicines' was basically solved nationwide, except for a few poverty-stricken areas with sparse population and inconvenient transportation. This created a certain material foundation for making basic medical services available for all. Nonetheless, many debates have accompanied the reforms. The focus of the disputes has been whether medical and health services should be market- and industry-oriented, or should be welfare- and cause-oriented. Along with the transition to the market economic system started in the late 1980s, more emphasis has been placed on market-oriented medical and healthcare services.

Since the 16th CPC National Congress, and especially after the 2003 SARS crisis revealed the weaknesses in both China's public health system and its rural health service system, the situation has changed. Both policy-making circles and the more academic 'theory community', and the decision-making levels have focused more on the welfare- and cause-oriented development of health services. The government has increased public finance inputs into the public and rural health causes, attempting to reverse a situation in which health care services were beginning to rely mainly on market-based services and market-sourced funding. Since 2002 a total of RMB 10.5 billion (including RMB 2.9 billion in special Central funds) has been invested in building an infrastructure of disease prevention and control centers at the provincial, municipal and county levels [Note that municipal includes 'prefectures' in some instances, and county includes 'districts' in some instances, throughout the following]. In a special line item, the Central government invested RMB 6.4 billion to build the medical treatment system for sudden public health events; medical supervision agencies have been set up in 98 percent of municipalities and 94 percent of counties, with an increased number of health supervisors.[6] The country also increased its support for the rural health services system, with the building of health centers at the township level regarded as the 'key effort' in order to further improve the three-level (county, township and village) health services network. Health services conditions and capabilities at the county, township and village level improved greatly after years of infrastructure building. By the end of 2006 the total building included 8,800 hospitals, 2,020 maternal and child healthcare centers (stations), 39,000 township health centers (including 38,000 government-run ones) and 609,000 village clinics (88.1 percent of which were in 'administrative villages'). These were either in counties or county-level cities. Each town had at least one government-run health center, which strengthened supervision and management of village clinics to ensure the provision of cheap and reliable drugs and services to villagers. To overcome the problem of 'overly expensive medical services' in this same period the country also strengthened the building of urban community health services systems[7] and increased financial inputs into community medical institutions to lower the medical expenses of residents and attract patients to seek treatment there. Each locality also set up emergency-relief or 'fair-price' hospitals and low-cost pharmacies in significant attempts to lower the cost of medical expenses for local residents. With the immense increase in the aggregate amount of health resources and the continuous improvement in infrastructure,[8] the rate at which residents utilized health services also increased (Table 6.1).

Table 6.1 Service and sickbed use at medical institutions countrywide

Year	2001	2002	2003	2004	2005
Diagnosis and treatment person-times (100 million)	20.87	21.45	20.96	22.03	23.00
at: hospitals	12.10	12.43	12.13	13.05	13.87
health centers	8.37	7.30	7.10	7.03	6.99
Hospitalized patients (10,000)	5,464	5,991	6,092	6,676	7,184
at: hospitals	3,625	3,997	4,159	4,673	5,108
health centers	1,705	1,654	1,626	1,621	1,641

Sickbed use ratio (%)	53.5	57.4	58.7	61.4	62.9
at: hospitals	61.1	64.6	65.3	68.4	70.3
health centers	31.3	34.8	36.2	37.2	37.8
Average days of hospitalization	9.5	8.7	9.0	9.1	9.2
at: hospitals	11.8	10.9	11.0	10.8	10.9
health centers	4.5	4.0	4.2	4.5	4.7
Person-times of diagnosis and treatment per doctor per day	4.6	5.2	5.0	4.8	5.3
Sickbeds in each doctor's charge per day	1.4	1.4	1.5	1.5	1.7

Note: In the table, 'Diagnosis and treatment person-times' exclude clinics, community health service stations and village clinics; 'Person-times of diagnosis and treatment per doctor per day' and 'Sickbeds in each doctor's charge per day' figures at general hospitals of the health sector.

Data Source: Bulletin on Development of China's Health Cause 2005 (Statistical Information Center, Ministry of Health).

Further progress was made after the tradition of 'patriotic health campaigns stressing prevention and the surrounding environment' was restored throughout the country (see Box 6.1).

Box 6.1 Public health environment control in rural areas as in drinking water and toilet renovation

Organized under the auspices of the State Development and Reform Commission, Ministry of Water Resources and Ministry of Health, the '10th Five-Year Program' for Drinking Water Safety in Rural Areas Nationwide was approved by the State Council in 2007. The Program aims to solve the issue of drinking water safety in rural areas by establishing a protection system to deal with the issue. By the end of 2007, around 900 million people had benefitted from drinking water improvements, accounting for 92.8 percent of the total rural population. Access to tap water in rural areas increased from 58.2 percent in 2003 to 64.1 percent in 2007, and access to sanitary toilets increased from 50.9 percent to 57 percent. After more than 20 years of ongoing water and toilet improvements in rural areas, the water conditions of rural China are vastly improved. Diseases relating to unclean water and intestinal problems have been brought under control, and the general health level of farmers and rural inhabitants is better as well.

Source: Zhang Zhenzhong, Wu Huazhang and Wang Xiufeng, *Health Security in China's New Social Welfare System* (Background Report, 2008).

Reform and development of the medical security system

Medical security is a fund-raising system of a government or social organization for spreading out the risk of an individual's unforeseen medical costs. There are many forms of bearing the expense of medical security, ranging from individuals bearing all to individuals bearing none. In countries or regions without a medical security system and a public medical service system, medical expenses are shouldered mainly by individuals and their families. This harbors the risk of impoverishing patients and families, and it also often leads to patients being unable to pay for services. In those countries and regions with a robust medical security system, individuals bear no medical expenses while public funds carry the burden. To prevent people from bringing poverty upon themselves due to ill health, those countries with medical security systems assume the majority of costs but individuals bear a certain percentage of expenses, in order to save on medical expenses and reduce waste in provision of medical services, as well as due to moral hazard. A sound 'medical security system' (with wide coverage, a rational proportion of costs carried by individuals, and harmonious relations with medical service supply systems) determines the effective functioning of a 'health security system'.

Establishment and development of China's medical security system

Following the founding of New China, three medical security systems covering urban and rural residents were gradually established. The first was the 'labor protection medical care' of enterprises, which was intended mainly for workers at state-owned and urban collective enterprises and their family members. Whether still employed or retired, workers could enjoy free medical service and were charged only a symbolic registration fee. The second was free medical care, provided mainly for workers at governmental organizations and institutions. The burden of medical expenses fell on public finance, while individuals assumed expenses for drugs and hospitalization in a certain proportion. The third was cooporative medical care, one of the fundamental systems in China's rural health work. Collective economic entities at the township level generally paid the remuneration to medical personnel, and farmers received medical care for free or with a symbolic registration fee but were required to pay drug expenses (see Box 6.2).

After reform and opening-up, as enterprises gradually became economic entities that operated independently and that were responsible for their own profits and losses, these economic entities paid more attention to accounting. They lowered investments in labor protection benefits, which meant that getting reimbursed for medical expenses became a major problem. Workers of bankrupt enterprises were particularly subject to losing all 'labor protection medical care'. It should be noted that the labor protection medical care under the planned-economy system also had obvious weaknesses, such as tremendous waste of medical resources, lack of constraints on parties involved in both supply and demand, lack of any society-wide mutual aid and social pooling function, and so on. These weaknesses became more apparent in the context of economic-system reform.

Box 6.2 Traditional rural cooperative medical care

Rural cooperative medical care aimed to solve the problem of medical care for rural residents. It officially appeared in 1955 when the movement to set up cooperatives in the countryside was at its peak. It refers to a form of 'organization for mutual aid', in which individuals, together with the 'production' parts of rural collectives or their administrative organizations jointly put up the resources for basic medical healthcare services; medical expenses are thereby redistributed among both healthy and sick people.[9] The system was voluntary and adhered to the principles of mutual benefit and moderation. In September 1965, the Central Committee of the Communist Party of China approved and passed on a 'Report on Placing the Emphasis of Health Work on Rural Areas'. This was prepared by the Party Committee of the Ministry of Health, and it greatly promoted the development of rural cooperative medical care. By 1976, over 90 percent of farmers were participating in cooperative medical care, and at a certain level this resolved the problems that rural people had experienced in getting any medical care at all.

Rural cooperative medical care was designed to provide health prevention and medical care for villagers within a commune. The basic unit for the system was the commune. The work was done by the production brigade, under the direct authority of the commune as administered by the commune's 'health center'. The property of a cooperative medical care station was collectively owned and any remuneration to doctors and health personnel was paid with collective funds; medical expenses were carried jointly by farmers and collective public welfare funds, at a ratio determined by the state of the collective economy. Either diagnosis and treatment fees could be waived (and paid collectively) or medicine costs could be waived (and paid collectively), or both.

Adapted to the needs of China's low level of economic development at the time, and to the fact of a medical system that allowed no connection between urban and rural areas, the system of cooperative medical care was local-community based and relied on the local collective's resources. As described by the World Bank and the World Health Organization, it was 'the sole example of collectively solving health funds among the developing countries' and it was regarded as a kind of 'Health Revolution'. Widespread access basically guaranteed the health of a great numbers of farmers,[10] effectively improved labor productivity, and contributed to the development of the then rural economy.

On October 12, 1983, a 'Notice' of the Central Committee of the Communist Party of China and the State Council was issued that related to separating out the functions of 'government' from 'communes' and establishing new Township Governments. As a result, the strength of the collective aspect of the rural economy began to decline and the traditional cooperative medical care lost its economic base and organizational structure. It therefore rapidly went downhill—by 1989 its coverage had decreased to 4.8 percent of people nationwide.

Source: Zhang Zhenzhong, Wu Huazhang and Wang Xiufeng, *Health Security in China's New Social Welfare System* (Background Report, 2008).

From the late 1980s many cities carried out a succession of reforms and pilot projects relating to free medical care systems and labor protection medical care. In 1993 the Third Plenary Session of the 14th CPC Central Committee decided to establish a 'basic medical insurance system for workers that integrated socially pooled funds and personal accounts'. After gathering together the experience and lessons of trial reforms in medical insurance across the country, in 1998, the State Council issued the *Decision to Establish a Basic Medical Insurance System for Urban Workers*. It called for the integration of socially pooled funds and personal accounts for the basic medical insurance for workers, and required all urban workers to participate in the basic medical insurance of the community in which they were located. To incorporate diverse forms of employment, in 2003–2004 the coverage of the basic medical insurance for workers was expanded to include all urban workers—and an increasing proportion of urban workers now began to be covered (see Figure 6.1). At the end of 2007 the number of urban workers enrolled in the basic medical insurance stood at 180.2 million, including 134.2 million incumbent workers and 46 million retirees. The total revenue of basic medical insurance funds for the whole year was RMB 225.7 billion, the expenditure was RMB 156.2 billion, and the year-end cumulative balance was RMB 247.7 billion.[11]

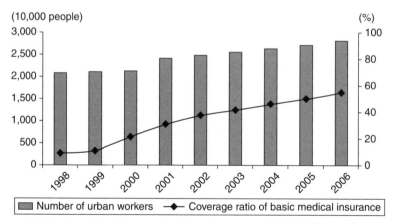

Figure 6.1   Number of workers enrolled in, and coverage ratio of China's basic medical insurance for workers.

Source: Statistical Bulletin on Development of China's Labor and Social Security Cause in 1998–2006. [Note: 1998 and 1999 data include workers enrolled in 'Pooled Fund for Serious Diseases' and 'Social Pooled Fund for Medical Expenses Incurred by Retirees'.]

Establishment and development of the new cooperative medical care system for rural areas

After the 1980s, as reform of the economic system advanced, the cooperative medical care in rural areas that had relied on the collective economy and people's communes went into decline. Throughout the 1980s rural cooperative medical care had been at a standstill, and the cooperative medical care system had already collapsed in most places.

Entering the twenty-first century, the vulnerable condition of the rural public health service system and increasing medical and healthcare expenses led to heightened awareness of such problems as: 'hard to get medical care and too expensive to get medical care'. Many farmers were forced to reduce or even cut out all medical services due to their inability to pay. The situation was seriously constraining China's stated goal of 'building a society of moderate prosperity in an all-round and harmonious way'. Farmers were falling back into poverty or simply succumbing to disease as a result of the inequalities in the way medical and health expenses were being financed in the country, with rural health services growing ever weaker. In 2003 the General Office of the State Council approved and passed on the *Opinions on Establishing a New Rural Cooperative Medical System* as devised by the Ministry of Health and other relevant departments. This document determined that trials should be launched in two or three counties in each province from 2003 onward. Successful experience was to be collated and acted upon, and by 2010 the country was to establish a 'new rural cooperative medical system covering rural residents nationwide'.

The first trials started in the second half of 2003, and four groups of trials were conducted thereafter. By the end of 2007, 2,451 counties had implemented the new cooperative medical care, accounting for 85.64 percent of the country's total number of counties. Some 726 million people had been enrolled, accounting for 83.54 percent of the agricultural population nationwide, with a ratio of enrollment of 86.20 percent (see Table 6.2).[12] According to the State Council's decision, the new rural cooperative medical care will be implemented in the remaining 292 counties in 2008, so that the system will cover all rural areas. [Note: certain 'counties' are designated 'cities' and certain 'provinces' are designated 'regions' or 'cities'. These jurisdictional distinctions are deleted in the above for ease of understanding the meaning of the text.]

Pilot projects testing a basic medical insurance system for urban residents

In July 2007 the State Council issued the *Guiding Opinions on Basic Medical Insurance Trials for Urban Residents* (No. 20, G. F. [2007]), which stipulated that primary and secondary school students, children, and other unemployed urban residents not covered by the basic medical insurance system for urban workers could, on a voluntary basis, participate in the basic medical insurance plan for urban residents. The basic medical insurance for urban residents relies mainly on

Table 6.2 Development of the new rural cooperative medical care in 2003–2007

Time	Trial counties	Farmers enrolled (100 million)	Ratio of enrollment (%)	People benefited (100 million)	Funds raised for the year (RMB 100 million)	Funds spent for the year (RMB 100 million)	Ratio of fund use for the year (%)
Sep. 2003	304	0.43	74.0				
Dec. 2004	333	0.80	75.2	0.76	37.6	26.4	70.05
Dec. 2005	678	1.79	75.6	1.22	75.4	61.8	81.95
Dec. 2006	1,451	4.10	80.7	2.72	213.6	155.8	72.95
Dec. 2007	2,451	7.26	86.2	4.54	428.0	346.6	80.99

Data source: Bulletin on China's Health Development in 2003–2007 (material read at the 2008 National Health Work Conference, Statistical Information Center, Ministry of Health); Information on the Work of New Rural Cooperative Medical Care, Issue 2 (36 issues in all), Office of Inter-Ministerial Meeting for New Rural Cooperative Care, the State Council; Developing New Rural Cooperative Medical Care in China: An Assessment Report on the Trial Work of New Rural Cooperative Medical Care, written by the Assessment Group for the Experimental Work of New Rural Cooperative Medical Care (People's Medical Publishing House, 2006) p. 21.

family contributions, with moderate subsidies from the government. The focus of the fund is to pay medical expenses for diagnosis and hospitalization of those residents who are enrolled. In 2007 pilot projects trials were made in 88 cities, and the number of urban residents enrolled stood at 42.91 million.[13] As required by the Guiding Opinions, efforts will be made in 2009 to undertake trials in over 80 percent of the cities and, by 2010, to cover all urban unemployed residents.

Establishment and development of urban and rural medical aid systems

'Basic medical insurance' for workers, 'medical insurance' for urban residents and the 'new rural cooperative medical care system' all require contributions for enroll-ment. A considerable number of poverty-stricken families in both urban and rural areas face hardships in getting enrolled, however, and cannot carry that portion of their own expenses even after enrollment. To address this problem, in 2003, the Ministry of Civil Affairs, the Ministry of Health, and the Ministry of Finance jointly published the *Opinions on Implementing Rural Medical Aid*. In 2005 the General Office of the State Council approved and transmitted the *Opinions on the Trial Work of Establishing the Urban Medical Aid System* as presented by the Ministry of Civil Affairs, the Ministry of Health, the Ministry of Labor and Social Security and the Ministry of Finance, and decided to establish an urban medical aid system. By the end of June 2007 urban medical aid trials had been carried out in 65 percent of the districts and counties, covering a population of 6.69 million. In 2007 medical aid services were provided for 29 million 'person-times' in rural areas. This was four times the number serviced in 2004, which had been 7.29 million. Medical aid services were provided for 4.42 million person-times in urban areas, which was nearly 4 times the number serviced in 2005, which had been 1.15 million.[14]

Main problems in the health security system

China's health security for urban and rural residents has achieved great progress in the past several dozen years, but it is still far from the objective of establishing a system that can adapt to our socialist market-economy system, that conforms to our national situation, and that meets the basic health needs of the people. Numerous problems remain in the current health security system.

A weakening governmental role in providing health security for citizens

The government's investment in public health continues to decline, with health expenditures as a percentage of GDP going from 1.3 percent in 1983 to a low of 0.7 percent in 1997, while health expenditures as a percentage of total expenditures are similarly falling, from 6.1 percent in 1992 to a low of 3.9 percent in 2002 (see Figure 6.2). Moreover, the government health budget is also falling in terms of total health expenses. In the 1970s and 1980s, government inputs into hospital revenues totalled more than 30 percent on average. Government health

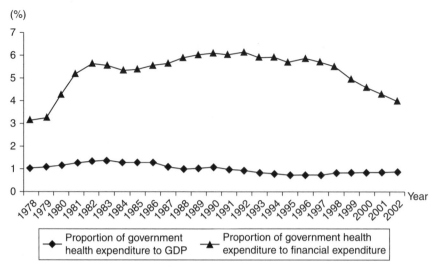

Figure 6.2 Proportions of government health expenditure to GDP and financial expenditure.

Source: Study Report on Aggregate Health Expenses in China, National Health Economics Institute, Ministry of Health, 2003.

expenditures as a percentage of total health expenses have been declining, however, from 32 percent in 1979 to 17 percent in 2003. Individuals' health expenditures, paid in cash, have risen from 20 percent to 56 percent (see Figure 6.3). After 2003, government health expenditures increased as a percent of total health expenses in the country, but were still much lower than in countries 'in economic transition' facing similar conditions (the figure in 2000 was an average of 70 percent) and also lower than the world's average (62 percent in 2000).

Since 'reform and opening up' began in China, one fairly prevalent mode of reform has been to 'provide the policy but not the money'.[15] With inadequate government inputs, any medical and health care has been supported mainly by citizens. Inequalities in the burden of healthcare expenses have simply led to worsening health conditions. Some 80 percent of all government health expenditures have been concentrated in cities, and 80 percent of that has gone to large hospitals in cities. Preventive healthcare and basic medical services with much greater social efficiencies have developed only slowly due to financing difficulties. The large number of grass-roots medical and health institutions in rural and urban areas that were providing medical services have been declining and can hardly get any local financial support at all. Medium- and high-level hospitals have been able to increase services and get State support as a result of this advantage. This has made limited funds in the health sector that much tighter; the State has largely retreated from medical and health services for rural residents. 'Division of tax' requirements have greatly cut the financial resources available to local

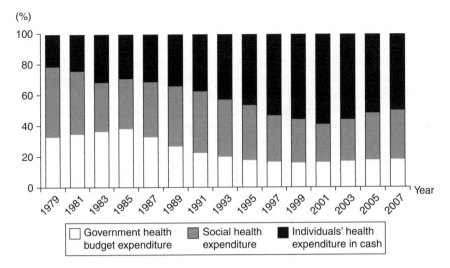

Figure 6.3 Structure of aggregate health expenses in 1979–2007 (percentage).

Source: Urban Medical Security System written by Li Ling, Jiang Yu and Chen Qiulin, 2008.

governments, meaning that economically backward areas have little or no funds for the health field. The Central government has increased subsidies to financially strapped provinces, but no effective transfer payment system has yet been formed within the country to balance public-service and health-service levels in different regions.

Decreasing efficiencies in how health services are allocated

Since the start of reform and opening-up policies, the government has introduced market competition as a way to improve the operating efficiencies of hospitals. The health services field is a market of imperfect competition, however. Increased operating efficiencies and financial indicators of hospitals mean that either prices of services per unit have increased or costs of inputs have been lowered, such as services or quality. As a result, patients' interests are harmed and the public's interests and rights in and demands for medical services are inadequately respected and satisfied. Measured from the overall perspective of the entire society, the overall efficiency of health services has actually decreased. Even as total health resources have expanded, the efficiency and quality of medical services provided by medical and health institutions has not increased accordingly.

Narrow coverage and low benefit levels of the medical security system

In the course of medical system reform, due to the bankruptcies or the restructuring of their employers, some workers who had previously enjoyed labor security medical care lost their coverage. Many people were also not covered during the decade that it took to develop the basic medical insurance for urban workers, from proposing the plan, conducting and expanding trials, to completion of the initial process. In the meantime, from establishment to expansion, the basics medical insurance system for urban workers has also needed a process during a time in which there was no medical security service. In addition, those who had enjoyed certain security benefits, such as college students covered by the original free medical care system and the family members of workers enjoying some security benefits from the previous labor protection system, were not included in the new medical security system. As the economy has developed, the forms of employment have also changed: the supply and demand sides of the labor market have been empowered to select working hours, working forms and labor contracts on a flexible and voluntary basis. The percentages of people employed 'flexibly' have been increasing, those who are casual laborers, hourly workers, domestic help, and workers in cooperative organizations. Our modern social insurance system, established on the basis of regular employment, has found it very difficult to adapt to other modes of employment. It has found it hard to expand, when the expansion room for regular employment was already very small. Affected by all these factors, the percentage of people enjoying medical security has decreased sharply. Since 2003 the number of workers (134.2 million) and retirees (46 million) participating in the basic medical insurance for urban workers has been increasing rapidly, and the basic trial medical insurance for urban residents has attracted 42.91 million. However, the number of incumbent workers enrolled accounts only for 45.8 percent of the total urban workers, and all urban residents enrolled (223.11 million) account only for 37.6 percent of the entire urban population. If one counts in workers at government organizations and institutions who enjoy free medical care but are excluded from statistics, the total number of people enrolled still only accounts for about 40 percent of the entire urban population. Some 60 percent of the urban population still has not been covered in the social medical security system. The new rural cooperative medical system has expanded considerably and already covers about 90 percent of rural residents, but the coverage of the remaining 10 percent is going to be hard to achieve. Limited by the low levels of funding, the biggest problem with the new rural cooperative medical system lies in its low levels of security [or benefits]. (The average percentage of costs for which farmers were compensated, for medical expenses for severe diseases, was less than 30 percent in 2006.)[16] Among other problems, incomplete financing mechanisms, weak managerial ability, inadequate supervision, and excessive fund accumulation in some places, have also affected the healthy development of the cooperative medical system.

Unsound management systems for health services and medical security

At the present time, China's public medical institutions are fragmented in terms of management, information systems, and ability to respond to emergencies. Their strength has been dispersed among various Central and local governmental departments, enterprises, institutions and the military system. Meanwhile, lines of authority among them are very unclear. This artificial fragmentation has led to a highly arbitrary use of medical resources, which has reinforced the unfair way in which they are allocated. This was just one of the key reasons for the obstructed information communications in the early days of SARS.[17] Another problem that the 2003 SARS event revealed was that response mechanisms against sudden public health events remained unsound; scientific and effective warning mechanisms had not really been established. In terms of regulatory systems governing medicine and healthcare, although a series of laws, rules and regulations, regulatory documents, various industry standards and specifications have been developed, the present admissible standards for various aspects of medical service organizations remain incomplete and the criteria for medical technology and equipment are not yet standardized.

In terms of the overall management of medical security systems, a multiple-management situation has existed for a long time. The basic medical insurance system for urban workers and the medical insurance system for urban residents are managed by human resources and social security departments. The new rural cooperative medical system is managed by health departments and the medical aid system is managed by civil affairs departments. These different lines of authority dismember the internal relationships between the medical security systems and the health service provision system. They work against any improvement in how resources are used efficiently and they lead to higher management costs. As of now, medical security administrative bodies have not been effective in serving as a third-party buyer of medical services. People enrolled in the medical security system must pay all or most medical expenses before they seek reimbursement from a medical insurance institution. That is to say, they are still at their own expense when seeking medical care, which means that so-called 'medical insurance management' focuses on controlling the behavior of patients rather than the behavior of hospitals. At the same time, the territorial or 'turf' nature of medical security management, and the lack of effective mechanisms for insurance transfer and renewal, also result in a legion of problems: difficulty in adjusting medical insurance fund balances among regions, concurrent existence of surpluses and deficits, ill-defined responsibilities of the Central and local governments, and difficulty in transferring medical insurance benefits.

Outstanding problems of 'hard to get medical care' and 'expensive to get medical care'

Since the 1980s, once China basically resolved the problem of shortages in medical services and drugs, the outstanding problem has been that it is both difficult to get care and it is very expensive. Due to the increasing prices of medicines, urban and rural residents who have no medical security have had to rely on their families to cover increasing medical expenses. As compared to 1997, in 2006 the total health funds raised nationwide increased from RMB 319.671 billion to

RMB 984.334 billion, and per capita health expenses rose from RMB 258.58 to RMB 748.84. The increase in medical expenses obviously outpaced the growth of GDP and per capita income. Together with the irrational mechanisms in place for sharing medical expenses and the inadequacy in quality health resources, this has left unresolved the problem of 'hard to get medical care and hard to pay for it'. In recent years, the State has moderately increased financial inputs into the health sector. It has established medical security systems that cover different groups of people, and introduced plans for a new round of medical and healthcare system reform. By considering opinions from all parts of society, in January 2009, the State Council adopted the *Opinions on Deepening the Medical and Health System Reform and the Scheme for Implementing the Medical and Health System Reform in 2009–2011*. It decided to invest RMB 850 billion within three years in basic public health services and basic medicines, to expand the coverage of the medical security system (up to 90 percent) and increase compensation standards. These measures are expected to relieve the problems of 'hard to get and too expensive'. To solve the fundamental problems, however, efforts must be made to expedite the building of a health security system with universal coverage.

Objectives of a 'developmental health security system'

China's developmental health security system should conform to the basic principles of a modern health security system, i.e. accessibility, impartiality and sustainability. By 2020 the objective is to achieve a situation in which 'Every person enjoys basic health services' and 'Every person is entitled equally to health security'.

Regarded as a key goal in 'achieving a moderately prosperous society in an all round way', 'Every person enjoys basic health services' is an important commitment of the Chinese government, and also a reiteration of its previous commitment.[18] It means that the government assumes a fundamental role in ensuring the health of people. Complying with the fundamental principles of a modern health security system and giving full consideration to the realities of China, the commitment is not an excessively high objective; it is within the carrying capacity of the present financial and medical systems.

In the process of building a moderately prosperous society, health security is not a system that provides general subsidies to income, nor is it a basic subsistence security system. Good health is not 'consumption' in the normal sense, but rather an important human capital investment. 'Health security' is a developmental social security project. It plays an important promotional role in increasing human capital and ensuring the overall development of people and harmonious socio-economic development. Health security should be regarded as an important part of building a moderately prosperous society and should be included in the overall plan for building such a society. The government should conscientiously take the lead and form a new health security system that is appropriate to a moderately prosperous society, provides all people with coverage, and is up to meeting their health needs.

From now until 2020, the above objective can be divided roughly into two stages, the first from 2009 to 2012 and the second from 2012 to 2020.

The emphasis of the first stage is to expand coverage of the health security system so that every person enjoys health security. Currently, the framework for basic medical insurance and health security systems has been formed in China; efforts should now be made to expand coverage of the medical security system in the process of reforming and improving relevant systems. The focus should be on the following four aspects. First, urban workers who should have participated in 'basic medical insurance' should be enrolled, with an aim to cover 90 percent of regular urban workers. Second, the building of 'basic medical insurance for all urban residents' should be accelerated to cover over 90 percent of all urban residents. Third, enrollment of farmers in the new rural cooperative medical care system should reach and be maintained at over 90 percent. Fourth, insurance enrollments and benefit transferability for migrant workers who move from one pooling region to another should be basically solved, so as to let them enjoy the basic benefits specified by the insurance enrollment system. The State should strengthen investment in, and management of, the grass-roots health service system in order to improve medical service quality. It should persuade more people to seek medical care at the grass-roots level so as to assure their basic health needs.

In the second stage, ending in 2020, basic medical and health systems covering both urban and rural residents should be established, including public health and medical service systems covering urban and rural areas, a medical security system covering urban and rural residents, a sound 'medicine supply' security system, and more scientific medical and health management and operating mechanisms. This second stage aims mainly to: (i) have the basic medical security system cover urban and rural populations and provide appropriate medical aid to all poverty-stricken people; (ii) lower the percentage of personal contributions in the medical security system, increase security levels and benefits, and strive to achieve a compensation ratio that is over 60 percent (thorough reimbursement of drugs under basic drug systems) for the basic medical insurance for urban and rural residents without lowering the present security benefits for urban workers, while increasing investment into and standards of social medical aid; (iii) gradually promote pooled funds at urban and rural levels, at the prefecture level, and at the outpatient level, establish coordination mechanisms among medical security and health service policies, from a macro-perspective, uniformly coordinate reform policies relating to health and medical security and their departmental implemen-tation, eliminate personal accounts and change the 'integration of social pooling funds and personal accounts' to an 'entirely social pooling fund'; and (iv) estab-lish a national framework for basic medical and health systems, sound urban and rural public health service systems, three-level rural medical and health service systems, and community health service systems, strengthen supervision and controls over medical services and expenses, establish relatively standard public medical institution management and operating mechanisms, and increase the efficiency of utilizing health resources.

Increase government investment, in order to maintain the public welfare nature of health security. Try to narrow the discrepancies in basic medical health services between urban and rural areas, regions and people with different levels of income, in order to further improve the level and quality of public health and basic medical services.

As for sourcing funds, apart from a portion of expenses that should be borne by enterprises, the society and individuals, the main sources of health security funds should be the country's financial appropriations and medical security funds. The country's financial appropriations for health security should be used mainly to build the public health service system and serve the objective: 'Every person enjoys basic medical and health services'. In 2006 the country allocated RMB 172.1 billion for health security. After deducting financial subsidies for medical security, the total came to RMB 118.8 billion, only RMB 7.5 per capita a month nationwide. If the monthly per capita amount reaches RMB 11 and RMB 20 by 2012 and 2020 respectively, provided that the present appropriation system remains unchanged, the required financial appropriations will be RMB 179.8 billion and RMB 354.9 billion. As for medical security funds, the government [should] not only provide insurance subsidies for various medical insurance (basic medical insurance for workers, basic medical insurance for residents, new rural cooperative medical care, supplementary medical insurance for severe diseases, etc), but [should] also assume medical expenses for non-participating personnel from government organizations and institutions as well as medical aid expenses for people with special difficulties. Based on end-2006 and end-2007 data, our estimation is that, given the numbers of people of various types that require coverage and their differing security standards, total subsidies required from national finance for medical security funds will be RMB 275.9 billion in 2012 and RMB 1028.1 billion in 2020. Adding together basic health services and medical security, the total national funding that will be required to meet the objective that every person enjoys basic health services and medical security will come to RMB 455.8 billion in 2012 and RMB 1,383 billion in 2020 (see Chapter 12 for detailed calculations).

Policy recommendations

Organic integration of grass-roots health service system building and medical security system building

In building a developmental health security system we follow the basic concepts of a modern health security system, namely, we aim to integrate the process of building both the health service system and the medical security system. In terms of providing services, this model provides urban and rural residents with medical services through the community health service system. It integrates prevention, basic medical care, healthcare, rehabilitation, health education and family planning functions as well as various forms of medical services. The community health service system is comprised of the urban and rural public health service system, the 'three-level rural medical and health service system', and the urban community health service system. It features convenient, economical, fair, comprehensive and equal grass-roots health services. It should meet community needs for basic health services and should play the dual role of service provider and medical security. The medical service system is composed of for-profit and non-profit medical institutions which compete with each other, under the rigorous supervision of the government, to provide citizens with multi-level and diverse medical services. Whether in terms of funding systems or medical security systems, the model must set up a basically 'full-coverage' security system that requires ongoing increases in governmental, social and individual financing. In this process the government takes a leading role and invests mainly in public health and grass-roots medical services. It also protects citizens from disease risks by means of a multi-level medical security system that consists of the basic medical insurance for urban workers, the basic medical insurance for urban residents, the new rural cooperative medical system, and the urban and rural medical aid system.

Strengthen the government's leading role in health security

As a field in which the market regularly fails to play its normal function, health services and medical security must be supported by the government. The government's leading role should be manifested in strengthening leadership, increasing inputs, making policies, and exercising rigorous supervision. Investments in health by both the Central and local governments should increase year on year with economic development, at a rate not lower than the growth in financial revenues. While increasing the total amount of investments, the structure of inputs should also be improved, to break out of the present situation of a divide between urban and rural, as well as among regions. Cross-regional transfer payments of health financing from Central sources should be improved. Investments in public health, urban community health, township health centers and health institutions in impoverished areas should be improved in particular, as well as basic medical services that provide coverage for all people. Barriers between regions, entities and industries should be removed, and resource provision for medical and health services should be reorganized in a scientific and rational way. We should gradually achieve the uniform management of hospitals at county-and-above levels that is conducted by municipal-level health authorities. We should allocate resources effectively as required by regional health plans, strengthen effective supervision by the government in the medical and health field, correct the profit-pursuing behavior of health service institutions, and guide the growth of large urban health service institutions in a more proper direction. We should tighten the eligibility for medical qualifications, standardize medical procedures, strengthen the assessment of medical quality, and reinforce supervision over prices of drugs and medical services. We should improve how we categorize in terms of management, strengthen government macro-controls and industry supervision, and effectively solve the irrational and inconsistent allocation of health resources. We should improve health information and education to raise knowledge of the general public about health issues as a way to modify unhealthy habits and lifestyles. We should actively launch 'patriotic health campaigns' and improve working and living conditions, to enhance the overall health of the entire nation.

Establish and improve a medical security system that provides coverage for all urban and rural citizens, and increase the efficiency with which medical security funds are utilized

The medical security system is an important way to transform 'accessible' medical and health services into 'attainable' ones. It is one of the critical measures in improving the impartiality of health services. In this regard our top priority is to expand the coverage of various medical security systems to include all laborers and urban and rural residents. Because the 'basic medical insurance for urban workers' was designed specifically for 'regular' employees, and cannot adapt to the situations of flexible employees, it will be necessary to design a medical insurance system with lower contributions and levels of security (for example, one that focuses on severe illnesses).

Rural migrant workers should be included in the present framework of medical security systems for urban workers. Given their high mobility and low income they should be allowed to enjoy different kinds of benefits. Existing arrangements should be maintained for rural migrant workers with regular employment who have been enrolled in the medical insurance for urban workers. Those without regular employment should be allowed to participate in the medical insurance system for urban residents. When they return home, the medical insurance relationships and funds of these people should be transferred to the new rural cooperative medical care system. In addition, a special aid system should be established for the floating population to disperse and ameliorate their basic medical risks. There should be elastic mechanisms to facilitate participants' transfer between different security systems, so that medical security relationships and benefits can be smoothly transferred between regions or departments. Outside the basic medical insurance system and the medical aid system, the development of supplementary medical insurance and commercial medical insurance should be firmly encouraged, supported and guided, in order to satisfy the medical and health needs of different levels of people.

With the building of a nationwide medical system and an increase of financing and compensation levels, expenses for medical and health services that workers and urban and rural residents receive will come mainly from medical insurance funds. This presents a challenge in terms of how we manage and how well we use medical insurance funds. First, we must resolve problems of inadequate funds, gross surpluses in some insurance funds and inequality in access to them, and in general address the low or nonexistent efficiency in fund utilization. Efforts should be made to lower the 'fund accumulation rate' that is employed by the basic medical insurance system. We must standardize the system of medical accounts for individuals, and actively explore ways to abolish the personal and family account systems (while giving consideration to local conditions), so that the problems of unsound mechanisms for payment of medical expenses and inappropriate payment structures can be solved. The critical role of the medical insurance fund management bodies in purchasing medical services should be fully exploited, in order to change the behavior of service institutions that use excessive amounts of resources simply to gain profits. The goal is to preserve resources while better protecting people's health.

Establish and improve the public health and preventive healthcare systems

The government should strengthen its support for public health, and for group-specific prevention activities. It should increase transfer payments to public health in western China and to the rural public health cause, in order to address the problems in those regions of extreme shortage of doctors and drugs. It should mobilize the transfer of medical personnel to grass-roots and western regions, strengthen the training of health personnel and improve standards in health service provisions; and mobilize both social forces at large and individuals to take part in the building of the public health system. Most public health problems are closely related to health awareness and behavior of citizens. Public involvement will not only expand public health resources but also facilitate effective health education, thus promoting the creation of healthier conditions and a change in public health behavior. At the same time, we should establish and improve response mechanisms to deal with sudden public health events, so that we can respond effectively to sudden infectious disease prevalence, serious food poisoning events, and public health events that arise from natural disasters and safety incidents. We must strengthen the prevention and control of major infectious diseases that pose a severe threat to people's health, such as AIDS, tuberculosis, schistosomiasis and hepatitis.

We must strengthen the prenatal care of pregnant women and the nutrition security of infants and children. These should be included in the developmental health security system by means of transfer payments in cash. We should actively coordinate other policies that affect public health, for example, environmental protection policies, measures for water resource protection and sewage treatment, as well as have an input into criteria for certain industries that have an extremely adverse health impact. We should conduct health assessments of the government's industrial plans and public policies, to ensure the health and welfare of the general public.

Deepen medical service system reform, and establish a standard, fair and efficient medical health service system

To achieve the primary objective that 'Every person enjoys basic medical services', the State should shift its conceptual framework in how it approaches investments in health, from 'focusing more on large entities and less on small ones', to 'focusing more on small entities and less on large ones'. It should increase support for rural grass-roots and community public medical service institutions, in order to improve the public health service system. The State should give priority to the development of urban community health service centers and rural township health centers. In this regard, it should establish an urban health service system that is based on community health services, and in rural areas, a three-level rural health prevention and healthcare network. It should be proactive in finding ways to fulfil the objective that states, 'Every person should enjoy basic medical services'. It should specify basic types of disease that must be treated, catalogue basic drugs, medical service items, and public health service items that the public health service system offers. It should establish a national 'basic drug' system, and organize the production, procurement and distribution of basic drugs by means of standard market-based operational mechanisms. At the same time, it should guide people toward using grass-roots medical and health services by changing payment methods for medical security. In transforming its mode of dealing with diseases, it should, strengthen early intervention in chronic diseases and commonly seen diseases. It should provide certain free medical services to poverty-stricken residents as well as elderly who are suffering from chronic diseases but who have no medical security.[19]

It should be noted that strengthening the government's leading role in health security does not mean that the government is to build and maintain all medical service institutions, especially medium- and large-sized ones. The basic concept is to 'focus on small entities while controlling large ones'. That is, have the government perform well at the grass-roots level, while it allows large medical institutions to compete but regulates their behavior. It should break the monopoly position of state-owned medical institutions, and encourage 'social forces' [i.e. non-governmental] to run hospitals and vigorously develop private medical institutions. The behaviors of medical institutions should be regulated through a scientific approach to adjusting the two payment methods of direct payment for health expenses and using medical security funds. The aim is to correct the tendency for unilateral pursuit of economic profit on the part of providers. It is to assure that health service institutions are real non-profit entities, rather than 'for-profit enterprises' that are using their monopoly positions to make maximum profits out of financial funds, medical insurance funds, and patients' medical expenses. The government must reform the macro-management systems and micro-operation mechanisms of medium- and large-sized public medical institutions. In macro terms, health authorities should become overall managers, planners and supervisors of the entire health sector. There must be a gradual separating out of governmental and institutional functions. 'Regulatory functions' should be separated out from 'management functions'. 'Hospitals' should be separated out from 'the suppliers of drugs'. In order to regulate them, we should make publicly-established hospitals become 'legal persons' [that is, place them under a legal framework in which they have legal-person status]. In micro terms, we should accelerate the creation of enforceable compensation mechanisms for medical institutions, form pricing mechanisms that are consistent with the natural laws of market competition and medical services, effectively solve the issue of 'relying on drugs for medical treatment', cut the practice of providing excessive services and drugs and reduce the consequent waste of resources, and control the phenomenal speed at which medical expenses are increasing.

Notes

1 Zhang Zhenzhong, Wu Huazhang and Wang Xiufeng, *Health Security in China's New Social Welfare System* (Background Report, 2008).

2 World Bank, *China: Long-term Issues and Countermeasures in Transition of Health Model* (China Financial & Economic Publishing House, 1994), p. 17.

3 Song Wenjiong Wu Ming, Li Weiping, Wang Pan and Wang Lin, 'Meet Challenges in the New Century through Institutional Innovation: Review and Comment on Urban Health Reform in the Past 20 Years', *Health Economics Research*, Issue 10, 1999, p. 32.

4 Wang Yanzhong and Feng Liguo, 'Where Should China's Medical and Health Reform Go: The Resource Gathering Effect and Improvement of the Unburdened Market-oriented Reform', *China Industrial Economics*, Issue 8, 2007, p. 25.

5 In September 1992 the State Council issued the Several Opinions on Deepening Health Reform. On the basis of this document, the Ministry of Health, in the spirit of 'relying on the state for construction and on oneself for subsistence', demanded that hospitals make new achievements in terms of 'aiding the medical sector by means of industry and reinforcing the main business with sideline'. Subsequently various 'innovative' measures able to create benefits were invented in hospitals, such as operation by designated doctor, special care, etc. In 2000 the State Council issued the Guiding Opinions regarding Urban Medical and Health Reform. In the document, such comments as 'various medical institutions are encouraged to organize into medical service groups via cooperation and merger; prices of medical services provided by for-profit medical institutions are deregulated so that they operate autonomously according to law and pay tax as required' were construed as a signal of allowing 'totally market-oriented operation' in the medical and health field. Ownership reform widely used in the state-owned enterprise reform was extended into the medical and health field.

6 *Bulletin on Development of China's Health Cause 2003–2007* (Statistical Information Center, Ministry of Health, 2008).

7 By the end of 2007, there was 24,000 community health service centers (stations) countrywide, including 2,500 health service centers (employing a total of 77,000 people, 31 persons per center on average, including 64,000 health professionals) and 21,000 health service stations (employing 80,000 people, 4 persons per station on average). See *Bulletin on Development of China's Health Cause 2003–2007* (Statistical Information Center, Ministry of Health, 2008).

8 By the end of 2007, there was 315,000 health institutions countrywide, including 19,900 hospitals, 40,000 health centers, 24,000 community health service centers (stations) and 3,007 maternal and child healthcare centers (clinics and stations); the total number of beds at these hospitals and health centers had reached 3,279,000, including 2,587,000 at hospitals and 692,000 at health centers, 2.54 per 1,000 people; the number of health personnel had stood at 5,7000,000, including about 950,000 village doctors and health workers and 4,680,000 health personnel, 1.56 practicing (assistant) physicians and 1.12 registered nurses per 1,000 people. These indicators were much higher than those in 2002. See *Bulletin on Development of China's Health Cause 2003–2007* (Statistical Information Center, Ministry of Health, 2008).

9 Song Shiyun, *Structure and Changes of the Social Security System in Rural China (1949–2002)* (People Press, 2003).

10 World Bank, *China: Long-term Issues and Countermeasures in Transition of Health Model* (China Financial & Economic Publishing House, 1994).

11 *Bulletin on Development of China's Labor and Social Security Cause in 2007*, Ministry of Human Resources and Social Security, May 21, 2008.

12 Office of Inter-Ministerial Meeting for New Rural Cooperative Care, the State Council, 'Information on the Work of New Rural Cooperative Medical Care', Issue 2 (36 issues in all), February 3, 2008.

13 *Bulletin on Development of China's Labor and Social Security Cause in 2007*, Ministry of Human Resources and Social Security, May 21, 2008.
14 National Bureau of Statistics of China, *China Statistical Abstract (2008)* (China Statistics Press, 2008), p. 196.
15 In 1979, the then Health Minister Qian Xinzhong advocated that 'health departments should also act on economic law', which was considered to be the first statement initiating the medical reform. See: Li Ling, '2006: Turning Point of China's Medical Reform', *China Health Economics*, Issue 4, 2007, p. 6.
16 Assessment Group for the Experimental Work of New Rural Cooperative Medical Care, *Developing New Rural Cooperative Medical Care in China: An Assessment Report on the Trial Work of New Rural Cooperative Medical Care* (People's Medical Publishing House, 2006), pp. 6–10.
17 Song Xiaowu, *Reform: Enterprises' Labor Security* (Social Sciences Academic Press, 2006), p. 403.
18 As early as the 1980s, the Chinese government made commitments to WHO's target 'Health for All by the Year 2000', and included it in China's 10-year plan for national economic and social development and its '8th Five-Year' plan. We have made great efforts in improving people's health and made remarkable achievements, but there is still a distance to the commitment made.
19 *Minor Diseases Treated Free of Charge in Zhuhai, at Government's Expense* (http://news.sina.com.cn).

7 Education security

Together with investment in good health, investment in education is a key part of investing in human capital, and increasing investments in human capital not only provide an active impetus to economic development, but are a significant way to achieve harmonious social development and promote human development. In countries with a sound market economic system, public education is usually considered a basic human right; it is an organic component of social welfare systems. 'Education security' refers to the allocations of public finance that are made for ensuring education. It means that the government will provide educational services for citizens through a variety of means, and incorporate basic education into the scope of what it considers State security. In China, compulsory education is currently the focus of the country's education security program.

A review of compulsory education in China

The Chinese government was well aware of the importance of education as long ago as the very early period of New China, after 1949. It launched a literacy campaign in the 1950s, and ongoing efforts to expand education contributed a certain amount to raising the educational level of the entire nation. Since the start of reform and opening up policies, all levels of government in China have worked to improve compulsory education, to the extent that China is in the forefront among developing countries in terms of basic education. According to the latest data provided in the UN's *Human Development Report 2007/2008*, in 2005 the literacy rate of Chinese young people aged between 15 and 24 stood at nearly 99 percent. This was 13 percent higher than the average level of developing countries, 2 percent higher than the average level of medium-income countries, 25 percent higher than the average level of low-income countries, and 12 percent higher than the world's average level (see Table 7.1).

The increase in literacy rates of the Chinese population cannot be divorced from the development of compulsory education. China's present nine-year compulsory education belongs to the basic type of public service. It is also an important component of the country's social welfare system. In 1952, shortly after the founding of New China, the enrollment rate of school-age children in primary schools in China was only 49.2 percent.[1] By the end of the twentieth century China had basically

Table 7.1 Literacy rates among young people (age 15–24) and enrollment rates in primary school: a comparison between China and the international community

	Young (aged 15–24) literacy rate		Primary school enrollment rate	
	1994	*2005*	*1994*	*2005*
China	94.3	98.9	97.0	99.0
Developing countries	80.2	85.6	80.0	85.0
Least developed countries	56.3	65.5	47.0	77.0
Latin American countries	93.7	96.6	86.0	95.0
South Asian countries	60.7	74.7	–	87.0
High human development countries	–	94.7	–	98.1
Medium human development countries	–	78.3	–	87.0
Low human development countries	55.9	–	96.0	95.0
High-income countries	99.0	–	96.0	95.0
Middle-income countries	93.1	96.8	92.0	93.0
Low-income countries	63.0	73.4	–	81.0
World average	83.5	86.5	83.7	87.0

Source: UNDP: *Human Development Report 2007/2008.*

achieved the establishment of nine-year compulsory education and 'basically' achieved the elimination of young and middle-aged illiteracy (this is known as the 'Two Basics'). As per plan [on schedule], coverage of the Two Basics stood at 85 percent; the primary school enrollment rate of school-age children (net enrollment rate) reached 99.1 percent, while the gross secondary school enrollment rate reached 88.6 percent (see Table 7.2). Nevertheless, rural areas in China's middle and western regions hold about 15 percent of the country's total population, but have failed to reach required enrollment rates. The coverage rate of nine-year compulsory education in China's western region in 2002 was only 73 percent.[2]

Table 7.2 China's progress in establishing compulsory education in 1990–2007 (unit: %)

Year	*1990*	*1995*	*2000*	*2005*	*2007*
Net primary school enrollment rate of pupils aged 6–11	96.3	98.5	99.1	99.2	99.5
Gross secondary school enrollment rate of children aged 12–14	66.7	78.4	88.6	95	98
Coverage rate of nine-year compulsory education	40	45	85	95	99
Illiteracy rate of young and middle-aged people aged 14–45	9.3	–	5	–	3.58

Source: Ministry of Education's Development & Planning Department, *China Education Statistical Yearbook 2006* (People's Education Press, 2007); *A Concise Statistical Analysis on Education Development in China* (2007).

When rural tax reforms began in the early twenty-first century in China, and the administrative reform of township governments was proceeding, the changes greatly impacted financial mechanisms for rural compulsory education. More than 80 percent of all funding for rural compulsory education gradually came to be the responsibility of public finance at the county and above. In 2003 the State Council held a national work conference on rural education, the first ever to be held in the country since the founding of new China. This conference articulated the strategic position of rural education as 'top priority'. It working out major steps to achieve nine-year compulsory education, including accelerating access to compulsory education in western rural areas, using any increase in educational allocations mainly for rural areas, and requiring that impoverished school-age populations in rural areas all be exempted from 'special fees' and textbook fees, and that students needing to live at schools receive subsidies (the so-called 'two exemptions and one subsidy'). These stipulations were made so they could complete nine-year compulsory education. In 2005 the State Council established a new 'rural compulsory education costs security mechanism' by which the Central government and local governments 'split the burden' in education costs, using certain percentages. In 2006 the National People's Congress adopted the *Compulsory Education Law (Amendment)*, which explicitly specified, for the first time, that no collection of 'special fees' could be required, and which obliged government departments at various levels to ensure access to compulsory education. All compulsory education expenditures were to be included in the scope of 'public finance security'. As per the requirements of basic public services, such resources as funds and teachers were to be allocated in a 'balanced manner'. Discrepancies between urban and rural areas, and among regions, and among schools in localities were thereby to be diminished as much as possible.

Beneficiaries of the 'two exemptions and one subsidy' policy have been growing in recent years. The policy began benefiting impoverished students in both rural and urban areas in 2003, it was expanded into all western rural areas in 2006, and it covered students in rural areas nationwide in 2007 [rural areas including so-designated counties and towns]. As a result, a total of 150 million students were not only exempted from tuition fees but also received free textbooks. This was at the time 85 percent of the country's total. The subsistence allowance standard for tens of millions of rural impoverished boarders in countryside schools also increased. This was an important milestone in the development of China's education. In 2007 the coverage rate of the 'Two Basics' in the western areas rose to 98 percent, and the national figure increased further to 99 percent. Nationwide, in 2007, the net primary school enrollment rate was 99.5 percent, and the gross secondary school enrollment rate was 98 percent.[3] Considering that 150 million students under compulsory education in rural areas had already been exempted from tuition fees, but more than 10 million urban students remain not exempted, on the basis of pilot trials, the State Council decided to exempt tuition and fees for urban compulsory education as well, from the fall of 2008. This was another major move to promote balanced development of compulsory education as well as educational impartiality.[4]

Box 7.1 An international comparison of compulsory education systems

The term compulsory education refers generally to the 'provision of a fixed number of years of universal, compulsory and free school education for school-age children, as required by national laws'. In 1619, the Duchy of Weimar passed a 'school law', which is considered to be the start of compulsory education. In 1763, Prussia promulgated school attendance regulations, requiring that children aged 5–13 must receive compulsory education. However, compulsory education was not originally designed as a social welfare program, but rather for preparing skilled labor forces for industrialized production. In the middle and late nineteenth century, one after another, industrialized countries began to enact compulsory education laws, such as the *Massachusetts Compulsory Education Law* of 1852, Britain's *Elementary Education Law* of 1870, France's *Jules Ferry Law of 1882* and Japan's *Primary School Decree* of 1886.[5]

According to UNESCO statistics, currently more than 170 countries worldwide have declared their implementation of compulsory education. All compulsory education laws of various countries have certain features in common: they explicitly state the recipients of the education, the purpose, content and number of years, as well as the government's duties and obligations in setting up and managing schools. They specify separation of education from religion, they state the responsibilities of parents with respect to compulsory education, they exempt tuition, and specify sources of funds and the distribution thereof. No country has so far been found to have declared, or mandated through legislation, that students should pay all fees for compulsory education.[6] The number of years of compulsory education is related in part to the level of economic development; compulsory education in developed countries or countries with small populations (for example, island countries) generally lasts for 10–13 years, and for 5–9 years in developing countries. After World War II, many countries enacted laws to extend the duration of compulsory education, but some developing countries have done the contrary due to regime changes or financial difficulties. Although economically developed countries generally have relatively longer compulsory education, these countries, even those with per capital GDP of tens of thousands of dollars did not rush to extend compulsory education when it had reached a certain level. They gave primary consideration to their own economic affordability and to the suitability of long compulsory attendance to individual needs.

Being free of charge is an important feature of modern compulsory education. Compulsory education cannot be implemented without the guarantee of government-supported free education, since parents could always use the pretext of not having enough money to refuse to send their children to school. The extent and scope of free compulsory education is affected by many factors: it is largely related to the economic strength of a country and sometimes also depends on such factors as ethnic traditions, the degree of importance attached to education and politics.

When a country cannot afford free compulsory education nationwide, it provides direct assistance to impoverished students through special subsidies, including establishing grants-in-aid and providing for free textbooks (some countries unable to provide free textbooks sometimes take the measure of using textbooks in rotation), school supplies, transportation, lunch allowances and so on. These measures usually start from economically disadvantaged areas and follow the principle of giving priority to the poorer and weaker social sectors, as well as to elementary education. Free compulsory education is usually not made available in one step, but is extended as socio-economic development proceeds, and it should be adjusted according to economic conditions.

Governments at different levels all share the joint responsibility of providing free compulsory education. To promote the balanced development of compulsory education, many countries have established effective responsibility mechanisms as well as financial transfer payment systems. In the US and Japan, transfer payments are an important source of funds for local governments, also an institutional guarantee that disadvantaged groups will receive compulsory education; Japan has also enacted a special education assistance law targeted at its islands and backcountry areas. South Korea's free compulsory education was carried out in succession from low to high grades, from islands, fishing villages, rural areas and other remote and impoverished areas to cities, and from medium and small cities to large cities. The policy generally adopted in many countries for impoverished areas and populations is to provide long-term assistance and help through such measures as special-purpose appropriations, subsidies, transfer payments and teacher mobility.

Source: Zhang Li, *Public Education Service in China's New Social Welfare System* (Background Report, 2008).

Problems facing China's compulsory education

Although extraordinary progress has been made in China's compulsory education, some problems still need to be solved. First, an outstanding problem is that quantity is emphasized more than quality. Second, remarkable disparities exist between urban and rural areas and between regions, either in the quantity or quality of compulsory education: rural areas lag behind urban areas and less-developed central and western areas lag behind developed eastern areas. Finally, the welfare level of compulsory education remains low—education resources are allocated irrationally.

In terms of educational quality, both 'software' and 'hardware' aspects of schools present problems to varying degrees. Concerns with the quality of compulsory education still exist, even in some developed areas. According to indicators published in Beijing's 2006 monitoring and assessment report on the teaching quality of compulsory education, certain problems are most prominent:[7] for example, the educational level of teachers remains low—the percentage of teachers with bachelor degrees is 40 percent in the urban areas of Beijing, but only 17 percent in the city's suburbs; 87 percent of classes each have more than 25 students (the most appropriate size of a class should be less than 25 students), and 46 percent have more than 36 students; the provision of specialized class-rooms at school is incomplete, and only 30 percent of primary schools have complete specialized classrooms; interdisciplinary teaching widely exists: math and language teachers who engage in interdisciplinary teaching account for 37 percent and 46 percent respectively, a phenomenon more obvious at primary schools. Math, language and social studies teachers who engage in interdiscipli-nary teaching account for 55.4 percent, 67.2 percent and 70.9 percent respec-tively. In contrast, the quality of compulsory education in central and western areas and economically less-developed areas is far lower, and the problems of inadequate educational funding, substandard school management, low-quality teachers and especially the low qualification rates of students still remain.[8]

Inadequate government spending is one important reason for the low quality of compulsory education. Statistically, governments at various levels have increased financial inputs into compulsory education, especially in central and western China, bringing about some changes in a situation in which government inputs had long been inadequate. Long-term deficits in this arena, over years of past 'history', mean, however, that short-term increases will not fundamentally change the reality of low educational quality in many areas. As Table 7.3 shows, in 1995 the total amount of national educational funds accounted for only 3 percent of GDP, and government spending on education accounted for 2.32 percent. Only in 2001 did the percentage of total educational funds to GDP break through 4 percent, but the percentage of government spending on education to GDP still remains below 3 percent. That is to say, the growth in educational funds in recent years comes from non-government spending. The increase of non-governmental funding is outpacing any increase in government spending.[9]

As a result of non-government spending outpacing government spending, the percentage of government spending on education to total educational funds has declined. As shown in Figure 7.1, in 1991, the percentage of government educa-tion spending in total educational expenditure was around 85 percent. This declined to 61 percent in 2005, a decrease of 24 percent. This does not mean that total financial inputs from either society or the government have declined; but it does mean that the 'social welfare' component in education has declined.

Relatively speaking, government spending on compulsory education and changes in that spending go a certain ways toward explaining the matter. From the mid-1990s to 2005, although the percentage of national educational funds to GDP increased, the percentage of educational funds devoted to primary and middle-school education was on the decline. As shown in Table 7.4, in total educational funds, the percentage of educational funds for primary and middle schools decreased from 56.5 percent in 1996 to 44 percent in 2000 and further to

Table 7.3 Percentages of different educational spending to GDP in China between 1995 and 2006

Year	Revised GDP (RMB 100 million)	Total educational funds (RMB 100 million)	Percentage of educational expenditure in GDP (%)	Percentage of government spending on education in GDP (%)	Percentage of non-government spending on education GDP (%)
1995	60,794	1,878	3.09	2.32	0.77
2000	99,215	2,849	3.88	2.58	1.30
2001	109,655	4,638	4.23	2.79	1.44
2002	120,333	5,480	4.55	2.90	1.65
2003	135,823	6,208	4.57	2.84	1.74
2004	159,878	7,243	4.53	2.79	1.74
2005	183,868	8,419	4.58	2.81	1.77
2006	210,871	9,815	4.65	3.01	1.64

Source: Statistical Bulletin on National Educational Funds, posted at the official website of Ministry of Education.

Notes:
1. In 2002, the percentage of China's government spending on education in GDP reach a record high, 3.41 percent, but was adjusted down to 2.9 percent, because the National Bureau of Statistics of China increase 2004's GDP base number up to RMB 2.3 trillion in 2005 according to the economic census results and revised data around 2002.
2. The pre-2005 data excludes funds for establishing Party schools, Communist Youth League schools and those run by women's organizations and labor unions, funds for staff training and training of Party, governmental and mass group carders, and funds of establishing military schools. The statistical scope of public expenditure on education was moderately expanded from 2006.

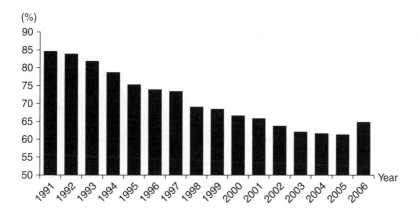

Figure 7.1 Proportion of government spending on education to total educational funds.

Source: Zhang Li, *Public Education Service in China's New Social Welfare System* (Background Report, 2008).

Table 7.4 Percentage of primary and middle educational funds in the total educational funds

Year	Percentage of educational funds to primary and middle schools in total educational funds	Percentage of government spending on primary and middle schools to total financial educational funds	Percentage of spending on primary and middle schools within financial budget to total education spending within financial budget
1996	56.48	57.10	53.69
2000	44.05	51.06	48.93
2005	41.97	53.38	53.83

Source: Zhang Li, *Public Education Service in China's New Social Welfare System* (Background Report, 2008).

42 percent in 2005. Government spending on primary and middle school education declined dramatically in 2000 relative to spending levels in the mid-1990s, and did not recover to those levels until 2005. These figures mean that there was decidedly not a tilt in the direction of compulsory education when it came to allocating educational resources.

Due to inadequate government spending for compulsory education, tuition and related fees increased considerably. Education costs shifted to individuals in the late twentieth century and early twenty-first century (see Table 7.5), causing the percentage of tuition and related fees to total educational expenses of primary and middle schools to rise greatly. Just as Figure 7.2 shows, compared to 1994, the share of tuition and related fees of primary and junior middle schools throughout the country increased remarkably in 2000; for all junior middle schools, it increased from 6.6 percent to 10.3 percent, and for rural junior middle schools, it rose from 7.7 percent to 11.8 percent. This undeniably put pressure on poor and low-income families in urban and rural areas (see Table 7.6). Fortunately, in the past few years, governments at various levels have introduced a series of new policies regarding free education, substantially decreasing fees that should be paid by individuals on compulsory education, and enhancing the welfare level of compulsory education. As shown in Figure 7.2, by 2006 the share of primary and junior middle schools' income from paid tuition in their educational funds had decreased to a very low level, and will continue to decline.

Table 7.5 Growth of government spending on education, tuition and related fees in different periods (unit: %)

Year	1991–2006	1991–1999	2000–2006
China's government spending on education	16.8	17.8	16.3
Tuition and related fees	29.4	39.5	17.3

Source: Zhang Li, *Public Education Service in China's New Social Welfare System* (Background Report, 2008).

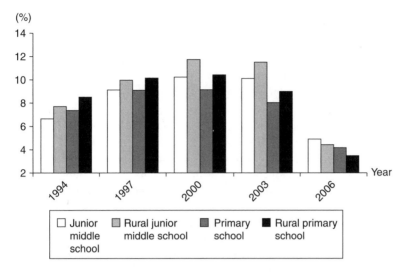

Figure 7.2 Share of primary and junior middle schools' tuition and related costs in their educational funds.

Source: Drawn using data provided in Zhang Li's *Public Education Service in China's New Social Welfare System* (Background Report, 2008).

Table 7.6 'Educational expenses' of urban households as a percentage of their annual income

	Average educational expenses (RMB)	Percentage of educational expenses to annual income of household (%)	Percentage of educational expenses to gross income of low-income household (%)
Primary school	2247	4.4	14.4
Junior middle school	3447	7.2	22.1
Senior high school	4529	9.3	29.0
Technical secondary school	2980	8.0	19.1
Junior college	3795	8.6	24.3
University	5337	9.3	34.1
Average	3431	6.9	22.0

Source: A sample survey conducted in 2007 on urban households of 15 provinces.

For a long time the trend has been to allocate more educational resources to urban areas than to rural areas. The overall level of rural compulsory education was very low, and has only begun to improve in recent years. Even at the beginning of the twenty-first century, per-student budgeted operational expenditures [*shi-ye fei*] and public expenditures were far lower in rural areas than in urban areas. As shown in Figure 7.3, in 2001 budgeted operational expenditure for each student in a rural primary school stood at 85 percent of the national level, those per student in rural junior middle schools at 80 percent. Budgeted operational expenditures and public funds per student in rural primary schools and junior middle schools were far less than the national level, 62 percent and 54 percent respectively. Figure 7.3 also shows, however, that from 2002 on, the disparities began to narrow between national and rural levels. This means that government spending began to be more equally allocated to primary and junior middle schools in both urban and rural areas.

Another reason for the lack of any improvement in quality of compulsory education is the unreasonable way in which funds are allocated among different levels of government. Governments at all levels have been enthusiastic about developing higher education, but they have neglected compulsory education development. The trend created a tilt in the direction of higher education when it came to allocating public funds, and that tilt has only recently begun to be corrected. As shown in Table 7.7, in 2000, the educational expenditure per student for higher education approximated RMB 16,000, including a budgetary expenditure of over RMB 8,600, while per student educational expenditure and budgetary

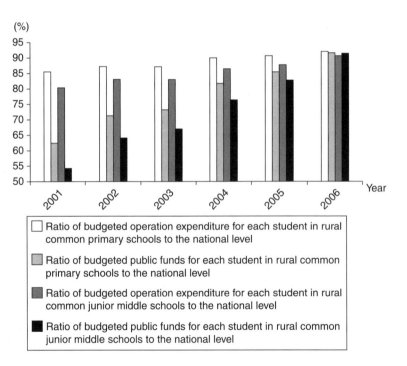

Figure 7.3 Comparison of budgeted operational expenditure and public funds for each student receiving the compulsory education in rural areas with the national level.

Source: Drawn using data provided in Zhang Li's *Public Education Service in China's New Social Welfare System* (Background Report, 2008).

Table 7.7 A comparison of expenditure per student at different education levels

Year	1990	1995	2000	2005	2006
Colleges and universities					
Expenditure per student		8,280.48	15,974.32	15,025.47	15,332.8
Budgetary expenditure per student	3,748.35	6,912.05	8,625.65	5,940.77	6,395.38
Senior high schools					
Expenditure per student		1,918.94	3,209.38	4,654.79	5,005.48
Budgetary expenditure per student	248.42	1,057.03	1,409.45	2,114.22	2,424.04
Junior middle schools					
Expenditure per student		918.92	1,211.32	2,278.35	2,669.49
Budgetary expenditure per student	248.42	507.95	698.28	1,562.01	1,962.92
Primary schools					
Expenditure per student		476.28	792.63	1,823.34	2,121.73
Budgetary expenditure per student	107.96	271.47	499.78	1,361.16	1,671.51
Colleges and universities/primary schools					
Expenditure per student		17.39	20.15	8.24	7.23
Budgetary expenditure per student	34.72	25.46	17.26	4.36	3.83

Source: Zhang Li, *Public Education Service in China's New Social Welfare System* (Background Report, 2008).

expenditure of common primary schools stood at RMB 792 and RMB 500 respectively. Expenditure per student in higher-education institutions was as much as 20 times that in primary schools, and the budgetary expenditure per student in higher-education institutions was as much as 17 times that in primary schools. Fortunately, by 2006, these figures decreased to 7.2 and 3.8 respectively (see Table 7.7).

Objectives of a 'developmental education security system'

'Students who would study will be taught.' Universal access to education is one of the primary objectives of the Chinese government in building a moderately prosperous society, and it is the basic objective of a developmental education security system. Therefore, this book recommends that, within a defined period of time, we should create conditions favorable to realizing the objectives of education security. The period of time is divided into a medium term, from now until 2012, and a longer term, from now until 2020. It should be noted that the developmental education security proposed here focuses on preschool education to senior middle school education, and is intended to solve basic problems of education security. Issues of higher education fall under the scope of higher-level 'education security' and are not a part of this book.

Taking the years 2012 and 2020 as reference time points, this report also provides the prospects of education at different levels and of various types as well as the prospects for increasing welfare resources. As seen from Table 7.8, given demographic fluctuations, the population aged 3–17 nationwide involved in preschool education through senior high school education will stabilize at about 280 million by 2012 and 2020. This report attempts to give a preliminary forecast and analysis of that period.

Table 7.8 A forecast of China's school-age population as well as the spread and fee exemption extent of compulsory education in 2012 and 2020

Year	2007	2012	2020
Total population (100 million persons)	13.21	13.6	14.5
Level of urbanization (%)	44.9	49	55
Population aged 3–5 (10,000 persons)	5267	5626	5737
Enrollment rate of preschool education (%)	44.6	>55	>65
Population aged 6–11 (10,000 persons)	10845	11003	11624
Net primary enrollment rate (%)	99.49	100	100
Population aged 12–14 (10,000 persons)	5912	5460	5350
Gross enrollment rate of junior middle schools (%)	98	100	>100
Population aged 15–17 (10,000 persons)	6818	5608	5388
Gross enrollment rate of senior high schools (%)	66	>80	90
Population aged 18–22	11739	10837	8922
Gross enrollment rate of higher education (%)	23	>30	>40
Total population receiving the nine-year compulsory education (aged 6–14, 10,000 persons)	16757	16463	16974
Total population receiving expanded compulsory education (aged 5–17, 10,000 persons)	30598	29572	30011
Total population receiving education (aged 3–22, 10,000 persons)	40581	38534	37021
Average years of education for population aged 15 and above	8.4	9.5	>10.5
Average years of education for new labor forces	10.5	12	>13
Ratio of government spending on education to GDP (%)	3.1	>4	About 4.5

Table 7.8 (continued)

Year	2007/2012	2020
Fee exemption and welfare scope of one-year preschool education	Free tuition and related fees for students from urban and rural impoverished or low-income families	Free or subsidized nutritious meals and free school safety insurance in rural areas
Fee exemption and welfare scope of nine-year compulsory education	Free tuition and related fees in both urban and rural areas; free textbooks in rural areas; subsistence allowances to impoverished boarders	Free or subsidized nutritious meals and free school safety insurance in rural areas
Fee exemption and welfare scope of one-year vocational education after graduation from junior middle school	Free tuition and related costs in the central and western areas and for urban and rural low-income families; free textbooks in rural areas; subsistence allowances to impoverished boarders	Free tuition and related fees and free textbooks in both urban and rural areas; subsistence allowances to impoverished boarders
Fee exemption and welfare scope of senior high school education	Subsidies to urban and rural medium vocational schools; reduced or exempted tuition for impoverished senior high school students	Free senior high school education for urban and rural low-income families

Source: National Population Census Office under the State Council and Department of Population & Employment Statistics (Social, Science and Technology Statistics) of the National Bureau of Statistics: Main Data from the Fifth National Population Census 2000 [R], 2001 edition, China Statistics Press; National Bureau of Statistics: Statistical Bulletin on National Economic and Social Development 2007 [Z], February 28, 2008; Report on National Population Development Strategy: Control China's Population Peak below 1.5 Billion [N], Beijing Daily, January 12, 2007; Gao Shuguo and Yang Xiaoming: A Report on Cultural Qualities of Chinese Population [R], 2004 edition, Social Sciences Academic Press.

Notes:
1. Total population and specific population data exclude Hong Kong, Macao and Taiwan.
2. All school-age population in 2012 and 2020 were estimated based on the demographic data by years since 2000.
3. The population of one-year preschool compulsory education was estimated according to ⅓ of the population aged 3–5.

Medium-term objectives, by the year 2012

A nine-year system for compulsory education

Without discrimination, the aim is coverage for a total of 170 million school-age children in urban and rural areas, including 110 million primary school students and

54 million junior middle school students. Rural students in primary and junior-middle schools should represent half of this figure, while children of people in the 'floating' or migrant population should total around 30 million.[10] The enrollment rate of primary school-age population nationwide should approach 100 percent, the gross enrollment rate of junior middle schools be 100 percent, and gender differences in enrollment should be eliminated. The nine-year compulsory education system will mainly be provided by public schools, and the government education spending will account for some 95 percent of total expenditures on compulsory education, coming mainly in the form of budgetary allocations. A balance in educational development should be achieved within regions, and most rural schools have come up to the country's uniform school running standards by this time. All urban and rural schools as well as special education institutions should be exempting students from any tuition fees or 'miscellaneous fees' by this time, while rural students should also receive free textbooks, and impoverished boarders should be given increased subsistence subsidies on a broad basis. The malnutrition of students living in schools in central and western rural areas should be resolved by using the country's special funds. The issue of which schools to designate as public schools in urban areas should be addressed, and teachers and schoolmasters in urban and rural schools should be assigned on a basis according to unified national criteria.

Expanded compulsory education

Compulsory vocational education will be provided for one year for free to students from urban and rural low-income families in the central and western areas who graduate from junior middle school but fail to enter senior high school. Coverage for senior middle school education should include all urban school-age population and most rural school-age population, with a gross enrollment rate of over 80 percent. Senior high school students from impoverished families should be exempted wholly or in part from tuition and textbook fees. The percentage of government spending on education to total educational expenditure should increase back to about 75 percent, and the remaining 25 percent should come mainly from tuition and related fees of regular senior middle schools as well as medium-level vocational schools that have a high payback [in terms of return on their investment] to individual. Incremental increases in budgetary allocations should go mainly in support of rural senior middle-school education, to continue to expand the number of rural students with reduced or exempted tuition. With regard to preschool: assuming a gross enrollment rate of three-year preschool education at more than 55 percent, preschool education ought to cover all urban children as well as rural children in relatively developed rural areas. Rural impoverished families and low-income families in both urban and rural areas should enjoy one year of preschool education for free. The number of kindergarten children should increase from 23.49 million in 2007 to 31 million; the percentage of public spending on kindergarten should stabilize at some 65 percent, and the remaining should be paid in the form of kindergarten admittance fees by parents. Private kindergartens have great room for development in this regard.

Long-term objectives by the year 2020 and beyond

A nine-year system for compulsory education

Without discrimination, the aim is coverage for a total of 170 million school-age children who are in both urban and rural areas. One hundred percent of children of primary-school age should enroll when it is time to enroll, and one hundred percent should also finish primary school. For junior middle school, one hundred percent should enroll, while those who finish should constitute no less than 99 percent. The nine-year compulsory education is mainly provided by public schools, with public finance constituting some 95 percent of total expenditures. Balanced educational development should be basically achieved within regions, and all rural schools have come up to nation-wide uniform standards for running schools. The teaching population should receive sufficient compensation. Students from central and western rural areas should be provided with differing levels of public-finance subsidies and also free nutritional meals.

Expanded compulsory education

Compulsory vocational education should be provided for one year for free to all junior middle school graduates who fail to enter senior middle schools. Budgetary funds should continue to support rural senior middle school education. Rural areas should implement free senior middle-school education and there should be tuition waivers, exemption of related fees, and free textbooks for children from impoverished families in urban areas. The gross enrollment rate of senior middle schools nationwide should rise to over 90 percent; the percentage of government education spending to total educational expenditures should stabilize at 75 percent, while systems relating to tuition and 'miscellaneous costs' should be regulated. One year of free preschool education should be provided nationwide. The enrollment rate for the first two years of preschool education should increase to over 65 percent, and that of the last year to 100 percent, including for all urban and rural children. The number of children in kindergarten should increase to between 37 and 50 million, and the percentage of public finance in kindergarten education should standardize at between 60–80 percent.

In terms of budgeting financial resources: in 2007 the annual per capita expenditure for primary schools was about RMB 2,200, and that for junior middle schools was RMB 2,800, with the weighted average of both being RMB 2,400—equivalent to RMB 200 a month. The number of children receiving nine years of compulsory education in 2007 totalled 170 million. Based on changing age structures as a result of changing demographics, this number should stay basically the same by 2020. To narrow discrepancies between urban and rural areas, incremental increases in educational expenditures should focus more on rural compulsory education. Our calculations are based on a 10 percent annual growth rate in per capita education expenditures, using 2007 as the base year. By 2012, public spending on the nine-year compulsory education system in urban and rural areas should total around RMB 657.1 billion, and RMB 1.41 trillion by 2020 (see Chapter 12 for detailed calculations).

To sum up, by 2020, the amount of public-finance type spending on education ought not to be below 4 percent of GDP, and the amount of non-governmental spending ought to be below 2 percent. Thus, a possible institutional arrangement may be as follows: basic public education services are able to satisfy all the people, especially low-income people; non-basic public education services are able to satisfy people with a certain financial capability, plus eligible low-income people are funded, given assistance, and basically satisfied; non-public education services are able to satisfy people with special needs and people who have the full ability to pay. We expect that by 2030, with an increase in overall national strength, there will be far more opportunities for children at different ages to receive the education that corresponds to their situation. The number of students should reach a new record. When government spending on education reaches 5 percent of GDP, the real 'welfare nature' of public education services will come into its own.

Box 7.2 Government duties and acts in public education

Levels of educational development are closely tied to levels of economic development. Educational equity has different emphases, and is generally a gradual process that proceeds in stages. The widespread international experience is that the first step is to allow more people to receive more education, that is, any education at all. The second step is to allow all people to receive basic education and let more people receive higher levels of education. The third step is to allow all people to receive as high a level of education as possible (including education from public education services and non-public services). Faced with different educational services, governments may categorize their actions as follows:

Obligatory acts: the government takes the full responsibility for and directly provides basic public education services as according to law. It does this mainly by allocating funds to public education institutions or directly providing funds to groups in need. For example, the government may play a bigger role in providing free compulsory education, to promote balanced and equal development of compulsory education between urban and rural areas, between regions and between schools. Even at the stage of non-compulsory education, in which the burden for paying is shared, favorable and supporting polices should still be addressed towards disadvantaged areas and groups as well as groups engaged in national defense and key projects.

Key acts: the government takes limited responsibility for non-basic public services according to law. It undertakes overall planning [budgeting] with regard to regular funds and to special financial aid and subsidies. It focuses on serving eligible disadvantaged groups, and on those areas in which the market fails to play a role. For example, helping meet human resources requirements in the basic disciplines of non-compulsory education and in remote and difficult industries. At the same time, the government continues to encourage enterprises and social forces to provide contributions and grants.

'Authorizing' behavior: through authorizations, licensing or trusteeship or by buying services, the government can play an indirect role in those educational services that are not basic public services and for which others can bear some of the costs. When it is inappropriate for the government to play a role but there would be benefits in terms of meeting social demand or improving efficiencies, the government can legally authorize nongovernmental organizations or 'third parties' to participate.

When direct action is unnecessary: the supply and demand of most non-public services is regulated by signals from the human resources market. The government need only specify equal-access and rules of competition when it identifies fields in which it does not want to intervene directly. For example, the government has no responsibility to directly fund and establish schools. At the same time, the government should strengthen legal supervision and regulation, take macro-measures and conduct overall supervision, and give encouragement or awards to school-administering practices that have a positive social impact.

The core of basic public-education services is compulsory education. Compulsory education will become one of the fundamental links in China's social welfare system. A portion of non-basic public education services can also be brought into the scope of the country's social welfare system, depending on the situation of beneficiaries, but the 'welfare' aspect should be determined by mode of public-finance support and by degree of coverage. Efforts should be made to avoid having the government meddle in things in which it should not be involved, and which it cannot handle, and alternatively having the government step back and leave a vacuum in areas in which it is needed.

Source: Zhang Li, *Public Education Service in China's New Social Welfare System* (Background Report, 2008).

Policy recommendations

Increase public finance to improve the welfare of, and expand the coverage of compulsory education

The term compulsory education refers generally to the 'provision of a fixed number of years of universal, compulsory and free school education for school-age children, as required by national laws'. This is the common understanding in the international community. According to UNESCO statistics, more than 170 countries worldwide have currently declared their implementation of compulsory education. All compulsory education laws of various countries have certain features in common: they explicitly state the recipients of the education, the purpose, content and number of years, as well as the government's duties and obligations in setting up and managing schools. They specify separation of education from religion, they state the responsibilities of parents with respect to compulsory education, they exempt tuition, specify sources of funds and distribution thereof. No country has so far been found to have declared, or mandated through legislation, that students should pay all fees for compulsory education.[11]

The number of years of compulsory education is related in part to the level of economic development; compulsory education in developed countries or countries with small populations (for example, island countries) generally lasts for 10–13 years, and for 5–9 years in developing countries. After World War II many countries enacted laws to extend the duration of compulsory education, but some developing countries have done the contrary due to regime changes or financial difficulties. Although economically developed countries generally have relatively longer compulsory education, these countries, even those with per capital GDP of tens of thousands of dollars did not rush to extend compulsory education when it had reached a certain level. They gave primary consideration to their own economic affordability and to the suitability of long compulsory attendance to individual needs.

Being free of charge is an important feature of modern compulsory education. Compulsory education cannot be implemented without the guarantee of government-supported free education, since parents could always use the pretext of not having enough money to refuse to send their children to school. The extent and scope of free compulsory education is affected by many factors: it is largely related to the economic strength of a country and sometimes also depends on such factors as ethnic traditions, the degree of importance attached to education, and politics.

When a country cannot afford free compulsory education nationwide, it provides direct assistance to impoverished students through special subsidies, including establishing grants-in-aid and providing free textbooks (some countries unable to provide free textbooks sometimes take the measure of using textbooks in rotation), school supplies, transportation, lunch allowances and so on. These measures usually start from economically disadvantaged areas and follow the principle of giving priority to the poorer and weaker social sectors, as well as to elementary education. Free compulsory education is usually not made available in one step, but is extended as socio-economic development proceeds, and it should be adjusted according to economic conditions.

China is a developing country and shares many aspects of compulsory education with other developing countries. China also has an economy that is growing very fast; over the past 30 years, it has grown faster than any other country. At the same time it has a tradition of valuing education highly and its economic growth has benefited from giving priority to educational development. Therefore, China should strive toward even higher goals in its educational development.

On the one hand, the 'welfare' aspect of China's compulsory education should be improved, and 'free' compulsory education should really be provided as it is now in name only. The fast growth of Chinese fiscal revenues in recent years provides financial guarantees for free compulsory education. How is it possible to tell when the 'welfare' aspect of educational resources is sufficient? One important indicator, that the international community has long paid attention to, is the ratio of public (financial) educational funds to GDP. In the early 1990s the world's average across the board for this indicator was 4 percent and it currently has increased to 4.4 percent, showing an increase of governments' inputs into public education. Evaluated by status of economic development, the figure in developed countries is as high as about 5 percent, and it is below 3.5 percent in developing countries.[11] In China, the figure is still below the average level of developing countries (see Table 7.3).

In another regard, the government should consider expanding the definition of compulsory education to include one year of preschool education and one year of vocational education for junior middle school graduates before employment.

Coordinate the allocation of resources for urban and rural education security, and achieve the same level of compulsory education in urban and rural areas

Generally speaking, in Chinese cities, the access to and quality of compulsory education is already at or close to the level of developed countries. In contrast, compulsory education in the rural areas still has a long way to go. Therefore, one of objectives of further educational development ought to be to narrow, as soon as possible, the discrepancies between urban and rural areas in terms of compulsory education development, by increasing inputs in rural compulsory education and thus improving educational quality, while reinforcing and improving urban compulsory education. For rural compulsory education, the emphasis should be placed on remote backward rural areas, and efforts should be made to improve quality and services there as soon as possible.

Attach importance to early education of children and provide one free year of preschool education

During recent years the international academic research has tended to support the idea that early childhood education and an individual's performance in the job market are closely correlated. Some research results suggest that early childhood care and certain educational methods are important determinants of their later career selection, income, and social status. In 2006, UNESCO and other international organizations passed *The Dakar Framework for Action*, setting six main objectives for follow-up work on the assessment of Education for All (EFA) by the year 2015, one being the expansion of early care and education for children.

Although China has attached increasing importance to early child care, it is still not enough. The most recent data shows that China's enrollment rate of children aged 3–5 in formal preschool education was only 35 percent in 2000 and only 45 percent in 2007.[13] That is still more than half of preschool children that are educated by families. Especially in rural areas the enrollment rate of preschool children still remains at a very low level and, similarly, children of rural migrant workers in urban areas still find it hard to enter kindergartens. A related study shows that in 2004 about 87 percent of children of migrant workers who were age 7 and under had no chance to enter kindergartens.

Strengthen occupational education and provide one year of compulsory vocational education for junior middle school graduates before employment

Junior middle school graduates and those with less education still occupy the largest percentage of China's labor forces. According to the data from the fifth national population census, conducted in 2000, among people aged 6 and above who received formal education, junior middle school graduates accounted for 45.4 percent, and those who received only primary education account for 34.4 percent. Of all people aged 6 and above, 79 percent had received no more than a junior middle-school education. According to estimates on the data from fifth national population census, among the population aged 15–19 throughout the country, in 2002, junior middle school graduates and dropouts accounted for 36.2 percent and primary school graduates and dropouts for 11.1 percent. Therefore, among the new labor force in the market, the percentage of people with a junior middle school education or less was still as high as 47 percent. Due to the imbalance between urban and rural education development, in rural areas this percentage was as high as nearly 60 percent.[14]

China's inadequate investment in human capital has led to various adverse impacts on economic development, one of which is the unbalanced structure between labor force supply and labor force demand. As China's economy is growing quickly, its economic structure is also changing dramatically and the labor market often exhibits unbalanced supply and demand. High-quality and hi-tech talent is under-supplied, while unskilled labor is in over-supply. It is not hard to imagine that such an unbalanced structure not only leads to unemployment and underemployment but widens the gap in wage earnings. Relevant studies suggest that educational attainments have had an increasing effect on widening income disparities in the past decade.

From the early twenty-first century, the Chinese government began to strengthen the training of the urban unemployed and migrant rural labors. In 2003 the Ministries of Agriculture, Labor and Social Security, Education, Science and Technology, and Construction and Finance jointly issued the *National Program for Training of Migrant Rural Workers in 2003–2010*, planning to

> provide 'guidance' training for 10 million rural workers who were transfer-ring into nonagricultural sectors or moving to cities (and to provide it before they transitioned out of agriculture), and to provide occupational training for

5 million of those in the period 2003–2005. In addition, in the period 2006–2012, to offer the guidance training to 50 million rural laborers who would be transferring to nonagricultural sectors or moving to cities, including occupational training for 30 million of these.

Due to limited financial resources, however, these training costs had to be paid jointly by the government, employers and migrant workers. To a certain degree this affected migrant workers' desire to participate in training. And because the government's training funds were used mainly for the 'guidance' training programs, which were simple and less technical, there was little effect on promoting employment.

Learning from the experience of some developed countries, a more effective policy would be to provide one year of compulsory vocation education for junior middle school graduates before they took up employment.

Link children's nutrition and health security to education security, letting education security better promote human development

Children are in an early stage of growth and development. Their nutrition and health not only relate to their growth and development and thus affect their physical condition at adulthood, but also directly affect their education and job performance. Surveys reveal that severe malnutrition still exists among primary and middle school students of the impoverished areas, which has become a direct obstacle to human capital development there. Currently, the country has introduced a series of policies to enable children to get a better education and more conveniently. These include merging schools for the integration and optimization of educational resources, and building boarding schools, where children can live as they go to school. Students studying and living in a centralized way provides conditions for the government to take intervention measures to ensure their nutrition. At present, many places and organizations have carried out experiments of providing nutrition security to students at boarding schools in poor areas and achieved good results. Based on summarizing the experience in various places, the government should include the supply of nutritious meals to students of poor areas in its scope of financial expenditures, providing better security for the nutrition and education of students.

Notes

1 Planning and Finance Department, Ministry of Education, *China's Educational Achievements 1949–1983* (People's Education Press, 1983).
2 Website of Ministry of Education (www.moe.gov.cn).
3 Ministry of Education's Development & Planning Department, *A Concise Statistical Analysis on Education Development in China (2007)*, February 2008.
4 Wen Jiabao, *Government Work Report*, given at the First Session of the 11th National People's Congress.
5 Gu Mingyuan (editor in chief), *Education Dictionary* (Shanghai Educational Publishing House, 1998).

6 Ci Hai editorial board, *Ci Hai* (Shanghai Lexicographical Publishing House, 2000); Wang Huanxun (editor in chief), *A Practical Dictionary of Education* (Beijing Normal University Publishing Group, 1995).

7 http://news.xinhuanet.com.

8 In 2007 a basic education survey group surveyed the quality of primary school education in western China. The exam results of primary school graduates presented by a local bureau of education revealed that the qualification rates of students at some schools stood at only about 20 percent, but these students were all smoothly admitted by junior middle schools (see 'Pay More Attention to Qualification Rate of Compulsory Education', http://shiping.haedu.cn).

9 Between 1991–2006, government spending on education increased 16.8 percent and non-government spending on education rose by 25.6 percent, leading to the continual decrease of the proportion of government spending on education—to 61.3 percent in 2005 from 84.5 percent in 1991, till 2006 when it grew to 64.7 percent (see Zhang Li, *Public Education Service in China's New Social Welfare System* (Background Report, 2008)).

10 According to 2007 statistics, throughout the country, the number children migrating with their parents from rural areas and receiving compulsory education is 7.657 million and left-behind children are 20.374 million, totaling 28.031 million. Estimated according to a non-enrollment rate of at least 2 percent, the number of school-age children for compulsory education of migrant rural workers approximates 29 million.

11 Ci Hai editorial board, *Ci Hai* (Shanghai Lexicographical Publishing House, 2000); Wang Huanxun (editor in chief), *A Practical Dictionary of Education* (Beijing Normal University Publishing Group, 1995).

12 http://www.unesco.org/general.

13 See Zhang Li, *Public Education Service in China's New Social Welfare System* (Background Report, 2008).

14 Estimated based on the data from the fifth national population census, among the rural population aged 15–19, in 2000 junior middle school graduates and dropouts accounted for 43.4 percent and primary school graduates and dropouts for 16.2 percent.

8 Employment security

'He who works will be paid' is regarded by the Chinese government as a key part of building a harmonious society, and the prerequisite to getting paid is being employed. To achieve full employment is an essential part of China's developmental welfare policy. It incorporates the various aspects of creating and implementing proactive labor policies, increasing the number of employment positions as appropriate, encouraging the start-up of private businesses and providing vocational training to young people of job age, especially migrant workers, in order to increase both their employability and entrepreneurial talents.

Economic restructuring and the evolution of employment policies

The planned labor system in urban areas, and implementing proactive employment policies

Reform of the urban planned labor system started after the Cultural Revolution, when a large number of educated urban youth returned to cities to try to take up jobs after their experience of being dispatched to the countryside. This marked the first peak in unemployment after Reform and Opening Up policies began in 1979. Large numbers of new entrants were coming on the job market at the time, even as educated urban youth were returning to the cities. In 1979 the number of urban youth waiting for employment exceeded 20 million, and the unemployment rate was over 5 percent. Given inadequate job opportunities and the fact that there was no alternative, a policy of 'getting employed through recommendations by labor departments, through voluntary organizations, or on one's own initiative' had to be adopted. This employment policy essentially destroyed the old planned employment system of 'centralized labor allocation'. It opened up channels for arranging employment in creative ways and also contributed to developing the nonpublic economy. It basically found jobs for enormous numbers of unemployed youth, euphemistically called at that time 'youth waiting for employment'.[1]

In the 1990s, as China established the reform objective of 'establishing a socialist market-economy system', the pace of market-based employment accelerated. On the one hand, employment provided by such emerging economic sectors as private businesses, foreign-invested and shareholding companies offered an increasing percentage of jobs in urban areas; on the other hand, the traditional employment system was continually being reformed to adapt to the changing external environment.[2] With ongoing reform of state-owned enterprises, a second unemployment peak appeared in the cities. Between 1992 and 2006, 77.84 million people (including 75.34 million employees) were laid off from state-owned and collectively-owned enterprises. Among these laid-off people, 32.39 million people (including 31.93 million employees) were cut in 1997 and 1998 following the Asian economic crisis.

To deal with this unemployment peak the Central government introduced a combined set of measures, including adjusting the economic structure to accelerate economic growth and thus promote employment, establishing re-employment service centers to provide re-employment assistance to the large number of laid-off workers, encouraging and supporting the start-up of businesses, and expanding enrollment in colleges and universities to defer unemployment pressure. The government developed unemployment insurance and improved what it called the 'Three Lines of Protection' among other comprehensive measures. Among these measures the government began 'proactive employment policies' that were highly effective in promoting employment and relieving the severe unemployment problems brought on by dramatic changes in the old planned-method of employing people.

The proactive employment policies, or 'proactive labor policies', was a labor market policy that corresponded to the social security system. Essentially, it provided support and assistance to the weaker participants in the labor market competition, in order to draw them back to employment.[3] Experiments in the proactive employment policies were initially conducted in several places in 2000, and the practices were clarified as 'policy' at a national re-employment working conference in 2002. The main aspects of this policy included the 'five main pillars', the 'six fields of activity' and the 'ten policy measures'. The five pillars were: a macro-economic policy of spurring employment, a policy supporting re-employment, a policy setting up labor market services, a policy on macro-controls, and a social security policy. The six fields meant the six different 'directions' or ways of creating jobs: the nonpublic economy, tertiary industries, small and medium-sized enterprises, labor-intensive sectors, flexible employment and export of labor services. The ten policy measures were: tax reduction and exemption, micro loans, social security subsidies, employment assistance, separation of auxiliary from main businesses, employment services, vocational training, unemployment regulations and control, public finance investment and social security.[4] 'Reform' and the implementation of the proactive employment policies made the job market in cities more 'marketized'. They increased the capacity of cities to absorb more jobs and more people, making them the main force behind employment for the increasing numbers of 'new entrants' to the job market as well as the swelling numbers of migrant rural workers now coming in from the countryside.

Development of rural labor markets

In freeing farmers from collective economy, rural reforms not only increased labor productivity and promoted the development of the rural economy, but also brought into sharp relief the problem of rural surplus labor. Using the rural labor productivity of 1978 as the baseline, by 1987 the increase in rural labor productivity was equivalent to an increase of 33.47 million agricultural workers.[5] The way in which the 'household registration system' blocked free movement between the countryside and cities, and blocked rural workers' access to jobs in cities, made it necessary for them to have to shift employment locally from agricultural to non-agricultural production. This was a major underlying reason for the later rapid emergence of rural township-and-village enterprises (TVEs) following economic restructuring.

The growth of (TVEs) has absorbed a tremendous number of rural laborers and has played the main role in developing rural labor markets. From 1978–2007, employees working in TVEs increased from 9.2 percent to 31.7 percent of all employees in townships and villages.

The fast growth of TVEs has become an important force not just for rural but for national economic development in China. It has given rise to the 'miracle' of transferring agricultural surplus labor 'on the spot' to new jobs, of 'leaving the soil but not the home'. The margin for further growth of these enterprises began to decline, however, as China confirmed its path of becoming a 'socialist market economy', as it opened to the outside world, and as market competition gradually changed the situation from being a seller's to a buyer's market. As the growth of rural labor supply remained steady, it became impossible to rely on rural areas alone for absorbing the enormous size of surplus labor. Inevitably, surplus labor gradually had to resort to cities.

In the process of reforming the urban planned-labor system, the entry of rural laborers on the scene underwent several stages. These included controlled or restricted migration (in the early 1980s), allowed migration (in the mid-1980s), restricted irrational migration (in the early 1990s), guided orderly migration (after 1992) and fairly treated migration (after China's accession to WTO).[6] In the 1980s not many migrant workers went to cities for work. In the late 1980s, affected by the 'improvement and rectification' campaigns, as well as the sluggish development of TVEs, the movement of migrant workers began to take shape. It began to involve some 30 million people. In the 1990s a transfer of rural labor that had been mainly to TVEs now began to gradually switch to the modes of 'floating employment' and 'migrating among different places'. In the face of the tremendous influx of migrant workers—the 'wave of migrant workers'—cities realized that migrant workers must be effectively guided rather than being merely 'blocked'. They issued employment and temporary residence permits to migrant workers, and some cities even reformed their household registration systems to create a more relaxed administrative environment for the movement of rural migrant workers. In the 1990s the number of migrant rural workers in urban areas stayed stable at around 60 to 80 million people. Since the beginning of the twenty-first century the number of migrant rural workers has again been increasing and is only getting larger. Migrant labor chooses where to go purely according to market forces. Not only have these people become disconnected from their own land, but they have become an important component of the urbanization. They are also the reason for further reform of the urban labor markets, and for developing a nationally unified labor market as soon as possible.

Formation of a nationally unified labor market

Since China's reform and opening up began, over 30 years ago, great changes have taken place in the country's economic system and socioeconomic structure. The planned-economy system with its high degree of centralization has been changed to a socialist market-economy system. China's accession to WTO in 2001 marked the international community's recognition of China's economic marketization reforms and its now-dominant market economy. China's economic marketization and its internationalization have also created the conditions for the development of a nationally unified labor market.

Labor marketization has greatly improved the efficiency with which labor resources are allocated. It has allowed China to use its latent resources in ways that maximize its greatest comparative advantage *vis-à-vis* other countries. It has provided maximum power for the country's economic growth. In return, 30 years of fast and sustained economic growth has served to provide secure employment in China. From 1979 to 2007 the average annual economic growth of China was 9.8 percent, and the number of employees increased annually by 2.3 percent on average. Though the elasticity of employment has taken on a downward trend as a result of the increasingly intensive use of capital, without the support of fast economic growth, it would have been impossible to achieve this kind of employment growth as well as structural change that is geared to modernization. (Labor elasticity was 0.235 on average in the period 1979–2007, 0.097 in the period 1991–2009 and 0.088 in the period 2001–2007.) It is safe to say that the market-oriented reforms over this entire period, the sustained growth in China's economy and employment, and the transformation in socioeconomic structure are all internally consistent.

The Central government's labor policies have basically met the requirements of reform and development. Unlike the rigid labor system adopted during the planned-economy period, which imposed restrictions on the movement of labor and prevented any structural change, the reformed labor policies have been subject to continual modification given changes in socioeconomic development. Whether it was the 'three combinations' policy advanced in the early days of reform, or the proactive policies implemented when large numbers of state-owned enterprise workers were laid off and unemployed in the 1990s, the 'on-the-spot' transfer of rural surplus labor that was promoted by developing TVEs, or finally the increasingly fair employment policies in support of the orderly movement of migrant workers, all have had the positive effect on creating employment.

China's labor policy now faces a new round of substantive adjustment and reform in the early twenty-first century. The underlying reason is that the total amount of rural surplus labor is approaching the 'Lewis Turning Point': the supply of rural surplus labor is indeed tapering off, and some shortages, especially structural shortages, are already appearing. Both pushing and pulling force for rural surplus labor to work 'outside' are weakening. In addition, differences between urban and rural household registration systems are being eliminated in an increasing number of places, and urban discriminatory policies against migrant rural workers are being reduced, both of which are providing favorable conditions for introducing a nationwide 'fair employment' policy.

The *Employment Promotion Law* and the *Labor Contract Law* enacted in 2007 by the National People's Congress came into force in 2008. By standardizing labor relations, the *Labor Contract Law* will help reduce inequalities in the market, build a fairer environment for competition, help employers establish long-term and stable labor relations with employees, and encourage corporate and individual investment in human capital. The four principles articulated in the *Employment Promotion Law* (increasing employment, market-oriented employment, equal employment and coordinated employment) not only pull together the valuable experience acquired in China's labor system reform and elevate it to the status of national law, but also enrich China's legal system of labor protection.[7] The law is a significant achievement in creating a legal structure for protecting the rights of workers in China. At the same time, there are differing opinions in the academic community as to some particular clauses of the *Labor Contract Law*. Particularly at a time when the international financial crisis is affecting employment, and many migrant rural workers as well as new college graduates are finding it hard to get a job, balancing the rights and interests of workers with the need to create more employment is not easy. As we move forward we need to take actual conditions into account and make adjustments when appropriate.

The establishment and development of an unemployment insurance system

Unemployment insurance is tied to the reality of unemployment. Under the planned-economy system, China refused to admit the unemployment that, objectively, did exist, due to the theoretical need for 'no unemployment' under the socialist system. The country practiced a labor employment system that guaranteed full employment. Jobs were arranged, under 'plans', for any person who entered the planned-labor system, whether it was college students or demobilized soldiers, enterprise workers or young people. Once 'arranged-for', these people could not be transferred, fired or laid off, except as organizationally required. In addition, their wages were set by planning departments in a unified manner, with minimal differences. The entire system was ultra-egalitarian. Labor protection during the planned-economy period belonged to the category of 'employment security', which was an ironclad protection system for employees. There was no recognized unemployment (other than a small number of young people for whom jobs would eventually be arranged), nor was there a labor market. Neither enterprises nor employers had any right to decide whom to employ or how much they would be paid. The situation was a classic case of 'iron rice bowl' and 'extreme egalitarianism'. Although there was a large amount of surplus labor in agriculture, it was regarded as 'underemployed' rather than 'unemployed'. At the same time, rural employment was not included within the scope of the 'planned-labor' system, so did not come under any kind of 'employment security'.

Establishment of the 'job-waiting insurance system' for workers in state-owned enterprises

In the mid-1980s, as economic restructuring began to require enterprises to become autonomous entities with responsibility for their own profits and losses, reform of employment systems in enterprises began to come to the fore. In 1986 the State Council promulgated such regulations as the *Temporary Regulations on the Labor Contract System for state-owned Enterprises*, the *Temporary Regulations on Worker Employment of state-owned Enterprises*, the *Temporary Regulations on Dismissal by state-owned Enterprises of Discipline-breaching Workers*, and the *Temporary Regulations on Job-waiting Insurance for Workers in state-owned Enterprises*. Recruitment of workers by enterprises shifted gradually from an 'unchangeable' form of employment to recruiting workers by signing contracts. The promulgation and implementation of the *Temporary Regulations on Job-waiting Insurance for Workers in state-owned Enterprises* was a milestone in terms of insurance for those who were de facto unemployed. This document specified those who were eligible to receive this insurance and how funds were to be raised and managed. The payment by enterprises was set at 1 percent of the gross standard wages of workers, as insurance premiums. This was used mainly as an 'unemployment relief fund' for the unemployed of state-owned enterprises.

In 1993 China set forth the goal of creating a 'socialist market-economy system' with a corresponding 'social security system'. In terms of unemployment security, the new *Regulations on Worker Waiting for Employment Insurance of state-owned Enterprises*, promulgated by the State Council to replace *Temporary Regulations on Job-waiting Insurance for Workers in state-owned Enterprises* in 1986, expanded its scope, adjusted the benefit levels of the insurance, changed the administrative level at which funds were pooled from provincial to municipalities and counties, and did certain adjusting of rates. Since the documents preceded a time when the term 'unemployment' could be used by the Central government, this insurance was called 'job-waiting insurance' rather than 'unemployment insurance'. However, after being introduced, despite the expanded coverage, the new system was limited to employees in state-owned enterprises. Funding as well as expenditures rose to a degree, with the number of people receiving unemployment benefits going from 1.53 million in 1995 to 3.31 million in 1996. By 1996 the per capita level of benefits stood at RMB 419.

Establishment of the unemployment insurance system for urban workers and the 'Three Lines of Protection in Social Security'

In response to the unemployment peak in all urban areas in the 1990s, and to address problems of limited coverage and low benefits in the previous system, in January of 1999, the State Council issued what it now called *Regulations on Unemployment Insurance* to officially establish an unemployment insurance system for urban workers. This law replaced the term 'job-waiting insurance' with 'unemployment insurance', and it replaced the term 'job-waiting relief funds' with the term 'unemployment insurance benefit funds'. It expanded the previous scope of security coverage from just employees of state-owned enterprises to various official urban workers other than civil servants. Unemployment insurance contributions were paid by enterprises at two percent and by individuals at one percent of their wages. All funds were now pooled at the prefectural level, and unemployment insurance benefits were linked to the minimum living allowance for urban residents (i.e. lower than the local minimum wage but higher than the minimum living allowance line). Unemployment benefits could be received for a period of 12 to 24 months. After being set up, coverage of the unemployment insurance system increased markedly, especially for regular urban workers.[8] Capacity of the system increased and it played an active role in relieving the unemployment peak at the time.

As the system of social insurance and relief was established other emergency security measures were also adopted in response to unemployment, early retirement and impoverished conditions of some workers. These included a basic living security allowance for laid-off workers and a minimum living allowance system for urban residents. These measures, together with the unemployment insurance system, formed the 'Three Lines of Protection' intended to meet the problem of unemployment.

As an unusual form of unemployment security, the 'basic living allowance for laid-off workers from state-owned enterprises' is unique to China, for it is directed at laid-off workers instead of open unemployment. From 1996 to 2000, the total number of laid-off workers that were registered at the end of each year exceeded the total number of registered unemployed. People formerly employed by state-owned enterprises constituted the bulk of these laid-off workers, whose numbers also exceeded the number of registered unemployed (see Table 8.1). Therefore, ensuring a living allowance for laid-off workers was essentially the same as establishing an independent unemployment security system. At the same time, the process tied the basic living allowance closely to the country's proactive employment policies. Laid-off workers from state-owned enterprises who registered at the re-employment service centers could now receive basic living allowances, have their social insurance relationships maintained there and, after finding their own means of livelihood, were entitled to tax reductions and preferential treatment for industrial and commercial registration and credit terms. On entering the 'Center' each laid-off worker had to sign an agreement. The time limit for being under the preferential terms of such a Center was three years. At the expiry of an

Table 8.1 Changes in numbers of urban laid-off workers and retirees from 1992 to 2006 (unit: 10,000 people)

Year	Registered unemployed people		Number of unemployment insurance benefit receivers	Year-end number of laid-off workers from SOEs		Retirees		
	Number	% up or down over the previous year		Number[1]	% up or down over the previous year	Total	Number of retirees from enterprises	% up or down over the previous year in number of retirees from enterprises
1992	364	12	30	—	—	2,598	1,681	595
1993	420	56	103	300[2]	—	2,780	1,839	158
1994	476	56	197	360[2]	—	2,929	2,079	240
1995	520	44	261	563[2]	—	3,094	2,241	162
1996	553	33	331	815[2]	—	3,212	2,358	117
1997	577	27	319	634	−181	3,351	2,533	59
1998	571	−6	158	610	−24	3,594	2,767	234
1999	575	4	271	653	53	3,730	2,864	97
2000	595	20	330	657	4	3,876	2,978	114
2001	681	86	469	515	−142	4,018	3,072	94
2002	770	89	657	410	−105	4,223	3,261	189
2003	800	30	742	260	−150	4,523	3,486	225
2004	827	27	754	153	−107	4,675		
2005	839	12	679	61	−92	5,088	3,842	356
2006	847	8	327	0	−61	3,966	124	

Source: Wang Mengkui, editor in chief, China after Asian Financial Crisis (China Development Press, 2007).

Notes:

1. China's data on laid-off workers has been incomplete. According to data provided in Lu Ming's Labor Economics, at p. 196, the numbers of laid-off workers in 1997, 1998 and 1999 were 9.95, 8.77 and 9.37 million, all of which included laid-off workers of non-SOEs. Also, according to data provided in The Changes in and an Assessment of China's Social Security System authored by Zheng Gongcheng et al., at p. 419, the numbers of laid-off workers in 1998, 1999 and 2000 were: at the beginning of the years, 9.95, 8.71 and 9.42 million, including those from SOEs standing at 6.92, 5.92 and 6.53 million; at the end of the years, 8.77, 9.37 and 9.11 million, including 5.95, 6.53 and 6.57 million laid-off workers from SOEs. While according to data given in Chinese Economy in a Period of Hypo-high Growth authored by Liu Yingqiu et al., at p. 276, the numbers of urban laid-off workers at the end of 1993, 1994, 1995, 1996, 1997, 1998 and 1999 stood at 30, 36, 36.5, 89.1, 11.51, 10.8 and 11.74 million, respectively.

2. In this table, 1993–1996 data are the total numbers of laid-off workers.

agreement, the laid-off worker had to end any labor relationship with his previous employer and, in the event that he had not yet found work, have his situation transferred to the category of 'unemployment insurance'.

Box 8.1 Three Lines of Protection

The 'Three Lines of Protection' are an important component of China's social security. They include the basic living allowance for laid-off workers of state-owned enterprises, unemployment insurance and the minimum living allowance system for urban residents, and they play a crucial role in ensuring the basic living of urban workers and residents, contributing ongoing reform, and maintaining social stability. They are tailored to China's unique circumstances. On April 29, 1999, the Ministry of Labor and Social Security, the Ministry of Civil Affairs and the Ministry of Finance jointly promulgated a 'notification' entitled, 'Notice Concerning how properly to link up the Basic Living Allowance System for Laid-off Workers of state-owned Enterprises, the Unemployment Insurance System and the Minimum Living Allowance System for Urban Residents'. This was Law No. 13 of the Ministry of Labor and Social Security. With regard to this proper 'linking up' of the three issues, the 'Three Lines of Protection' specify:

1   When the contract at a 're-employment service center' ends, for any previously laid-off worker of a state-owned enterprise, and that workers has failed to find a job in the meantime, the labor contract between the laid-off worker and the enterprise shall come to an end. In a timely manner, the enterprise shall issue a certificate to the laid-off worker, informing him of his right to enjoy unemployment insurance benefits as provided, and submitting a list of the unemployed to the relevant unemployment insurance agency for registration within seven days of the date the labor contract was terminated or rescinded. Such unemployment insurance agency shall grant unemployment insurance benefits in full amount as scheduled to any eligible laid-off worker.

2   If the unemployed has still failed to find a job at the expiry of his unemployment insurance benefits and needs to apply for the 'minimum living allowance for urban residents', the relevant unemployment insurance agency will provide relevant documentation and give one month's prior notice to the relevant civil affairs department, in the form of a list of those whose unemployment insurance benefits have expired. The civil affairs department shall have such persons registered and grant relief to eligible persons.

3   For laid-off workers from urban collectively-owned enterprises that have established re-employment service centers as prescribed by provincial governments, the above-stated procedures shall be consulted

when providing basic living allowance, unemployment insurance and minimum living allowance for urban residents. If laid-off workers of urban collectively-owned enterprises without re-employment service centers need to apply for minimum living allowance for urban residents, they shall carry the relevant certificate issued by such enterprises and apply to the local civil affairs department or sub-district offices having jurisdiction over them.

Source: http://www.51labour.com.

The policies that established unemployment insurance and improved the 'Three Lines of Protection' contributed greatly to China tackling the unemployment peak that occurred in the mid and late 1990s. In 2000, for example, 3.3 million unemployed people nationwide received unemployment insurance benefits, about 6.5 million laid-off workers of state-owned enterprises received living allowances, and more than 3 million impoverished urban residents enjoyed the minimum living allowance; a total of 12 million people receiving benefits and accounting for some 6 percent of total urban employees. Recipients of unemployment benefits and living allowances for laid-off workers approximated 10 million, more than 60 percent of total urban laid-off workers. In the course of 'deepening' the systemic changes in China and adjusting the country's economic structure, these policies ensured the basic living of laid-off workers, maintained social stability, and laid the foundation for a new round of economic growth.

Incorporating laid-off workers into the 'unemployment' and 'employment assistance' systems

The 'basic living security system for laid-off workers' was a transitional measure. It was designed to function within only a certain scope and period of time. In 2000 the State Council specified in the *Experimental Plan for Improving the Urban Social Security System* that from January 1, 2001, no re-employment service centers would be founded by state-owned enterprises, and no more laid-off workers would be registered at the re-employment service centers. Incorporating laid-off workers into the general category of 'unemployed' was to be finished, in incremental steps, within three years. Work was gradually done in various places to have laid-off workers leave the 'centers', and those having trouble finding jobs were included in the category publicly recognized as being 'unemployed', and were enrolled in unemployment insurance. Due to the vast numbers of laid-off workers, this work took more than five years. By 2006, the incorporation of 'basic living security for laid-off workers from SOEs' into 'unemployment insurance' had basically been accomplished. The 'Three Lines of Protection', aimed at laid-off and unemployed people, were then changed to the 'Two Lines of Protection': unemployment insurance for the unemployed insured and minimum living allowance for urban low-income families.[9]

As a form of income compensation for participants, unemployment insurance is always limited in how long it lasts. To provide assistance to those long-unemployed people with special difficulties, China has implemented an 'employ-ment assistance system' with reference to practical experience in its proactive employment policies. The *Employment Promotion Law* enacted in 2007 makes it clear that governmental institutions at various levels should establish and improve upon 'employment assistance' systems. Through such measures as tax reductions or exemptions, loan subsidies, job allowances and the provision of public-welfare posts, the aim is to strengthen the work of grass-roots employment assistance. The numbers of people finding jobs in labor markets in 2007 and 2008 decreased,[10] showing that fewer urban households facing employment problems were either willing or able to get jobs, and that employment assistance policies played a certain role in helping them out.

Main problems of the unemployment insurance and employment security systems

Future pressure and labour flexibility

In the past 30 years of 'reform and opening up', the country's nearly 10 percent rate of economic growth has basically dealt with the problem of employing new urban labor as well as the shift of more than 200 million agricultural laborers into different industries. (Over 100 million of these have been migrant rural workers.) However, it is very hard for both these sets of people to get unemploy-ment insurance. Once 'unemployed' they cannot get social relief from wherever they are newly located, which means that their rights and interests are not fully protected. Due to the vast number of laborers in China, both the shift of rural labor to new forms of work and the urbanization of the population in general are still confronted with formidable tasks. The massive employment pressure makes it imperative that China keep an appropriate balance between 'improving employment quality and a degree of unemployment security', and 'maintaining employment vitality and labor market flexibility'. The *Labor Contract Law*, introduced in the context of a 'scarcity of migrant rural workers', that appeared in coastal areas several years ago was aimed at improving the quality of employment and protecting the basic rights and interests of laborers. With accelerating urbanization and a decreasing number of 'rural' people and agricultural labor, this must be the overall direction of employment security. Under current conditions, however, especially when the world's financial crisis has already severely affected China's exports and economic growth, China faces the new formidable challenge of not being able to provide college graduates, migrant rural workers and others with an adequate number of jobs. The emphasis of our employment security policy must therefore change to 'stable labor relations' and a 'stable labor situation'.[11] Therefore, how to balance improvement in labor conditions and still maintain labor market flexibility, and how to balance trying to increase employment with unemployment security are going to be long-term factors that govern China's labor market and economic development. These are also precisely the main problems for the country as we try to improve our new social welfare system. Conceptually, many problems still exist with respect to how we should build our institutions, and how we should actually put theories into practice.

Labor market segmentation and employment discrimination

Labor mobility and integration in China has been improving. The labor market is still broadly segmented, however, given factors that had long-standing importance in the traditional employment system—such things as status, urban–rural dual structure and regional segmentation (see Figure 8.1). In addition to the problem of migrant rural workers' receiving the lowest levels of protection, the mobility of other labor is also limited due to various factors. Barriers limit the mobility of labor with different status (civil servants, workers in institutions, and workers in enterprises), and across regions and sectors, making it very difficult for the market mechanisms to play an effective role. Although such laws and regulations as the *Labor Law*, the *Employment Promotion Law* and the *Labor Contract Law* advocate and protect equal employment and oppose employment discrimination, there is in fact severe employment discrimination as a result of labor market reforms being out of step with current laws and also insufficient enforcement of

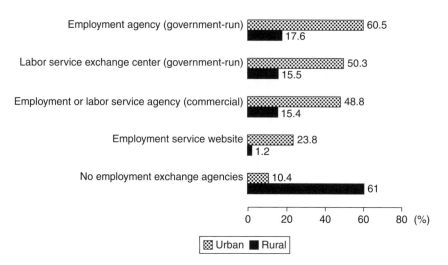

Figure 8.1 A comparison between urban and rural areas in information provided in employment information exchange market.

Source: *Manual of Public Index Assessment on Public Services in China in 2008*, Horizon Research Consultancy Group.

current laws. Migrant workers ['laborers coming from 'outside',], especially migrant rural workers [*nong-min-gong*], have no chance of getting equal treatment from employers. Very substantial differences exist in the status and treatment accorded to regular workers and that accorded to 'contract workers' within an enterprise. This leads to both unequal status and unequal pay for equal work. Due to differences in how people view labor protection and differences in conceptual framework, women encounter severe gender discrimination in finding jobs.

The unemployment insurance system is unsound and unable to function effectively

Coverage of unemployment insurance is too narrow

From a global perspective, unemployment insurance systems are related closely to levels of economic development; they are far less developed than pension and medical security programs. Currently, in the early twenty-first century, only 82 countries and regions in the world have established social security systems. China established a socialized unemployment insurance system in the course of its economic structural transition, which replaced the previous employment security benefits provided by state-owned and collectively-owned enterprises. The coverage afforded by the system has grown and, by 2007, 116.45 million people had been included, accounting for about 40 percent of all urban employees. However, this number still does not match just the number of workers of state-owned and collectively-owned enterprises in the mid 1990s. Affected by such factors as unstable employment relations, the difficulty of expanding the unemployment system is even greater than that facing the more imperative pension, medical, and even on-job injury insurances. The security system for laid-off workers has already been incorporated into unemployment insurance. Therefore, the employment assistance policy, which was previously directed at laid-off workers of state-owned enterprises, is aimed mainly at the 'regular unemployed', [people who had previously worked in regular jobs]. This makes it very difficult for people who were not previously enrolled in unemployment insurance, including temporary employees, migrant rural workers and the 'youth waiting for employment', to get any help. In addition, urban newly unemployed groups, such as college graduates and workers of TVEs, cannot get help.

Poor management of the unemployment insurance system

Contribution rates for insurance funds in China are not high, only around 3 percent, but there are severe omissions and arrears in collecting funds. In 2007 unemployment insurance funds, when calculated on the average wage of workers and the number of workers enrolled, should have reached over RMB 86 billion, but only RMB 47.2 billion had actually been collected—only 55 percent of the intended amount. In terms of fund payment, the time period in which unemployment insurance benefits may be received is divided into three stages, within a range of 12 to 24 months. This is notably longer than the foreign average (which in most countries ranges from 6 months to 1 year, with the average standing at 47.57 weeks[12]) and indeed is the longest in the world. The over-long length of payment is not conducive to encouraging re-employment.[13] Also, this approach does not accurately reflect the relationship between contributions paid in and benefits received, which does not inspire enthusiasm to work hard. In addition, as benefits are geared to the minimum wage and minimum living allowance and are therefore quite low, they do not allow contributions to correspond to rights and obligations. They lack provisions that allow for benefit standards decreasing with time, which again is not conducive to encouraging re-employment of the unemployed.

Low numbers of beneficiaries and low substitution rates of the unemployment insurance system

China's unemployment insurance system rules that the following three basic conditions be met in order to receive unemployment insurance benefits: i) participants in unemployment insurance, and their previous employer, must have contributed for a full year; ii) participants must be 'unwillingly' unemployed; and iii) participants must be 'registered unemployed who need to get a job'. Limited by these conditions the percentage of unemployment insurance beneficiaries is low, and stood at only 38 percent in 2006 (see Table 8.2). At the same time, determined according to the minimum living allowance, unemployment benefits are not linked to contribution standards; so the actual substitution rate is low, about 1/5 to 1/4 of the average wage of workers (see Table 8.3), making it very difficult to ensure the basic living of the unemployed.

Table 8.2 Number of unemployment insurance beneficiaries in China

Year	Registered unemployed people (10,000)	People receiving unemployment benefits (10,000)	% of people receiving unemployment benefits in registered unemployed people
1999	575	109	18.96
2000	595	190	31.93
2001	681	312	45.81
2002	770	440	57.14
2003	800	415	51.88
2004	827	419	50.67
2005	839	362	43.15
2006	847	327	38.61

Source: Ministry of Labor and Social Security, *Statistical Bulletin on Labor and Social Security Development.*

Table 8.3 Changes in substitution rate of unemployment insurance benefits since 2000

Year	Year-end people receiving unemployment benefits (10,000)	All-year unemployment benefits granted (RMB 10,000)	Unemployment benefits per capita (RMB)	Average monetary wage of workers	% of unemployment benefits per capita in average monetary wage
2000	190	56,198	296	9371	3.16
2001	312	832,563	2,668	1,0870	24.55
2002	440	1,167,736	2,654	1,2422	21.36
2003	415	1,334,448	3,216	1,4040	22.90
2004	419	1,374,983	3,282	1,6024	20.48
2005	362	1,323,767	3,657	1,8364	19.91

Source: Based on *China Statistical Yearbook* and *China Labor Statistical Yearbook*.

Unemployment security funds are used for relief rather than for creating or promoting employment

The main purpose of the unemployment insurance system is to provide proper living security for the unemployed and to counter the risk of having no income while unemployed. The best way to counter that risk is to improve employment skills, however, and overcome obstacles to re-employment—to get people back to work. Currently, unemployment insurance funds are used mainly as benefits, with little support for such aspects of employment as training subsidies and job recommendations. Of the RMB 10.17 billion in unemployment insurance funds paid out in 2001, 82 percent was used as unemployment insurance benefits, while only 13 percent was used for vocational training subsidies and job recommendations.

Box 8.2 Denmark's employment promotion program

The unemployment insurance system of Denmark is based on the following principle: any person who is able should live on his or her own labor, be entitled to rights but also take on obligations. Therefore, the unemployed have the obligation to find, accept and value jobs. If one fails to find a long-term job immediately, however, he or she is entitled to financial aid only after participating in the appropriate 'employment creation program'. If the person fails to fulfil this obligation, the person is punished, for example, by taking away all or part of the financial aid that he or she previously enjoyed.

For the above purpose, the Danish government, especially at the municipal level, has implemented an employment creation program. People must acquire skills through education or training before entering the labor market. Participants in the employment creation program must obtain required qualifications in a certain way (for example, through vocational training courses and job opportunities offered by employers), so that they either begin to receive some education or find jobs. Second, they must be positive and aggressive. The unemployed must perform with a positive attitude to be entitled to financial aid during the employment creation program. Without a justifiable reason (such as illness), program participants may not be absent from the training course or arranged work. They must accept any work provided under the employment creation program; otherwise, they are likely to lose all or part of any initial assistance or cash subsidies.

For the insured unemployed, the purpose of the employment creation program lies in strengthening their skills, so that they find new jobs as soon as possible. The Danish *Labor Market Reform of 1997* combines 'flexibility' (i.e. accept the job offered, or lose all allowance) and rights in an organic way. The *Social Aid Act*, promulgated in 1997, further specifies that the unemployed have no right to receive public allowance and can only receive arrangements by local governments.

The Danish government has established the following five main policies designed to help the unemployed find jobs: i) providing vocational training, to improve the employment abilities of the unemployed; ii) providing free public employment service or employment assistance service; iii) directly creating jobs, for example, by launching public works, service projects or community service projects, to arrange temporary employment for the long-term unemployed; iv) providing pay or employment supplements to enterprises employing the unemployed or to self-employed individuals; and v) helping the unemployed found micro-enterprises for the purpose of self-employment.

Source: Du Zhixin, *A Survey Report on Social Welfare of Denmark* (China Development Research Foundation, 2008).

China's unemployment insurance system lacks effective links to other security systems

At the expiry of unemployment insurance benefits, an unemployed person directly enters the status of receiving the 'minimum living allowance', the benefits of which are equivalent to the 'basic cost of living allowance'. Once these people receive certain income, such allowances are reduced or even removed. This presents the problem of having unemployment insurance become divorced from employment promotion and assistance, which is unfavorable when trying to grow employment. The risk of unemployment is uneven, however. Those who have little probability of unemployment are not incentivized to participate in unemployment insurance under unified compulsory contribution rates. The ties between the unemployment insurance system and minimum living allowances and pension schemes are also imperfect, which does not help the long-term unemployed and those old-age unemployed who are near retirement to transfer smoothly to other security systems. In addition, due to the low administrative levels at which funds are pooled, the amount of funds in pooling regions is small and their ability to respond to structural unemployment is limited. This makes it difficult to ensure any impartiality of unemployment security between different industries and different regions. Given the increasing mobility of labor, the present unemployment insurance system and the minimum living allowance system, both established on the basis of the household registration system, are powerless to provide security to people coming in to work from regions outside their own pooling regions.

Objectives in building a 'developmental employment security system'

Compared to developed countries, China's per capita GDP in 2007 was only some $2,500, less than 1/10th that of the US and Japan. Even if China's economy continues to maintain a relatively high growth rate over the next 5 to 12 years, GDP per capita will still lag considerably behind developed countries. On the premise that fast economic growth will continue, China's levels of social security and social welfare (including employment security) should increase at a relatively fast rate, but the rate should definitely be 'appropriate'. Over the next 10 years or more the basic pattern of an oversupply of labor will remain unchanged in China. In light of formidable pressure to create jobs, and in light of the enormous number of unemployed in China, too generous employment security will harm both the enthusiasm of employers and the spirit of workers. By taking the experience and lessons of developed countries as reference points, we should transform passive unemployment compensation to proactive employment assistance and welfare. By implementing a broader proactive labor policy, we should build a developmental unemployment security system that maintains the vitality of the labor market. In the context of the global financial crisis the slowdown in China's economic development has already affected employment growth. Special attention should be paid to any potential unemployment peak that may arise from the economic downturn.

A 'developmental employment security system' has the following objectives: first, provide laborers with continual and different levels of training, enabling them to improve skills and working ability—thereby increasing employment quality, actively promoting employment and stability, and increasing the size of employment. Second, ensure the basic living of the unemployed, and increase as appropriate the benefit levels of unemployment insurance. Third, provide coverage for all eligible urban residents, while expanding the coverage of unemployment insurance as much as possible; on the one hand, mobilize laborers to participate in the labor market, and on the other hand, provide them with access to a fair, just and relatively stable unemployment environment. Establish harmonious labor relations, instead of merely focusing on combining the unemployment insurance system with proactive employment policies we should create an organic unity between these two aspects of providing security while building the labor market. While improving the labor market we should let market mechanisms, government interventions and social assistance play supportive roles in reducing unemployment and creating employment.

In the first stage, namely from 2009 to 2012, the following tasks should be fulfilled: first, help laborers improve their competitiveness through training and business start-up support. Provide proactive employment assistance to those with job problems, to enable them to stay voluntarily in the labor market rather than merely depending on welfare. Combine unemployment benefits with the granting of public-welfare jobs, training participation and re-employment in better ways. Second, realize unemployment insurance coverage of all urban laborers, and expand it to rural laborers. Third, further improve the operations and management of the unemployment insurance system, determine the contribution base amounts in a rational way, improve benefit release methods, and improve as appropriate the benefiting and substitution rates of the registered unemployed person. Fourth, explore an unemployment security system that is appropriate for temporary employers, migrant rural workers and rural non-agricultural laborers (TVE workers), whose levels of contributions and release of benefits should differ in appropriate ways from the unemployment insurance system, in order to maintain certain flexibility.

In the second stage, from 2013 to 2020, on the basis of ongoing expansion in unemployment security, the primary task is to continually improve training and the quality of employment on the basis of expanding employment security—to provide training and assistance to all the unemployed and people having difficulties in finding a job, thereby forming long-lasting mechanisms to create new employment. To strengthen the development of a labor market, eliminate urban and rural segmentation in labor market policies, further improve the labor market service system of job recommendation, training, mobility and creation, and accelerate the integration of the labor market.

Policy recommendations

Further clarify the strategic imperative of building a developmental employment security system

Developmental employment security is key to, and a core part of, improving social welfare. It is associated directly with employment creation. It integrates 'social development' and 'social protections' in an organic way, by applying market mechanisms to expanding employment and maintaining economic vitality. That is, it integrates two concepts that are often seen as being in conflict. To build China's developmental employment security system in the new period, we must establish unemployment insurance and minimum living allowance systems that are appropriate both to our national situation and stage in development. We must ensure the basic living of the unemployed and make them share more effectively in the outcome of socioeconomic development. More emphasis should be placed on the building of a secure labor market system, in order to promote and expand employment and increase the quality of employment.

Put considerable effort into implementing and improving active labor policies

Active labor policies encourage workers to stay in the job market, through such means as employment training and business start-up support, and provide proactive employment assistance to those who cannot find jobs. For any who are willing and able to work, we should create opportunities through special policies, so as to maximally achieve employment equality, narrow income disparities, and reduce welfare expenditures. There are many types of active labor policies. The practices of various regions should be summarized and appropriate measures should be taken, according to the actual needs of different groups with job problems, so that scarce resources can have a greater effect. Job creation should be regarded as an important objective of stimulating economic growth in public-finance-invested projects.

The government should increase its investment in active labor market policies. It should establish an effective labor market system, to truly provide the underlying conditions for 'market-supplied' employment. This will also be an effective method of freeing the government from having to be directly involved in arranging for the unemployed. In 2007 the financial expenditures for implementing active labor market policies came to RMB 37.1 billion; they should increase annually by 10 percent, to reach RMB 60 billion by 2012, and RMB 120 billion by 2020.

Improve the unemployment insurance and relief systems

The *Regulations on Unemployment Insurance* contains many provisions which are inconsistent with international experience and are also behind the pace of socioeconomic development in China. We recommend determining contributions and benefits based on type of coverage for the participant, so that unemployment insurance rights and obligations are in agreement with each other. Efforts should be made to improve the coverage of unemployment insurance and increase the contribution rates to 80 percent, and even above 90 percent as soon as possible, in order to strengthen the security function of unemployment insurance funds. We should determine the length of time that unemployment benefits are paid out in a more rational way, and we should formulate unemployment benefit standards in a more scientific manner, shorten as appropriate the time of receiving benefits, and be determined to reduce the rate of accumulation of unemployment insurance funds by either increasing investment into the positive labor policy or improving as appropriate the benefit levels for the unemployed. We should also set benefit levels of unemployment insurance according to contributions that are themselves determined by level of wages, and establish a benefit reduction mechanism to exert the role of insurance in encouraging people to be proactive about finding jobs. We should raise the administrative level at which funds are pooled, and establish as soon as possible an unemployment benefit system that is consistent within provinces and that comes under national regulations.

Since it is hard for the unemployment insurance system to cover temporary employers, migrant rural workers and new job seekers, contribution rates and benefit standards can be reduced for these categories of people. For those with a small probability of unemployment, an incentive system with a lower rate of contribution can be established and individual unemployment compensation can be designed accordingly.[14] Those who become unemployed before retirement may receive unemployment benefits as prescribed. If an individual has never received unemployment benefits before retirement, a sum of compensation can be refunded to his or her pension account on the basis of the accumulated amount in the account upon retirement. But if the individual has received unemployment benefits before retirement, he or she will enjoy no such compensation after retirement. The unemployment compensation account and its effective link to the pension account are meant to encourage laborers to participate in insurance, to be proactive about finding jobs and to add funds to their pension accounts.

With the process of urbanization accelerating, and in order to promote the stable employment of migrant workers who are now permanently settled in one place, it is necessary to reform the system that relies on 'household registration' to determine minimum allowances. We need now to establish unemployment relief systems that are associated with the regions where migrant rural workers are employed, so that they can receive local assistance and support.

Build a labor-market services system that integrates urban and rural markets, and provide practical and effective vocational training

A healthy labor market must be backed by an efficiently operating labor-market services system. Efforts must be made to break down the market segmentation that is caused by urban, rural, regional, industrial, status and other factors, and to strengthen the building of an integrated labor market. We must promote rational mobility of labor, develop human resources, and achieve an effective allocation of labor resources. Unemployment insurance, unemployment compensation and re-employment promotion should be tightly linked.

A nationally uniform information system covering the supply and demand of labor should be established as soon as possible and it should be authoritative and reputable. As registered unemployment figures are released, unemployment data based on surveys should also be released in order to provide full information on which to make decisions. Employment system reforms should be in line with the trends in the market—the information network that should cater to the needs of market-oriented employment system reform. Through nationwide surveys on labor resources, both urban and rural, we should make reliable forecasts of labor demand and be timely in providing information on supply and demand. At the same time we should take advantage of the role information can play in guiding action, and make quality information services available to both laid-off workers and rural surplus labor. We should excel in the process of collecting, sorting, storing, exchanging, promulgating and consulting about information that is associated with this effort.

To facilitate the employment of flexible employers, migrant rural workers and rural non-agricultural employers, as well as the re-employment capacity of the unemployed, an educational and training system guided by labor market demands should be established. Training markets should be actively fostered and developed, and various vocational and skills training facilities should be encouraged. According to the relevant foreign experience, consideration can be given to: i) enacting laws and regulations, strengthening vocational training by mobilizing national forces as legally required, calling for social recognition and support of vocational training, and prescribing predetermined objectives to be accomplished by vocational training and education; ii) reforming the training management system and better mobilizing the initiative of private enterprises and social groups; the government doesn't participate directly in employment training but transfers responsibility of training to NGOs and private enterprises, which can not only reduce the burden of the government but also make training more effective; iii) providing various forms of training, including class training, field training as well as such services as job recommendation, consulting and basic technical training; iv) establishing socialized vocational training centers; establishing vocational training centers funded by the government and operated by social groups specially for migrant workers and laid-off workers, providing free vocational training and employment information to those who need to find jobs.

Strengthen the legal framework for employment, to help in job creation and to provide employment security

In recent years, China's creation of a legal system that addresses labor market issues has progressed considerably, but we need to go much further in improving the quality, relevancy, and effectiveness of laws and regulations. For example, we need to strengthen labor protections as appropriate and provide employment support for people who haven't enrolled in unemployment insurance. We need to reinforce the ability of the labor market to be flexible, by amending or adjusting relevant legal clauses. We need to adopt more flexible policies for employers of medium and small-sized enterprises.

Take proactive and flexible measures in response to the peak in unemployment that may arise from the economic crisis

Affected by the global financial crisis, China is currently facing a new peak in unemployment. The government should attach great importance to this: it should place equal emphasis on solving employment problems and maintaining economic growth. It should set up a 'flexible labor' system, preserve the vitality of the labor market, set up third-party arbitration mechanisms, expand the coverage of group labor contracts, adopt measures that allow for flexible hiring practices, flexible times, flexible wages. It should organize training, and in general facilitate labor issues that arise during this time of crisis. Unemployment insurance funds and government funding should increase their level of support to enterprises that are in trouble in terms of keeping on employees: especially to medium- and small-sized enterprises. Efforts should be made to strengthen guidance and management for enterprises when they have to reduce their number of employees. Such efforts should be proactive in preventing and properly dealing with the problem of wage arrears of enterprises. They should establish and improve communications and coordination systems that address major issues to do with labor relations. It should be noted that unemployment is a chronic and tenacious disease that accompanies the whole process of economic growth. Any mitigating measures should be moderate and undertaken on the basis of capability. Anti-crisis measures taken during the unemployment peak should be connected organically with the fundamental functioning of labor-market mechanisms, so that in the end we are able to create a sounder labor market system.

Notes

1 According to Xiao Donglian's research, in 1979–1981 new jobs were arranged for 26,226,000 people in cities, 63.3 percent of them arranged by state-owned entities, 32.9 percent by collectively-owned entities and 36 percent by the self-employed. Feng Lanrui's research reveals that during the period, the non-state-owned sector arranged 63 percent of jobs in many coastal cities. See Xiao Donglian, 'China's Employment Crisis and Development Opportunity of Non-state-owned Economy in Cities in the Late 1970s' (http://www.usc.cuhk.hk).

2 A 1990s survey reveals that urban employment channels became more market-oriented and diverse, including national arrangement at 38.7 percent, self-employment at 29.8 percent, recommendations at 22.3 percent and advertising at 67 percent. See Wang Yanzhong, *Labor and Social Security Problems of China* (Economy & Management Publishing House, 2004).

3 Wang Yanzhong. *Labor and Social Security Problems of China* (Economy & Management Publishing House, 2004).

4 Liu Danhua, *Main Policy Measures for Employment and Re-employment Promotion in China; Department of Training and Employment* (Ministry of Labour and Social Security): *An Interpretation and Analysis of the Positive Employment Policy* (China Labour and Social Security Publishing House, 2008).

5 Lin JY, 'Rural Reforms and Agricultural Growth in China', *American Economic Review*, Vol 82, 34–54, 1992.

6 Du Yang, Cai Fang and Wang Dewen, *Mobility of Rural Laborers*, Working Paper (Institute of Population and Labour Economics, CASS, 2008).

7 Mo Rong, *Employment Promotion, Employment Assistance and Unemployment Protection Systems* (Background Report, 2008).

8 In 1998, 79 million workers were enrolled in unemployment insurance, accounting for some 50 percent of total urban workers across the country. In 2000, more than 100 million (exactly 104.08 million) were enrolled, accounting for 77 percent of total urban workers. By 2003, although the number of enrolled workers did not increase, they had already accounted for 99 percent of total urban workers, as a result of the decrease in the number of urban workers. See Chen Jiagui and Wang Yanzhong, *Report on Social Security Development in China* (Social Sciences Academic Press, 2004).

9 Ming Chun, Liang Liqun and Gao Peng, 'A Survey of the Joining of "Three Security Lines" and Re-employment Policy', *Budget Control and Accounting Monthly*, Issue 11, 2005.

10 Mo Rong, *Employment Promotion, Employment Assistance and Unemployment Protection Systems* (Background Report, 2008).

11 Ministry of Human Resources and Social Security, All China Federation of Trade Unions, China Enterprise Confederation/China Enterprise Directors Association,

Guiding Opinions on Dealing with the Present Economic Situation and Stabilizing Labor Relations. See such media as the website of Ministry of Human Resources and Social Security and People's Daily Online (http://news.163.com).

12 The US Social Security Administration, *Global Social Security 1995* (Chinese Edition) (Huaxia Publishing House, 1997). The figures here are the author's statistical result based on data contained in the book.

13 Yang Wenzhong, 'Make the Most of Integrated Service Functions of Unemployment Insurance', *China Social Security*, Issue 11, 2003, p. 19.

14 Li Shaoguang, *An Economic Analysis of Deepening Social Security Reform* (China Renmin University Press, 2006).

9 Housing security

Housing security is an important part of the social welfare system. In the transition from planned economy to a socialist market economy, a series of reforms were adopted with respect to China's housing system. The 'urban housing security system' developed, bringing substantial improvement to the housing conditions of urban residents. To achieve the harmonious social objective of 'housing afford-ability', however, and build a framework of 'developmental housing security systems', we now need to go further in solving the housing problems of low-income groups; finding solutions to housing problems of middle-income groups, and improving housing security measures aimed at rural households. The latter includes bringing migrant workers who have long worked in cities into the scope of housing security. This must all be done with an eye to China's national conditions.

The process of housing reform

Dramatic changes have taken place in China's urban housing system in the past 60 years. The process of housing reform brings into relief problems in the government–market relationship in distributing housing. At the same time it also reveals that it is unfeasible to adopt either marketized practices or the traditional planning mode in entirety, since housing distribution relates to the short and long-term interests of millions of households. A more effective approach might be as follows: the real estate market is allowed to play the dominant role in meeting the housing needs of moderately high- and high-income groups, while the government is responsible for solving the housing problems of middle- and low-income groups.

Housing security under the planned system

From the founding of New China to the early days of the reform, China practiced separate housing security systems for urban and rural areas, which was done within the context of an overall 'dual-system' for urban and rural. In the cities, in line with the planned-economy system and the low wages that prevailed at the time, public housing was 'allocated' to employees. The phrase describing the system at the time was that it was 'government-funded, under unified [state] management, allocated in unified fashion, and rents that were collected paid for upkeep'. Specifically, housing was built with government-disbursed funds, or with funds raised by state-owned or collective units. The land on which housing was built was allocated by the State at no cost. Housing was distributed directly to the worker in the form of an in-kind benefit by the worker's 'unit', according to seniority and size of family. The worker was expected to pay a low rent. Since rents changed only slightly over a long period of time, the percentage of family income that workers paid out in rent constantly declined. The housing was owned either by the State, an enterprise, or a collective. It could not be transferred by individuals at their own discretion, and it was maintained and managed at no charge by the 'unit' who had 'property rights' to the property.

As one component of the whole social welfare security system under the planned-economy system, the urban housing distribution system was complementary to the medical, educational and other security systems for urban residents at the time. However, as the economy grew and the urban population kept increasing, more and more of the drawbacks of this housing distribution system became apparent. It not only hindered the development of the real estate industry but also caused inequities in public housing distribution. In short, it was a low-level, low-efficiency and unfair way to distribute housing.

In contrast to the way in which housing was distributed for urban residents, in the countryside the government provided farmers with 'home sites' and let them build homes for themselves. Immediately after 'land reform' in the early 1950s, rural land, including 'home sites', was declared to be the private property of farmers—this was officially stated in and was given protection by *The 1954 Constitution*. Following the collectivization of agriculture, land became collectively owned; *The 1962 Draft Amendment to the Regulations for Rural People's Communes* stipulated that 'home sites' of farmers were owned by the production brigade and that farmers were now allowed apply to the collective for permission to have a 'home site' and to build a home on it, depending on the number of people in their households. 'Home sites' could not be rented, bought, or sold. The housing arrangements of any vulnerable groups were the responsibility of the rural collective. The national government took very little to no responsibility at all.

The process of urban housing reform

To address the defects of the housing distribution system under the planned economy, in 1980, Deng Xiaoping came up with the concept, which was an overall general approach at the time, of selling public housing, raising rents, and encouraging people to build or buy their own homes. This opened the curtain to the ensuing housing system reforms, which occurred in roughly the following four stages.

The first stage, from 1980 to 1993, began with experiments in increasing housing rentals, granting subsidies, and selling public housing. In June 1980 the State formally ratified and then publicly announced the policy of 'commoditizing' housing [i.e. making it a commodity that could be bought and sold], with the focus placed on selling newly built housing at subsidized prices. In June 1991 the State

Council issued the *Notice on Continuing to Carry out the Reform of Urban Housing System in a Stable Way* (No. 30 State Issued [1991]). It set the tone for the reform by establishing such principles as focusing on rent increases, and housing sale, and stressing 'mechanism transformation' [i.e. creating new mechanisms for transferring property].

The second stage, from 1994 to 1997, explored a variety of housing supply systems and took the first steps in establishing a 'housing accumulation fund'. In the mid-1990s the State Council issued the *Decision to Deepen Reform of the Urban Housing System*. It defined an 'affordable housing system' for middle and low-income groups, and a 'commercialized housing system' for high-income groups. It required the nationwide implementation of the housing accumulation fund and defined regulations relating to its establishment and management. At the same time it actively promoted reform of the public housing rental system, and called for taking deliberate steps toward being able to sell public housing and toward developing a market for buying and selling [exchanging] housing.

The third stage, from 1998 to 2006, saw the abolition of the system that had provided housing as a welfare benefit. It saw the growth of a housing market, and the establishment of a multi-level housing supply system. In 1998 the State Council issued the 'Notice on Further Deepening Reform of the Urban Housing System and Accelerating the Building of Affordable Housing'. This explicitly required the discontinuation of any distribution of welfare housing, nationwide, from the second half of 1998. It gradually began the process of monetizing housing, and setting up a multi-level and multi-channel housing supply system. The following year [1999], the Ministry of Construction promulgated the *Measures for Urban Low-rent Housing Administration*, and printed and distributed the *Notice of Several Opinions Regarding Affordable Housing Development*. This clearly defined all aspects of developing low-rent and affordable housing, including purpose, principles, planning process, pricing and property management.

The fourth stage, from 2007 to the present, has been marked by strengthening institutional support for middle and low-income households with housing difficulties. In 2007 the State Council issued *Several Opinions on Solving Housing Difficulties of Urban Low-income Households*, which further established China's housing security system, and defined low-rent housing as the core and the main focus of the system, and low-rent and affordable housing as the main way to solve housing difficulties of low-income urban residents. At the end of 2007 the new *Low-rent Housing Security Measures*, the *Administrative Measures for Affordable Housing*, and the Ministry of Finance's *Administrative Measures for Low-rent Housing Security Funds* were introduced in succession. These policies have stimulated housing marketization in China and gradually improved housing conditions for both urban and rural residents.

Current housing conditions of urban and rural residents

After 30 years of reform, China has greatly improved the housing conditions of its people. As shown in Figure 9.1, the per capita living space has increased quickly.

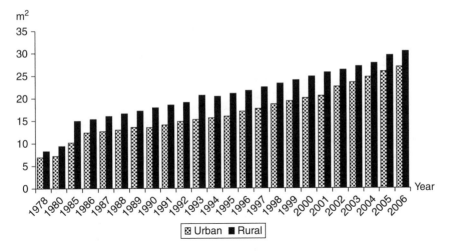

Figure 9.1 Housing area increase of urban and rural residents, 1978–2006.

Source: Based on National Bureau of Statistics of China (2008) *China Statistical Abstract 2008.* Beijing: China Statistics Press, p. 103.

Between 1978 and 2006 the living space per urban resident increased by 4 times, by 0.73m² per annum, while the living space per urban resident rose by 3.8 times, by 0.81m² per annum.

The degree of 'marketization' of housing in urban and rural areas has risen continually but the market has gained particular momentum since the overall reform of the housing system in 1998. This is reflected by the considerable decrease in the percentage of public housing and the increase in the percentage of housing purchases. According to a 2005 sampling survey of 1 percent of the population, only 13.3 percent of urban households lived in rented public housing that year, while the percentage had been nearly 60 percent in 1995.[1] Aside from a small number of households that still rented public housing, other urban households lived in more or less market-oriented houses. Around half lived in housing that was either self-built, purchased commercial or affordable housing, and rented commercial housing. The percentage would have exceeded 80 percent if purchased public housing had been added (Table 9.1) [i.e. people purchasing the public housing that they had formerly rented].

Although the living space of urban and rural residents has constantly increased, the quality of housing has yet to be improved. A considerable percentage of rural residents are badly housed. As shown in Table 9.2, in 2005, nearly 8.4 percent of rural residents lived in 'very inferior' housing, and nearly 16 percent lived in housing that was even worse (Table 9.2).

Deficiencies also exist in the provision of such public services as tap water, cooking fuel, kitchens, toilets and bathing facilities. Take tap water as an example: in 2005 only 31 percent of rural residents had access to tap water as their drinking water, but the figure was 69 percent for urban residents, and 24 percent of rural migrant workers in cities had no access to tap water at all.

Table 9.1 Sources of housing in China's cities, towns and rural areas in 2005

Source of housing	Households in cities		Town households	Rural households
	Registered urban residents		*Registered rural residents*	
1. Self-built housing	10.99	0.21	57.22	93.82
2. Purchased commercial housing	23.19	5.26	10.85	0.89
3. Purchased affordable housing	8.79	0.98	4.92	0.51
4. Public housing later purchased by individuals	34.63	1.93	8.47	0.63
5. Rented public housing	13.32	5.79	4.52	0.32
6. Rented commercial housing	5.50	38.67	9.00	1.29
7. Other	3.58	7.16	5.02	2.54
Total	100	100	100	100

Source: Based on a sampling survey of a 1% population in 2005.

Table 9.2 Housing construction in China's cities, towns and rural areas in 2005

Source of housing	Households in cities		Town households	Rural households
	Registered urban residents		*Registered rural residents*	
1. Reinforced concrete structure	39.94	23.42	25.45	8.82
2. Composite structure	47.75	35.84	31.91	21.15
3. Brick–wood structure	11.59	35.87	33.81	45.71
4. Wood–bamboo–grass structure	0.19	1.56	2.53	8.39
5. Other	0.53	3.32	6.29	15.93
Total	100	100	100	100

Source: Based on a sampling survey of a 1% population in 2005.

The Fifth Plenary Session of the Sixteenth Communist Party of China's Central Committee set forth the historic mission of building a socialist 'new countryside', which led to the implementation of a series of important policies on supporting and benefiting rural residents. As a part of the campaign, great efforts were made in various regions to improve those public utilities for which farmers have the greatest need, such as improving the safety of drinking water, broadening the

Table 9.3 Proportion of households with housing difficulties in different urban income groups (%)

Income decile groups	Proportion of households with housing difficulties	Income decile groups	Proportion of households with housing difficulties
Lowest income group	12.5	Group 6	2.5
Group 2	4.2	Group 7	2.4
Group 3	3.2	Group 8	1.8
Group 4	4.5	Group 9	1.8
Group 5	1.8	Highest income group	0.5
Total	3.5		

Source: A 2007 sampling survey on urban households in 15 provinces.

use of such clean energies as methane and straw-produced gas, building biogas-generating pits as a step in renovating pigpens, toilets and kitchens, separating residences from pigpens, and ameliorating rural sewage and waste problems. These infrastructure projects have greatly improved the housing conditions of farmers, as well as improved their drinking water, power supply, fuel supply, and road supply. The countryside surrounding Beijing is one example. In Beijing's efforts to build a 'new countryside' it focused on improving the working and living conditions of farmers to the extent that, in 2007, the toilets of 100,000 farming households were renovated, 175 public toilets were built, and 430,000 farmers were ensured access to safe drinking water.[2]

Although urban housing has increased considerably in quantity, a large percentage of low-income households are inadequately or poorly housed. Table 9.3 shows the percentages of households living in poor conditions as according to income groups, based on a 2007 survey of urban households. It is not hard to see that the lowest-income group, some 10 percent of the population, lives in inadequate housing.

Urban and rural housing security systems at present

Comprehensive reform of housing systems began in 1998, and since that time the housing market has developed extremely quickly in China. By 2007 the aggregate sum of housing resources in urban and rural China had reached 42 billion square meters, which included urban housing resources of 12 billion square meters. The figures increased particularly fast after the beginning of the twenty-first century. Since 2000, housing has increased annually by 1.3 billion square meters, including an increase of 0.6 billion square meters in urban areas; and housing investment has grown by 19.8 percent each year. The per capita living space of urban residents increased markedly in this period, going from 13.7 square meters in 1990 to

27 square meters in 2006. During the same period, the living space of rural residents increased from 17.8 to 31 square meters.[3] Meanwhile, however, housing prices have soared in urban areas. Most of the low- and middle-income households cannot afford housing if they have to rely on their own resources. This has become an extremely prominent social issue. Given inadequate government efforts in the arena of housing security it is not likely to be resolved at any time in the near future.

Recognizing that inadequate housing security is having a serious impact on society, the Chinese government raised the importance of 'improving a housing security system' by 'putting it on the agenda'. By now, the basic framework for an urban housing security system has taken shape. It consists of housing relief (mainly in the form of the low-rent housing), housing assistance (mainly in the form of the affordable housing, plus reasonably-priced commercial housing) and mutual aid (mainly the housing accumulation fund system).

Housing relief

Aiming mainly to reduce poverty, the housing relief system can be categorized as the basic level of security. It provides basic housing for households or groups unable to solve their housing problems on their own. Mainly in the form of low-rent housing, the system offers ordinary housing to urban poverty-stricken households at a low rent. Besides having poor housing conditions, eligible recipients should be either the especially poor (those that are disabled, the widowed elderly or those unable to work); or low-income groups who have the ability to work but earn only slightly higher than the local income threshold for minimum living allowance. The relief includes rent subsidies, provision of low-rent housing, and reduced rent. China's low-rent housing system has gradually evolved, as described in Box 9.1.

Box 9.1 Legal framework established for low-rent housing in China's urban areas

Year	*Content*
1998	The Notice by the State Council on Further Deepening the Urban Housing System Reform and Accelerating Housing Construction (No. 23, *guo fa* [1998]) proposes for the first time the establishment of the low-rent housing system. This Notice points out that lowest-income groups may have access to low-rent houses provided by the government or employers, and such low-rent houses may be converted from old public housing that has been vacated, or newly built through the investment of the government or employers, and the rent is fixed by the government.
1999	In the spirit of the document (No. 23, *guo fa* [1998]), the Ministry of Construction formulated the Administrative Measures for Urban Low-rent Housing (No. 70, Order of the Ministry

of Construction), which established a policy framework for low-rent housing.

2003   The Notice by the State Council on Promoting the Healthy and Sustainable Development of Real Estate Market (No. 18, *guo fa* [2003]) requires strengthening the government's role in housing security, and stabilizing the sources of housing security funds with focus placed on the government's budgetary funds. The housing relief includes rent subsidy, provision of low-rent houses, and reduced rent. In the same year, the Ministry of Construction, jointly with other departments concerned, revised and promulgated Measures for the Administration on Low-rent Housing for Urban Lowest-income Households (Order No. 120, Ministry of Construction), marking the establishment of the low-rent housing system.

2005   The General Office of the State Council Forwarding the Notice by Ministry of Construction and Other Departments on Stabilizing Housing Prices (No. 26, *guo ban fa* [2005]) requires the municipal and county governments to report to the provincial governments on their performance concerning the urban low-rent housing system and be held accountable for that. The notice marks the establishment of the low-rent housing promotion mechanism. In the same year, the Ministry of Construction, jointly with other departments concerned, issued the Measures for Rent Administration of Urban Low-rent Housing (No. 405, *fa gai jia ge* [2005]) and the Administrative Measures for Low-rent Housing Application, Approval and Exit of Urban Lowest-income Households (No. 122, *jian zhu fang* [2005]), which further improved the low-rent housing policy.

2006   The General Office of the State Council Forwarding the Notice by Ministry of Construction and Other Departments on Adjusting the Housing Supply Structure and Stabilizing Housing Prices (No. 37, *guo ban fa* [2006]) requires that the fund raising for low-rent housing should be in place and that the municipal governments should use a certain percentage of net income from land transfer for building low-rent housing. In the same year, in the spirit of this document, the Notice by Ministries of Finance, Construction and Land and Resources on Securing Funds for Urban Low-rent Housing (No. 25, *cai zong* [2006]) was issued, which further expanded the funding sources of low-rent housing.

August 2007   Opinions by the State Council on Solving Housing Difficulties of Urban Low-income Households (No. 24, *guo fa* [2007]) stresses that the main component of housing security is low-rent housing, and that the coverage shall be expanded to include low-income households. This document contains

| | specific regulations on such aspects as land source, security fund and working mechanism and includes for the first time housing security as an indicator to assess the municipal governments' performances. |
| November 2007 | The nine departments, including the Ministry of Construction, printed and distributed the Low-rent Housing Security Measures. The Ministry of Finance's Administrative Measures for Low-rent Housing Security Funds was promulgated, which makes clear the stable sources and channels for low-rent housing funds and strengthens the support of government budget at various levels to low-rent housing. |

Source: Ren Xingzhou, *Housing Security in China's New Social Welfare System* (Background Report, 2008). [Note: in the above, '*guo fa*' refers to a State Council-issued document, '*cai*' refers to a document issued by the Ministry of Finance, '*jian*' refers to a document issued by the Ministry of Construction.]

By the end of 2006 a total of 512 cities in the country had established, and started to implement, a low-rent housing system. Total funds allocated to this effort came to RMB 7.08 billion (see Table 9.4); a total of 547,000 households had improved their housing conditions through the system. Among them, 167,000 households received subsidies for rented housing, 77,000 were allocated low-rent housing, 279,000 benefited from reduced rents and 24,000 improved their housing conditions through other means.

Housing assistance

The so-called 'housing assistance system' is one in which the government provides assistance to households unable to solve housing problems completely on their own. The assistance policies and the level of subsidies differ, depending on the recipient's financial circumstances. The main forms of housing assistance include i) the 'affordable housing system', in which the government sells housing to low-income and poorly housed families at preferential prices, so long as regulations relating to housing design, floorage and construction standards are met, and ii) the 'reasonably-priced commercial housing' policy, which adopts a market way in which the government is responsible for organizing and supervising the process. The government allocates land on which developers are allowed to build, and uses a bidding process to select the developer. The housing is aimed at urban middle and low-income households. The two policies are consistent in that housing prices are lowered through the government's preferential policies, making housing affordable for middle and low-income groups. At the present time the 'affordable housing system' is the main form of housing assistance. This system began in 1994, and has gradually evolved in terms of its nature and positioning (see Box 9.2).

Table 9.4 Development of the low-rent housing system (cumulative totals, by the end of 2006)

Region	Cities	Cities with established system	Households benefiting from low-rent housing system					Sources of funds (RMB 10,000)					
			Total	Subsidy for rented housing	Allocation of low-rent housing	Rent reduction	Other	Total	Government budgetary funds	Net income from land transfer	Income from accumulation fund increment	Social donations	Other
Country-wide	657	512	547,292	166,568	77,544	278,864	24,316	708,421	321,466	31,023	197,863	2,102	155,972
East China	263	219	296,828	87,039	28,925	178,184	2,680	419,015	182,938	4,379	151,931	1,574	78,192
Central China	227	182	133,435	47,663	17,376	66,055	2,341	105,723	25,175	10,791	26,640	81	43,039
West China	167	111	117,029	31,866	31,243	34,625	19,295	183,683	113,353	15,853	19,292	447	34,741

Source: China Economic Net, February 14, 2007.

Box 9.2　Legal framework established for affordable housing in China's urban areas

Year	*Content*
1994	The Decision by the State Council to Deepen the Urban Housing System Reform (No. 43, *guo fa* [1994]) mentioned for the first time the establishment of an affordable housing supply system directed at middle and low-income households and in the nature of social security. In 1995 the 'Comfortable Housing Project' was launched.
1998	The Notice by the State Council on Further Deepening the Urban Housing System Reform and Accelerating Housing Construction (No. 23, *guo fa* [1998]) required the establishment and improvement of a multi-level housing supply system with emphasis placed on affordable housing that are supplied mainly to urban middle and low-income households and for sale only.
2003	The Notice by the State Council on Promoting Continual and Healthy Development of the Real Estate Market (No. 18, *guo fa* [2003]), which positions affordable housing as social security-oriented commercial housing, and requires the strengthening of such an orientation through controlling construction standards, defining eligibility of applicants, implementing preferential policies and exercising strict control over bidding and selling price. In the same year, the Ministry of Construction, together with other ministries, formulated more detailed rules, the Administrative Measures for Affordable Housing.
2006	It is stressed in the General Office of the State Council Forwarding the Notice by Ministry of Construction and Other Departments on Adjusting the Housing Supply Structure and Stabilizing Housing Prices (No. 37, *guo fa* [2006]) that efforts should be made to develop affordable housing in a standard way, improve the affordable housing system and earnestly solve the problems with housing construction and sales. Particularly geared to the needs of the new situation, this document explicitly positioned affordable housing as catering to low-income households, thus defining the subsequent development direction of the system.
August 2007	The State Council promulgated Opinions on Solving Housing Difficulties of Urban Low-income Households (No. 24, *guo fa* [2007]), specifying that 'affordable housing belongs to policy-oriented housing and the buyer owns limited property rights' and that 'affordable housing are supplied to urban low-income households with housing difficulties'. It also defines an exit

mechanism: affordable housing may not be traded directly on the market until five years after the purchase; the buyer may then obtain full property right if he or she pays land income and other proceedings to the government; if the family owning an affordable house buys another property, the affordable house may be taken back by the government according to relevant regulations.

December 2007	Seven departments, including Ministry of Construction, printed and distributed the Administrative Measures for Affordable Housing.

Source: Ren Xingzhou, *Housing Security in China's New Social Welfare System* (Background Report, 2008).

The process of housing 'marketization' has accelerated with ongoing housing reforms. The development of systems for supplying housing has meant that 'affordable housing' has been constantly modified and improved in terms of its scope of eligible applicants and beneficiaries. A whole series of problems in actual implementation still need to be addressed, however.

'Reasonably-priced housing', a housing assistance policy introduced in some places in recent years, focuses on urban medium-low income groups, i.e. those 'squeezed in the middle'. This is housing that is 'commoditized', or sold on the market, but for which prices must be kept below a certain range. It is 'restricted-price housing'. Problems with the policy include imperfect policy design, lack of consistency in implementation across the country, and failure to achieve its designed end; thus it needs further experiments and improvement. The drawbacks of reasonably-priced housing become apparent, particularly when housing prices fluctuate (and especially when market prices fluctuate downwards).

Box 9.3 Housing policy of the United States

The United States is one of those countries that have been relatively successful in resolving its housing problems. Most land is privately owned, so the US government achieves goals of housing affordability mainly through project financing, tax incentives, and other house financing and development policies.

1 Housing supply by different categories. The US first began to implement a system of housing supply by different categories in 1930. Under this system, 'commodity' housing [housing as a good for sale] is supplied to the 20 percent of total households who earn a high-income. For the 62 percent of middle-income people, in addition to such measures as providing them with long-term mortgage loans and reducing

---

taxes by being able to deduct the interest of homebuyers, low-interest loans are provided to real estate companies, encouraging them to build more 'social housing' for which prices are controlled; the 18 percent low-income people may live in a house for a rent below the rate prescribed by the government, with the government providing a subsidy equal to the part of the rent above 25 percent of the tenant's income. The high-, middle- and low-income lines are announced by cities each year.

2   Tax and interest reduction for homebuyers. The US government allows middle-income people who buy a home with mortgage loans to deduct from their income taxes a certain percentage of the monthly interest on the loan. In addition, there is no tax on the increase in value of the property [no value-added tax]. For example, in 2003, 150 million people across the country benefited from being able to deduct mortgage loan interest from their income when paying federal individual income tax. In 2004, interest reductions and exemptions on housing mortgage loans, together with other tax preferences for homeowners, exceeded $100 billion.

In addition to the exemption of individual income tax concerning interest expenditure for housing mortgage loans, other tax policies for homeowners include reduction and exemption of real estate tax and capital gains tax on housing sales, and low-interest loans supported by tax-exempt bonds for first-time homebuyers. The tax incentive policies relating to rented housing mainly include: housing tax subsidies for low-income people, tax subsidies for historic-monument protection and low-interest loans supported by tax-exempt bonds.

3   Housing subsidies. In addition to the above-mentioned tax preferences, the federal government also provides three types of subsidy. The first is project-based, in support of the construction of specific housing projects, including the public housing program originated in 1937, as well as the subsidy under 'Section 8: New Projects'[4] for housing building for all low-income people. The second is helping low-income people obtain housing on the private housing market. The government provides low-income households with housing rent coupons to pay the part of the maximum locally acceptable rent above 30 percent of the tenants' before-tax income. The third is providing funds to state and local governments, letting them develop housing programs of their own. The main form is that the federal government provides funds to state and local governments and the latter develop specific housing programs by themselves.

Currently, nearly 6.9 million low-income households receive a certain type of housing rent subsidy, mostly in the form of government subsidies to low-rent private houses (2 million dwellings in total). Besides, 1.8 million dwellings are backed by 'housing renting coupons' and 1.2 million by the public housing programs. The remaining

1.9 million dwellings receive low-income housing tax subsidy, tax-free multi-dwelling housing bonds and HOME program subsidy. The US government has financially aided a majority of households in the form of housing subsidy, which is a reflection of the social equity principle.

4 Housing mortgage loan and guaranty. Middle-income homebuyers may apply for a combination of policy-oriented loans (at lower interest rates) and commercial loans for a term up to 30 years, with the property purchased as collateral and 30 percent of the housing price paid for the first instalment. At the same time, the government would provide guaranty for residents buying housing.

5 Financing support. The US government supports the establishment of a policy-oriented housing banking system, to provide financial support to middle- and low-income residents for building, buying or renting houses. Combined with the large number of commercial banks, the government-supported housing loan system has played an important role in improving house financing, raising funds for housing construction and providing policy-oriented and commercial mortgage loans.

The US house financing model has also caused problems recently. Loan agencies grant housing mortgage loans to households with low credit standing and income, which leads to a large number of sub-prime loans. These loans, after securitization, are sold worldwide. When the real estate market goes up, these packaged securitized products bring considerable profits to commercial and investment banks, and more and more banks are driven by high profits to participate in the waves of sub-prime loans and grant sub-prime loans to increasing numbers of people ineligible for credit standards. When housing prices go down, cases of repayment in arrears and banks revoking mortgage keep increasing, and the properties of many households become negative assets overnight. In mid-2007, a sub-prime crisis emerged and severely affected the financial market and system of the US and even of the entire world.

Source: Alex F. Schwartz: *Housing Policy in the United States*, China CITIC Press, 2008. Li Jian and Zhu Xiaohui: 'Social Housing Security Systems in European and American Countries and Their Inspiration to China', published in *China Real Estate Finance*, Issue 8, 2004. Bao Zonghua, 'Housing for Middle and Low-income People: What Should the Government Be Responsible for', published in *Outlook Weekly*, Issue 41, October 2005.

Mutual aid system

China's 'mutual aid system' is an arrangement among homeowners to assist each other. It is also a government-backed housing security system, with the housing accumulation fund as one of its important components. Essentially, the fund is co-paid by employers and their employees in equal amount and individual accounts are set up for employees so that funds are used for the specific purpose. A management committee, led and supervised by the government, formulates rules for the pooled accumulation fund; local accumulation fund management centers are in charge of fund operations. Accumulated funds are exempted from individual income tax. Pooled accumulated funds may be used to repay housing loans as prescribed, at an interest rate lower than the prevailing housing loan rate of commercial banks. At present the operation and management of the fund is governed mainly by the State Council's *Regulations on Management of Housing Accumulation Fund* (as revised in March 2002).

By the end of June 2007 the total number of urban employees enrolled in the housing accumulation fund system had exceeded 100 million, with over RMB 1.4 trillion in pooled funds. Nearly RMB 550 billion were drawn by employees for buying or building housing, or upon retirement, and personal housing loans granted amounted to over RMB 730 billion; 42 million employees across the country improved their housing conditions by drawing from the fund and by taking out an accumulated fund loan.

China has made initial steps in constructing the overall framework for a housing security system, given the three main types of housing policies above.

Current housing security system problems

Although a legal framework has been introduced for housing security, many problems still exist due to China's rapid urbanization and its ever-widening income disparities. Problems include implementation of the policies, range of security provided and so on, and they are in urgent need of attention.

Problems with implementation of the low-rent housing system

The main problems with the implementation of the low-rent housing system are as follows: first, inadequate coverage. By the end of 2006, 70 cities at the prefectural level and above and most counties nationwide had not yet established the 'low-rent housing system'. Housing security beneficiaries are most often defined as 'recipients of minimum living allowances' in the urban areas, which represents a failure to cover all those in need. According to a 2005 housing survey by the Ministries of Construction and Civil Affairs on minimum living allowance recipients, 4,439,000 households across the country were eligible for local low-rent housing, but only 7.7 percent of them, or 341,000 households, had actually benefited from the policy. By May 2005, a total of 14,000 households in the eight urban districts of Beijing had benefited from the low-rent housing policy, accounting for only 1 percent of the registered population of these districts. The policy had not been implemented at all in some outer suburban areas of the city (after the State Council's No. 24 document was announced and implemented in 2007, local governments have sped up their implementation of the policy, and the coverage has expanded significantly).

Second, lack of stable funding sources: housing security funds are severely inadequate, especially in the economically less developed region of western China. According to a 2005 national survey conducted by the Ministry of Construction jointly with the Ministry of Civil Affairs in 12 western provinces, 1.5 million families receiving minimum living allowances had an average housing area of 45 square meters, and only 58,000 of them benefited from the low-rent housing.

Third, incomplete management agencies: currently, the majority of cities and counties have no specifically designated low-rent housing management departments that are equipped with full-time personnel. Especially at the grass-roots level, management resources are not readily available, department functions are not clearly defined, and there are no independent departments responsible for policy publicity, demographic census, examination and approval, proclamation and other essential work related to social security-oriented housing. This had led to low-quality basic management. The absence of the necessary information systems concerning housing ownership and individual credit have made it hard to identify the income and housing conditions of beneficiaries of housing security policies, and has limited their effectiveness in actual implementation.

Fourth, incomplete legal system for housing security: the policies intended for low-income households are inadequate and the legal system is incomplete. Departmental rules and regulations that have already been introduced have not yet effectively protected the housing rights and interests of low-income households. At present, the low-rent housing system provides either monetary subsidies or designated low-rent dwellings. 'Monetary subsidies' mean that the local government grants a subsidy to urban low-income households with housing problems, who may then rent a house of their own choice. 'Designated low-rent dwellings' mean that the local government may provide designated dwellings to them, and collect the stipulated rent. Among the two methods we must focus firmly on the latter, providing low-rent dwellings rather than a subsidy to improve the housing conditions of low-income households. The top priority for the moment is to increase the quantity of such dwellings. For those cities short of low-rent dwellings, more of them should be made available either through procurement or new developments.

With regard to creating more low-rent housing, innovative policies should also be explored. It is by no means necessary for the government to invest in all the low-rent housing; it may also be funded by other investors, and the government may take out a long-term lease at a rational price and use it for low-rent facilities. In fact this is an effective way to leverage limited amounts of government funds and bring about the maximum possible benefit in housing security. As long as the long-term rent that the government pays to the builder is higher than the prevailing bank rate for deposits, this approach can be quite feasible. For non-government investors this approach will bring them stable income over a long period of time; for the government, it can obtain low-rent houses without investing large sums of money. At present, some local governments are purchasing housing from market by means of 'reverse auction' and distributing them as affordable housing.

Problems with implementation of the affordable housing system

The affordable housing system has had different goals in the different stages of China's housing reform. However, judgments made in the early days, and systems design based on those judgments, are no longer in alignment with current reality. In actual implementation of 'affordable housing' policies, therefore, certain problems have become extremely pronounced and the negative social response to these problems has been intense.

First, decreasing supply. With real estate markets developing fast, urban land and housing prices have been rising extremely fast. To increase income from land transfers, some municipal governments, who were affected by a certain mentality of having to 'operate' the city [in a way that turned a profit] were less than proactive in carrying out the affordable housing policy. This was manifested by decreasing investments in and decreasing supply of supply of affordable housing. In 1998–2003 the aggregate area of affordable housing completed nationwide stood at 477 million square meters, which had helped ameliorate the housing problems of more than 6 million middle- and low-income households. By 2004, however, negative growth took place in affordable housing investment, and its percentage in total real estate investment decreased from 9 percent to 6.8 percent in 2003. In many places the building of affordable housing stopped altogether. In 2005 investment in affordable housing stood at RMB 51.9 billion, 4.8 percent of the total real estate investment and also the lowest since 1998 (see Table 9.5). The supply of affordable housing that could meet the needs of local residents was severely inadequate in medium-sized and large cities in particular. A notable increase in supply came after [policy changes in] 2007.

Second, unfairness in supply. According to the initial policy design, affordable housing should be geared to urban middle-income and low-income households. In reality, much 'affordable housing' was sold to medium-high and even high-

Table 9.5 National affordable housing investment, 1997–2006

Year	Commercial housing (RMB 100 million)	Affordable housing (RMB 100 million)	Affordable housing investment as a proportion of total investment in commercial housing (%)
1997	1,539.38	185.5	12
1998	2,081.56	270.85	13
1999	2,638.48	437.02	17
2000	3,311.98	542.44	16
2001	3,216.68	599.65	14
2002	5,227.76	589.05	11
2003	6,776.69	621.98	9
2004	8,836.95	606.39	6.8
2005	10,860.93	519.18	4.8
2006	13,638.41	696.84	5.1

Source: Ren Xingzhou, *Housing Security in China's New Social Welfare System* (Background Report, 2008).

income households, due to such factors as being overly highly-priced for the intended income groups and due to lack of transparent operations. More affluent people acquired more 'affordable housing' than poorer households, leading to the policy's failure to truly benefit those households in urgent need.

Third, poor management and inappropriate distribution. Local governments are not motivated to build affordable housing, and so fail to apply any kind of effective management to the process. The eligibility of buyers is defined in very vague terms, examination and approval procedures are loose, and the selling and management processes are non-transparent. In addition there is no control over construction standards. In many cities, overly large-size units are built, well beyond the 'basic security' standards, most constituting more than 80 square meters and some even 100 to 150 square meters. Some places, due to such considerations as getting an adequate return off inner-city land and the lower cost of more distant land, build affordable housing in the fringe areas of cities, where public transport is inconvenient and basic infrastructure is incomplete. This leads to considerably increased costs for the person living in the housing in terms of getting jobs, paying for commuting, and paying for schooling and, as a result, a lowered quality of life overall.

The affordable housing system has allowed a certain number of people with limited means to resolve their housing problems, but actual implementation of the policy has led to unintended consequences. The government has modified certain things due to this problem of results diverging from intentions. In the end, however, little has been achieved in terms of eliminating inequities arising from how affordable housing is distributed. Further exploration and improvement is needed.

To improve the affordable housing system innovative efforts should be made in the following respects: first, we should explore new operating and exit mechanisms, i.e. changing from open exit mode (direct selling on the market) to quasi-closed

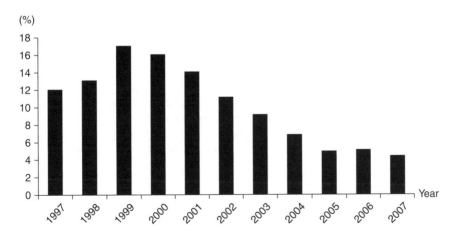

Figure 9.2 Affordable housing investment as a proportion of total investment in commercial housing, 1997–2007.

Source: Graph based on figures given in Table 9.3.

operating and exit mechanisms, under which the transaction process involves mainly government buyback, in order to guarantee the 'affordable' and 'security' aspect of the system. If affordable housing is allowed to be sold directly on the market, more rigorous conditions should be instituted, and a considerable part of the income from such sales should be handed over to the government to be used for building new affordable housing. Second, we should explore new ways of providing affordable housing subsidies and assistance. The current subsidy, the so called 'brick subsidy', concentrates mainly on the housing development and construction process [i.e. providing the 'bricks and mortar']. As a replacement, a 'headcount subsidy' should be gradually explored that provides cash subsidy directly to eligible applicants for housing security. Trial experiments have been made in this regard (see Box 9.4). The 'headcount subsidy' is easier to operate, more open and transparent, and requires less one-off investment from the government, which makes implementation of exit mechanisms far easier. In the long run, subsidies for building affordable housing should be reduced and replaced with monetary subsidies. Many countries have experienced such a progression as they implement housing security policies.

Box 9.4 Shift from 'brick subsidy' to 'headcount subsidy'

From 2003, Rizhao City of Shandong Province began to reform the way it handled the affordable housing security system. The reform was called 'marketizing land use, monetizing subsidies, giving people power to determine their own purchases, and making the process transparent'. This marked a shift from a 'brick subsidy' to a 'headcount subsidy'. The land used for affordable housing construction was sold by the various means of tenders, public auction, and listing. The net income from land sales was transferred into a special subsidy account for eligible applicants. Eligible low-income households with housing problems could buy the housing they selected. They received subsidies only after they had made the purchase. This new policy had excellent results. In the two years that followed, the government granted affordable housing subsidies of RMB 60 million, which mobilized the purchasing power of about RMB 200 million on the market. Some 94 percent of homebuyers bought second-hand housing, which in return spurred an increase in the trading volume of second-hand housing. In the meanwhile, no appeal to the higher authorities regarding affordable housing was filed. The policy of granting subsidies only for 'headcount' was effective in curbing corruption and abuse of power.

Source: Ren Xingzhou, *Housing Security in China's New Social Welfare System* (Background Report, 2008).

Lack of any 'mutual aid' of the housing accumulation fund system

Tremendous changes have taken place in the underlying environment in which the 'housing accumulation fund' operates, given the growth in the housing market over the past dozen or more years. Changes have also occurred in China's whole housing system reform. First, government-provided housing has switched to market-based distribution, and the ability of urban residents to buy housing has been improved by across-the-board subsidies from the government. Second, the framework for a multi-level housing security system has taken shape, covering all different levels of households and groups of people. At the same time, however, many problems have begun to exhibit themselves with regard to the housing accumulation fund. They are in tandem with the process of ongoing reforms in how China handles housing issues and the resulting very fast development of the real estate market. The most outstanding problem is that the fund has not at all served its mutual aid function. Not only has it not provided housing security to low-income people, but it has had the effect of worsening the disparities in income distribution. Contributions to housing accumulation funds are linked to personal wages and therefore also to the performance of the employers. As the income gap widens, there is an increasing gap in the percentage of subsidies put towards high-income and low-income people. The employer puts in 12 percent of a person's wages. If a person makes more, more goes into the accumulation fund for him, and the same is true of the government's contributions, since they exempt individual income tax. Contributions to the housing accumulation for different people vary dramatically. High-income employees are benefiting far more than those with low income. In addition, the system benefits those who are already not in need of it. Most high-income employers have their own housing, so housing accumulation funds have become a type of housing subsidy to them. Since high-income employees benefit most from the system, the whole process is exacerbating income disparities in cities. Another problem is inadequate coverage of the policy. The policy stipulates that

> In places where conditions permit, employers and the migrant rural workers they hire may make deposits into housing accumulation funds; private business owner and freelancers in urban areas may apply to make contributions to housing accumulation funds, with the wage base for monthly contributions calculated according to the monthly average taxable income in the previous year.[5]

In fact, however, many middle- and low-income employees, such as those from small private enterprises, do not currently have individual accounts in the housing accumulation fund, or they contribute nothing to their individual accounts due to the fluid state of their employment. Their wages contain no allowance for housing consumption, making them ineligible for applying for public cumulative fund loans. This has excluded those who are most in need of support from coverage under the policy.

Inadequate coverage

First, migrant rural workers and their families who enter cities to live and work are urgently in need of housing. Their housing problems have gradually attracted the attention of the Chinese government. In January 2008 five ministries, including the Ministry of Construction and the National Development and Reform Commission, jointly issued the *Guidance on Improving Housing Conditions of Migrant Rural Workers* (No. 276, *jian zhu fang* [2007]). This mandated improvement in the housing conditions of migrant rural workers, via multiple channels, and with considerable support from the government. Those firms which are employing the migrant workers should play the main role at the current stage in providing them with housing that meets basic health and safety conditions. Ideally, they can provide free or low-rent housing or dormitories to these workers, or they can provide housing through renting and purchase. Collective dormitories for migrant rural workers may be built on land that can be used for that purpose if it is within the legally granted rights of the enterprise and if the dormitories meet local planning requirements. If migrant rural workers can afford housing on their own, employers should provide them with subsidies and provide for it in labor contacts. As another option, housing appropriate for migrant rural workers can be built in places with favorable conditions according to policies that encourage low-rent housing construction—it can be leased at affordable prices. In addition, residents in city outskirts should be guided and encouraged to lease their houses to migrant rural workers (see Box 9.5). Looking at the problem from an overall perspective, China already has more than 140 million migrant rural workers, and the country has an urban population growing at faster than 1 percent every year. In the long run, this means that the massive number of migrant rural workers will gradually be incorporated into cities. However, the current housing security system does not yet cover migrant rural workers and their families in cities. It provides only in principle for improving the housing conditions of this group of people, 'through multiple channels'. It relies mainly on local governments and employers to build and provide collective dormitories. There have been no well-defined security system arrangements and specific policy measures to deal with housing for this group. From a long-term strategic perspective, to meet the demands of urbanization, it is absolutely necessary and utterly urgent that we provide migrant rural workers with access to housing.

Box 9.5   Local experience in solving the housing problems of migrant rural workers

1   Laiwu City, Shandong Province: migrant rural workers are entitled to the government's housing subsidy. According to regulations, they can receive a housing rent subsidy of about RMB 3,000 each year from the government as long as they have worked in Laiwu for three or more years. In addition, 96 'urban villages' of Laiwu have also been included in the government's housing security program. Laiwu regulations stipulate that any low-income households with housing difficulties in the 'urban villages', whether rural or non-rural households, may apply for a subsidy to rent or buy housing, and that the amount of rental subsidies has been increased from 50 percent to 60 percent of the average market rent.

2 Suzhou and Wuxi, Jiangsu Province: a group of dormitories and residential housing with basic facilities and public services has been built specifically for migrant rural workers. The process has used multiple channels, including the government building large-scale, standardized housing, enterprises building collective dormitories for their employees and rural collectives building apartments by using collective land.

3 Changsha, Hunan Province: apartment-like collective dormitories intended for migrant rural workers, together with low-rent housing with small living spaces, have been built in the outskirts of Changsha.

4 Chongqing: guided by the government, local neighborhood committees have turned vacant buildings and hostels into facilities that have the key features of being 'low-rent' and 'comfortable'. These are being called 'Porters' Apartments' and 'Sunshine Apartments' for migrant rural workers.

5 Huzhou, Zhejiang: a housing accumulation fund system for non-public enterprises has been established to create the underlying conditions to allow workers from other places to settle in and buy housing.

6 Dalian, Liaoning: the collective dormitories on all construction sites are required to equip each person with a single bed, rather than providing wide beds for a number of people, and to comply with unified regulations and standards that apply to dormitories, facilities, ventilation, lighting, toilets, kitchens, canteens and telephone booths.

Source: Ren Xingzhou, *Housing Security in China's New Social Welfare System* (Background Report, 2008).

Second, middle-income and low-income households with housing difficulties have no housing security. Debates continue as to whether or not to include these people into the housing security system. One view is that middle-income households should solve their own housing problems through market means since they have a degree of purchasing power, and that the government cannot include middle-income households within the scope of security, as that would bring even more pressure to bear on the government. Unfortunately, the rise in housing prices far outpaces the income growth of middle-income households. They are in fact unable to solve their housing problems solely on their own. According to international practice, a family's income should be one-fourth to one-sixth of the price of housing that the family purchases—this an appropriate amount to spend on housing. If loans are taken into consideration, annual outlay on housing should be below 40 percent of family income. In China the amount spent on purchasing housing is more than six times the average income in most large and middle-sized cities. In large cities such as Beijing, Shanghai, Shenyang, Guiyang, Nanjing, Guangzhou, Dalian and Xi'an, people spend 10 times their annual household income to purchase their own housing.

Take Beijing as an example: in 2007 the per capita disposable income of the middle-income population was RMB 19,883, and the average household income was RMB 57,661 as calculated by the statistical size of 2.9 persons per household. When calculated on the loosest housing price/income ratio at 10:1, the average housing price affordable to middle-income citizens was RMB 576,610 for an apartment. In terms of housing area, in 2008, the per capita housing area of the middle-income population was 39.54 square meters, and 29.50 square meters for low-income population. On that basis, the housing area of middle-income households should be 115 square meters, and 85 square meters for low-income households. To ensure an area of 115 square meters of housing space for middle-income households, the housing price per square meter should be RMB 5,014. It should be RMB 6,784 to ensure the least area of 85 square meters. But in 2007 the average housing price in the city was already RMB 10,661 per square meter. This shows that housing prices in the city are far beyond the affordability of middle-income citizens. It should be noted that 'residency rights' in China have a duration of only 70 years, equivalent to a 1.4 percent annual depreciation.[6]

Under the present system in China, 'local government' derives all of the income from land assets and retains the major part of any property taxes paid on land. They depend heavily on real estate development and real estate taxes to make up budgetary shortfalls and to stimulate the local economy. In 2001–2003 income derived by local governments from transfers of land came to RMB 910 billion, about 35 percent of all local financial revenues nationwide during the same period. In 2004 total land transfer fees came to RMB 589.4 billion, which was 47 percent of local financial revenues during the period. In 2005, in the context of stringent government policies that were attempting to stem the outflow of land resources, the land transfer fees still amounted to RMB 550.5 billion. In 2006 the total land transfer income stood at RMB 767.7 billion. Land transfer income has thus become a second source of financing for local governments.[7] At the same time, there is no motivation for local governments to create social security-oriented housing, since there is no pay-out from it. According to statistics the local governments' investment in affordable housing for middle- and low-income households has been small to negligible. In 2004, national investment in affordable housing began to take on negative growth. Investment in affordable housing, as a percentage of investment in all real estate development, decreased from 6.1 percent in 2003 to 4.6 percent in 2004; in 2005–2007 the percentage was only about 3 percent.[8] During this period local governments took in huge amounts of net income from land and various taxes as housing prices increased. After acquiring the land-use rights from local governments, real estate developers transferred the costs to housing buyers, causing housing prices to soar. In the meantime the limited quantities of social security-oriented housing made it hard for lower-income households to find housing.

Box 9.6 Home ownership policy in Singapore

Singapore had a total population of 1.58 million when it achieved autonomy in 1959. Out of 1.58 million, 750,000 people had no housing at all and 500,000 lived in slums and sheds. To solve the basic housing problems of people in the context of too great a population for very limited land, in the 1960s the Singaporean government enacted the *Housing & Development Act*, and set up the Housing & Development Board (HDB) to implement a plan called 'Home Ownership'. This was aimed at resolving the housing difficulties of low and middle-income residents. By the mid 1990s, HDB had implemented seven 'Five-Year Plans for Housing & Development'. According to the Singaporean population census conducted in 2000, in that year, 88 percent of households lived in public housing and 92 percent of the population was 'housed', showing that the housing security problem had basically been solved. Singapore has realized the goal of Home Ownership within a period of less than 50 years. The main lessons derived from this are as follows.

1   Robust financial support for construction. As a statutory agency subordinate to the Ministry of National Development, HDB is the largest housing developer and public housing management body in Singapore. HDB has the following three funding sources. The first is government housing loan. This loan is transformed from the housing accumulation fund; collected by the Central Accumulation Fund Board, except for the provision of money to be drawn by the members, the rest of the accumulation fund is all used to purchase state bonds that are loaned to HDB. The loan interest rate is 2 percent higher than the deposit interest rate of accumulation fund, and 2 percent lower than the market rate, which was 5.1 percent in 1995; the loan has a 20-year term, and the amount each year stands at about SGD 1 billion. The second is housing purchase loan. Residents may pay by instalments when buying housing. When a resident has bought housing from HDB, HDB will provide an instalment credit and advance a working fund, thus requiring housing purchase loan from the government; the interest of this loan is 0.1 percent higher than the deposit rate of accumulation fund, which was 3.1 percent in 1995, with a term of 20 years. The government has so far provided HDB with a total of housing purchase loan of SGD 13 billion since 1968, when it introduced its scheme of purchasing public housing with accumulation funds. The third is government subsidy—because the rent and price for public housing are determined by the government, which are far lower than the market prices, HDB operates at a loss. Therefore, the government arranges a subsidy to HDB each year from its financial budget. From the founding of HDB in 1960 to the end of 1994, the government had provided HDB with a total subsidy of SGD 5,060 million. The actual beneficiaries of this subsidy are those living in public housing.

2   The government's land policy. In Singapore, land is owned by both the state and private persons. Some 80 percent of all land is owned by the state. In 1966 the Singaporean government enacted the *Land Acquisition Act*, which provided that any land, anywhere in Singapore, can be

acquired to build public housing, and HDB can acquire land at a purchase price far lower than that at which private developers could acquire it. HDB's acquisition of massive quantities of land at lower prices ensures successful construction of public housing. To date, HDB occupies more than 40 percent of all land in Singapore.

3   Housing supply by classifications. In Singapore, very rich residents account for about 3 percent of the country's population. HDB is not responsible for providing public housing to these people, who purchase housing directly from the real estate market. The government allocates land for building housing for them, but charges high land transfer fees when they are being built, and relatively high annual management fees [*wu-ye-fei*] when these people settle in these houses.

The 80 percent of middle-income residents purchase public housing provided by HDB. To accelerate fund turnover and thus increase the speed of housing construction, the government encourages households to buy public housing. Households with monthly income at SGD 800–5,000 may buy public housing, and those with monthly income at SGD 5,000–8,000 may purchase higher-grade apartments. Buyers may pay by installments, with the first installment being 20 percent of the housing price, and for the remainder they can apply to HDB for a loan with a term ranging from 5 to 25 years, with the interest rate 0.1 percent higher than the deposit rate of accumulated funds and 2–4 percent lower than the market interest rate. If the loan is paid by instalments over 25 years, the deposit in ordinary account of housing accumulation fund is enough to set off the monthly instalment. A total of 80 percent of Singaporean residents have bought public housing, the 3 percent richest residents have bought housing intended for them, and the remaining 17 percent cannot afford public housing. Singapore divides these 17 percent residents into poor and very poor households, each being roughly 8.5 percent of the total population, and has taken measures to solve their housing problems as the national economy grows. The measures taken in recent years include: subsidies to enable each poor household to buy around 60 to 70 square meters of inexpensive second-hand housing; and renting 42 square meters of low-rent housing to every very poor household, by charging a symbolic amount every month of some 10 Singaporean dollars. Having solved the housing problems of poor and very poor households, the country has achieved its goal of providing every citizen in the country with access to housing.

Sources:

1 Wang Ningnan, *Public Housing Policy in Singapore and Its Value of Reference*, published in *Southeast Asian Affairs,* Issue 2, 2001.
2 Bao Zonghua, *The Importance of Housing Price Control as Seen from Singaporean and Germany Experience*, published in *China Real Estate Information*, Issue 8, 2004.
3 Zhang Qiguang, *Housing and Accumulation Fund Systems in Singapore and Their Reference Value to China*, published in *Beijing Real Estate*, Issue 10, 1996.

Finally, the housing problems of rural poor households have not yet been raised to an institutional level. At present, although there is plenty of available data on trial practices (see Box 9.7), this task has not yet been lifted to the policy-making process. Each place carries out its own methods, with no timely summing-up of experience and application to other places, and with none of the necessary institutional arrangements and policy guidance.

Box 9.7 Shanxi's exploration and practice in providing 'housing assistance' to rural poor households

Shanxi Province has already initiated a project to provide 'housing assistance' to rural poor households. The project aims to arrange housing for 3,000 households in 2008, to solve the housing problems of 70,000 very poor households living in sub-standard housing within 5 years, and to basically have solved the housing problems of rural poor residents by 2020. The major housing problems rural poor residents face is that either housing is very badly built and has also not been repaired for a long time, or that it is primitive and crude. According to survey, there are 400,000 households with housing problems in Shanxi's rural areas, accounting for 6.46 percent of all rural households. Among them, about 70,000 households, or 17.5 percent, live in dilapidated housing. Attaching great important to this issue, the provincial Party committee and government listed the project of 'housing assistance' among the important tasks of the provincial government for 2008, and decided to make initial pilot experiments in Youyu County. The project targeted those 'recipients of five guarantee households' (unable to live in a centralized way) who live not only without housing but at a level substantially below the rural poverty line, MLA (minimum living allowance) recipients, and marginal poor people who, though not qualified for MLA under the current system, have been trapped in serious financial difficulties. The project plans to subsidize every such household with a sum of RMB 11,000, with contributions in a 4:3:3 ratio from provincial, municipal and county finance. Subject to the household's decision, one of four different methods can be chosen—new building, rebuilding, repair, or replacement—are adopted for centralized arrangement or decentralized solution. The standard for the newly built houses is that one-person households enjoy an area of about 25 square meters; two-person households enjoy about 45 square meters. Currently, construction at six sites for building new houses for 401 households in Youyu County has commenced, and houses of 599 households are under repair or replacement. Youyu County is one of the 35 counties designated as 'poverty-stricken' by the Central government. What can be done in Youyu County can surely also be done elsewhere.

Source: Ren Xingzhou, *Housing Security in China's New Social Welfare System* (Background Report, 2008).

Objectives of housing security systems

China's housing security is currently the bottleneck of the entire social security system. The country's housing security policy focuses on social fairness and the basic housing needs of residents, aiming especially at affordability. The income growth of most urban residents is slower than that of housing prices and it is difficult for middle and low-income people to get access to housing via the regular market. Therefore, a complete housing security system must be established in order to meet the housing needs of these people. Of course it will take a long time for China, as a developing country, to establish a complete housing security system for both urban and rural residents.

The principles and framework governing the housing security system

The basic principle governing housing security is 'universal coverage, basic security and sustainability'. 'Universal coverage' means that the housing security system should cover both urban and rural residents, including migrant rural workers who are facing particular problems. 'Basic security' means that the housing security system should provide appropriate security as appropriate according to the income level of households, housing price/income ratio, housing affordability and current housing conditions. 'Sustainability' means that the housing security system should take the country's conditions into consideration and determine a moderate level of security that accords with the supporting capacity of public finance and the economy, and the carrying capacity of land and resources—once determined, it should gradually improve upon that level. Housing security should be provided for two levels of need: 'relief' in more urgent cases, and 'assistance' in less urgent cases.

The overall framework for the process involves improving the housing 'relief' and 'assistance' systems on the foundation of the existing housing security system. Housing relief mainly takes the form of providing low-rent housing; housing assistance focuses on improving affordable housing and providing housing subsidies. Within this framework, our tasks are the following: definitively solve the housing problems of low-income people; explore solutions to housing difficulties facing urban middle-income groups, those 'caught in the middle'; gradually incorporate households who have worked in cities and lived in substandard housing into the housing security program; and adopt and improve measures to solve housing problems confronting rural households (see Table 9.6).

Appropriate security standards

Basic housing security standards should be established on the basis of the national conditions, after taking into consideration both the basic housing needs of assisted residents and the limited land and resources. Somewhat lower security standards may be fixed at first and then be gradually improved as the economy develops. In this regard the experience of other countries in matching their level of housing security to their level of development may be used. China's current level of

Table 9.6 The future framework of China's housing security system

Beneficiary	Modes	Measures	Approaches	Providers
Urban middle-income households	Housing assistance	Reasonably-priced housing Affordable housing Housing subsidy	Mainly sold, with interest subsidy and tax reduction Mainly sold Subsidy in cash	Government, employer
Urban low-income households	Housing assistance Housing relief	Affordable housing Housing subsidy Low-rent housing	Mainly sold Subsidy in cash Provide directly to eligible applicants, subsidy	Government
Urban lowest-income households	Housing relief	Low-rent housing	Provide directly to eligible applicants, subsidy	Government
Households of migrant rural workers	Housing relief	Low-rent housing	Provide directly to eligible applicants, subsidy	Government, employer
Rural poor households	Housing relief	House building subsidy	Subsidy	Government, village committee

industrialization and urbanization is roughly equivalent to what Europe and Japan experienced in the 1960s. Their standards at the time provide a valuable benchmark for China. In 1958 Europe's standard housing space per 3-person family was 46 square meters, or around 15.3 square meters per capita. Europe's available space was greater, and its population density lower, than that of Japan which had less space per person: about 39 square meters in building area for 3-person family, equivalent to about 35 square meters in useable floor area, meaning 11.6 square meters per capita. The per capita floor area in China's cities currently stands at about 26 square meters. If we set the 'housing security standard' for per capita space at 50 percent of the urban average, namely 13 square meters, that should be a feasible goal. At the same time the security should assure that basic needs of people are met, such as independent kitchens and toilets.

Coverage

The new housing security system aims at providing every citizen in the country with access to housing. In this system, housing relief and assistance, and low-rent housing in particular, are mainly aimed at solving the housing problems of low-income households. They constitute a part of China's anti-poverty policies. In our way of reckoning, low-income people in China are mainly divided into three categories: i) recipients of the 'minimum living allowance', most of whom are elderly people with no family, those who are disabled and those who cannot work—all those who clearly are unable to get housing on their own; ii) low-income households who have severe housing problems and cannot improve the situation since their income can only meet their basic subsistence needs; iii) the rural floating population, mainly migrant rural workers, who still fall into the category of low-income groups when they work in cities. These three groups should be the main targets of housing relief and assistance. Housing assistance is intended mainly to solve the housing problems of middle- and low-income households with buying ability. As the economy develops, its percentage of middle-and low-income households will constantly increase and these households will become an important mainstay for China, key in increasing domestic demand and maintaining social stability. Through specific policies the government should guarantee supply of social security-oriented housing, should effectively regulate and control housing prices, and should provide affordable housing to these households by means of interest subsidies, tax reductions, rent subsidies and so on.

Staged objectives

The implementation of the housing security system can be divided into the following two stages. These stages are a part of the overall the process of building a moderately prosperous society in an all-round way by the year 2020.

Stage 1: 2009–2012 (4 years). Gradually improve upon the current housing security system. Major tasks:

- Improve the urban housing security system. All the cities at county level and above should ensure provision of low-rent housing and rent subsidies to eligible minimum living allowance recipients. (According to a survey conducted by relevant government departments, in 2005 there were 4 million such recipients living in less than ten square meters' housing per capita.) About 50 percent of urban low-income households with housing difficulties should be covered by the housing security system (mainly the low-rent housing system), and the housing conditions for low-income households should be considerably improved. Assistance of various forms will be provided to middle and low-income households with housing difficulties.
- Put our best efforts into improving the housing situation of migrant rural workers. That should be the primary task in our efforts to solve housing problems facing urban low-income households. When conditions permit, resident migrant rural workers should be incorporated into the urban housing security system, to allow them to enjoy the same housing security standards as urban residents. In addition, we should take proactive policy measures to assure that 10 percent of cross-regional migrant rural workers have access to low-rent housing by 2010, and to assure that the housing conditions for all of them will be considerably improved by the early '12th Five-Year Plan' period.
- Explicitly put 'solving the housing problems of rural poor households' on the government's agenda of implementing the housing security system, and gradually repair the dilapidated housing of rural 'minimum living allowance'

recipients. We should try to provide housing building subsidies to 2.6 million rural poor households by 2012, with the amount of subsidy arriving at RMB 7,200 for each household.

Stage 2: During the eight years between 2013 and 2020, basically form a new housing security system that provides appropriate housing to urban and rural households. In building this system the main tasks are: further improve the urban housing security system, improve the present forms of security and explore new ones, and provide middle- and low-income groups of people with access to effective security measures; provide housing subsidies to all urban low-income households with housing difficulties; include households of migrant rural workers who usually live and work in cities in the housing security system, allowing them to enjoy the same housing security level as urban residents. By 2020, assure that 30 percent of all cross-regional migrant rural workers receive housing security subsidies. Basically make sure that all migrant rural workers who live in substandard housing in cities are covered. Improve the social relief and assistance systems for rural households with housing difficulties. In addition, set up a housing relief system that is targeted at rural poor residents, seek funding through multiple channels and relief approaches. By 2020, seek to completely resolve the housing emergencies of the poorest and most needy in the country.

Policy recommendations

Accelerate the legislative process that addresses housing security, in order to provide the legal foundation for implementing this system

As an important social policy, our housing security system must have the assurance of long lasting and stable institutional security. It therefore requires effective legal support. The international practice is to have housing security included in all general comprehensive laws, such as the constitution and the civil code. These mainly specify the following: i) that it is the basic right of citizens to enjoy appropriate housing;[9] ii) that providing housing security is an objective of governmental activity; that guaranteeing the basic housing conditions of its citizens is a key manifestation of a government; and iii) the precise means of achieving housing security.[10] Special housing security laws state in a detailed way the housing security objectives, security standards, sources of security funds, setup of special management boards and the division of authority, and specify the division of labor and responsibility between Central and local governments and between special agencies. Currently there is no such housing security law in China. Many housing policies have been promulgated in the form of official documents ('red-headlined documents'), but their authority and degree of severity are inadequate. This has led to *ad hoc* or irresponsible implementation, due to the lack of any legal constraints. We recommend that, at the earliest possible time, the government undertake research for the drafting of a law called *Housing Security Regulations*. In legal terms, this should specify the targeted population of 'housing security' (the 'objects'), security standards, level of security, sources of security funds, security management agencies and punishments for infringing the law. This should be promulgated as soon as possible, so that the housing security system has a legal foundation.

Develop national and local housing security programs as required by the new institutional framework, and put them into effect as soon as possible

The new housing security system framework, which was designed according to the principle of 'universal coverage, basic security and sustainability', is visionary to a certain degree but is also feasible. It is consistent both with the concept of being 'human-oriented', and with our stated purpose of aiming for 'scientific' development. We should attempt to publicize its importance nationwide, as soon as possible, to form a common understanding at high political as well as grass-roots levels. We should then, as required by the framework of the new system, realize Five-Year Plans at both the national and local level, and annual implementation plans. We also should try to specify housing security objectives in the national and local '12th Five-Year' plans, as well as annual implementation plans and measures, so that the housing security system can be implemented in a down-to-earth manner. In addition to strengthening housing security objectives and measures for urban low-income residents with housing difficulties, these plans should specify the housing security objectives and measures for migrant rural workers. Eastern cities with favorable conditions should be encouraged to include housing for migrant rural workers into their urban housing security systems. In addition we should specify housing assistance measures for urban middle- and low-income people.

Ensure that government spending is the primary source of housing security funds and that housing security funds are raised through multiple channels

The capacity of public finance to pay for the system is the key to its sustainability; to a great extent, methods of financing the system will determine how effective it will be in its operations. To ensure sustainability, expenditures for housing secu-rity must definitely be included in fiscal budgets, and the percentage allocated to housing should be specified. In the immediate period, proper oversight should ensure that funds for the system come from local land transfers. The policy is that 'a specific percentage of local net income from land-transfer transactions (no less than 10 percent) must be used for low-rent housing construction'. (In 2005 the net income nationwide from land transfers totaled about RMB 218 billion. If 10 percent of this amount had been used for low-rent housing construction, the amount would have been 3.1 times the actual investment in low-rent housing construction across the country in 2006.) In the future, specific percentages of budgets should be marked for housing security. This should be done as we reform the tax system and adjust the government budgeting system. Specified channels and specified percentages should be earmarked from both State and local budgets for the purpose of housing security, so that we gradually reduce the percentage of housing security expenditures that come directly from land transfer income. Urban land transfer fees in various regions differ considerably. In 2005, for example, the eastern region took in 62.4 percent of all land-transfer revenue, the central region 16.7 percent, and the western region 20.8 percent. Even within the same region some small cities and western cities had small amounts of land transfer fees. Therefore the percentage of such revenue devoted to low-rent housing expenditures should differ by regions: land transfer income should take a bigger proportion in economically developed eastern areas, while in economically less-developed central and western China, government spending at various levels should take a bigger proportion. In addition, efforts should be made to explore possible funding channels for housing security through the means of financial innovation. For example, funds can be collected through trust funds of real estate investment trusts, to provide long-term financial support to low-rent housing. In the meantime, the governments should also provide special 'housing-reform subsidies' to middle- and low-income groups, to be used for subsidizing interest rates, for market adjustments, and for preferential tax treatment of various kinds. The idea is to use centralized policy measures to address the housing difficulties of middle and low-income groups as well as migrant rural workers.

Improve the operational mechanisms for housing security

The present housing security mechanisms are inadequate. We should specify the eligibility, rotation and retreat mechanisms for various programs, to ensure that policies will not be skewed in practice, and that participants in the programs truly do benefit. At the same time, since housing security management is quite a specialized skill, it is also very necessary to build the organizational capacity to handle it. We must establish and improve related management bodies and improve the housing security management system. Resolving housing problems is a long-term and complex task, so we should encourage the timely analysis of local experience, summarize it and apply it to the overall planning and coordination. We want to make sure that useful experience is publicized in a timely fashion so that problems can be solved more effectively.

Explore new modes of developing and constructing social security-oriented housing

At present, social security-oriented housing is built on the outskirts of cities, which is not only inconvenient for low-income residents but increases the costs of finding and commuting to jobs, as well as schooling costs. We recommend that the two issues of spatial layout of security housing and urban land transfers be combined. That is, the construction of social security-oriented housing and housing for resettlement should be built into the process of tenders, auctions and listings for land, so that people with different incomes can enjoy urban public spaces and facilities. This will facilitate the daily lives, employment and schooling of low-income residents, and help create a more harmonious society.

Promote the steady development of the housing market and reduce the negative effect of real estate bubbles

The healthy and steady development of the housing market relates to the implementation of the housing security system and security policies in a very direct way. Housing prices and the structure of supply and demand are tightly linked to housing security policies. Both domestic and foreign real estate market practices suggest that, when the market develops steadily and the housing price/income ratio (the ratio of the household's spending on buying housing to its annual income) remains at a rational level, pressure on the government is relatively small and the purchasing capacity of low-income groups is relatively strong. When the housing price/income ratio increases considerably, the purchasing capacity of low-income households becomes weak, housing difficulties grow and the government's security burden gets heavier. Therefore, promoting healthy development of the housing market is also an important part of building the housing security system. Price hikes in the market should be avoided by means of necessary regulation and control policies, especially the land transfer policy.

Improve the land policy and stabilize the supply of land for constructing social security-oriented housing

In those countries in which the government owns a portion of the land, one means of providing affordable housing for low- and middle-income people is to transfer that land at low prices for the use of low-rent housing. The government is able to control land costs and housing prices as a result. This measure is used in addition to national credit policies for homeowners, subsidies and the use of capital markets. In China, land transfers are an important source of income for local governments. China should continually change its land policies in this regard, so that land transfer becomes a less important source of income for local finance. At the same time, when they make their annual land-supply plans, local governments should be encouraged to give priority to land supply for the construction of social security-oriented housing. Local governments should supply land for building middle- and low-priced ordinary housing of modest-to-small size, to ensure supply to middle- and low-income people. Localities should avoid building low-rent housing in dense clusters, but should spread such housing out among 'commodity' or more upscale housing, so as to prevent the creation of slums. Localities should also guard against building low-rent housing in remote areas that only increase the housing and transport costs of low-income households.

Pay attention to and strengthen housing assistance to middle-income households with housing difficulties

A very large percentage of the Chinese population is now 'middle-income'. Since Chinese real estate prices are rising much faster than the income of these people, however, despite their purchasing power, they cannot solve their housing problems all by themselves. If this situation continues it will be hard to reach the goal of creating a harmonious society through making housing available to all. All countries recognize that resolving housing for its middle class is of extreme importance. Learning from international experience, the Chinese government can help this group get access to housing in such ways as subsidizing lower interest rates, providing preferential tax policies, and subsidizing rent. This is done to ensure a steady supply of housing and to stabilize real estate prices.

Strengthen the accountability system for local governments as they implement the housing security system

The housing security system is implemented mainly by local governments. Therefore, under the present policy framework, with an incomplete legal system to address the problems, more efforts should made to strengthen the accountability of local governments as they implement housing security measures. Local governments must be made to recognize that they have a responsibility to conserve land. They also have a responsibility to carry out housing security measures so that each citizen of China is able to be properly housed.

Notes

1 See Li and Zhao, 'Changes in the Distribution of Wealth in China, 1995–2002' in Jim Davies (ed.), *Global Distribution of Personal Wealth* (Oxford University Press, 2008).
2 *Beijing Statistical Yearbook 2008.*
3 See *China Statistical Abstract 2008.*
4 It is stated in Section 8 of *the Housing and Community Development Act* amended by the Nixon administration in 1974, that any households with family income below 40 percent of the local average family income are regarded as low-income households and entitled to subsidy; the benefitted households, regardless of how much they earn, use 30 percent of their family income as housing rent, and the balance between the remaining income and market rent is subsided in the form of rent subsidy coupons granted by the government. This famous Section 8 has proved to be very successful over the 30-plus years and helped the majority of low-income classes mitigate the burden of housing consumption.
5 *Guiding Opinions on Several Problems with Management of Housing Accumulation Funds*, issued jointly by the Ministry of Construction, the Ministry of Finance and the People's Bank of China, published on People's Daily Online (http://politics.people.com.cn).
6 Calculated according to *Beijing Statistical Yearbook 2008.*
7 Website of the Ministry of Land and Resources (http://www.mlr.gov.cn).
8 *China Statistical Yearbook 2008.*

9 For example, it is stated in the Swedish Constitution that 'it is the social right of the national people to enjoy good residential environment and spacious housing conditions'.

10 For example, Australia developed a detailed housing subsidy scheme that is regulated and guaranteed through legislation, and introduced the Housing Subsidy Act of 1989 and the Housing Subsidy Act of 1996. The laws ensured the effective implementation of housing policies and schemes.

10 Basic living allowance system

In China, the term that is usually used for 'providing a basic standard of living' is the 'minimum living allowance'. This is the 'last line of defense' in modern social security systems—it is the ultimate safety net. Meant to ensure poverty alleviation, help maintain social security and stability, and achieve 'bottom-line justice', it is also the quintessential governmental duty—the welfare program deemed essential for the entire social system. The Chinese government focuses a great deal on this segment of the population and aims to help the very large number of poverty-stricken people in the country cover their most basic needs. The term 'minimum living allowance' can be used in a broader and a more narrowly defined sense. In its broader sense, it implies various anti-poverty policies and measures that the country adopts in a discrete period of time, including poverty relief, temporary subsidies to people in need, disaster relief, the five guarantees system for *wubaohu* and certain development programs. In a more narrow sense it refers mainly to a system that provides income compensation to both urban and rural citizens who are below the poverty line. This chapter mainly deals with the 'minimum living allowance' system in the narrow sense, although it may refer to the system in the broader sense on some occasions.

The development of the minimum living allowance system

As early as the 1950s, enterprises and institutions in China were already providing a relief system for urban workers living in poverty, and the five-guarantee system was implemented in rural areas. Not until the 1990s, however, was there a minimum living allowance system that had the unique feature of being backed by Central government spending. In the early 1990s the system was implemented as a trial program in various cities in tandem with reform of state-owned enterprises. Towards the end of the 1990s the program was expanded throughout China's urban areas. During this time the system was also adopted in some rural areas. In 2007 the Chinese government specified a policy objective of implementing the system in all of China's rural areas. It also specified the plan for building the framework for a low-level 'minimum living allowance' system in both urban and rural areas.

Rural anti-poverty and social assistance systems since 1978

The various policies implemented during the period of China's planned economy ensured the subsistence and basic living of urban and rural residents, but living standards remained low and a considerable number of people lived in poverty. In 1978, 250 million people living in rural areas in China were 'distressed poor'—30.7 percent of the rural population. The social assistance system at the time was designed for only a small number of extremely poor people, mainly disaster-stricken people as well as those not able to work or those who had no source of income or lawful supporters. The vast majority of poor people were not covered by the system at all. Economic reform and a fast growing economy in rural areas were essential to the fight against poverty there. By 1985 the number of poor people who did not have enough to eat or to wear had declined to 125 million, or 14.8 percent of the rural population. At the same time as it gradually advanced rural reforms, the Chinese government set aside dedicated funds in support of the economic development of some 'extremely poor' areas. In 1984 the Central Committee of the Communist Party of China and the State Council promulgated the 'Notice on Helping Poor Areas change the face of Poverty as Soon as Possible', and set up a special fund for assistance to these areas. In 1986, the National People's Congress put the poverty-reduction issue of poverty-stricken areas into the 7th Five-Year Plan for National Economic Development (1986–1990). This formally established a developmental policy aimed at poverty alleviation. It was funded by earmarked loans for poverty alleviation. It conducted poverty alleviation measures such as work relief programs (working in return for assistance), and financial development-fund plans in the poorest of counties. The numbers of rural poor further declined to about 80 million in the period 1986–1993. Most poor were now living in the central and western areas with adverse natural conditions which made poverty alleviation development work difficult. In 1994 the Central government put forward a national program for poverty alleviation that it called 'eight–seven' and was designed to cover the period 1994 to 2000. This redefined 'poverty-stricken counties', and considerably increased funds to be spent on lifting the 80 million rural poor out of absolute poverty within the seven years (8–7) By 2000 the number of the rural poor had decreased to 32.09 million. In the years that followed, the program was modified to place emphasis on 'villages' as opposed to 'counties'. More than two decades of economic reform policies and poverty alleviation objectives have contributed greatly to lifting 200 million people, who had been living in absolute poverty, up to a level of 'adequacy' in terms of food and clothing. However a considerable number of people are still living in poverty. A 2003 Ministry of Civil Affairs survey revealed that 25.42 million people in rural areas were especially vulnerable, including 5.7 million *wubaohu* and 19.72 million 'particularly distressed'.[1]

The establishment and development of the minimum living allowance system for urban residents

Urban poverty was not a conspicuous problem during the planned-economy period, and as a result assistance was basically only provided for the 'three withouts', i.e.

without the ability to work, any source of income, or help from family. After the start of the country's reform and opening up policies, the ever deepened enterprise and labor-system reforms resulted in an increasing number of laid-off workers, and these became the the newly poverty-stricken in cities. Traditional urban relief systems aimed at the 'three withouts' were unable to deal with the new problems. These people are now urgently in need of expanded coverage from China's security systems, to assure their own basic living conditions and also to maintain overall social stability. In June 1993, Shanghai proposed a minimum cost-of-living guarantee plan, the earliest minimum living allowance program for urban residents in China. This was later ratified and disseminated by the Ministry of Civil Affairs. Subsequently, Qingdao, Guangzhou and some other coastal cities began similar trial experiments. By the end of May 1997, 206 cities had established such systems. In September 1997, the State Council issued the 'Notice on Establishing a Minimum Living Allowance System for Urban Residents Nationwide'. This required all cities and towns that serve as county seats governments to establish a minimum living allowance system for urban residents by 1999. On October 1, 1999, the State Council promulgated the *Regulations on Minimum Living Allowances for Urban Residents*, heralding the implementation of the system throughout all urban areas. The system was aimed at local governments nationwide, but the result was that they failed to spend the necessary amounts to ensure full coverage in most places. As a result, in 2001, the General Office of the State Council issued a more stringent *Notice on Further Strengthening the Work of Minimum Living Allowances for Urban Residents*. This required local governments to increase their investment in the program to a sufficient degree to cover all eligible people in the system. In recent years some cities with ample funding, for example Beijing, have extended the minimum living allowance benefits to the 'marginal poor' who, though not qualified under the current system, have been trapped in serious financial difficulties (see Box 10.1). Overall, more poor people have benefited from the urban minimum living allowance system with the increases in funding. The target population increased to 22 million in 2002, before basically stabilizing (see Figure 10.1). The targeted population of ultra-poor was 22.709 million in 2007 and 22.728 million in September 2008.

Box 10.1 Beijing's marginal poor people receive aid based on computer ordering

In the past, the focus of aid efforts in China was mainly on those people living below a certain poverty line, a threshold amount of income set for the minimum living allowance system. Those above that threshold received little in the way of assistance. To remedy the inadequacies of the present policies, Beijing's Dongcheng District [eastern part of the city] launched the 'Social Assistance Information System'. Precise information on poverty-stricken families was entered into this computerized system, enabling an orderly way of classifying them, and aid was provided—with priority given to those most in need. The Social Assistance Information System stores information including personal information, financial circumstances, degree of poverty, aid needed and aid provided. Each entry may contain up to 188 fields. The aid is not based on an egalitarian distribution of social relief nor does it depend on income as the sole qualifying standard, but uses a computerized rating of the candidates according to their degree of poverty. In this way, those not meeting MLA criteria but in urgent need of help can be supported in a timely manner by particular policies. Considerations include, for example, people thrown into poverty due to expensive schooling or medical bills or a sudden accident, or those who have received other aid but still face great financial difficulties.

Source: Poverty-stricken Families Aided through Computer Ordering, http://www. beijing.gov.cn.

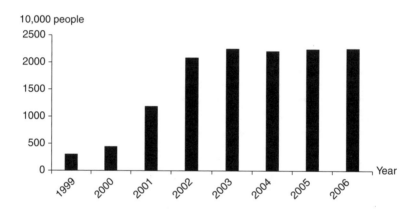

10,000 people

Figure 10.1 Number of MLA recipients in urban China, 1999–2006.

Source: National Bureau of Statistics of China (2007) *China Statistical Yearbook 2007 for Civil Affairs.* Beijing: China Statistics Press.

The establishment of a rural minimum living allowance system

While setting up the minimum living allowance system for urban residents, China has also explored how to establish its rural counterpart.

Social assistance to the rural poor includes the following arrangements: i) the system of supporting the 'five-guaranteed' types of people, including elderly who 'lack three necessary means of support', other adults who do not have the ability to work, those that are disabled, underage orphans; ii) the temporary relief system, also started in the early 1950s, and covering inadequately fed and clothed people; iii) relief aid systems that extend specific amounts of aid on an ongoing routine basis. These systems are aimed at perpetual poverty and they provide relief and/or grain rations. This system started in the 1980s and was implemented only on a limited basis; and iv) the medical aid system.

Influenced by the establishment of minimum living allowance systems in cities, from the 1990s onward, some coastal areas lsuch as Shanghai, Guangzhou and Zhejiang began exploring rural minimum security systems on the basis of the regular supply of ration-based aid. In 1996 the Ministry of Civil Affairs issued the Opinions on Accelerating the Establishment of a Rural Social Security System; it focused on the minimum living allowance system, and specified that the required funding had to come from public finance of the various levels of local government and the village collectives. From 1997 the rural minimum living allowance system was launched in areas where conditions permitted its implementation. By the end of 2002, 10 provinces had introduced local laws or regulations regarding the rural minimum security system. In 2007 the State Council promulgated the 'Notice on Establishing a Rural Minimum Living Allowance System throughout the Country', which gave notice that the system was going to be implemented nationwide. By September 2007, 2,777 agricultural counties in 31 provinces had established the rural minimum living allowance system. In September 2008, the aggregate national amount paid out monthly was RMB 2.02 billion. The average monthly standard was RMB 81.8 and the average monthly per capita expenditure was RMB 43.

Effectiveness and problems of a minimum living allowance system

Effectiveness of the system

The establishment of the minimum living allowance system for both urban and rural residents has been a milestone in building China's social security system. The system has played an important role in alleviating poverty and stabilizing society, and has served as a 'last line of defense' in the social security system.

The system ensures basic subsistence for the poorest people

Through the system, the government provides the poorest people with a fixed amount of 'essential' and regular aid, a stable source of income to cover their basic cost of living. By May 2008 the number of rural people covered by the five guarantees system had increased to 5,286,000; the national per capita average benefits stood at RMB 2,229 per year for those provided for at a special facility and RMB 1,691 for those provided for at individual homes, accounting for 53.8 percent and 40.8 percent of the per capita net income (RMB 4,140) of rural residents in 2007, and for 69.1 percent and 52.6 percent of their per capita consumption expenditure (RMB 3,224), respectively. By September 2008, the average income threshold for each qualified urban resident was RMB 206.2 per month, and 10.84 million urban households or 22,728,000 people were included in the system. These security measures can cover the basic living cost of urban and rural poor and help alleviate pressures of the most basic existence. The MLA system contributes to poverty alleviation and improves the income and living standard of poverty-stricken people. It grants a benefit to urban and rural households that is equivalent to 10.8 percent and 10.7 percent respectively of their per capita income. As the MLA system grants differentiated subsidies, i.e. more benefit goes to low earners, it guarantees the basic subsistence of recipients and serves as an effective means of poverty alleviation.

MLA has become a cornerstone of China's social security and welfare system

Specially designed for the poor, it is the primary means for a modern society to implement its anti-poverty strategy. Poverty relief usually aims at rescuing people from starvation, but the MLA system pays a benefit appropriate to help the recipient maintain the acceptable minimum living standard, or in internationally acknowledged terms, the lowest standard for 'living a decent life in dignity'. It provides assistance or subsidies by means of direct transfer payments, producing immediate effect in alleviating poverty and narrowing income gaps. At the same time, it offers a solution to people's financial predicaments, provides subsistence and living necessities and helps maintain social stability and equity.

Problems with the MLA system

Low level of benefits and obstacles to raising the benefits

At present, the benefits paid by social assistance plans (except for the 'five guaranteed', or the *wubaohu*) remain at a very low level, accounting for only about 10 percent of income per capita. This low level makes it extremely difficult for the impoverished to extricate themselves from poverty. In the central and western rural areas, in particular, the income threshold for minimum living allowance is calculated largely based on the absolute poverty line, and the benefit available for each person may be as low as RMB 10 or so in some counties. This amount is unable to do anything to mitigate poverty (see Table 10.1). On the other hand, raising the benefit threshold is limited by such factors as inadequate local funds and large numbers of marginal poor. In rural areas, given the system's efforts to expand and cover all those who are eligible, the number of recipients has steadily increased. By the end of September 2008, it had reached 38,577,000, people in 17,861,000 households. A rise in the income threshold and the inclusion of more people in the system would put insupportable strains on the financial resources of local governments. This is precisely the reason the income thresholds cannot be increased.

MLA income threshold varies with places and gaps exist between urban and rural areas and between regions

The MLA system is budgeted for and implemented by local governments who will have a say in the income criteria. The MLA criteria may vary greatly at different places due to their economic status and availability of financial resources. By December 2007, among the 36 most important cities, Shenzhen had the highest

Table 10.1 MLA standards, 2005–2007 (unit: RMB/person/month)

Index	2005	2006	2007
Average income threshold of an urban MLA program	156.0	173.9	182.4
Average benefit paid from an urban MLA program	72.3	83.6	102.0
Average income threshold of a rural MLA program	76.0	70.9	70.0
Average benefit paid from a rural MLA program	38.0	34.5	37.0
Average income threshold under a rural *wubaohu* program	–	102	141
Average benefit paid from a rural *wubaohu* program	136.0	78.3	98.0

Source: Based on National Bureau of Statistics of China (2008) *China Statistical Abstract 2008*. Beijing: China Statistics Press, p. 196.

(monthly) income threshold, RMB 361, followed by Shanghai (RMB 350), Beijing, Tianjin and Guangzhou (RMB 330). The city at the bottom of the list is Urumqi, with only RMB 156.[2] In small cities and counties of undeveloped regions, the income threshold is a meager RMB 100 or even less. In rural areas with a much lower income and living standard, residents may receive only a few dozen RMB on average as the monthly benefit. The great difference has led to obvious inequity in the MLA system between urban and rural areas and among regions, and has affected the unity and fairness of the system.

As a 'comprehensive' aid system, it develops only very slowly and contributes at such a low level that it can hardly meet the basic needs of those who receive assistance

Seen from an overall perspective, China's urban and rural comprehensive aid system is still in its infancy, leaving many of the needs of poverty-stricken people unaddressed. In 2007 the average level of per capita medical aid to the hospitalized stood at RMB 940 for cities and RMB 850 for rural areas, a drop in the ocean for those with serious diseases. The comprehensive aid system focuses on people who are qualified for MLA, but excludes those marginal poor people whose financial predicament is increasingly prominent. Ineligible for MLA, these households can neither receive the MLA benefits nor other related social assistances such as medical treatment, education, housing and heating. The desperate situation of these people is becoming ever more apparent.

Role of a minimum living allowance in a developmental welfare system

Features of the MLA system

The following features of the MLA system distinguish it from social insurance. First, the system is not based on contributions; it is mainly funded by the government at various levels rather than by contributions by a prospective beneficiary.

Second, benefit granting is needs-based, i.e. benefits are paid not based on one's contribution to the social security fund or tax payment, but on one's needs. The third is the noticeable anti-poverty function; the benefits paid under the system are mainly based on the fact that the recipient's family income is lower than the locally specified poverty line. The aid is used to make up the difference required to keep all the families above the poverty line. The fourth is the limited and focused nature of benefits; benefits paid under the MLA system are only to meet the basic living needs of recipients, not all needs. Once one is registered as an MLA recipient, however, one can easily receive other assistance provided by the government and society, to the extent that marginal poor above the poverty line wish they could be considered below the poverty line to get the same treatment. The fifth lies in its welfare nature and the ambivalent nature of its ultimate good. The MLA is a quintessential form of social welfare. Income thresholds rise as income increases, so if no appropriate measures are taken the system encourages people to stay below the line in order to get the benefits. This rigidifies the system. For a considerable number of MLA recipients, the receipt of minimum security benefits can help them mitigate poverty, but not get out of poverty. The system itself therefore contributes to a quintessential 'welfare dependency' or 'poverty trap'. For society as a whole, the MLA system may act like a double-sided blade: it can combat poverty and narrow income disparities on the one hand, while on the other hand it is liable to increase unemployment and financial pressures on the government. In the end, it only contributes to social enervation. How to bring the system's strengths into play and limit its adverse impacts are usually the priority and focus of welfare system reform.

The position of the MLA system in a developmental welfare system

In the early days of transitioning from one economic system to another, the primary task for China's social security was to establish a new social insurance system that enabled reform of state-owned enterprises. Today the tasks are different: they are to to make the current social security and welfare systems more comprehensive and to take them to a higher level through improved institutional-ized arrangements. Increasing contribution-based programs was formerly the primary goal, while still embodying the principles of both equity and efficiency. Now the greatest weakness in China's current systems lies in the glaring inade-quacies of non-contribution-based programs. This must be remedied as soon as possible, so that non-contribution based programs can develop in tandem with contribution-based programs in a harmonious way. As the main component of non-contribution-based programs the minimum living allowance is the foundation of the entire social security and welfare system. Since China has already established a widely recognized basic framework for the system, expendi-tures for which are both controllable and affordable. Improving it became a break-through in building China's new social security and welfare system, so that it can form the underlying a 'line of defense' in keeping all of the population above the poverty line.

Objectives of the MLA system and measures for its improvement

Economic growth is the ultimate basis for improving the minimum living allowance system. As the system plays a fundamental role in China's developmental welfare systems, it must be based on the reality of the country's economic growth. As a quintessential part of China's social welfare systems its future development needs to be backed up by a powerful economy and the adequate financial resources of the government. It needs to correspond to the economic status of the country and the stage of its economic development (see Box 10.2). Fast economic growth over the past 30 years has provided the conditions for China to improve its minimum living allowance system. In 2007, per capita GDP in China went over US$2,000. The momentum for growth is expected to continue for a long time to come, which should lay a solid foundation for a sound social security system.

Box 10.2 Foreign MLA systems for rural areas

France: the pressures of 'rigidified' welfare. France introduced an MLA system in 1988, which was called '*Revenu Minimum d'Insertion*' (RMI). A beneficiary may participate in voluntary medical insurance without paying any premiums and may have access to medical treatment at no cost. The benefits paid to a beneficiary, who must be above 25, are based on an examination of family financial data, and are allowed after the deduction of other benefits being received from other welfare policies. RMI is completely funded out of state tax revenues. Since its inception, the number of RMI beneficiaries has continually increased. In the early 1990s, France's budgetary outlays on RMI benefits stood at about 20 billion francs. The rigidified welfare has put extreme financial pressure on the government, so that it has had to have the welfare indexed, tightening the criteria year by year.

The United States: reform of the welfare-payments type system. By definition, a family is deemed to be poor in America when one third of its expenditure is used for buying food. Social assistance should be provided accordingly, and should include unemployment benefits and free medical assistance as well as family allowance. Welfare recipients are supported by such measures as Supplemental Security Income (SSI), child care subsidies, house rent subsidies, child nutrition subsidies, affordable housing programs, aid for education and employment training assistance. These social assistance programs are co-funded by the federal and state governments, but state governments have more decision-making power as to the amount of the benefits. After the 1990s, due to great financial pressure, calls to reform the system have been increasing.

Germany: voluntary insurance plus public assistance. In Germany, social aid as a supplement to social insurance is provided to people excluded from the job market, the unemployed and the old, to cover their spending on food,

---

fuel or other living expenses, to contribute to housing subsidies and pay for medical insurance and old-age insurance. Only one third of social aid funds come from the government and charity organizations; the rest is carried by duly incorporated social insurance management organizations under a kind of self-governing social system.

Sweden: universal relief. Sweden is the ultimate model of a country that provides universal relief. In this country with 'active labor market policies', the universally applied welfare has led to an ossified labor market. In 1993, the country reported an official unemployment rate of 8 percent, the highest since World War II. In 1994, Sweden's welfare budget deficit reached 13 percent of its GDP, and the government deficit stood at 80 percent of its GDP. Beginning in the 1970s, the negative incentives and welfare rigidity arising from the excessively generous welfare programs had severely hindered the country's macro-economic development, leading to a financial crisis for the government. From 1992 Sweden had to reform its welfare system.

India: a less-developed country with significant achievements in its welfare programs. As a developing country, India has implemented a successful rural welfare policy. Older farmers who cannot work can receive a basic living allowance from the government; homeless farmers can receive home-building subsidies from the government; poor people can buy food at a low price; schooling of poor children is subsidized by the Central and State governments. Primary education is free in India, and in richer states secondary education is also free. Students can receive books free of charge, and even free lunches in certain states.

Source: Zhu Lifang, 'Foreign MLA systems in Rural Areas', *Rural Work Newsletter*, Issue 19, 2008.

The objectives of China's MLA system

Before 2020, the MLA system should be geared towards the following objectives. First, it should cover all urban and rural residents eligible for MLA and all residents living below the MLA poverty line. Given the percentage of population covered by similar arrangements in low-income, medium-income and developed countries, China should incorporate about 5 percent of its population, or over 70 million, into the MLA system in order to assure a firm safety net. Second, it should accelerate the process of bringing the income thresholds of urban and rural families into line with each other, as well as the thresholds for various regions, in order to improve the equity of the program. Third, it should gradually increase income thresholds and benefits, so as to lift poverty-stricken people out of poverty and give them the security of adequate food and clothing and to bring into full play the poverty-reduction role of the system. Fourth, it should increase Central government spending in the MLA system, and promote, through such measures as transfer payment, the uniformity of the system throughout the country and the balance of MLA income thresholds among regions. Finally, it should develop comprehensive security measures for poverty-stricken people, including those on the verge of poverty, such as education relief and health aid, and establish a comprehensive relief system that matches the MLA system and serves to improve the financial conditions of poverty-stricken families.

Stages and tasks of the MLA system

To develop the program prior to 2020 we need to carry out the following measures in two stages.

The first stage should last from 2009 to 2012, a key period for improving the system, with the emphasis on ensuring the coverage of all those eligible and duly increasing benefits. In this stage the primary task is to solve the problem of extreme poverty. In 2005 there were 570,000 orphans throughout the country, and 200,000 rural orphans who were receiving no social relief. Some were even resorting to begging or theft for a living. Some seriously ill patients have no access to immediate relief; some especially poor rural residents live in shacks, and housing is also an outstanding issue for a number of urban poor. In view of the urgency of fighting extreme poverty and the limited financial resources available, providing assistance to the extremely poor, as a first step towards the improvement of the MLA system, will produce the most noticeable and comprehensive social effects within the shortest period of time. It is worth noting that relief to the extremely poor should include not only provision for basic subsistence, but also medical, educational and housing aid, and meanwhile a social welfare system covering orphans and disabled old people should be put in place. In January through October 2008, the urban MLA program paid a monthly benefit of RMB 133 per person, while the rural program paid RMB 44. This huge gap between urban and rural benefits should be narrowed along with the establishment of a uniform household registration system for both urban and rural areas. One of the goals to achieve by 2012 is to have more than 27 million urban residents and over 35.5 million rural residents covered by the MLA system, each receiving a monthly benefit of about RMB 200 and RMB 100 respectively. The five-guarantee system for *wubaohu* should refer to the urban MLA program in terms of benefit payment. It should cover all eligible people and benefit more than 5.3 million people in total. The expenditure for the above three schemes will come to some RMB 120 billion.

In the second stage, namely from 2013 to 2020, full coverage should be achieved for the urban and rural MLA programs and the rural five-guarantee system, and continued efforts should be made to improve the social relief system and establish a mechanism for benefits adjustment. The emphasis of the MLA system should be gradually shifted to system unity and increased security standards. By 2020 the income criteria should be raised and an annual benefit of RMB 4,440 should be paid to each urban beneficiary and *wubaohu*, and RMB 3,190 to each rural beneficiary, so as to further narrow the urban–rural gap. The government spending for the urban and rural MLA programs and the rural five-guarantee system will be some RMB 270 billion. At the same time the social relief and welfare service system should be improved to realize balanced and equitable access to basic security and welfare services for all people.

Policy recommendations

Over the next three to five years, China's rigidly controlled household registration system, that defines 'urban' and 'rural' differently, will be moving towards urban–rural integration. As this happens the challenge for the MLA system is going to be to unify its urban and rural components as soon as possible, and to redefine the measures of calculating family income. The task will require adequate theoretical and institutional preparation. An even greater challenge is going to face the system over the next 10 years: as China's economy grows the entire system should be replaced by a basic living allowance program, in line with China turning into a medium-level developed country. This will lead to considerable hikes in the security standards, requiring thorough research and preparation.

First, financial support for the MLA system needs to be bolstered. Governments at various levels are continuously increasing their financial investment in the MLA, but the overall level of the program's funding remains extremely low. In 2007, total governmental expenditures on civil affairs accounted for only 2 percent of spending for the year, with only one percent of that being used for MLA and relief. According to the 'two-step' development strategy of the MLA system, total funding for MLA and relief should double from the current level by 2012, and it should quadruple by 2020. At the same time, the amount of government spending addressed to MLA programs should increase accordingly.

Second, the structure of financial investments in social security needs to be adjusted and the standard and consistency of the MLA system needs be improved. Government spending on social security and welfare increased from RMB 151.76 billion in 2000 to RMB 539.6 billion in 2007. Spending on basic social relief, employment assistance and temporary hardship subsidies took only a small part of this (RMB 75.85 billion in 2007, only 14 percent of government spending on social security), only half of which was used for the MLA. Meanwhile, in many regions local government spending is the dominant source of funding for MLA, leading to great inconsistencies among regions in defining the MLA threshold. In addition, local government spending focuses on urban areas. Rural areas receive less in the way of social security funds, leading to a greater urban–rural gap in terms of MLA benefits. This funding structure is not conducive to reinforcing the fundamental position of the MLA system, increasing standards, or to promoting the uniformity of regulations. Efforts should be made to increase MLA expenditures as a percentage of the total welfare and relief expenditures and as a percentage of all government spending on social security. The percentage of Central-government spending on MLA should be increased; support for rural and poor areas should be increased, and MLA standards and the standardization and consistency of the MLA system should be steadily improved. With government spending raised in this regard, we should first standardize the MLA system throughout the country, then gradually realize the relative balance and basic uniformity of MLA income threshold and benefits.

Third, the management of the system should be improved through building organizational infrastructure and making staff more professional. Current problems include beneficiary identification, fund allocations, management procedures, the application of IT measures and greater specialization of management. Both material and human-resource inputs need to be improved. At the same time we should constantly review local practices and learn from them in enhancing our MLA system, learn from international experiences, transform irrational management systems and procedures into more rational procedures, push forward legislation so as to promote standard and scientific management and, overall, constantly improve the managerial quality of China's social security and welfare system.

Fourth, we should gradually expand the 'basic living allowance' component of our social relief system into a system that is more comprehensive in terms of both relief and security. The minimum living allowance should not be seen in isolation but should be a part of a combination of various measures that help recipients climb out of the 'subsistence trap'. The MLA system currently helps recipients stay alive, but it hardly provides them with dignity or equal development opportunities. Therefore, social relief and support should be given in other aspects such as basic medical care, education and housing. Currently, policies regarding medical relief, educational assistance and low-rent housing for MLA beneficiaries have been initiated, but both the benefits and coverage are limited and can hardly meet basic needs. The financial predicament of some seriously ill patients is not addressed in particular. Policy adjustments must be made so that these people can receive relief in time. At the same time we must avoid concentrating an excessive number of relief measures on MLA beneficiaries, so as to prevent over-reliance on the system. After a reasonable level of benefits has been decided for MLA recipients, comprehensive relief measures should be carried out that are based on actual needs of all poor people, rather than simply concentrating on MLA beneficiaries, so as to avoid the waste of resources and to ensure appropriate relief to marginal poor people who are not under the poverty line. With a rise in government investment, developmental social policies should be more effectively implemented, the comprehensive security system should be improved, and the real purposes of the MLA system should begin to be more in evidence.

Fifth, we should summarize and disseminate good local practices, and actively explore a developmental MLA system that takes existing realities into account. Currently, China's MLA system needs improvement in both theoretical and operational aspects. When making the names of beneficiaries public, a more considerate or humanitarian approach should be adopted. Greater effort should be put into improving the working skills of beneficiaries and providing better information and other services to help them secure a job. For those having great difficulty finding a job, public-service jobs may be arranged in urban areas. Even in rural areas, job opportunities may be created, for example in the 'new rural development plans' that will need help in the areas of 'environmental greening' [landscaping through plantings], road construction, improving public health through 'cleaning things up' and various community services.

Notes

1 China Development Research Foundation, *Eliminate Poverty Through Development* (China Development Press, 2007).
2 See the website of the Ministry of Civil Affairs (http: //dbs.mca.gov.cn).

11 Social welfare systems for special groups

Prior to industrialization the social assistance systems focused mainly on security for special groups. Modern social welfare system still regards the security of special groups as a key element. Modern welfare systems include programs for children, the disabled and senior citizens, but in developed countries, children's welfare systems are generally created first, followed by those for the disabled and then senior citizens. Countries regard children's welfare as fundamental and devote considerable importance and a large number of programs to it, hence a large percentage of their resources. Social welfare system programs are extremely diverse in developed countries, for example France has 422 welfare programs. Due to such diversity of approaches, the term 'special group' is not clearly defined either in terms of what it connotes or how far it extends. This chapter will focus on China's social welfare programs for the disabled, senior citizens, women and children.

Development of welfare for the disabled

Disabled persons form a vast special group in China, totaling more than 83 million, with 260 million people directly affected when family members are included. To ensure the basic subsistence and special needs of disabled persons, China has gradually developed special social welfare program, to constantly improve the life, education and employment status of this group.

Minimum living allowance and relief

In view of the large population of disabled people and their varying conditions, China has taken different measures to address different conditions so as to secure basic subsistence and special needs. Severely disabled persons who have totally or partially lost the ability to work, or who were unable to work to begin with, who have no legal guardians to support them, and who have no source of income, are included by the government in the urban and rural minimum living allowance system or other relevant assistance systems. According to a 2007 monitoring report on the status of the disabled nationwide, 19.7 percent of urban disabled persons enjoy the local minimum living allowance, and 22.2 percent receive

Table 11.1 Basic social subsistence assistance accessible to the disabled in China (%)

	Data of second national sample survey on disabled persons in 2006		Major data of national monitoring on status of disabled persons in 2007	
	Urban disabled persons	Rural disabled persons	Urban disabled persons	Rural disabled persons
Minimum living allowance	13.3	5.1	19.7	12.5
Regular or irregular relief	9.8	11.7	22.2	26.6

Source: Zhang Shifei, *Social Welfare System for Special Groups* (Background Report, 2008).

regular or irregular relief (cash or food). In rural areas these figures are 12.5 percent and 26.6 percent respectively (see Table 11.1).

Employment support and welfare service

It is common in countries throughout the world to provide employment support for those disabled persons with a certain ability to work (Box 11.1 introduces Japan's experience). In China, favorable policies for employment promotion and protection mainly include pro rata employment arrangements, preferential tax policies and other support and protection measures that encourage the employment of disabled persons in various ways. Relevant government bodies have utilized social forces to create welfare enterprises for disabled persons, including massage services by blind people and other institutions of a welfare nature to create jobs for disabled persons. At the end of 2007 a total of 26,000 welfare enterprises created jobs for 556,000 disabled persons.[1] The State offers preferential tax treatment to employers who employ a certain percentage of disabled persons (companies in which disabled persons account for more than 25 percent of the staff), and provides them legally required support in terms of production, operations, technology, funds, material and land. The State encourages disabled persons to seek jobs and create businesses on their own. If disabled persons engage in private business, the government will give preferential tax treatment as per the law, and provide support in terms of location of the business, micro-loans and other aspects. The State encourages and gives support to public employment service institutions in providing disabled persons with such free services as advice on government policies, job vacancy information, career guidance and job introductions, in terms of targeted assistance. It offers priority support to those disabled persons who find it particularly hard to be employed. At the end of 2005, employed urban disabled persons totalled 4.636 million, including 1.402 million employed under the pro rata employment arrangement, 1.241 million under the concentrated employment arrangement, and 1.992 million engaged in private business.

Box 11.1 Employment service for disabled persons in Japan

There are currently around 5 million disabled persons in Japan, 5 percent of the total population. This figure includes 2.722 million people with physical disabilities above the age of 18, and includes roughly 360,000 people who are mentally disabled. To help these people get jobs, the Japanese government has specified in the *Law on Disabled Persons' Employment Promotion* that non-profit public institutions should employ disabled persons at a rate of 2.0 percent of their total staff, while the figure is 1.9 percent for profit-making public institutions, large enterprises and groups respectively, and 1.6 percent for common private enterprises.

In November 1993, enterprises and non-profit-making institutions with more than five employees hired a total of 344,000 people with physical disabilities, and more than 60,000 people with mental disabilities.

Employers who fail to meet the requirements have to pay a fine; those who employ disabled persons above the requirements are granted an award. At present, in Japan, disabled persons account for 1.44 percent of the total staff in private enterprises, 1.91 percent in companies and profit-making public institutions, and more than 2 percent in not-for-profit public institutions.

As to occupational guidance, the instructor is required to understand information about a disabled person in an indirect way, take a warm and honest attitude and avoid discriminatory expressions and behavior. He is required to observe and judge whether the state of the disabled person is stable or in line with the disabled persons' diagnosis; to assess the vocational ability of the person through testing, and suggest jobs that suit and tap their potential.

The employment agency is required to obtain detailed information on a job applicant and the potential employer, for example, the interest, will, physical ability and occupational ability of the job applicant, and the will, working conditions and requirements of the employer; assess the remaining ability of the person, and ability of the disabled person to use aids; notify both parties of their respective information in detail; and carry out a one-year follow-up instruction two weeks after the recommendation via direct interview, phone interview and correspondence.

Any discrimination and wilful ignorance during the occupational guidance process will be considered illegal behavior once the disabled person submits verified complaints.

If an enterprise employs a disabled person, a mentally disabled person in particular, the government will subsidize a quarter to one third of the salary for this person for one year to 18 months after the employment, depending on the extent of disability. In addition, the Japanese government plans to raise the subsidy to half of the salary for a disabled employee (two-thirds in the case of small and medium-sized enterprises), and two-thirds of the salary for a severely disabled employee (three-quarters in the case of small- and medium-sized enterprises) as of March 31, 1995.

Generally, an enterprise must contact a local employment agency and make sure a new job is available before it dismisses a disabled employee.

The vocational training and employment agencies for disabled persons in Japan are run by the government, civil society and private investors. These institutions are usually near or even integrated with rehabilitation hospitals for disabled persons, so as to train disabled persons after treatment, and even carry out training during treatment.

Source: Zhao Hong, Wu Jiang, 'Employment Service for Disabled Persons in Japan', *Labor Theory and Practice*, (2), 1995.

China has taken certain steps to meet the special needs of disabled persons in daily life and social activities. For one, the country has built welfare service facilities and rehabilitation institutions to provide basic services for disabled persons. For another, it provides assistance to the families of disabled persons that meet certain requirements, in the form of medical services, low-rent housing, education, employment and legal advice. The exclusive care institutions for disabled persons built in China include social welfare houses and welfare houses for children and the mentally disabled, as well as rural nursing homes. Those cared for in these institutions are mostly severely disabled persons who have no other means of support.

Rehabilitation services for disabled people in China observe the principle of practicality, easy implementation and the broadest possible benefit. The socialized rehabilitation service system that has gradually formed has professional rehabilitation institutions as the backbone, community rehabilitation as the foundation and disabled persons' families as the support. The rehabilitation programs for disabled persons have been broadened from the 'three rehabilitations', namely corrective surgery for physical disabilities, audio and linguistic training for deaf children, and surgery for removal of cataracts, to include iodine supplementation, treatments for poor vision, treatment for people with mental health issues, treatment for people who are mentally disabled, community 'health restoration' services and supplies for disabled people.

As to the education and training of disabled persons, China focuses on nine-year compulsory education for disabled children, and incorporates the education of disabled children into the national and regional compulsory education systems. As mandated by State law, any county with a population of over 300,000 people and a relatively large number of disabled children who are of school age should set up a special school to provide nine-year compulsory education for disabled children. In 2005 there were 1,662 special schools for disabled persons, with 562,000 students, and the enrollment rate of children with visual, auditry and mental disabilities had reached 80 percent.

Some 75 percent of all disabled persons in China live in rural areas. With regard to these people, the State first stresses the implementation of poverty elimination and development plans to help in poverty alleviation. This also constitutes an important part of China's poverty elimination and development strategy. The poverty elimination and development for disabled persons in impoverished counties is incorporated into the overall poverty elimination planning of the local [municipal] government, and enjoys priority in terms of budget allocation. In counties that have a 'moderate' level of poverty the state mainly provides the national rehabilitation and poverty elimination loans as well as other special funds. In 2001–2005 China spent a total of RMB 4.52 billion on elimination of poverty among disabled persons—this was used to support 11.659 million poor disabled persons in rural areas, meet the basic subsistence needs of 6.997 million people, and provide 4.545 million people with practical technology training. A total of 2,106 counties across the nation have used the rehabilitation and poverty elimination loans, and more than over 60,000 disabled persons from more than 50,000 households have benefited from the housing reconstruction program that is funded by the lottery fund established for this purpose.

Development of social welfare for senior citizens

Basic living allowance for senior citizens

Other chapters of this book focus on the security system for senior citizens in China, which mainly includes the basic pension system for enterprise employees, the basic pension system for employees of public institutions that is currently under construction, and the pension system for civil servants. In 2007 more than 50 million senior citizens enjoyed benefits from the above systems, and about RMB 500 billion was paid out in pensions. Surveys indicate that, in 2006, 78 percent of Chinese urban senior citizens enjoyed retirement pay (pension), 8.9 percent more than had received pensions in 2000, while the 2006 figure was 4.8 percent in rural areas, an increase of 1.5 percentage points over 2000. In 2006 the average monthly retirement pay for qualified urban senior citizens was RMB 990, while the average monthly retirement pay for rural senior citizens participating in the rural pension insurance was RMB 684, an increase of 61.8 percent and 64.9 percent over 2000 respectively. In 2006, 74.1 percent of urban senior citizens enjoying various medical security services, an increase of 22.5 percent over 2000; 44.7 percent of rural senior citizens had medical services, an increase of 35.8 percent over 2000 (see Table 11.2).[2]

There are some 90 million senior citizens above the age of 60 who do not enjoy pensions. With respect to this group, China is now actively exploring various pension security systems in urban and rural areas, such as the rural pension system and the subsidy system for urban senior citizens. Of course these systems only cover a small portion of senior citizens at present. The majority of senior citizens without pensions still rely on their children. Overall, family-based support for the elderly can play a role to some extent, but faces increasing challenges. The poverty of the elderly still remains a significant challenge for China.

Table 11.2 Pension and medical security for senior citizens in 2000 and 2006 (%, RMB)

	2000		2006	
	Urban senior citizens	*Rural senior citizens*	*Urban senior citizens*	*Rural senior citizens*
Enjoying retirement pay (pension)	69.1	3.3	78.0	4.8
Average annual income	7,392	1,651	11,963	2,722
Enjoying various medical security	51.6	8.9	74.1	44.7
Enjoying no social insurance	48.4	91.1	25.9	55.3

Source: Zhang Shifei, *Social Welfare System for Special Groups* (Background Report, 2008).

The Chinese government has incorporated the mitigation and elimination of poverty of the elderly into its national anti-poverty strategy and developmental programs. Depending on the profile of the target group it adopts corresponding measures as follows: for needy senior citizens that meet the requirements, the state has established minimum living allowance systems for urban and rural residents and a relief system for extremely impoverished rural households. It distributes regular minimum living allowances or 'temporary life assistance' to these senior citizens. In 2007, 6.96 million rural senior citizens were incorporated into the rural minimum living allowance system, more than 70,000 rural senior citizens received a certain quantity of assistance on a regular basis as 'extremely impoverished rural households', and the number of senior citizens enjoying Five Guarantees reached 5.257 million nationwide.[3] Rural households that observe the family planning policy and have only one child or two daughters are covered by the 'award and support system' for family planning households after the parents are 60 years old. By the end of 2006, 1.87 million people had benefitted from this system. In 2006 the Central government and local governments earmarked RMB 1.11 billion for the system.[4]

Basic public services for the elderly

To satisfy the growing demand of senior citizens for social services, China is now striving to build a social service system that is based on family-based care, supported by community services, and supplemented by institutional maintenance. Major measures include:

1   building community service facilities to provide necessary services for senior citizens. Since 2001 the Chinese government has been implementing the Starlight Plan to build community welfare service facilities for senior citizens with a total investment of RMB 13.4 billion. To date, 32,000 Starlight Senior Citizens' Homes have been built that cover such functions as home care, emer-

gency aid, daily care, health and rehabilitation, and entertainment. The Plan has benefitted over 30 million senior citizens. At the end of 2005 there were 195,000 community service facilities throughout the country and 8,479 comprehensive community service centers. Across the board, every 'street' has an average of 1.32 welfare institutions for senior citizens and there is one welfare institution for senior citizens for every 9.8 'community committee' areas.[5]

2   Promote services for family-based care for senior citizens in an all-round manner. Community entertainment rooms in urban areas covered 70.8 percent of senior citizens in 2006, and nursing homes covered 31.2 percent of senior citizens in urban areas. These figures in 2000 were 51.2 percent and 11.7 percent respectively.[6] In 2008, the China National Committee on Ageing and other departments jointly distributed the *Opinions Promoting Community-based Home Care Systems in an All-round Way*, clearly specifying that urban communities should basically build home-care network in various forms and with extensive coverage, and rural communities should rely on such existing facilities and resources as township rest homes and village-level institutions. They should step up the construction of integrated welfare service centers for senior citizens that combine such functions as accommodation, community care and home care.

3   Actively develop institution-supported service for the elderly. The State has built 'old-age apartments', rest homes, care centers and rural senior citizens' homes for senior citizens who have no income, children and support and who meet certain requirements, and has provided them with institution-supported services. In 2005 there were 39,546 institutions such as social welfare charity houses, senior citizens' homes, rest homes, old-age apartments and care centers for senior citizens nationwide, which have 1.497 million beds in total. In 2005 there were 29,861 township rest homes, with 895,000 beds in total.[7]

Development of social welfare for women and children

Social welfare for women

The Chinese government considers eliminating gender discrimination an ineluctable responsibility. This includes gender discrimination at work, equal access for men and women to social welfare, and female employees' access to special labor protection. As early as 1953, the Government Administration Council, the predecessor of the State Council, revised and issued the *Regulations of the People's Republic of China on Labor Insurance* which provided maternity rights to women workers and women staff; in 1988 the State Council decreed and implemented the *Provisions on the Labor Protection of Women Staff*, and in 1994 the Ministry of Labor published the Provisional *Measures on Maternity Insurance for Urban Employees*. Given these documents, the State has adopted relatively complete labor protection measures for women workers. For example, it is forbidden to assign women workers to work in mines and do underground work that is inappropriate for them. The State has stipulated and implemented protective measures for women workers during menses, pregnancy and lactation. According to relevant surveys, more than 76 percent of the women employees have signed employment contracts with employers, over 90 percent of the employers implemented the labor protection measures and abided by maternity leave provisions for women workers, and 94 percent of the pregnant employees can receive regular prenatal examinations.[8] With the reform of the labor and employment systems, the protection system for women employees is gradually evolving to become a social insurance program, and maternity insurance has come into being. Enterprises are to pay maternity insurance premiums at a certain percentage of total salaries to a social welfare institution (not to exceed 1 percent in general). Women employees can take the maternity leave according to the law and regulations, and receive the maternity subsidies and reimburse maternity medical expenses after delivery. In 2006, 64.59 million people participated in the maternity insurance program across the nation, and 1.08 million people enjoyed the maternity insurance treatment.[9]

Social welfare for children

China's social welfare for children mainly covers orphans and street children at present. The Chinese government focuses in particular on the security of orphans. After the founding of the People's Republic of China, government at all levels established welfare institutions to adopt homeless, helpless and income-less orphans and abandoned babies. It strove to secure the interests of orphans and their right to survive. Since reform and opening up policies began, and in recent years in particular, the Central government has announced a series of policy measures to promote the social welfare cause for orphans. The Future Plan, implemented in 2004 to treat disabled orphans through surgery and rehabilitate them, has benefited more than 35,000 disabled orphans; the *Opinions on Strengthening the Assistance to Orphans* and the *Opinions on Strengthening our Work with respect to Vagrant Minors*, both issued in 2006, have extended the definition and programs of social welfare for orphans from 'fostering' to '[ph]'education, medical service, rehabilitation, as well as housing and employment after they grow up. In the arena of building infrastructure, China has implemented the *Eleventh Five-Year plan for Construction of Children's Welfare Institutions*, the *Eleventh Five-Year plan for Construction of the Assistance and Protection System for Vagrant Minors* and the *Eleventh Five-Year plan for Construction of the Community Service System*, which have clearly incorporated construction of children's welfare institutions, assistance and protection institutions for vagrant minors and community service institutions into key public service projects supported by the Central government, and greatly promoted the development of children's social welfare.

In terms of social security provisions for orphans, China implements the 'basic security for orphans', which includes a combination of two different forms of caring for orphans, one in family homes and the other in institutions. Orphans whose families have legal guardians or foster parents should be fostered in families. Orphans who are 'dispersed in' society and fostered by legal guardians and those who are dispersed in rural areas are included within the scope of 'Five Guarantee' fostering, the minimum living allowance system for rural residents, and the relief system for extremely poor rural households. Orphans who are 'dispersed in' cities are incorporated into the minimum living allowance system for urban residents and are given key-status protection. If orphans' families have no legal guardians or foster parents, or legal guardians or foster parents are unable to care for them, the civil affairs department will designate social welfare institutions to care for them in a centralized way. Welfare facilities have been built to adopt orphans and abandoned babies. In April 2005 about 69,000 of all the 573,000 orphans across the nation lived in public children's welfare institutions; 295,000 received social assistance, including 54,000 who received the minimum living allowance for urban residents, 125,000 obtained the minimum living allowance for rural residents, and 116,000 received relief funds for extremely poor rural households.[10] In 2006, various social welfare institutions adopted 121,000 children in total, including 72,000 orphans and abandoned babies. Children's welfare centers adopted 32,000 children among the 121,000.[11] Nearly half of the children living in welfare institutions in China are disabled. China has tried to launch rehabilitation services. In May 2004 the Ministry of Civil Affairs launched the Tomorrow Plan to treat more than 35,000 disabled orphans in 1,109 welfare institutions across the country through surgery and rehabilitation.[12] The State encourages orphans' relatives and society at large to adopt orphans, become foster parents of orphans, and to take on the living and educational expenses of orphans. As to those orphans who cannot be adopted or entrusted, in particular the children who become orphans due to their parents' being infected by AIDS/HIV, local governments are building single-unit family facilities in communities, which adopt the 'small-family care mode' in providing necessary living and educational conditions for orphans.

With regard to the protection of minors, China offers social assistance to vagrant minors in the specific ways described below—there are between one and one-and-one-half million such people.[13] Policies to assist them include the following: if minors can provide family information, then the local civil affairs department or other relevant department will contact their parents or other legal guardians in a timely manner and help them return home. If their parents or other legal guardians cannot be found, then the civil affairs department will send them to an 'assistance and protection' institution to be cared for and educated. If the stay of such minors in such institutions extends for a period of time, then the minors will be taken to social welfare institutions for fostering and education in line with relevant provisions. Minors under the age of six, about whom no family information can be found, will be sent to social welfare institutions after reporting to relevant government organs. Vagrant minors' 'assistance and protection' institutions include 'assistance and protection centers', 'assistance and protection sub-centers', local 'street service stations' and 'community service stations'. By the end of 2005 there were 1,026 assistance management stations across the nation, and 130 either attached or independent 'assistance and protection centers' for vagrant minors with over 5,000 beds.[14] Assistance and protection institutions for vagrant minors offer universal services, and take various measures to secure the life, education, management, return to home and arrangement of these groups of people. According to the statistics, 325,000 vagrant minors have been assisted since the implementation of the *Measures for the Administration of Relief for Vagrants and Beggars without Assured Living Sources in Cities* in 2003.[15]

Problems underlying social welfare for special groups

The above measures for special groups have basically solved the survival problem of these groups. However, compared to normal people, the problems faced by these groups still remain outstanding. Service facilities are insufficient, the service level is relatively low, income disparities between special groups and normal people are expanding, and 'special groups' are almost invariably poor.

A very large number of the people included in 'special groups', especially those in rural areas, have not been able to extricate themselves from poverty

The social assistance system, which focuses on the minimum living allowance, represents the major institutional arrangement to relieve poverty. However, 'social assistance' and 'social welfare' often overlap in terms of contents and institutional arrangements for the special groups who need support and assistance. Restricted by insufficient financial and resource input, China's current assistance and welfare system has failed to help the special groups listed above in conquering poverty. According to the second national sample survey on disabled persons in 2005, the per capita annual income of the families of disabled persons was RMB 4,864 in cities and RMB 2,260 in rural areas, compared to the per capita annual income of people overall of RMB 11,321 in cities and RMB 4,631 in rural areas in the same year. The per capita income of the families of disabled persons is less than half that of the national average. Meanwhile, the per capita income of 12.95 percent of the rural families of disabled persons was below RMB 683 per year. Even worse, 7.96 percent of such families had per capita incomes that ranged from RMB 684 to RMB 944. In China, almost 10 million disabled persons living in rural areas are still faced with the problem of mere survival. In cities, 2.75 million disabled persons live at an income level that is less than the minimum subsistence level. According to a follow-up survey on the status of the urban and rural elderly population in China in 2006, nearly 20 percent of the senior citizens in cities have an annual income of less than RMB 4,600. Fifty percent of senior citizens have incomes that are lower than the median annual income level of the senior citizens in cities. The annual income of 1.35 million urban senior citizens is below the local minimum subsistence security line. Nearly 27 percent of rural senior citizens have an annual income of less than RMB 750, 50 percent lower than the median annual income level of the senior citizens in cities. The income of 21.6 million rural senior citizens is below the income threshold for rural assistance. The status of orphans across the nation is not optimistic, either. Judging from the national picture, in 2006, the orphans fostered by various social welfare institutions across the nation accounted for less than 13 percent of the total orphans. More than 200,000 orphans didn't receive any regular assistance in 2005, almost one third of total orphans.[16]

Special labor protection for female employees, in particular those in nonpublic enterprises, is not being properly implemented

Since reform and opening up policies began, measures designed to protect women are not having their desired effect, in particular in such non-public economic sectors as enterprises [private enterprises]. These either do not sign any employment contracts with female employees or they fail to respect the contracts. Although some enterprises sign employment contracts with female employees, such contracts do not contain provisions for special protection and social insurance for women employees. Most non-public enterprises do not participate in maternity insurance, do not implement the *Provisions on the Labor Protection of Female Employees*, and do not carry out the protection for these employees during the 'four periods' that women generally undergo (menstrual period, duration of pregnancy, prenatal period and lactation). In addition, women rarely have the opportunity to have regular gynaecological checkups.

Service facilities for special groups are inadequate

Special groups not only need regular public services, but also need special services. China's facilities obviously cannot satisfy the special needs of vast special groups in terms of quantity and service quality.

1 Special education. With minimal coverage, schools providing special education are poor in condition and vary considerably from region to region. In 2006, 74 prefecture-level cities (22.7 percent of all prefecture-level cities in China) and 483 counties (39.56 percent of the total) had not built special schools.[17] Poor schooling conditions and low quality represent two common problems in the existing special education schools. About 70 percent of the schools need to build classrooms and purchase necessary educational and rehabilitation training facilities.[18]

2 Children's welfare facilities are small in quantity, size, simple equipment and basic functions. In 2005, 130 'assistance and protection' institutions for vagrant minors had been established in just 39 percent of cities above the 'local' level. Of these 130, 128 were attached to 'assistance management stations' and had primitive infrastructure and facilities. There were 5,000 beds that were to help vagrant minors. The facilities could provide for feeding and accommodating just 114,000 vagrant minors for no more than 16 days. That number accounted for just 10 percent of the total in need.[19] In 2006 various social welfare institutions across the nation only fostered 72,000 orphans, less than 13 percent of the total. There were only 249 children's welfare institutions, which had 30,716 beds. The existing children's welfare facilities are having a very hard time covering and securing the basic needs of all the orphans and disabled children in terms of basic living, medical services, rehabilitation, special education and skills training.

3 Social welfare institutions for senior citizens are hampered by insufficient supply, sluggish development and low quality. Nationally, a survey shows that

there is a potential demand of 22.61 million beds in social welfare institutions in 2006. However, social welfare institutions for senior citizens only have 1.49 million beds, less than one twelfth of the total demand.[20] Research shows that for every 100 senior citizens aged 60 and above in Beijing, there are only 1.58 nursing-home beds on average. This is much lower than the five to seven beds in developed countries. Most social welfare institutions for senior citizens suffer from insufficient public funds, and find it hard to keep operating.

Basic public services aimed at special groups are in serious shortage

Not taking into account special needs that cannot be fully met, even basic public services available to special groups lag considerably behind the average level of society. The enrollment rate of disabled children in schools, especially those in the central and western regions, is markedly low. In 2005, only 80 percent of disabled children were receiving compulsory education. At present, 243,500 disabled children of school age do not go to school at all, and more than 80 percent of these children live in the central and western regions. One of the major reasons these children are not going to school is that there are not enough schools in these areas.[21] At the same time, the employment rate of disabled persons is very low. In Shaanxi Province the employment rate of the disabled population who are at an age to work, including males aged 16–59 and females aged 16–54, was merely 56.46 percent, only 70 percent of the employment rate of all the population surveyed at the same age bracket. Specifically, the employment rate of the disabled aged 25 to 29 was only half that of the surveyed population, while that of the disabled aged 35 to 44 was only 60 percent that of the surveyed population.[22] The reasons for low employment of disabled persons in China are multiple: for example, the disabled persons are not well educated in general, they are relatively poor in vocational skills and they cannot meet the demands of a broad range of industries and occupations. However, other important reasons include the bias and even discrimination against disabled persons among some employers. Employers also find it hard to obey many of the State laws and regulations concerning promoting and protecting disabled persons. In addition, most disabled persons have no access to practical rehabilitation services. According to the second national sample survey on disabled persons, only 8.45 percent of urban and rural disabled persons have received any rehabilitation training and services, while merely 7.31 percent have received the equipment and service of auxiliary devices. However, 27.69 percent of the disabled persons have requested rehabilitation training and services, while 38.56 percent have asked for auxiliary devices. Major factors that lead to the big gap between the rehabilitation demand of disabled persons and the actual services supply include: first, rehabilitation facilities for disabled persons are few and incomplete. The coverage ratio of community services for disabled persons remains a mere 14.3 percent.[23] Second, rehabilitation technicians are in severe shortage. There are currently only 5,000 rehabilitation technicians across the country, but there is demand for another 350,000.[24] Third, poor disabled persons cannot afford rehabilitation. According to the national monitoring results on the status of disabled persons based on a questionnaire survey conducted in Beijing Municipality, Henan

Province and Sichuan Province in 2006, 32.06 percent of the persons with intellectual disability and 60.76 percent of those that are mentally disabled and in need of treatment and rehabilitation training, as well as 42.53 percent of the persons with auditory disability and 31.09 percent of the linguistic disability demanding auxiliary devices cannot afford these services.[25] As to services for the elderly, China has not yet created an adequate social service system for an aging society. At present there are only 11.6 beds in social welfare institutions for every 1,000 senior citizens in China. This means that, at most, 1.16 percent of senior citizens can enjoy the services provided by the social welfare institutions, while senior citizens choosing to live in rest homes and other senior citizens' centers are 6–8 percent of the total. The home care service is in serious shortage. At present, only 15.9 percent[26] of the home care service demand is satisfied. Because the building of the rural old-age social service system has just started, the long-term care for rural senior citizens faces even greater challenges.

The social welfare system for special groups, particularly those in rural areas, is very unsound

Many of China's current social security programs have narrow coverage, and fail to cover special groups. According to major monitoring data on national disabled persons in 2007, less than 40 percent of the urban disabled persons aged above 16 participated in the basic pension scheme and the basic medical insurance, the proportion for the unemployment, industrial injury and maternity insurances was below 4 percent, and 58 percent did not participate in any social insurance programs. Less than 10 percent of the rural disabled persons above the age of 16 participated in the basic pension scheme and the basic medical insurance, less than 1 percent participated in unemployment, industrial injury and maternity insurance programs, and 89.2 percent participated in none of these programs.[27] This indicates that social security for China's disabled persons, and rural disabled persons in particular, is seriously absent. The follow-up survey on the state of urban and rural senior citizens shows that in 2006, 22 percent of the urban senior citizens did not receive any retirement pay (pension), 25.9 percent of the urban senior citizens could not enjoy any medical security, only 4.8 percent of the rural senior citizens enjoyed the pension security, while less than half (44.7 percent) of the rural senior citizens had access to medical security. In 2006 the coverage ratio of the maternity insurance among urban female employees was only 52 percent, still far less than the '90 percent by 2010' specified under the China Women's Development Outline.

Creating social welfare for special groups: objectives and methods

Development of social welfare system for special groups: objectives

The needs of different special groups are diverse and complex, due to the many types of special groups. Here, we will look at the overall objectives and trends of the so-called 'development of the social welfare for special groups, in two stages', mainly according to the economic and social trends in China. The objective for the first stage (2009–2012) is to ensure that special groups have access to the minimum living allowance and are extricated from poverty in terms of daily needs, that infrastructure for the basic living and rehabilitation of special groups is developed, and that the institutional framework for a basic public service system is built. The objective for the second stage (2013–2020) is to further step up the investment to meet the demands of social welfare for special groups, raise the basic living allowance as well as the quantity and quality of the public services available to special groups in a dramatic fashion, further improve the infrastructure for social welfare, and basically satisfy the minimum subsistence security needs of special groups (see Table 11.3).

Regarding the minimum living allowance: the work during 2009 to 2012 will focus on accelerating the transition from 'full coverage of the system' (of the minimum living allowance system) to 'full coverage of groups'. This transition is meant to ensure that all eligible people can, by and large, be provided for. At the same time, much should be done with regard to rural residents in raising the income threshold for minimum living allowances. As the economy develops the income thresholds for both urban and rural areas should constantly be raised.

Table 11.3 Objectives for development of social welfare for special groups in the future

Social welfare program	Stage 1 (2008–2012)	Stage 2 (2013–2020)
Basic living allowance	Realize universal coverage of all residents. By 2012, an annual subsidy of RMB 2,400 per capita will be offered to Five-Guarantee households, while this figure is RMB 1,200 per capita in rural areas.	Eliminate unreasonable urban–rural difference step by step; by 2012, an annual subsidy of RMB 4,440 per capita will be offered to Five-Guarantee households, while this figure is RMB 3,190 per capita in rural areas. Also establish basic service system for special groups.
Basic public service	The key work is to incorporate special groups, particularly rural special groups, into the social security system.	The major task is to build sound special systems, such as those for rehabilitation, education, employment and pension for special groups; and strengthen the linkage between different systems.
Infrastructure construction	Ensure the important special projects supported by the Central government are realized on schedule, and arrange new important special projects.	Coordinate the construction of infrastructure for special groups and the construction of urban and rural public service facilities, and strengthen the construction of social work talent teams.

Meanwhile, a basic security system targeted at special groups should be gradually established.

Regarding basic public services: China will accelerate the setting up of a basic public service system during the years 2009 to 2012, It will provide rural special groups with the most basic public services. To meet the special needs of these groups China will gradually improve special systems. For example, China will continue the national key rehabilitation projects to help the rehabilitation of the disabled, and research and build rehabilitation assistance systems for disabled children. As to the education of disabled persons, China will make an effort to solve the education problems faced by severely disabled children, and continue implementing the project of building special schools in the central and western regions. As to services for the elderly, China will push to improve community-based home care services in an all-round manner, and research and establish a nursing insurance system for senior citizens. By 2020, China will form a sound basic public service system for special groups mainly by integrating the rehabilitation of disabled persons into the national basic medical and health system as well as the basic medical service system. The country will build a service system for the elderly that covers urban and rural residents, and will establish a nursing-home system in economically developed regions. It will make sure that disabled children have nine-year compulsory education, it will step up employment promotion for disabled persons, and expand the areas and quantity of employment for disabled persons.

Regarding the construction of service facilities for special groups: to meet the basic needs of special groups in education, rehabilitation, assistance and special education, China will, in the 2009–2012 period, ensure the scheduled completion of children's welfare institutions, vagrant minors' 'assistance and protection' systems, the community service system, special schools in the central and western regions, and rehabilitation projects supported by the lottery public welfare fund. It will expand the community-based home care service network and other public service projects supported by the Central government. By 2020, China will basically complete construction of the urban and rural public service facilities and the service system. By giving play to the forces of the government, the market and society, it will grow the service industries that serve special groups. It will foster a professional team of people who engage in the field of social work, and make sure that public services for special groups improve in structural terms as well as in both quantity and quality,

Development of social welfare system for special groups: principles and requirements

Providing special groups with basic guarantees for their livelihood and basic public services, appropriate to the level of economic and social development, enables all citizens to share in the fruits of economic and social development, and contributes to building a harmonious society and embodies the progress of social civilization. However, for quite some time to come, China's economic development will not be able to improve to a massive degree. Meanwhile, the huge differences between urban and rural areas, as well as among regions, remains. The development of the social welfare for special groups must proceed from this reality. It must adhere to the overall principle of realizing universal coverage, satisfying basic needs, maintaining an appropriate level, and seeking steady development and improvement. To this end, we put forward the following principles.

- The first is the principle of equal participation and universal access. Development of social welfare for special groups should gradually shift from the relief-oriented model to the moderate universal coverage, so that all special groups who are eligible have the right and ability to receive security and welfare services provided by the government and the society, thereby fundamentally eliminating poverty faced by special groups.
- The second is continuing to adhere to a combination of the 'basic system' and 'special-category support'. Like regular people, special groups also need the basic institutional arrangements in life, medical services, education, employment, housing, social insurance and social services. In some sense, the actual demand of special groups for the basic systems is even greater than that of regular people. However, special groups have unique welfare needs, which must be satisfied through special social welfare programs. Examples include employment promotion for disabled persons; social services, professional nursing and community-based care services for senior citizens; and the fostering of and care for orphans. The social welfare programs designed for special groups should organically combine the basic institutional arrangements and special support policies.
- The third is adhering to the combination of subsistence security and service security. The basic objective of the social welfare system is to secure the basic life of all citizens. However, unlike basic life assistance for regular people, the minimum living allowance alone is insufficient for special groups, disabled persons and orphans in particular. Instead, the principle is to provide assistance according to the local living standards. At the same time, the social welfare policy should also take into full consideration the special needs of special groups in education, medical services, rehabilitation, employment, housing and long-term care, and should provide basic service security in these regards as well.
- The fourth is adhering to a combination of government leadership and social participation. The importance of government leadership should be particularly emphasized in developing social welfare for special groups. That does not mean that the government should undertake all the social services. It must actively foster and encourage the extensive participation of social forces, and maximize the roles of family, community and social organizations [civic organizations] to realize the purpose of sharing and building the system in common.
- The fifth is to adhere to a combination of urban–rural coordination and local adaptation. The current social welfare systems for special groups feature

obvious urban–rural and regional differences. For example, more than 80 percent of the disabled young children of school age who do not go to school live in the central and western regions. The social security for rural disabled persons is seriously insufficient, and rural senior citizens are basically excluded from pensions. Children's welfare institutions differ greatly from the urban and rural areas in their standards. The State's policies must adhere to the urban–rural coordination and balanced development between regions in future development of social welfare. At the same time, the innovative capacity of government at all levels and social organizations should be tapped, to actively explore the social welfare services and basic security modes that are suited to local conditions.

Policy recommendations

- First, focus more on the development of social welfare for special groups. Providing social welfares for such special groups as disabled persons, senior citizens and children allows them to participate in social life as equals, and to share in the results of our reform and opening up policies together with other citizens. The degree to which social welfare for special groups is focused upon represents the extent of the security and welfare of a country. Since the market, families and communities are able to play only supporting roles in protecting vulnerable groups, the State and the government must undertake greater responsibility in guiding the development of social welfare for special groups, to ensure they live with dignity and enjoy basic public services.
- Second, take firm hold of the process of establishing a system of 'basic living allowances' for special groups, in particular those who are impoverished. Currently, the basic livelihood of needy special groups in China is secured mainly through the 'social assistance' system. Due to their special needs, a basic living security system that is independent of the minimum living allowance system should be gradually created for special groups. This will help prevent the direct influence that high-risk poor families have on their family members who are included in 'special groups'; it will help design support policies for them based on their special needs. (1) Establish the children's welfare system at a moderate level. Unify standards for caring for orphans, and begin to provide disabled orphans with more intensive care; (2) expand the subsidy system for senior citizens to provide subsidies for those above 80 who have no pension, nationwide, as soon as possible. Set the standard at RMB 100–200 per month; (3) build the subsidy system for severely disabled persons, identify the total number of these persons and distribute the subsidies in a uniform way.
- Third, be thorough and conscientious in incorporating special groups, particularly rural special groups, into the social security system—'everybody should be covered by social security'. This is the most direct and practical issue that these special groups are concerned about. It is also an important method of breaking through the divide between urban and rural, and of

constructing a social welfare system that covers both. Strengthen supervision and inspection to ensure that both urban disabled persons and female employees participate in basic pension, medical, employment, industrial injury and maternity insurance programs. Implement and perfect the participation of the basic pension subsidy system for those urban disabled persons who engage in private business. Provide support for urban children and needy disabled persons so that they can participate in the basic medical insurance system, and for needy rural disabled persons so that they can participate in the new rural cooperative medical system. Implement the 'awards' policy for urban families who abide by family planning rules. Help rural needy disabled persons to participate in the rural social pension scheme. Implement the pension subsidy system for urban and rural senior citizens who do not participate in pension or other security programs, with subsidy amounts not lower than the local income threshold for minimum living allowances.

- Fourth, accelerate and improve the process of building an infrastructure for social welfare. As an important medium for advancing the work, and as a basic platform, the infrastructure directly determines the capacity, content and level of service security. Incorporate welfare service facilities for disabled persons, senior citizens, and children into the key public service projects supported by the Central government. Concentrate financial resources, bring sufficient resources to bear on building social welfare institutions, special schools and comprehensive community service facilities to provide a favorable environment for the daily life, education, rehabilitation, assistance and protection of children, disabled persons and senior citizens.

- Fifth, build the social welfare system and the public service system in a way that forms an organically unified system. Building the social welfare system is an important component of creating people's well-being and social environment. It plays an important role in promoting equal access to basic public services. Social security programs cannot function without public services. In addition to funding security programs, attention should also be paid to the provision of basic public services. Equalization of basic public services is important for ensuring basic living standards of the vast numbers of people of medium-income, but in particular for ensuring those standards for low-income groups.

- Sixth, step up the development of professional services for special groups. In addition to welfare funds and infrastructure, special groups most need social public services, particularly professional services, to meet their special needs. We must focus on the professional services needed to meet the special needs of these groups, such as human resource teams. We must mobilize social forces to participate in the construction of the welfare service system, further enhance the fiscal support for those social organizations engaged in social welfare programs aimed at special groups, and cultivate a well structured team of people who are high level professionals.

- Seventh, focus on targeted special services for special groups of people. Special groups are particularly vulnerable, and have unusual needs. They not only need the sunshine of the general public service system, but also need targeted special services. For example, the disabled population more needs rehabilitation facilities and high-level rehabilitation services in addition to the basic living allowance. We must keep developing the vocational education and training for disabled persons depending on their type of disability, promote their employment, and vigorously provide community-based jobs and welfare-related jobs suitable for disabled persons, as well as employing a certain percentage of disabled people in regular jobs. As to children, the State should energetically develop family welfare and children's welfare with universal access. More importantly, appropriate intervention measures should be taken to address such issues as school dropouts, rural children who are 'left behind' when their parents go to cities to work, orphans and children whose family conditions aren't conducive to their growth. We must improve the environment for the growth of these special children through the combined efforts of professional social-work teams and local communities.

Notes

1 2007 Statistical Communiqué on Civil Undertakings Development (http://www.mca.gov.cn).
2 The Follow-up Survey on the State of the Aged Population in China's Rural and Urban Areas (http://www.cpirc.org.cn).
3 2007 Statistical Communiqué on the Developing of Civil Undertakings (http://www.mca.gov.cn).
4 2006 Statistical Communiqué on Basic Condition of Implementing the Award and Support System for Family Planning Households in Some Rural Areas (http://www.chinapop.gov.cn).
5 Planning on Community Service System Development in the Eleventh Five-year Plan Period (http://www.sdpc.gov.cn).
6 The Follow-up Survey on the State of the Aged Population in China's Rural and Urban Areas (http://www.cpirc.org.cn).
7 State Council Information Office of the PRC: Development of China's Undertakings for the Old Age (http://www.china.com.cn).
8 Survey and Research Group on Labor Protection for Female Employees, *Report on Investigating Labor Protection on Female Employees in Beijing* (2002) (http://www.qianlong.com).
9 2006 Statistical Communiqué on the Development of Labor and Social Security Undertakings (http:///www.Molss.gov.cn).
10 Shang Xiaoyuan, Cheng Jianpeng, *Analysis on the Situation of Orphans in China* (published on China Youth Study, the 10th issue, 2006).
11 Zhang Mingling, Provide Category-based Relief and Comprehensive Protection to Promote the Development of China's Welfare Undertakings for Children (http://www.chin.net.cn).
12 Li Liguo's Speech on the Concluding Video Conference on the National 'Tomorrow Plan on Surgeon and Rehabilitation for Disabled Orphans' (http://bod.mca.gov.cn).
13 Planning on Constructing Assistance and Protection System for Vagrant Minors in the Eleventh Five-year Plan Period (http://fss.mca.gov.cn).
14 Planning on Constructing Assistance and Protection System for Vagrant Minors in the Eleventh Five-year Plan Period (http://fss.mca.gov.cn).

15 Study on Policy and Major Progress on the Development of Women and Children in China (2001–2006) (http://www.foredu.com.cn).
16 Vice Minister Li Liguo's Speech Work Conference about the Planning and Implementation of Constructiong Civil Affairs Undertakings in the Eleventh Five-year Plan Period (http://cew.mca.gov.cn).
17 Planning on Constructing Special Schools in the Middle and Western Regions in China During the Eleventh Five-year Plan Period (2008–2010) (http://www.moe.gov.cn).
18 Planning on Constructing Special Schools in the Middle and Western Regions in China During the Eleventh Five-year Plan Period (2008–2010) (http://www.moe.gov.cn).
19 Planning on Constructing Relief and Protection System for Vagrant Minors in the Eleventh Five-year Plan Period (http://fss.mca.gov.cn).
20 The Follow-up Survey on the State of the Aged Population in China's Rural and Urban Areas (http://www.cpirc.org.cn).
21 Planning on Constructing Special Schools in the Middle and Western Regions in China During the Eleventh Five-year Plan Period (2008–2010) (http://www.moe.gov.cn).
22 Xu Lin, Zhang Hui, 'The Government's Responsibility in Supporting Vulnerable Groups Reflected by the Employment of the Disabled in the Western Region of China', *Journal of Henan Normal University (Philosophy and Social Sciences)*, Volume 34, issue 6, 2007.
23 Planning on Constructing Special Schools in the Middle and Western Regions in China during the Eleventh Five-year Plan Period (2008–2010) (http://www.moe.gov.cn).
24 Tang Xiaoquan's Speech at the 22nd Working Conference of China Disabled Persons' Federation (http://temp07.cdpj.cn).
25 Develop Public Undertakings for the Disabled and Secure Their Rights – An Interview with Shen Zhifei, the Deputy Director of China Disabled Persons' Federation (http://www.cdpf.org.cn).
26 The Follow-up Survey on the State of the Aged Population in China's Rural and Urban Areas (http://www.cpirc.org.cn).
27 Report on Major Statistics on Monitoring the State of the Disabled across the Country in 2007 (http://temp07.cdpj.cn).

12 Social welfare programs supported by public finance

As we build our social welfare system, a strategic effort of vital importance to our social development, we must adjust the structure of our public spending accordingly. As the system changes, our spending must keep changing. There is a positive correlation between spending on social welfare and economic development. Although every country adopts a different model for its social welfare system, the rule holds true that the more economically developed the country, the more it spends on social welfare. Building a new social welfare system [in China] that benefits all citizens and that continues to be in alignment with changing stages of economic development will call for the strong support of public finance. This chapter presents what we believe the demands on public finance will be for the new system, and estimates the ability of China's public finance to support the system.

Government spending on social welfare programs: trends and analysis

Relationship between social welfare development and public finance

The level of benefits under a social welfare system and the percentage of total government spending that is devoted to providing the benefits are influenced by such factors as economic development, type of system, tax regime, and reform and transformation of the social insurance system. To analyze relative percentages of government spending on different kinds of programs, we have selected Russia, the Czech Republic and Hungary to represent transitional states, Britain and Switzerland to represent welfare states, Germany and Japan to represent social insurance states and America to represent a market-oriented state (see Table 12.1).

The social welfare in developed countries is generally of a high level. Among these, 'welfare states' provide complete programs, universal coverage of all citizens, fundraising through taxation, considerable governmental duties, and a high percentage of total public finance spent on the system. 'Social insurance states' give a larger role to social insurance programs, which provide basic living allowances for the insured, and are funded by premiums paid by employers and employees; the government undertakes more limited duties in these states, but the social welfare benefits are high and the percentage of government spending is also

Table 12.1 Social welfare expenditures of some countries in 2002

Country	Proportion of social welfare expenditure[1] in GDP (%)	Proportion of social welfare expenditure[2] in government spending (including social insurance) (%)	Total government spending	In which: social welfare expenditure	Social insurance tax
America	12	33.6	3,727,942	1,252,265	745,900
Britain	13.5	32.4	435,707	141,079	70,253
Germany	27.1	55.9	1,023,870	527,850	367,190
France	23.8	44.4	816,788	362,700	250,264
Sweden	20.7	35.4	1,368,849	484,940	346,337
Japan	16.8	44	190,089	83,581	49,167
The Czech Republic	19.6	35.4	1,257,431	445,122	362,982
Hungary	16.4	31.2	8,814,085	2,747,080	220,2320

Source: The data on America, Britain, Germany, France, Switzerland, the Czech Republic, Japan and Hungary come from the OECD website (http://www.oecd.org/dataoecd/42/47/33784603.xls) 'Summary of general government aggregates and balances'.

Notes:
1. Social welfare expenditures in the table include everything from pensions, survivor's benefits, disability benefits, industrial injury, medical, maternity and unemployment insurance, to family, educational and housing subsidies, social relief and other payments in cash or in-kind.
2. The amount of expenditure is expressed in USD 1 million, GBP 1 million, Euro 1 million, SEK 1 million, JPY 1 billion, CZK 1 million and one million Hungarian Forint, respectively.

high. States that espouse the 'guiding role of the market' stress the equal standing rights and obligations; the government is only responsible for the most fundamental social welfare system with moderate benefit levels. The levels of relief it provides for the poor and the levels of social welfare in general are not as high.

In comparing the specifics of different countries, it is not possible to rank the types of social welfare systems according to welfare levels and amount of spending, due to the complexities of variables that must be considered. These include differences in how taxation is handled, differences in tax rates, and the status of the reform of various systems. In 2002 all developed countries spent more than 30 percent of total public monies on social welfare. The figures for the countries were: Britain—32.4 percent, Switzerland—35.4 percent, Germany—55.9 percent, Japan—44.0 percent and America—33.6 percent.

The percentage of GDP that transitional countries are spending on social welfare systems is not necessarily low, indeed it is sometimes higher than the percentage of GDP spent in developed countries such as Britain and America. In 2002 this indicator was 9.6 percent in Russia in 1999, 19.6 percent in the Czech Republic, and 16.4 percent in Hungary. In terms of the percentage of total public spending put into social welfare systems, the figures are much the same as in developed countries. They were: Russia—35.8 percent (2001), the

Czech Republic—35.4 percent (2002) and Hungary—31.2 percent (2002). If the social insurance tax and corresponding government expenditure are deducted out of public finance, however, the government spending on social welfare in these countries is lower than that in developed countries.

Government spending on social welfare programs in China: trends and analysis

(1) Percentage of government spending on social welfare is somewhat declining. China's social welfare expenditures as a percentage of GDP are notably low. Over the past five to ten years, China's fiscal revenues have maintained very fast growth. They topped RMB 1 trillion in 1999, RMB 2 trillion in 2003, RMB 3 trillion in 2005 and RMB 4 trillion in 2006, RMB 5 trillion in 2007 and RMB 6 trillion in 2008. Fiscal revenues also increased as a percentage of GDP, going from 11.7 percent in 1995 to 20.8 percent in 2007. However, China's total welfare expenditures, including spending on compulsory education, only accounted for 5 percent of GDP in 2005,[1] far below the percentage of countries listed in Table 12.1.

It should be noted that fiscal revenues in China are relatively low as a percentage of GDP, therefore social welfare expenditures as a percentage of GDP may be misleading when compared to other countries. Another indicator, namely the percentage of social welfare expenditures to total government spending, may make more sense. Even when measured by this indicator, however, China's social welfare expenditures still remain at a low level. In 2005 China's social welfare expenditures only occupied 27.1 percent of government spending (including social insurance spending), lagging far behind most of the countries noted above.

In recent years the percentage of China's government spending put to social welfare has been declining, reinforcing the above trend. Though government spending on social security jumped from RMB 222.9 billion in 2001 to RMB 395.5 billion in 2005, it occupied a lower percentage of total government spending, going from 12.7 percent in 2001 to 11.7 percent in 2005 (see Table 12.2). It therefore failed to meet the goal of 15–20 percent that was specified in the *Outline for the Development of Labor and Social Security Cause in the Tenth Five-Year Plan*.

(2) Pronounced decline in the percentage of government funds spent on education, which is increasingly financed by other sources. Education is another field in which government spending is occupying an ever-smaller percentage. China's total educational expenditures on education, including non-compulsory education, almost quadrupled in the period 1997 to 2006, going from RMB 253.1 billion to RMB 981.5 billion. In that same period, government spending overall more than tripled, from RMB 186.2 billion to RMB 634.8 billion. Despite the fast growth of the figure, education occupies a smaller percentage of the total, down from 20.17 percent in 1997 to 15.7 percent in 2006. The percentage of government spending in total funding for education is declining very swiftly. It went from 73.57 percent in 1997 to 61.30 percent in 2005, only coming back somewhat in 2006. See Table 12.3 for details.

Table 12.2 Government spending on social security in China (unit: RMB 100 million, %)

Item	2000		2001		2002		2003		2004		2005	
	Amount	Prop.	Amount	Prop.	Amount	Prop.	Amount	Prop.	Amount	Prop.	Amount	Prop.
Total	1,918	12.7	2,229	12.3	2,894	3.5	938	12.4	3,440	12.1	3,955	11.7
Medical expense of government departments and public institutions	215	1.42	241	1.33	258	1.21	290	1.21	324	1.14	306	0.91
Consolation money, social welfare and relief	213	1.41	267	1.47	373	1.74	499	2.11	563	1.98	707	2.10
Retirement pay of government departments and public institutions	479	3.16	625	3.45	789	3.69	895	3.78	1,028	3.61	1,148	3.41
Social security subsidy	526	3.47	786	4.34	1.17	4.76	1,181	5.00	1,372	4.82	1,599	4.74
Subsidy to national social security fund	485	3.2	310	1.71	457	2.14	77	0.32	153	0.54	195	0.58

Table 12.3 The government's educational expenditure as a percentage of total fiscal revenues, as a percentage of government spending and as a percentage of GDP, 1997–2006 (unit: %)

Year	Percentage of fiscal revenues (%)	Percentage of government spending (%)	Percentage of GDP (%)	Percentage of total educational expenditures (%)
1997	21.53	20.17	2.36	73.57
1998	20.58	18.82	2.41	68.92
1999	20	17.34	2.55	68.29
2000	19.13	16.13	2.58	66.58
2001	18.66	16.17	2.79	65.92
2002	18.47	15.83	2.9	63.71
2003	17.73	15.62	2.84	62.02
2004	16.92	15.68	2.79	61.66
2005	16.31	15.21	2.81	61.30
2006	16.38	15.70	3.01	64.68

Source: Based on *China Education Statistical Yearbook, China Statistical Yearbook 2007.*

(3) Percentage of the government's spending for health is somewhat declining. The same problem exists in the health sector. The government's budget for health rose from RMB 58.7 billion in 1998 to RMB 155 billion in 2005, but health spending as a percent of total government spending went down over the same period from 5.46 percent to 4.57 percent (for details, see Table 12.4).

It is worth noting that the percentage of personal health expenditures has remained high, up to 52.2 percent in 2005. This is not only higher than in developed countries, but also well above the world's average of 43 percent.

Table 12.4 China's aggregate health expenditure (unit: RMB 100 million)

Year	Government budget for health	Social health expenditures	Personal health expenditures	Percentage of government budget to total government spending (%)
1998	587.2	1,006.0	2,183.3	5.46
1999	640.9	1,064.6	2,473.1	4.86
2000	709.5	1,171.9	2,705.2	4.47
2001	800.6	1,211.4	3,013.9	4.24
2002	908.5	1,539.4	3,342.1	3.92
2003	1,116.9	1,788.5	3,678.7	4.53
2004	1,293.6	2,225.4	4,071.4	5.54
2005	1,550.1	2,589.3	4,520.5	4.57

Source: National Bureau of Statistics of China (2006) *China Statistical Yearbook 2006.* Beijing: China Statistics Press.

Public financial resources needed for building a developmental social welfare system

A developmental social welfare system that covers all citizens and is able to adapt to ongoing economic development calls for the strong support of public funding. This section estimates the necessary extent of that funding, in specific stages, between now and 2012, and on to 2020. Estimates are based on the suggestions proposed in the preceding chapters. Our estimates use a baseline of actual government expenditures in 2006 or 2007. We estimate the costs of programs as recommended and come up with public finance needs for 2012 and 2020. For ease of calculations, constant prices are used, with no consideration for inflation.

Funding requirements for improving the old-age social security system

Pensions generally derive from two direct sources of funding, from the pension fund or from public finance. The former mainly consists of contributions made by the insured and their employers, while the latter mainly includes the tax exemptions of the pension fund, management and operational expenses of operating the system, and fund deficits that are subsidized by the government. Pension insurance funds, and especially their 'socially pooled' component, have incurred sizeable deficits since the end of the twentieth century, which have had to be covered by increasing subsidies from public finance at all levels of government. The deficits have been due to such factors as the transitioning of our economic system, the low percentage of the laborers participating in pension schemes, and a relatively early retirement and age at which one can draw a pension. In 2007, subsidies for urban pension plans reached RMB 126 billion. If the subsidized amount grows 10 percent on average every year from 2008–2012, RMB 202.9 billion will be needed in 2012. If the growth rate declines to 8 percent from 2013–2020, due to improvements in the urban pension system, the subsidy will amount to RMB 375.6 billion in 2020.

At present, pensions for retirees from government departments and public institutions are paid out directly by public finance. Given our upcoming pension system reform, the trend is going to be an ever-smaller gap in funding that has to be covered by the government, for these people as well as all urban and rural residents. In 2007 the total amount of pensions paid out in China was RMB 182.6 billion. If we adopt 'incremental' reform by improving the pension system without transforming its framework, and we assume an 8 percent annual increase in the amount of government subsidies for pensions of retirees from government departments and public institutions (from the 2005 level), then, RMB 337.1 billion will be needed in 2012 to subsidize pensions for these retirees alone. If the annual increase in subsidized amount slows to 6 percent in the period 2013 to 2020, then government subsidies for pensions of retirees from governmental departments and public institutions in 2020 will be RMB 559.7 billion.

In order to set up a system that covers rural residents as fast as possible, the State will also need to subsidize rural pension funds, in order to attract more of the agricultural population to participate. If the monthly subsidy for each insured is RMB 50, by 2012, the total subsidy for rural areas will be some RMB 310 billion. Subtracting out, however, 60 million uninsured senior citizens who are subsidized in other ways, and estimating that full coverage will affect 250 million people in rural areas,[2] actual subsidies will come to around RMB 150 billion. By 2020, if we increase subsidies per capita to RMB 100, and if the number of rural insured falls to 170 million due to urbanization, then the subsidies from public finance will come to RMB 203.2 billion.

In addition, in order to realize a system in which everyone is covered, the State will need to ensure that senior citizens have access to pensions. It will need to finance subsidies for those who are not currently participating in pension insurance. Beijing, Shanghai and some other places have explored ways to provide old-age subsidies for such uninsured senior citizens, but the cost is unaffordably high for the rest of the country. This report recommends that the old-age subsidy for urban senior citizens who are not currently covered by a social security plan should be raised to a monthly RMB 300 per capita in 2012, and further to RMB 555 in 2020. Subsidies for the elderly in their rural areas should be increased to RMB 100 in 2012, and further to RMB 285 in 2020, thereby gradually narrowing the disparity between rural and urban. We estimate that if there are 80 million senior citizens aged 65 and over who are enjoying a pension subsidy by 2012, which includes over 60 million elderly in rural areas, then we will need total funding for those subsidies of RMB 130.4 billion in that year. By the year 2020, as universal coverage of the pension system improves and fewer elderly need the subsidies, we estimate that RMB 234.7 billion will be needed to cover a reduced number of 50 million older people, including 30 million in rural areas.

Funding requirements for improving the health security system

As with other welfare programs, except for certain costs borne by enterprises, 'society', and individuals, the main funding for health security in modern society should come from public finance allocations and health insurance funds. Public finance appropriations for health are used mainly to improve the public health services system and to assure that 'everyone has access to basic medical and health care'. In 2006 the State's public finance appropriations for health came to RMB 172.1 billion. Subtracting out subsidies for various 'medical security programs', a total of RMB 118.8 billion was spent on public health, representing a monthly per capita spending, nationwide, of RMB 7.5. This report recommends that public health expenditures grow at no less than the average annual growth rate of the economy. If the current health appropriation system remains unchanged, and we assume a growth rate of 8 percent, then in 2012 the per capita monthly expense will be RMB 11 and in 2020 it will be RMB 20. Total government appropriations for health will come to RMB 179.8 billion in 2012, and RMB 354.9 billion in 2020.

With regard to 'medical security funds', the government not only subsidizes participants in various medical insurance schemes (basic medical insurance for employees, basic medical insurance for residents, the new rural cooperative medical system and the supplementary medical insurance for serious diseases), but also pays the medical bills of those employees in government departments and public institutions who are not covered by the above programs, as well as costs of 'medical assistance' for the vulnerable and the poor. Based on benchmark data from 2006 and 2007 that shows the number of people covered in various groups and the different benefits for which they are eligible, we have made the following calculations. Total government subsidies required for the medical security fund will be roughly RMB 275.9 billion in 2012 and RMB 1,028.1 billion in 2020. Adding the two cost items together, in order to provide universal access to both basic health services and medical security, total government spending required will be RMB 455.8 billion in 2012 and RMB 1,383 billion in 2020.

An itemized calculation follows: in 2007 the medical expense for employees of government departments and public institutions stood at RMB 53.2 billion. Given the fact that these medical expenses grew very fast over the past 10 years, if we assume a 10 percent rate of growth in the period 2007 to 2012, then we will need public funding in the order of RMB 85.7 billion in 2012. If growth stands at 8 percent from 2013 to 2020 (the decrease anticipated due to ongoing reform of the medical system), then we will need RMB 158.6 billion in 2020. The medical insurance subsidy for urban residents was RMB 7 per capita each month in 2006, and covered 42.91 million residents. We recommend expanding the coverage to 267 million urban residents by 2012, and increasing the monthly subsidy to RMB 17 per capita. That would require government funding of RMB 55.8 billion. With the development of urbanization, the medical insurance subsidy for urban residents will cover 531 million people in 2020, and the monthly subsidy will reach RMB 37 per capita each month. As a result, by 2020, government spending on medical insurance subsidies will reach RMB 237.9 billion. The new rural cooperative medical system currently covers a population of 726 million, but the subsidies are still relatively low. We recommend a gradual increase to RMB 14 per person per month in 2012 (which would require government funding of RMB 111.6 billion in that year), and further to RMB 34 in 2020. This latter figure assumes that benefits will grow at an annual rate of 12 percent after 2012. Given the decline in rural populations by that time, the subsidized population will decline to 673 million in 2012 and then further to 504 million in 2020. We therefore estimate that government spending on the new rural cooperative medical system would come to RMB 207 billion in 2020.

With the further improvement of the basic medical insurance for employees, this report recommends that the subsidy to cover its deficit should be increased from RMB 2.19 billion in 2006 to RMB 13.3 billion in 2012, and further to RMB 40.6 billion in 2020. In addition, from now until 2020, public spending on both urban and rural medical assistance should increase dramatically and this report recommends that government subsidies be increased by 15 percent every year from 2008 levels.

Funding requirements for expanding compulsory education

In 2007, 170 million people received nine-year compulsory education in China nationwide. This figure is expected to stay basically the same until 2020, given ongoing changes in the age structure. In 2007 the annual costs of primary education came to RMB 2,200 per student and junior high school costs were RMB 2,800 per student. A weighted average of the two sums results in an average per-student cost of RMB 2,400 per year, or RMB 200 per month. To close the gap between urban areas and rural areas, more of the additional fund will go to the rural area. Future annual educational costs per student are calculated on the assumption that they will grow 10 percent year per year from a base figure in 2007. Given that we want to close the gap between rural and urban areas, more of the increase in funding every year should go to rural areas. By 2012, government spending on subsidies for urban and rural compulsory education will be roughly RMB 657.1 billion, and by 2020, it will be RMB 1.4 trillion.

We recommend that one year of pre-school education be offered at no cost, and that coverage reach 50 percent by the year 2012 and 100 percent by the year 2020. Per student funding of that should be 90 percent of the cost of funding the nine-year compulsory education. Given these assumptions, the one year of free pre-school program will benefit 9 million children in 2012, requiring government spending of some RMB 31.3 billion, and it will benefit 16 million children in 2020, requiring government spending of around RMB 119.3 billion.

Coverage of the one-year of free vocational education for junior high school graduates before they take jobs should reach 80 percent in 2012, and rise further to 100 percent in 2020. Forecasts predict that 80 percent of the junior high school graduates will continue with their high school studies in 2012. The remaining 15 percent will start to take on jobs. We recommend that one year of free vocational education be provided to this segment, and we expect coverage of this segment to reach 85 percent by 2012. The cost per student in vocational schools or technical schools was roughly RMB 5,020 in 2007. We recommend that this be increased to RMB 8,880 in 2012 and to RMB 19,000 in 2020. In addition, this book recommends that subsidies be provided for the roughly 10 percent of senior high school students whose families face financial difficulties, for such things as tuition exemption or reduction. With the free year and the subsidies for the poorest, government spending will be RMB 62.2 billion in 2012. Further, we recommend instituting free senior high education in rural areas, in a staged fashion, by the year 2020. The cost of this, together with the one year of free vocational education and the subsidies for the poorest, will mean that 22.7 million students are covered by educational security programs by 2020, at a cost of RMB 432.2 billion in government subsidies.

Funding requirements for improving employment security

Employment security forms an important component of the new social welfare system. We must use all ways and means to carry forward proactive employment policies and to expand employment. Doing so will help realize greater fairness in employment opportunities, will help reduce income disparities, will reduce the burden of welfare expenditures and will contribute to maintaining social stability. Employment training, an important element of the employment promotion policy, needs step-up government spending in order to improve job prospects for the flexibly employed, migrant rural workers, non-agricultural employees in rural areas, and those who are currently jobless and need to be reemployed. In 2007 the government spent RMB 37.1 billion on employment assistance, training and subsidies. We recommend that this be substantially increased in the future, namely, to RMB 60 billion in 2012 and then doubling to RMB 120 billion in 2020.

Funding requirements for improving housing security

As stated above, our thinking with regard to housing reform is that we should address the housing problems of low-income urban residents through low-rent housing programs. The government subsidize low-income families who live in overcrowded housing, that is, housing in which per person living space is less than 13 square meters, which is the specified line for housing security. The subsidies will be paid based on the difference between the actual living space and the speci-fied lower limit, as well as the headcount of such families. Local governments may explore their own modes of providing low-rent housing in line with their own conditions. For example, eligible people may rent regular housing on the market, with the government providing monthly subsidies to cover rent differentials. Or the government may build a certain amount of low-rent housing each year to solve the housing problems of part of urban low-income households. By 2012, low-rent housing security should cover 50 percent of urban low-income families who live in overcrowded housing, which will benefit approximately 22 million people. If the monthly subsidy is RMB 200 per person, the total subsidy will add up to some RMB 40 billion. In 2020, low-rent housing security should cover 100 percent of urban low-income families with housing difficulties and should benefit more than 39 million people. If the monthly subsidy is RMB 400 per person, at that point the total subsidy will come to some RMB 190 billion. Housing issues faced by urban medium- and low-income groups will principally be settled through affordable [low-cost] housing, reasonably priced housing, tax exemptions and reductions, and other assistance-oriented methods. This will call for government spending of RMB 200 billion in 2012 and RMB 300 billion in 2020 to cover all those who are eligible.

The housing problems of migrant workers who have lived in cities for a long time will principally be solved through low-rent housing. The government should earmark funds to provide subsidies for these people and their families. In 2012, the total number of transient rural workers, who are migrating from one region to another for work, is expected to come to some 150 million. By 2020 that figure is expected to be 190 million. We aim to subsidize 10 percent of such workers in 2012, with housing subsidies of RMB 100 per person per month. The total amount needed will be RMB 18.3 billion. We aim to subsidize 30 percent of such workers by 2020, with a monthly amount of RMB 200 per worker. The amount of govern-ment spending required for these subsidies will come to RMB 204.3 billion.

With regard to those low-income rural inhabitants who have inadequate housing, the government will in future be offering a one-off building subsidy for help in constructing a home. At present, about 7.5 million rural households have difficulty building housing—affecting 30 million people. If building subsidies started in 2009 and are offered to 650,000 farmers each year, by 2012, 2.6 million rural low-income households will be subsidized. At a one-off cost of RMB 7,200, the total government spending required in 2012 will be RMB 4.7 billion. In 2020 all rural low-income households will be entitled to the building subsidy, and total government spending will come to RMB 9.7 billion, if the subsidy is lifted to RMB 15,000 per household.

Funding requirements for improving the basic living allowance system

Two factors influence the funding requirement of the basic living allowance system if supply is not considered—coverage rate of the system and benefits. In 2007 the recipients of the minimum living allowance in both urban and rural areas reached 58.38 million people, which, together with 5.31 million recipients of Five Guarantee relief, accounted for about 4.82 percent of the total population. Based on the internationally accepted poverty rate of 5 percent, if the total population grows to 1.36 billion in 2012 (the population grew by 7.35 million people from 2002 to 2007), recipients of the basic living allowance will be about 68 million people, and if the total population grows to 1.40 billion in 2020, recipients will be about 70 million people, an increase of 5 million and 8 million over 2007 respectively. With respect to the amount of benefits, the basic living allowance fund totalled RMB 49.85 billion in 2007. Subsidies for urban low-income residents, rural low-income residents and Five Guarantee residents were RMB 1,224, 444 and 1,176 per capita per annum, respectively. If the subsidies for urban low-income residents and Five Guarantee residents grow 8 percent year on year in terms of constant 2007 prices, the subsidies will rise to RMB 200 and RMB 370 in 2012 and 2020 respectively. The income threshold for living allowances in the rural areas, if growing at 13 percent year on year, will reach RMB 100 in 2012 and RMB 266 in 2020. Government spending on pensions is expected to amount to roughly RMB 120.6 billion in 2012 and RMB 273.4 billion in 2020.

Funding requirements for developing the social welfare system for special groups

Funding for social welfare for special groups mainly comes from government appropriations. Charity donations, social welfare lottery income and income of welfare enterprises will in future also be playing a considerable role. Looking first at social welfare undertakings in the narrow sense, which are administered by the Ministry of Civil Affairs, government spending in 2007 was less than RMB 3 billion, representing a per capita expenditure below RMB 3 for the national population of 1.3 billion. Even when employment assistance and other welfare

Table 12.5 Forecast of public finance needs to fund the social welfare system

Item		2007			2012			2020		
		Annual beneficiaries (10,000 people)	Fund needed per capita (RMB/month)	Total fund needed (RMB 100m)	Beneficiaries	Fund needed per capita (RMB/month)	Total fund needed (RMB 100m)	Beneficiaries	Fund needed per capita (RMB/month)	Total fund needed (RMB100m)
Old age security	Subsidy to uninsured urban senior citizens				1,850	300	666	1,960	555	1,306
	Subsidy to uninsured rural senior citizens				6,150	100	738	3,040	285	1,031
	Pension for government departments and public institutions (2005)	1,114	1,366	1,826	1,200	2,341	3,371	1,250	3,731	5,597
	Deficit subsidy for urban pension scheme			1,260			2,029			3,756
	Subsidy for rural pension scheme	5,171			25,000	50	1,500	17,000	100	2,032
Medical security	Public health fund	132,000	7.5	1,188	136,000	11	1,798	145,000	20	3,549
	Medical expense of government and other organs			532			857			1,586
	Urban residents' medical insurance subsidy (2006)	4,291	7	34.3	26,700	17	558	53,100	37	2,379
	Subsidy to new rural cooperative medical system (2008)	72,623	6.7	326.4	67,300	12	1,116	50,400	37	2,070

Category	Service									
	Medical assistance (2008)			92.9			162			497
	Subsidy to loss of basic medical insurance program for employees (2006)	1,8020		21.9	23,000		65	25,000		200
Public education	9-year compulsory education	17,000	200	4,080		322	6,571	17,000	690	14,085
	One-year preschool education		180		900	290	313	1,600	621	1,193
	Subsidy to one-year vocational education of junior high school graduates, and benefit for poor senior school students		420		700	740	622	2,470	1,587	4,322
	Housing and housing reform subsidy to medium- and low-income residents			1,620			2,000			3,000
Housing security	Subsidy to urban low-income families with housing issue				2,230	200	399	3,950	400	1,897
	Housing security for migrant rural workers				1,530	100	183	5,680	300	2,043
	Building subsidy for needy farmers				260		47	260		97

(Continued overleaf)

Table 12.5 (Continued)

Item		2007			2012			2020		
		Annual beneficiaries (10,000 people)	Fund needed per capita (RMB/month)	Total fund needed (RMB 100m)	Beneficiaries	Fund needed per capita (RMB/month)	Total fund needed (RMB 100m)	Beneficiaries	Fund needed per capita (RMB/month)	Total fund needed (RMB100m)
Welfare for special groups	Benefit to the survivors of killed servicemen or disabled veterans	545.7	286	186.8	650	417	325	800	670	643
	Welfare for disabled, women and aged	80,000	0.3	29.6	80,000	5	480	80,000	10	960
	Child nutrition subsidy			10,000	30	360	20,000	50	1,200	1,200
Employment security	Employment assistance, training and subsidy			371			600			1,200
Basic living allowance	Minimum living allowance for urban residents	2,272	102	278	2,720	200	653	3,500	370	1,555
	Minimum living allowance for rural residents	3,566	37	158	3,550	100	426	3,000	266	957
	Five Guarantee households	531	98	62.5	530	200	127	500	370	222
Total				12,079.4			25,966			57,377

Notes:
1. Used for interest exemption or reduction, market adjustment and experiments and reforms of taxation preferences in a bid to fully address the housing problems of the medium-income group and migrant rural workers.
2. 2006 expenditure for affordable housing.
3. Benefit per capita, i.e. income threshold for minimum living allowance minus current income of beneficiary. 4, 5, 6, 7, 8, 9, 10 and 11 all indicate benefits per capita.

Future explanatory notes on the table:

(1) The numbers of the uninsured senior citizens receiving the subsidy in 2012 and 2020 are both estimates. The population of uninsured senior citizens is estimated at 80 million in 2012, including 18.50 in urban areas, and 61.50 million in rural areas. With the improvement of the pension security system as well as the accelerated urbanization, such a population will reduce to 50 million, including 19.60 million in urban areas and 30.40 million in rural areas;

(2) 250 million people in rural areas are expected to enjoy the pension subsidy (excluding 60 million uninsured senior citizens subject to another kind of subsidy). Together with the development of urbanization, this figure is expected to decline to 170 million (excluding 30 million uninsured senior citizens subject to another kind of subsidy);

(3) The total population of China in 2020 is calculated at the upper limit of 1.45 billion;

(4) The population covered by the medical insurance for urban residents and the new rural cooperative medical system in 2012 and 2020 are estimated based on such factors as total population, urbanization rate and coverage;

(5) The number of students receiving the compulsory education in 2012 and 2020 are both estimates, and the educational fund per student is calculated on the basis of an annual growth rate of 10 percent over 2007. To close the urban–rural gap, the rural areas will be prioritized for increases in educational fund;

(6) It is expected that the total junior high school graduates will hit 17 million in 2012, and 80 percent of them will proceed with their learning in senior high schools. The remaining 20 percent will choose to take up a job; and it is suggested to provide the one-year free vocational education for 85 percent of these prospective workers, i.e. roughly 2.90 million graduates. Among the students who continue with their high school studies, an estimated 10 percent will come from low-income families, and they will receive tuition exemption or reduction or other subsidies. The senior high school program will take three years 4.10 million students are estimated to benefit. Then, 7 million students will benefit from this welfare program in 2012;

(7) The objective is to provide free senior high school education in rural areas in 2020, which will benefit 19.40 million students there. In addition, about 10 percent of the junior high school graduates who don't proceed with their study will receive the one-year free vocational education, which will benefit 1.60 million students. Among the urban students who enroll in senior high schools, about 7 percent of them are estimated to come from low-income families. These students, estimated at 1.70 million will receive tuition exemption or reduction and other subsidies. In total, 22.70 million students are expected to benefit from this educational welfare program in 2020;

(8) The number of migrant rural workers is calculated based on an annual growth of 7 million people over 200 million in 2007. An estimated 65 percent of all the migrant rural workers move from one region to another;

(9) All the welfare expenditures in 2012 and 2020 are based on the constant price level in 2007.

expenditures are added, the total comes to only some RMB 40 billion. For the 80 million disabled persons, more than 100 million senior citizens, 240 million children and the women who constitute half of the entire population, this welfare spending is at an extremely low level. There is an extreme contrast here between supply and demand. For these welfare programs, in which supply is the decisive consideration, the State should do its utmost to increase financial support. This category is an important component of China's 'developmental social welfare system'. In the context of strong economic and financial capacity right now in China, expenditures in this arena should be substantially increased, particularly for children's nutrition, disability handling and rehabilitation, and for protecting the rights and interests of women, children and senior citizens. The social welfare programs for these special groups will need an investment of RMB 116.5 billion in 2012 and RMB 280 billion in 2020.

Based on the above, the government will need to spend RMB 2596.6 billion to build a new 'developmental social welfare system for all', and ensure full 'system' coverage in 2012. By 2020, to ensure full basic coverage of 'all groups', the government will need to invest RMB 5737.7 billion.

Estimated capacity of public finance to support the building of a social welfare system

The previous section focused on the demand side of the equation, in terms of how much public funding is required to achieve the objectives described herein. This section focuses on the supply side of the equation. What assumptions have to be made if we expect China's government to be able to pay for the social welfare system envisioned in this report?

If we accept certain assumptions, we can roughly estimate the ability of public finance to support the developmental social welfare system recommended in this report. The Chinese government has set forth the objective of doubling GDP by the year 2020 over what it was in the year 2000. In 2007, fiscal revenues accounted for 20.8 percent of GDP, while spending on social welfare required 27.08 percent of fiscal revenues. Those figures give us some benchmarks. We further assume that GDP will grow at a rate of 8 percent per year. [Note: fiscal revenues in 2007 were RMB 5,130.403 billion. GDP in 2007 was RMB 24.6619 trillion.]

Our calculation show that public finance will not be able to pay for the welfare system, as put forth in the sections above, if fiscal revenues stay at 21 percent of GDP and if spending on welfare stays at 27.08 percent of fiscal revenue, even if GDP does grow as assumed at 8 percent each year. The shortfall will come to RMB 530 billion in 2012 alone and RMB 1.9 trillion in 2020. That is to say, unless the two percentages are modified, economic growth alone will not allow us to support this welfare system.

The question then becomes how much of an adjustment must be made in public spending in order to meet the recommendations in this report. First, we continue to assume that economic growth maintains an 8 percent rate in the 12 years to come, but we allow for a period of adjustment in other respects to counter the impact of the global financial crisis. We assume that the adjustment period lasts from 2008 to 2011, within which fiscal revenues stay roughly the same percentage of GDP, a stable 21 percent. After that period, however, we make the assumption that they then rise by 1 percent per year from 2012 to 2016. They reach 26 percent and then remain stable. In addition, we make the assumption that the percentage of government spending on welfare grows by 1.2 percentage points each year to reach 33 percent in 2012, later rising to 35 percent and remaining stable. If we make these new assumptions, then public finance will indeed be able to fund the welfare system we are recommending, whether that be the goals for 2012 or those for 2020 (see Table 12.6 for details).

Looking at current trends, and given the improvement in the economic situation, fiscal revenues will probably continue to grow at a rate that is higher than the rate of economic growth. In addition, many kinds of government revenue that were heretofore not included in the category of 'fiscal revenue' are gradually going to be incorporated into that sum, with the deepening of fiscal reforms and better regulation of taxation. Even given the necessity to adjust to the global financial crisis, to have fiscal revenues reach 26 percent of GDP and to have welfare spending reach 35 percent of all government spending in the years to come is not at all impossible. Indeed, such percentages are still on the low side (see Table 12.1), when compared to other countries, and also when compared to the realities of what is needed in China in the way of expanded programs and

Table 12.6 Government spending on social welfare, 2007–2020

Year	GDP	Fiscal revenue		Welfare expenditure		
	Annual growth of 8% (RMB 100m)	Proportion of GDP (%)	Aggregate (RMB 100m)	Proportion of fiscal revenue (%)	Aggregate (RMB 100m)	Proportion of GDP (%)
2007	246,619	20.80	51,297	27.08	13,891	5.63
2008	266,349	21	55,933	28.20	15,773	5.92
2009	287,656	21	60,408	29.40	17,760	6.17
2010	310,669	21	65,240	30.60	19,963	6.43
2011	335,522	21	70,460	31.80	22,406	6.68
2012	362,364	22	79,720	33.00	26,308	7.26
2013	391,353	23	90,011	34.00	30,604	7.82
2014	422,662	24	101,439	35.00	35,504	8.40
2015	456,475	25	114,119	35.00	39,942	8.75
2016	492,993	26	128,178	35.00	44,862	9.10
2017	532,432	26	138,432	35.00	48,451	9.10
2018	575,026	26	149,507	35.00	52,327	9.10
2019	621,029	26	161,467	35.00	56,513	9.10
2020	670,711	26	174,385	35.00	61,035	9.10

expanded coverage. China's government spending can absolutely afford the increases in these two percentages. Moreover, as will be discussed in the next section, the State will face even less in the way of financial pressures if more financing channels are encouraged.

To some extent this calculation reveals that it is necessary for China to maintain an annual economic growth rate above 8 percent for an extended period of time, at least until 2020. Based on our calculation, even if the proportion of the welfare expenditure in GDP is boosted to the level expected in this report, the State will be unable to fund a social welfare system (even if it is at a lower level), if economic growth falls short of 8 percent. Only when the economic growth keeps a certain momentum, can the basic needs of social development be met. People always talk about keeping the growth rate at or above 8 percent ['hold the line at eight!'], and focus on its significance for employment. Actually, employment alone is not sufficient to justify the rate, as the same economic growth rate may have varying effects depending on the types of jobs created. The 8 percent growth rate is better understood, however, when we consider the need to improve social welfare. We have forecast a scenario under which annual GDP growth is 7 percent. Under this scenario, the public finance system cannot support the recommendations, whether in the long term or the short term.

Building a 'developmental welfare system for all' in the next 4 to 12 years is definitely going to be a magnificent feat in the history of China and, perhaps, of all humanity. As a major socioeconomic reform in China, it will also lay the foundations for changing our old economic pattern of high savings, investment and export, while continuing low consumption and domestic demand. However, we should also bear in mind there is no free lunch. To resolve so many significant issues within a short term will require State finances and society to put in very considerable investments.

Establishing a social welfare system is a long term process of system creation, affecting all aspects of the economy and society. Therefore, our planning needs to be comprehensive and we need to systematically analyze and estimate the aggregate demand for social welfare and the aggregate availability of financial resources as well as their future trends. Currently, government organs are working separately to push forward the welfare programs for which they are responsible and to promote the importance and urgency of their own programs over others. This research is significant in that it integrates and aggregates all the relevant programs, in order to find out under what conditions State finance can support a social welfare system with universal coverage, and what welfare levels the State can truly afford. This will allow us to have a full picture, even when we are making policy decisions about only part of the welfare system or programs. When we are setting policy, priorities can be more easily identified.

This forecast also warns us against setting up overly ambitious goals for the social welfare system. Our fiscal capacity can only maintain a basic and low-level welfare system for all. The free welfare programs should still focus on low-income groups for an extended period of time, except for the compulsory education. Social insurance programs for those medium-income groups and above in both urban and rural areas are still going to have to rely on the payment of premiums. Therefore, various types of payment-based welfare arrangements are still going to have to be the core of our welfare system.

It's worth noting that the above forecast does not take into account the operating costs required to expand the welfare. We assume the operating cost will be covered by State finance as part of the government's operating expenditures. The forecast as above will be unable to support the welfare system recommended in this Report, even if operating costs are estimated at only 10 percent of the total welfare expenditure. Either fiscal revenues as a percent of GDP are going to have to rise, or welfare spending as a percent of total government spending is going to have to be increased.

Developmental social welfare system: fund raising and management

Expansion of financing channels for social welfare system

The social welfare system consists of multiple programs, each with its own functions and financing pattern. Generally, these programs can be divided into two major categories. The first is contribution-based social insurance programs, such as pensions, medical care, unemployment, industrial injuries, and maternity insurance. They are mainly funded by the premiums paid by employers and employees, while State finance mainly performs the following functions: (1) to pay into the programs for government employees; (2) subsidizes the vulnerable groups participating in these programs; and (3) acts as lender of last resort when the insurance fund incurs a deficit. The second category is free social welfare programs, such as the minimum living allowance, compulsory education and medical assistance. These programs are accessible to all (such as compulsory education) or only to people in need (such as minimum living allowances and medical assistance), and they offer free services to beneficiaries while binding them to no obligations at all. The choice of welfare mode differs from one country to the next, as does the choice in financing approaches. Like most countries, China's social insurance programs are the major form of its welfare system, which are then supplemented by free welfare programs. Thus, financing is done principally through the contributions paid by employers and employees. To date, social insurance programs for employees of urban enterprises have been widely implemented. Employers pay 30 percent and employees pay 11 percent of the employee's salary into the fund, on average. For details of contribution rates, see Table 12.7.

In 2007, the total income of five insurance programs stood at RMB 1081.2 billion, while total expenditures were RMB 841.5 billion, leaving an accumulated balance of RMB 1123.4 billion. Of the five programs listed above, the largest amount of government funding goes to pensions, and it is also appropriated first. However, government funding still only accounted for 18.5 percent of the pension fund. See Table 12.8 for income breakdown of the pension fund in the past five years.

Table 12.7 Average contribution rates of enterprises and individuals in the social insurance programs (%)

	Pension	Medical care	Industrial injury	Unemployment	Maternity	Total
Corporate contribution	20	6–8	1 (on average)	2	0.8	30
Individual contribution	8	2	0	1	0	11

Source: National Bureau of Statistics of China (2007) *China Statistical Yearbook 2007*. Beijing: China Statistics Press.

Table 12.8 Income breakdown of corporate pension fund, 2002–2007 (unit: RMB billion)

Year	Total	Contribution income	Government subsidy	Local government subsidy*	Interest	Others
2002	278.4	217.9	55.3	4.7	2.5	2.7
2003	320.9	259.5	54.4	5.2	2.9	4.1
2004	372.8	308.8	56.8	7.2	4.2	3.0
2005	449.2	374.7	64.9	8.2	5.4	4.1
2006	563.3	458.1	94.1	13.2	7.1	4.0
2007	701.1	574.0	110.3	19.8	11.5	5.3
Increase from 2002	422.7	356.1	55	15.1	9	2.6
Annual growth rate (%)	20.3	21.4	14.8	33.3	35.7	14.4

Source: National Bureau of Statistics of China (2007) *China Statistical Yearbook 2007*. Beijing: China Statistics Press.
* Indicates the amount of subsidy provided by local treasury.

To accelerate the establishment of a security system with universal coverage, we are going to need to expand funding channels through every means possible. In addition to adjusting the structure of government spending and increasing government spending on social welfare, we can also consider raising funds through the following channels.

1 Introducing new taxes. For example, the government can levy a high consumption tax on the purchase of villas, luxury cars, yachts and golf to fund the secondary distribution. Or the government can impose estate taxes and put a part of interest tax income into a social welfare fund. The government can also introduce resource taxes to moderate the extremely high incomes currently being earned by the petroleum, coal and electric power

companies as a result of their monopoly status. This will not only raise funds for social welfare but will also help promote social equity.

2   Allotting a part of state assets to the social welfare system. The government can transfer state-owned shares to welfare purposes through such means as repurchase of its own shares and placement of new shares. Moreover, in 2007 alone, State-own enterprise realized a profit of RMB 1.62 trillion. A budget can be set up from the operating earnings of State capital that takes in one-third to one-fourth of earnings for social welfare. A part of the proceeds from the transfer of land-use rights may also be transferred to social welfare programs.

3   Issuing more social welfare lotteries to raise funds. In 2007 the government obtained RMB 21.7 billion from social welfare lotteries and RMB 12.7 billion from sports lotteries, which it put into welfare funds. The sales of the two types of lotteries have increased rapidly since 1994, but there is still plenty of margin left for issuing social security lotteries.

Establishing a social security fund budget

We can consider setting up a separate social security budget and make the expenditures and income of a social security fund separate from recurrent expenditures and incomes, and independent from the government's public budget and the budget for state-owned capital. The social insurance fund is mainly composed of corporate and individual contribution. Its pooled fund is owned in common by the beneficiaries, while individual account funds belong to each individual and are not of a 'public funds' nature. The receipt of funds into, payments out of, and operations of the social insurance fund are distinct and different from those of public finance funds. A number of actions will be necessary in helping keep a long-term balance in the income and payments of the social security fund. These include: establishing one social security budget, bringing various social security funds under the unified management of government budgets, instituting a double-entry budgeting system under public finance, standardizing management of social security expenditures that come from public funds, improve the efficient use of capital and providing fiscal support for social security. The following is a suggested framework for budgeting social security funds.

Budgeting procedure

The draft budget will be made by the labor security departments and financial departments in the local pooling area, and submitted to the local government for examination, then on to the local people's congress for review and approval. After local people's congresses have approved local budgets, the government will authorize 'social insurance' and relevant departments to implement the local budgets if approved at the national level. The draft budget of the national social security fund will be drawn up by the relevant department in the State Council. It will then be submitted to the State Council for examination [and confirmation] and to the National People's Congress for review and approval.

Fund account

The government should set up an independent account for the social security fund, which is to be managed by the People's Bank of China. Once a separate budget is set up for the social security fund, it will no longer be possible simply to use extra-budgetary capital accounts for handling social security funds. Instead a special account, as per the approach of managing treasury accounts, will be set up that effectively separates the social security fund from public finance funds in general. This will assure the 'completeness' [integrity], independence and security of the fund, and will prevent the fund intermingling that makes it easy for siphoning off money into other purposes. Setting up such a special account is in line with creating a separate budgeting process for the social security fund. It is also in line with current trends in reforming account management. Its most striking features are its independence from other accounts (for example, the treasury or special fiscal accounts), its being established at the Central bank (instead of a commercial bank), and its management by the Central bank (instead of social insurance departments or financial departments). It is neither the same as public finance accounts that financial departments of the government or social security institutions currently set up at state-owned commercial banks, that are 'income and expenditure accounts', nor is it the same as the accounts that social insurance institutions used to set up in commercial banks before 1998.

Meanwhile, managing the special account for the social security fund also helps the Central bank prevent and control financial risk overall.

Fund income

The premiums paid in by enterprises and individuals constitute the major part of the social security fund. The fund's budget will come from premiums, returns on the fund's investments, budgeted social security subsidies, and [public finance contributions to] social assistance, social welfare and special benefits (such as benefits to the survivors of killed servicemen or disabled veterans). Each item will be listed so as to reflect an accurate and complete accounting for sources of the fund. At the same time, public finance subsidies to the social security fund, when listed as discrete budgetary items, will clearly reflect the contributions of the government budget to social insurance.

Budget classification

In view of the history and development of China's social insurance system, the social security budget should also consist of two parts—budgetary revenues and budgetary expenditure, in the same manner as public finance budgets and the budgets for state-owned capital. They should be drawn up by 'program', and by type of insurance.

Budgetary revenue is composed of three parts. The first is the fund's general revenue that was formerly incorporated in a regular budget and used to cover the social welfare expenditures, including direct appropriations, surplus transfers and lump-sum subsidies under the regular budget, as well as earmarked appropriations. The second is the 'additional budgetary revenue' of the social insurance fund, including the revenue from basic pensions, medical, unemployment, industrial injury and maternity insurances. Thus, the budget can both reflect the overall situation of the social security fund, and the resources for a specific type of insurance. In addition, the second part also includes revenues from the disabled persons' employment security fund, the social welfare fund, the housing accumulation fund, the late fees paid by enterprises or individuals, revenue off fiscal subsidies, and the investment income of the social insurance fund. The third part includes other revenues derived mainly from the appreciation of state-owned assets and donations. The former represents the government's support for the social security cause, while the latter encompasses the donations from foreign governments, institutions, enterprises and individuals. Added together, this third category forms an important part of the social security budget revenue.

Budgetary expenditures consist of such items as social insurance, social relief, social welfare, social assistance and specific service expenditures. To match expenditures to revenues, expenditures may also be divided into three categories based on funding source and purpose. The first is the social security expenditures under the regular budget, mainly including public health expenditures, special benefits and relief expenditures, the fund for retirees of government departments and public institutions, urban employment assistance expenditures and poverty reduction expenditures. The second includes expenditures budgeted for the social insurance fund, including the subsistence subsidies, pensions, medical subsidies and other insurance-like expenditures paid by the government out of various funds to ensure the basic subsistence of every social member in case of old age, illness, disability and unemployment. The third is 'other outlays' to be met by proceedings from the appreciation of state-owned assets and donations. These are mainly used as an incremental supplement to boost the payment levels of social relief, social insurance and social welfare.

Budgetary level

Unlike government budgets created at different levels, each social security fund budget is drawn up mainly based on the pooling level of the fund. That is to say, for a fund pooled at the national level, only the national-level budget is needed, while, for a fund pooled at the provincial level, only the provincial-level budget is needed. [Note: in certain cases, municipalities are accorded provincial status. Beijing is one instance.] Budgeting according to the pooling level can, for one thing, reinforce the responsibility of the local government at that level and help break through barriers between jurisdictions. For another, it can help reduce administrative interference in the fund and thus help protect its independence and security.

Responsibilities of governmental departments

After a separate budgeting system is established for the social security fund, department responsibilities need to be clearly defined. The social security department will work together with the finance department in drafting the budget, and will join with other departments in managing the fund, as per the law. The auditing, taxation and regulatory departments will be responsible for overseeing and monitoring the fund, with the responsibilities of each spelled out as per the law.

Notes

1 See Table 1.3.
2 The current population engaged in agricultural activities stands at roughly 300 million.

13 Policy recommendations

This report feels that building a developmental social welfare system should be done in two stages. By 2012 the initial steps in creating a systemic framework will have been taken. By 2020 the 'developmental social welfare system' will basically have been created, and implementation will have begun. By 2020 all China's residents will be ensured more equitable rights in social welfare programs and benefits. They can maintain a decent living and have access to appropriate public services, and the difference in provision of public services in urban and rural areas will be essentially eliminated. The proposed system includes pensions, health security, education security, housing security, employment assistance, unemployment insurance, minimum living allowance and social security for special groups. Policy recommendations for each section that were detailed in the preceding chapters are summarized below.

Pensions

First, accelerate the establishment of a basic subsidy plan for uninsured senior citizens. A government-funded subsidy plan should become the fundamental pillar for the pension system in China. Subsidies are to be granted based mainly on age rather than on contributions. They may be lower than benefits paid by a basic pension plan, but should be no lower than the minimum living allowance or it will be hard to be effective in reducing poverty among the elderly. For the specific form of basic pension system, we may refer to the practices in such places as Beijing and Shanghai, and improve the system gradually. The Central treasury should provide certain financial support to economically less developed areas, so that this system meets the needs of the elderly nationwide; local governments may provide additional financial support depending on local living standards.

Second, establish a unified operational mechanism for basic pensions. Two programs may be considered. Program 1: the basic pension is pooled at the national level. We need to promote provincial pooling before it is achieved throughout the country by the end of 2009, and on the basis of this, realize the national pooling of basic pensions by 2012. A Central pooling fund should be established by then, putting basic pensions that were previously the responsibility of local authorities under Central management. Program 2: change the 'surcharge'

[fee] into a tax, and uniformly collect a social security tax that functions as a basic pension, nationwide. That portion of basic pensions currently paid from socially pooled funds should be separated from the current system, and be funded by a specific national tax paid by employers and collected by the national tax departments countrywide. The tax is to be imposed on all urban workers including those working for township enterprises; the basis for the tax is the total income of a taxpayer. In this way we should be able to eliminate the difference in basic pension granted to a worker due to his or her 'identity' [or 'status', *shen-fen*] (i.e. a worker in enterprises, government departments, public institutions or other organizations). To adapt to the new tax system all urban employees should be registered and an individual file should be created for each. The personal tax payment may vary depending on the payer's employment status. The employee may suspend or terminate tax payments due to such reasons as unemployment, the closing of a business, because he is going to school, and so on, but tax must be paid whenever the person is employed and it must be paid by both the employer and the employee. A retiree is entitled to the basic pension if he or she has paid the tax for a total number of 15 years. An increase of 0.5 percentage points in the replacement rate will accrue (no more than 35 percent at maximum) for each additional tax-paying year after the 15-year period. If the individual pays the tax for less than 15 years, then the pension will be reduced accordingly. When the new system is implemented, the years for which an employee or retiree has already participated in a pension plan or has been regarded as contributing to the plan shall be counted as part of his or her tax-paying years, and the pension will be granted accordingly.

Third, improve the financial soundness of the individual accounts fund. Individual accounts accrue as a result of personal contributions and investment returns. The amount of the monthly payout upon retirement will be determined by the fund's financial resources and life expectancy. The basic idea of improving the fund's financial soundness is to build upon the experience of 13 provinces that have already been carrying out trials. From 2010 onward, starting from a rate of no less than 3 percent, accounts will be made 'solid' by increasing one percentage point every two years until an 8 percent status is reached by 2020. The deficits in any provincial fund will be addressed mainly by expanding the coverage; the Central government will continue to subsidize the central and western regions as well as old industrial bases. All 'zero-balance' accounts before 2010 will be fully funded through multiple channels, such as cash income from state-owned assets, fees for assignment ['transfer'] of State land, excess profits of monopoly industries, income from use of concession resources, special transfer of personal income tax, and issue of special bonds. Individual account funds are managed by local governments and are 'mobile', i.e. can be transferred when a participant moves. The portability and renewability of the funds is the responsibility of the local social insurance department. Accumulated individual account funds are to be managed by financial institutions on a commission basis, subject to the supervision of relevant government departments, financial regulatory agencies and other supervisory bodies.

Fourth, establish and improve the pension system for migrant rural workers. The pension system proposed for migrant rural workers must have a new conceptual framework that is tailored to their situation: low premium rate, more centralized pooling and improved financial soundness of the individual accounts funds, meaning they are not being operated through deficit financing. A low premium rate should apply with the premium borne by employers and migrant rural workers. An enterprise should pay the premium at 12 percent of its total payroll, where 6 percent will go to the pooled fund, under national uniform management, and 4 percent to the individual account. An individual will pay 4 percent of his salary into the individual account, and obtain an individual account card. The card will record the premium payment status, and will allow for inquiries, but will not allow for premature withdrawal. At the same time a national pension settlement system will be established to pay migrant rural workers upon retirement according to national pooling regulations. The responsibility for the insurance procedures and the account management in principle rests with the labor security department or system from top to bottom. Migrant rural workers' personal account funds may be managed separately from urban insurance funds. Policies and measures should be formulated that allow funds to be invested indirectly in State infrastructure and key projects and to be operated through market-oriented investment, and special bonds may be issued to ensure the funds appreciation. Efforts should be made to ensure a 50 percent enrollment of migrant rural workers in the pension scheme by 2010 and 100 percent or so by 2012.

Migrant workers in the formal sector who are enrolled in the social insurance plan for urban workers shall remain in the plan, entitled to equal benefits. Employers should pay social insurance premiums for them. Migrant workers in the informal sector, especially in the cities' service industries where businesses are small and jobs are unstable, can gradually be incorporated into the urban pension system, just as informally employed urban workers are included in the system.

Fifth, build a new pension system for farmers. The new system should be modelled along the principles of the new rural cooperative medical system. By giving consideration to farmers' disadvantages, such as the absence of any employer to make contributions, low incomes, and inadequate ability to pay, such a system uses the 'basic pension + individual account' model featuring co-contributions by the State, collectives and individuals. The government should provide the bulk of financial support. A detailed description is given below. The State will pay the basic pension since it is not contribution-based. For example, a monthly benefit of RMB 50 per person will be set aside in the annual budget for what we can call an 'old-age subsidy'. Local governments may increase the basic pension in line with the local financial conditions. Farmers' individual accounts will consist of personal contributions, collective subsidies and investment returns plus government subsidies. Personal contributions may vary, at personal discretion, between 5 and 10 percent of the local net income per capita of the year. In addition to local governments, village-based collective enterprises and township enterprises may also subsidize individual accounts. The age at which one becomes eligible for benefits under the new system is fixed at 65, before which farmers who lose the ability to work may receive the minimum living allowance. In addition to basic pensions, rural residents may also receive pensions from their individual accounts, if any. All efforts should be made to assure a basic pension that is equal to 30 percent of the net income per capita of the local farmers; added to individual account benefits, this should be able to ensure that a person can support himself with dignity.

Sixth, establish a pension system for such other urban residents as flexible workers and the self-employed. Similar to the proposed pension plan for migrant rural workers, the premium rate may be lowered from the present 20 percent to 14 percent (8 percent into individual account and 6 percent into pooling fund). As incomes of the self-employed and flexible workers differ greatly and are unstable, a unified contribution base should be determined according to the average wage of local workers. In terms of pension payments, the rules of the enterprise pension scheme should apply, i.e. taking the local monthly average wage of the previous year and the average of one's indexed monthly wage as the base for basic pensions and granting 1 percent for every year of contribution. The pension payout from the individual account is the balance of individual account savings divided by the estimated number of months for pension payment, which is determined by such factors as the life expectancy of the urban population when the contributor retires, his or her retirement age and investment income.

Seventh, actively promote an occupational annuity system. Under the market economy, the government, in addition to promoting the pension plan, should also formulate policies in support of accelerating the establishment of an occupational annuity system. While the principle of 'equity' operates with respect to the basic insurance system, in balancing the interests between regions, departments, industries or occupations, the principle of 'efficiency' should operate with respect to the annuity system. This system should reflect income-based differences in pension benefits. It should encourage the enterprising attitude of people and their enthusiasm to create social wealth. When combined, the two systems should achieve a balance of equity and efficiency.

Eighth, raise the mandatory retirement age as appropriate and establish a long-lasting mechanism in response to aging. The working life of the population may be gradually extended according to international practices. The mandatory retirement age may be progressively raised to 65 based on the supply and demand situation for labor, and based on demographic changes. To support the late-retirement policy, a benefit-based incentive mechanism should be introduced, lowering pensions paid to early retirees and increasing the benefits to late retirees.

Ninth, explore a long-term nursing system for the old and actively develop socialized services for the elderly. Old-age security means not only the economic independence of an older person, but also the availability of essential social services when needed. In developing a mechanism that allows communities to take the lead in delivering home care services for the old, we can consider community-based care centers where the elderly are looked after while their children leave for work or other reasons, as well as recreational locations for the elderly. We may also consider nursing homes where the old are taken care of by what will need to be an expanding contingent of social workers. To solve underfunding in elderly care, market mechanisms can be used to develop old-age industries, produce products for the elderly and create job opportunities.

Tenth, accelerate legislation relating to the old-age security system and improve its management. The process of social security legislation must be accelerated, in particular the *Social Relief Law*, *Social Insurance Law* and *Social Welfare Law* should be put into effect. We must clarify rights and responsibilities among regions and between Central and local governments with respect to how social security funds are managed, especially pension funds. We should remove barriers to portability of social security insurance and to investment of individual account funds and other accumulative pension plans, and build the institutional arrangements for the smooth operation of the old-age security system. We should make full use of the favorable conditions that information technology has created for China's social security reform, accelerate the building of information-based social security and old-age security, maintain records on contributions and benefits on a nationally networked basis. We should make individual accounts an important carrier and information platform for records, portability, investments and benefits distribution. The application of IT technologies will guarantee the success of China's old-age security and also its social management systems. We should accelerate the training of professionals, providing an intellectual guarantee for the development of the country's old-age security system. Efforts should be made to remove, as fast as practical, the policy barriers for the portability of social security plans, and to formulate national portability rules so as to promote the rational flow of labor. We should excel at learning from international experience, but we must respect and proceed from our own realities in establishing a modern old-age security system that fits the country and that can be constantly improved on the basis of practice.

Health security

First, the work from 2009 to 2012 focuses on expanding coverage and improving levels of security in the system. This includes four dimensions: first, improving the coverage of the basic medical insurance for urban employees, up to 90 percent; second, accelerating the establishment of a basic medical insurance for urban *residents* to cover more than 90 percent of those urban workers and residents who cannot participate in the basic medical insurance system for urban *employees*; third, maintaining the percentage of rural residents participating in the new rural cooperative medical service program above 90 percent; and fourth, basically resolving the portability of insurance plans of migrant rural workers.

Second, between 2013 and 2020, the emphasis is on establishing a universal public health service system and medical service system in both urban and rural areas. Major objectives include: first, incorporating all urban and rural population into the basic medical security system; second, reducing the percentage of personal payments under the medical security system, improving the level and benefits of the security, and improving the percentage of reimbursement under the basic medical insurance system for urban and rural residents to over 60 percent (drug expenses under the basic drug system will be reimbursed in full) while maintaining the current security benefits for urban employees; third; establishing the basic medical and health system framework nationwide, building a relatively sound urban and rural public health service system, a 'three-level' rural medical and health service system, and the new urban medical and health service system based on the community medical service, and establishing the beginnings of a regular public medical institution management and operation mechanism.

Third, provide urban and rural residents with medical services through the community health service system that combines the functions of prevention, basic medical services, health, rehabilitation, health education and family planning [planned parenthood] as well as other medical services systems of various forms. The community health service system will consist of the urban and rural public health services system, the 'three-level' rural health services system and the urban community health services system. The medical services system will be composed of for-profit and not-for-profit medical institutions that compete against one another under strict governmental supervision, and provide diversified medical services at different levels for residents. The government will play a guiding role in terms of providing leadership, increasing investment, making policies, and providing supervision. The Central government and local governments will maintain a rate of investing in health sector that is no less than the growth rate in tax revenues. The separation between urban and rural areas and among regions regional separation will be addressed, as Central finance strengthens fiscal transfer payments for the health sector across regions.

Education security

First, the recommendation is to increase governmental investment in education, and balance educational funding for urban and rural areas and among different regions. Government spending on education as a percent of GDP should steadily increase to 4 percent in 2012, and further to above 4.5 percent in 2020. The difference in educational investment between urban and rural areas and among regions should be reduced. The Central government should undertake more responsibility with regard to the extended '1+9+1' compulsory education.

Second, we should realize a 100 percent enrollment rate in primary schools of school-age children, and a 100 percent gross enrollment rate in junior high school. We should basically eliminate the difference in enrollment rates of boys and girls who are of school age; we must boost the percentage of government spending (mainly budgeted appropriation) in total compulsory education expenditures to 95 percent. We must basically achieve balanced development between different regions, build most rural schools in compliance with the uniform standards of the State, exempt all tuitions and fees in urban and rural schools, and special schools provide rural students with free textbooks, offer boarding students in the central and western poor regions free nutritious meals, and resolve the issue of selecting which schools are to be publicly funded in urban areas. One year of compulsory vocational education is to be provided for students in the central and western regions and for children of urban and rural low-income families who graduate from junior high school but fail to go on to senior high school education, before they find work. The gross enrollment rate in senior high school (including vocational education) should be above 80 percent; the percentage of government spending on education in total educational expenditures should return to 75 percent; tuition and textbook expenses for senior high school students from poor families should be partially or totally exempted. Preschool education should cover all urban children and children in relatively developed rural areas, based on a gross kindergarten enrollment rate of 55 percent on the basis of three years of preschooling; students from poor rural areas and urban and rural low-income families should enjoy one free year of preschool education; and the percentage of government spending with respect to preschools should remain stable at about 65 percent.

Third, compulsory education should cover the entire urban and rural population without discrimination in the period from 2013 to 2020. The graduation rate of junior high school will be no less than 99 percent, the budgetary expenditure for the nine-year compulsory education will account for more than 95 percent of the total expenditures, and all rural schools will meet the uniform schooling standard of the State. One year of compulsory vocational education for the students who graduate from junior high school but fail to enter senior high school should be provided. Free senior high school education will be provided in rural areas, and the exemption and reduction of the tuition, surcharges and textbook expenses will be expanded to senior high school students from urban poor families. The gross enrollment rate in senior high school should exceed 90 percent, while the percentage of government spending in total expenditures should remain stable at 75 percent. One year of free preschool education will be provided for preschool children nationwide. The gross kindergarten enrollment rate in the first two years before school will be improved to above 65 percent, the gross kindergarten enrollment rate in the last year before school will be increased to 100 percent, and the percentage of government spending in total expenditures will remain stable at 60–80 percent.

Employment assistance and unemployment insurance

First, the major task in the first stage from 2009 to 2012 is to actively expand the coverage of unemployment insurance and make sure all urban employees are incorporated into the unemployment insurance system by 2012. The operations and management mechanisms for the unemployment insurance system will be further improved, the base figure for contributions will be firmed up, benefits distribution procedures will be improved, and the number of and substitution rates for the registered unemployed will be increased as appropriate. Active efforts will be made to see if the unemployment insurance system accessible to flexible/temporary employees, migrant rural workers and rural employees in non-agricultural sectors (for example, employees of TVEs), can be conducted on a flexible basis. That is, that the level of premiums and benefit distributions can differ from the regular unemployment insurance system. Vigorous efforts will be made to implement proactive employment policies, step up vocational training and investment in employment agencies, and better combine the provision of unemployment benefits with training and re-employment. We will actively explore ways in which unemployment insurance benefits and pensions and social welfare benefits can be organically integrated.

Second, the major task in the second stage from 2013 to 2020 is to improve the quality of 'employment protection' while expanding the coverage of unemployment insurance. Training and assistance will be provided for all unemployed and all those who have difficulty in finding a job, and long-term mechanisms will be formed to promote employment. In addition, we must improve how labor markets function, break down the barriers between urban and rural policies in this regard, further improve services and include employment agencies, occupational training, job mobility and job creation, and accelerate the integration of the labor market.

Housing security

First, with respect to low-rent housing security, we must increase the supply of low-rent housing and improve how the system works. For those cities most in need, we can adopt two approaches, both building new housing and acquiring older buildings, so as to increase the housing supply for eligible persons. By 2012 we should have provided low-rent housing or housing subsidies in cash for more than 22 million urban residents. The low-rent housing security program should by that time cover all urban low-income families with housing difficulties.

Second, we will overcome the housing difficulties of migrant rural workers in a variety of ways. The housing security of migrant rural workers who have lived in cities for a long time will principally be solved through low-rent housing system. The government should provide these people with housing subsidies. By 2012, the percentage of migrant rural workers receiving subsidies should account for 10 percent of all cross-regional transient workers; by 2020 the figure should be 30 percent. The government and employers should be jointly responsible for solving the housing difficulties of other migrant rural workers in various ways; the government should offer preferential policies for building and renting out collective dormitories that employers build for migrant rural workers. Municipal- and county-level governments should support these collective dormitory projects with respect to site selection, provision of land, and supporting facilities. The government should include the housing for migrant rural workers who live in cities for a long period into its urban planning process with respect to housing construction. Residents in city outskirts should be actively guided and encouraged to lease housing to migrant workers.

Third, a one-time subsidy should be offered to help low-income rural families with housing difficulties. From now until 2020, subsidies should be provided for 650,000 low-income families with housing difficulty on average every year. The average subsidy should be RMB 7,200 in 2012, rising to RMB 15,000 in 2020. By 2020 this housing subsidy should have covered all rural low-income families with housing difficulties.

Fourth, we must also focus on the housing problems of the middle-income group. The group incorporates a considerable number of people in China. Since real estate prices have been rising faster than incomes, many in this group are unable to solve their housing difficulties. If this situation remains unchanged, it will be impossible to 'make housing available to each citizen in a harmonious society', as our policy requires. Many countries attach great importance to the housing issues of the middle-income group. Learning from international experience, China's government can help this group gain access to housing in such ways as interest subsidies, preferential tax treatment, and rent subsidies, in addition to the fundamental measures of ensuring adequate housing supply and stabilizing real estate prices.

Fifth, the government has a responsibility in controlling real estate prices. By adopting a variety of measures, it should bring them back to a level that is affordable to the middle-income group.

Minimum living allowance

First, step up the funding support for the minimum living allowance (MLA). By 2012 the total amount of funds used for MLA and for 'relief' should at least double, and it should further double by 2020. The percentage of MLA funds in total government expenditures should also maintain an upward trend. At the same time, the percentage of Central finance funding in total expenditures for MLA should also increase. Priority should be given to rural areas and impoverished areas, and the income threshold for MLA should be raised incrementally, nationwide.

Second, formulate the developmental social policies and concepts that help MLA recipients extricate themselves from the poverty trap. In addition to providing the means to maintain a basic livelihood, such assistance and social support as basic medical services, basic education and basic housing should be provided so that the MLA recipients can live in dignity and enjoy equal social development opportunities. At the same time, attention should be paid to the status of other marginalized groups to prevent various assistance measures from concentrating excessively on MLA recipients.

Social welfare systems for special groups

First, by 2012, we must assure that the minimum living allowance is made available to all special groups, including disabled persons, senior citizens, children and women, in order to help lift them out of poverty. At the same time, the infrastructure for daily life and rehabilitation of special groups should be developed. By 2020, the level of MLA as well as the quantity and quality of public services for these people should be dramatically improved, with an increase in investments in social welfare undertakings. Basic life-support needs of these people should basically be met.

Second, accelerate the building and improvement of the social welfare infrastructure. Explicitly incorporate welfare service facilities for disabled persons, senior citizens and children into the key public service projects that are supported by the Central government. Consolidate financial resources in order to create social welfare institutions, special schools and comprehensive community service facilities, to provide a favorable environment for daily life, education, rehabilitation, assistance and protection of children, disabled persons and senior citizens.

Third, adhere to a combination of government leadership and social participation. The government leadership should particularly stress developing social welfare projects for special groups. At the same time, civil society must also participate in as active and extensive a way as possible. We must maximize the roles of family, community and social organizations, to realize the goal of making a better situation for all.

Budget for a social security fund

A separate budget for social security should be established. The receipts and expenditures of the social security fund should be separated from the regular current receipts and payments of public finance in general and from the budget that handles State capital. The social insurance fund consists primarily of payments made into it by employers and individuals, and the pooled part of the fund is owned in common by all social insurance beneficiaries. Each person's individual accounts fund is owned by the individual. It is not of a 'public funds' nature. Unlike the way public funds are managed, the social insurance fund is distinct in terms of collection, payment and operation. Setting up a separate social security budget, and incorporating various extra-budgetary social security funds into the overall government budget, will help in utilizing funds efficiently, providing funds only for social security programs, and assuring a long-term balance between receipts and expenditures. At the same time, setting up a double-entry bookkeeping system and having unified management procedures will assure that managing the funds is standardized nationwide.

Raise the percentage of welfare expenditures in GDP and government spending

Our calculations indicate that we will need government investment of around RMB 2.6 trillion by 2012 and RMB 5.74 trillion by 2020 if we want to create a 'social welfare system for all' that provides benefits at the most basic level by 2020. Furthermore, our forecast shows that if we maintain the current percentages of public spending for welfare in GDP and total government spending, then we will not be able to support the welfare system recommended by this report. Therefore, over the next 12 years, the following measures should be taken. First, the percentage of government welfare expenditures in GDP should be increased from the current 6 percent to above 9 percent. Second, we must increase the percentage of fiscal revenues [tax revenues] in GDP. We should expand sources of tax revenue, and tax collection should be standardized. Third, we should continue to dramatically increase the percentage of welfare spending in our total public spending, so as to provide a solid financial basis for the improvement of social welfare.

Appendix

Table A.1 2006 Human development index (HDI) of different provinces[1]

	HDI	Life expectancy index	Education index	GDP index	Rank
China	0.787	0.800	0.832	0.728	
Beijing	0.920	0.918	0.924	0.919	2
Tianjin	0.886	0.862	0.912	0.885	3
Hebei	0.801	0.823	0.844	0.737	9
Shanxi	0.789	0.797	0.862	0.706	14
Inner Mongolia	0.788	0.762	0.837	0.765	15
Liaoning	0.835	0.845	0.882	0.779	7
Jilin	0.800	0.811	0.865	0.724	11
Heilongjiang	0.794	0.793	0.858	0.729	12
Shanghai	0.923	0.919	0.909	0.941	1
Jiangsu	0.838	0.839	0.849	0.825	5
Zhejiang	0.846	0.850	0.846	0.842	4
Anhui	0.743	0.800	0.779	0.650	26
Fujian	0.801	0.806	0.821	0.776	10
Jiangxi	0.765	0.788	0.846	0.662	23
Shandong	0.822	0.834	0.838	0.793	8
Henan	0.773	0.797	0.825	0.697	20
Hubei	0.782	0.808	0.842	0.696	17
Hunan	0.779	0.810	0.849	0.678	18
Guangdong	0.836	0.835	0.850	0.823	6
Guangxi	0.767	0.805	0.843	0.654	22
Hainan	0.783	0.843	0.818	0.688	16
Chongqing	0.790	0.838	0.848	0.685	13
Sichuan	0.765	0.818	0.818	0.658	24
Guizhou	0.674	0.720	0.744	0.557	30
Yunnan	0.703	0.722	0.758	0.631	29
Tibet	0.635	0.693	0.558	0.656	31
Shaanxi	0.775	0.802	0.842	0.681	19
Gansu	0.705	0.751	0.738	0.627	28
Qinghai	0.724	0.743	0.753	0.676	27
Ningxia	0.757	0.807	0.787	0.677	25
Xinjiang	0.772	0.769	0.832	0.716	21

Source: National Bureau of Statistics of China (2007) *China Statistical Yearbook 2007*. Beijing: China Statistics Press.
Note: Life expectation index is calculated according to life expectation statistics in 2005, other indices are calculated according to data of 2006.

Table A.2 2006 Per capita GDP and GDP index of different provinces

	Per capita GDP (Yuan)	Per capita GDP (PPPUSD)	GDP index
China	16,084	7,843	0.728
Beijing	50,467	24,608	0.919
Tianjin	41,163	20,072	0.885
Hebei	16,962	8,271	0.737
Shanxi	14,123	6,887	0.706
Inner Mongolia	20,053	9,778	0.765
Liaoning	21,788	10,624	0.779
Jilin	15,720	7,665	0.724
Heilongjiang	16,195	7,897	0.729
Shanghai	57,695	28,133	0.941
Jiangsu	28,814	14,050	0.825
Zhejiang	31,874	15,542	0.842
Anhui	10,055	4,903	0.650
Fujian	21,471	10,470	0.776
Jiangxi	10,798	5,265	0.662
Shandong	23,794	11,602	0.793
Henan	13,313	6,492	0.697
Hubei	13,296	6,483	0.696
Hunan	11,950	5,827	0.678
Guangdong	28,332	13,815	0.823
Guangxi	10,296	5,020	0.654
Hainan	12,654	6,170	0.688
Chongqing	12,457	6,074	0.685
Sichuan	10,546	5,142	0.658
Guizhou	5,787	2,822	0.557
Yunnan	8,970	4,374	0.631
Tibet	10,430	5,086	0.656
Shaanxi	12,138	5,919	0.681
Gansu	8,757	4,270	0.627
Qinghai	11,762	5,735	0.676
Ningxia	11,847	5,777	0.677
Xinjiang	15,000	7,314	0.716

Source: National Bureau of Statistics of China (2007) *China Statistical Yearbook 2007*. Beijing: China Statistics Press.

Table A.3 2006 School enrollment rate and education index of different provinces

	Primary school enrollment rate (%)	Junior high school enrollment rate (%)	High school enrollment rate (%)	University and college enrollment rate (%)	Synthetic school enrollment rate (%)	Adult literacy rate (%)	Education index
China	0.993	1.001	0.692	0.209	0.683	90.69	0.832
Beijing	1.000	0.999	1.006	0.579	0.860	95.53	0.924
Tianjin	1.042	0.983	0.864	0.486	0.817	95.9	0.912
Hebei	0.994	0.991	0.633	0.174	0.660	93.58	0.844
Shanxi	0.996	0.989	0.643	0.212	0.675	95.58	0.862
Inner Mongolia	0.997	1.008	0.791	0.194	0.697	90.64	0.837
Liaoning	0.998	0.996	0.757	0.309	0.728	95.88	0.882
Jilin	0.992	1.021	0.695	0.249	0.700	94.79	0.865
Heilongjiang	0.989	0.989	0.543	0.267	0.674	95.03	0.858
Shanghai	1.000	1.000	1.019	0.470	0.827	95.08	0.909
Jiangsu	0.999	1.013	0.810	0.296	0.736	90.64	0.849
Zhejiang	1.000	1.009	0.894	0.276	0.742	89.8	0.846
Anhui	0.997	1.000	0.633	0.174	0.662	83.7	0.779
Fujian	0.998	0.996	0.757	0.193	0.689	88.69	0.821
Jiangxi	0.996	0.995	0.753	0.293	0.721	90.79	0.846
Shandong	1.000	1.006	0.750	0.216	0.698	90.87	0.838
Henan	0.999	0.997	0.604	0.141	0.647	91.36	0.825
Hubei	0.995	1.025	0.753	0.286	0.723	90.17	0.842
Hunan	0.995	1.015	0.682	0.190	0.678	93.48	0.849
Guangdong	0.997	0.973	0.648	0.151	0.653	94.89	0.850
Guangxi	0.993	1.012	0.629	0.137	0.650	93.99	0.843
Hainan	0.998	0.952	0.546	0.183	0.643	90.5	0.818
Chongqing	0.999	1.019	0.832	0.288	0.737	90.3	0.848
Sichuan	0.995	1.035	0.820	0.197	0.706	87.44	0.818
Guizhou	0.986	0.978	0.483	0.103	0.606	81.21	0.744
Yunnan	0.966	0.963	0.503	0.109	0.603	83.5	0.758
Tibet	0.965	0.931	0.415	0.123	0.587	54.35	0.558
Shaanxi	0.994	1.024	0.744	0.257	0.712	90.65	0.842
Gansu	0.989	0.996	0.691	0.150	0.661	77.73	0.738
Qinghai	0.971	0.972	0.751	0.106	0.646	80.7	0.753
Ningxia	0.993	0.994	0.735	0.155	0.671	84.56	0.787
Xinjiang	0.992	1.015	0.510	0.129	0.628	93.34	0.832

Source: National Bureau of Statistics of China (2007) China Statistical Yearbook 2007. Beijing: China Statistics Press.

Table A.4 2000 and 2005 Life expectancy index of different provinces

Region	2000 Life expectancy	2005 Life expectancy	Increase of life expectancy during 2000–2005 (%)	Increase of life expectancy in 2005 (%)
China	71.4	73.0	1.02	0.800
Beijing	76.1	80.09	1.05	0.918
Tianjin	74.91	76.71	1.02	0.862
Hebei	72.54	74.38	1.03	0.823
Shanxi	71.65	72.83	1.02	0.797
Inner Mongolia	69.87	70.70	1.01	0.762
Liaoning	73.34	75.71	1.03	0.845
Jilin	73.1	73.67	1.01	0.811
Heilongjiang	72.37	72.60	1.00	0.793
Shanghai	78.14	80.13	1.03	0.919
Jiangsu	73.91	75.32	1.02	0.839
Zhejiang	74.7	76.00	1.02	0.850
Anhui	71.85	73.00	1.02	0.800
Fujian	72.55	73.37	1.01	0.806
Jiangxi	68.95	72.25	1.05	0.788
Shandong	73.92	75.02	1.01	0.834
Henan	71.54	72.82	1.02	0.797
Hubei	71.08	73.48	1.03	0.808
Hunan	70.66	73.60	1.04	0.810
Guangdong	73.27	75.10	1.02	0.835
Guangxi	71.29	73.29	1.03	0.805
Hainan	72.92	75.55	1.04	0.843
Chongqing	71.73	75.27	1.05	0.838
Sichuan	71.2	74.11	1.04	0.818
Guizhou	65.96	68.20	1.03	0.720
Yunnan	65.49	68.29	1.04	0.722
Tibet	64.37	66.56	1.03	0.693
Shaanxi	70.07	73.11	1.04	0.802
Gansu	67.47	70.06	1.04	0.751
Qinghai	66.03	69.55	1.05	0.743
Ningxia	70.17	73.44	1.05	0.807
Xinjiang	67.41	71.12	1.06	0.769

Source: National Bureau of Statistics of China (2006) *China Statistical Yearbook 2006*. Beijing: China Statistics Press.

Table A.5 Basic indices for population in different provinces in 1995 and 2006

Region	Total population at the end of the year (10,000 persons)		Urban population at the end of the year (10,000 persons)		Share of urban population end of the year (%)		Birth rate (‰)	
	1995	2006	1995	2006	1995	2006	1995	2006
China	121,121	131,448	35,174	57,706	29	44	17.12	12.09
Beijing	1,251	1,581	946.2	1,333	76	84	8	6.26
Tianjin	942	1,075	545.57	814	58	76	10.23	7.67
Hebei	6,437	6,898		2,652		38	13.9	12.82
Shanxi	3,077	3,375		1,452		43	16.6	11.48
Inner Mongolia	2,284	2,397	873.1	1,166	38	49	17.2	9.87
Liaoning	4,092	4,271	1,780.9	2,519	43	59	9.9	6.4
Jilin	2,592	2,723	1,157.46	1,442	45	53	12.07	7.67
Heilongjiang	3,701	3,823		2,045		54	13.23	7.57
Shanghai	1,415	1,815	1,022.73	1,610	72	89	5.5	7.47
Jiangsu	7,066	7,550		3,918		52	12.32	9.36
Zhejiang	4,319	4,980	730.8	2,814	17	57	12.66	10.29
Anhui	5,923	6,110		2,267		37	16.07	12.6
Fujian	3,237	3,558	609.6	1,708	19	48	15.2	12
Jiangxi	4,063	4,339	968.92	1,678	24	39	18.94	13.8
Shandong	8,705	9,309	1,589.1	4,291	18	46	0	11.6
Henan	9,100	9,392		3,050		32	14.41	11.59
Hubei	5,772	5,693	1,730.4	2,494	30	44	16.18	9.08
Hunan	6,392	6,342		2,455		39	13.02	11.92
Guangdong	6,868	9,304	1,245.7	5,862	18	63	18.1	11.78
Guangxi	4,543	4,719		1,635		35	17.54	14.44
Hainan	724	836	248.1	385	34	46	20.12	14.59
Chongqing		2,808		1,311		47	13.16	9.9
Sichuan	11,325	8,169	1,938.7	2,802	17	34	17.1	9.14
Guizhou	3,508	3,757	552.58	1,032	16	27	21.86	13.97
Yunnan	3,990	4,483		1,367		31	20.75	13.2
Tibet	240	281	34.24	79	14	28	24.9	17.4
Shaanxi	3,513	3,735		1,461		39	15.93	10.19
Gansu	2,438	2,606		810		31	20.65	12.86
Qinghai	481	548		215		39	22.01	15.24
Ningxia	513	604	149	260	29	43	19.28	15.53
Xinjiang	1,661	2,050		778		38	18.9	15.79

Sources: National Bureau of Statistics of China (1997) *China Statistical Yearbook 1997*; and National Bureau of Statistics of China (2007) *China Statistical Yearbook 2007*. Beijing: China Statistics Press.

Table A.6 2005 Employment structures of different provinces

Region	Total employment at the end of the year (10,000 persons)	Employment structure				Employment of the tertiary industry		Percentage of employment in informal sector
		Employment in the primary industry		Employment of the secondary industry				
		(10,000 persons)	(%)	(10,000 persons)	(%)	(10,000 persons)	(%)	(%)
China	75,825	33,970.0	44.8	18,084.0	23.8	23,771.0	31.4	0.19
Beijing	920.4	62.2	6.8	226.4	24.6	631.8	68.6	0.38
Tianjin	426.9	80.5	18.9	173.3	40.6	173.1	40.5	0.30
Hebei	3,467.3	1,562.3	45.1	1,048.4	30.2	856.6	24.7	0.22
Shanxi	1,476.4	641.9	43.5	385.8	26.1	448.8	30.4	0.15
Inner Mongolia	1,041.1	560.5	53.8	162.8	15.6	317.9	30.5	0.19
Liaoning	1,978.6	718.9	36.3	504.4	25.5	755.2	38.2	0.28
Jilin	1,099.4	523.9	47.7	201.8	18.4	373.8	34.0	0.18
Heilongjiang	1,625.8	787.7	48.4	339.7	20.9	498.4	30.7	0.17
Shanghai	855.9	61.1	7.1	331.3	38.7	463.5	54.2	0.60
Jiangsu	3,877.7	1,076.7	27.8	1,493.4	38.5	1,307.6	33.7	0.33
Zhejiang	3,202.9	791.1	24.7	1,339.9	41.8	1,071.8	33.5	0.29
Anhui	3,484.7	1,778.2	51.0	762.7	21.9	943.8	27.1	0.18
Fujian	1,868.5	702.5	37.6	582.3	31.2	583.7	31.2	0.15
Jiangxi	2,107.5	967.4	45.9	464.3	22.0	675.8	32.1	0.17
Shandong	5,110.8	2,056.5	40.2	1,558.6	30.5	1,495.7	29.3	0.21
Henan	5,662.4	3,138.8	55.4	1,251.7	22.1	1,271.9	22.5	0.11
Hubei	2,676.3	1,133.9	42.4	521.9	19.5	1,020.6	38.1	0.14
Hunan	3,658.3	1,962.0	53.6	639.4	17.5	1,056.9	28.9	0.16

Guangdong	4,702.1	1,548.7	32.9	1,443.1	30.7	1,710.4	36.4	0.22
Guangxi	2,703.1	1,518.7	56.2	302.1	11.2	882.2	32.6	0.13
Hainan	377.7	215.1	57.0	40.1	10.6	122.5	32.4	0.26
Chongqing	1,720.8	779.5	45.3	370.6	21.5	570.7	33.2	0.14
Sichuan	4,603.5	2,329.9	50.6	845.8	18.4	1,427.8	31.0	0.15
Guizhou	2,215.8	1,272.0	57.4	228.5	10.3	715.3	32.3	0.08
Yunnan	2,461.3	1,709.2	69.4	245.1	10.0	507.0	20.6	0.22
Tibet	140.4	86.3	61.4	13.0	9.2	41.2	29.3	0.14
Shaanxi	1,882.9	956.4	50.8	348.3	18.5	578.2	30.7	0.26
Gansu	1,347.6	770.5	57.2	184.8	13.7	392.3	29.1	0.12
Qinghai	267.6	131.6	49.2	46.5	17.4	89.6	33.5	0.28
Ningxia	299.6	145.1	48.4	66.7	22.3	87.8	29.3	0.18
Xinjiang	764.3	407.1	53.3	101.8	13.3	255.4	33.4	0.24

Source: National Bureau of Statistics of China (2006) *China Statistical Yearbook 2006.* Beijing: China Statistics Press.

Table A.7 Registered number of unemployed and rate of unemployment in 1990, 2004, 2005 and 2006

Region	Registered number of unemployed (10,000 persons)				Rate of unemployment (%)			
	1990	2004	2005	2006	1990	2004	2005	2006
Beijing	1.7	6.5	10.56	10	0.4	1.3	2.11	2
Tianjin	8.1	11.8	11.71	12	2.7	3.8	3.7	3.6
Hebei	7.7	28	27.82	29	1.1	4	3.93	3.8
Shanxi	5.5	13.7	14.27	16	1.2	3.1	3.01	3.2
Inner Mongolia	15.2	18.5	17.74	18	3.8	4.6	4.26	4.1
Liaoning	23.7	70.1	60.4	54	2.2	6.5	5.62	5.1
Jilin	10.5	28.2	27.64	26	1.9	4.2	4.2	4.2
Heilongjiang	20.4	32.9	31.3	31	2.2	4.5	4.42	4.3
Shanghai	7.7	27.4	27.5	28	1.5	4.5		4.4
Jiangsu	22.5	42.9	41.62	40	2.4	3.8	3.56	3.4
Zhejiang	11.2	30.1	28.97	29	2.2	4.1	3.72	3.5
Anhui	15.2	26.1	27.77	28	2.8	4.2	4.4	4.2
Fujian	9.0	14.5	14.86	15	2.6	4	3.95	3.9
Jiangxi	10.3	22.4	22.83	25	2.4	3.6	3.48	3.6
Shandong	26.2	42.3	42.9	44	3.2	3.4	3.33	3.3
Henan	25.1	31.2	33.02	35	3.3	3.4	3.45	3.5
Hubei	12.7	49.4	52.64	53	1.7	4.2	4.33	4.2
Hunan	15.9	43	41.86	43	2.7	4.4	4.27	4.3
Guangdong	19.2	35.9	34.49	36	2.2	2.7	2.58	2.6
Guangxi	13.9	17.8	18.5	20	3.9	4.1	4.15	4.1
Hainan	3.5	4.7	5.08	5	3.0	3.4	3.55	3.6
Chongqing		16.8	16.88	15		4.1	4.12	4
Sichuan	38.0	33.3	34.3	36	3.7	4.4	4.61	4.5
Guizhou	10.7	11.6	12.13	12	4.1	4.1	4.2	4.1
Yunnan	7.8	11.9	12.97	14	2.5	4.3	4.17	4.3
Tibet		1.2				4		
Shaanxi	11.2	18.5	21.54	21	2.8	3.8	4.18	4
Gansu	12.5	9.5	9.25	10	4.9	3.4	3.26	3.6
Qinghai	4.2	3.5	3.63	4	5.6	3.9	3.93	3.9
Ningxia	4	4.1	4.35	4	5.4	4.5	4.52	4.3
Xinjiang	9.6	13.3	11.13	12	3.0	3.5	3.92	3.9

Source: National Bureau of Statistics of China (2007) *China Statistical Yearbook 2007*. Beijing: China Statistics Press.

Table A.8 2006 Local fiscal revenue and expenditure of different provinces

	Local fiscal revenue (10,000 Yuan)	Local fiscal expenditure (10,000 Yuan)	Local fiscal revenue per capita (Yuan)	Local fiscal expenditure per capita (Yuan)
Beijing	11,171,514	12,968,389	7,066	8,203
Tianjin	4,170,479	5,431,219	3,880	5,052
Hebei	6,205,340	11,803,590	900	1,711
Shanxi	5,833,752	9,155,698	1,729	2,713
Inner Mongolia	3,433,774	8,121,330	1,433	3,388
Liaoning	8,176,718	14,227,471	1,914	3,331
Jilin	2,452,045	7,183,588	900	2,638
Heilongjiang	3,868,440	9,685,255	1,012	2,533
Shanghai	15,760,742	17,955,660	8,684	9,893
Jiangsu	16,566,820	20,132,502	2,194	2,667
Zhejiang	12,982,044	14,718,593	2,607	2,956
Anhui	4,280,265	9,402,329	701	1,539
Fujian	5,411,707	7,286,973	1,521	2,048
Jiangxi	3,055,214	6,964,361	704	1,605
Shandong	13,562,526	18,334,400	1,457	1,970
Henan	6,791,715	14,400,878	723	1,533
Hubei	4,760,823	10,470,041	836	1,839
Hunan	4,779,274	10,645,177	754	1,679
Guangdong	21,794,608	25,533,399	2,342	2,744
Guangxi	3,425,788	7,295,172	726	1,546
Hainan	818,139	1,745,366	979	2,088
Chongqing	3,177,165	5,942,543	1,131	2,116
Sichuan	6,075,850	13,473,951	744	1,649
Guizhou	2,268,157	6,106,411	604	1,625
Yunnan	3,799,702	8,935,821	848	1,993
Tibet	145,607	2,001,969	518	7,124
Shaanxi	3,624,805	8,241,805	970	2,207
Gansu	1,412,152	5,285,946	542	2,028
Qinghai	422,437	2,146,628	771	3,917
Ningxia	613,570	1,932,089	1,016	3,199
Xinjiang	2,194,628	6,784,723	1,071	3,310

Source: National Bureau of Statistics of China (2007) *China Statistical Yearbook 2007*. Beijing: China Statistics Press.

Table A.9 The quantity and composition of per capita disposable income of urban citizens in different provinces in 2006

	Per capita disposable income	Income from wages and salaries	Net operating income	Property income	Transfer income
National average	11,759.45	8,766.96	809.56	244.01	2,898.66
Beijing	19,977.52	16,284.17	236.37	270.52	5,626.09
Tianjin	14,283.09	9,259.72	742.97	165.05	5,308.3
Hebei	10,304.56	7,065.29	779.27	113.49	2,929.14
Shanxi	10,027.7	7,877.3	377.03	159.43	2,380.14
Inner Mongolia	10,357.99	7,552.68	955.6	209.77	2,093.82
Liaoning	10,369.61	6,611.44	688.16	146.49	3,783.94
Jilin	9,775.07	6,576.52	786.22	117.26	2,765.28
Heilongjiang	9,182.31	6,028.06	1,032.13	99.33	2,562.37
Shanghai	20,667.91	16,016.4	958.5	300.26	5,533.42
Jiangsu	14,084.26	9,501.35	1,259.84	259.57	4,227.9
Zhejiang	18,265.1	13,015.77	2,172.13	888.78	3,877.35
Anhui	9,771.05	7,430.86	680.25	148.27	2,315.13
Fujian	13,753.28	10,164.49	956.46	508.74	3,472.69
Jiangxi	9,551.12	6,897.94	653.39	106.95	2,356.34
Shandong	12,192.24	10,442.06	558.18	220.66	2,001.96
Henan	9,810.26	6,861.49	770.4	129.72	2,577.6
Hubei	9,802.65	7,573.56	486.9	122.79	2,350.08
Hunan	10,504.67	7,401.73	929.83	287.22	2,527.3
Guangdong	16,015.58	13,031.33	1,339.38	565.47	2,789.37
Guangxi	9,898.75	7,419.4	890.81	189.81	2,124.28
Hainan	9,395.13	6,954.45	727.12	231.24	2,168.9
Chongqing	11,569.74	9,266.42	525.23	192.87	2,564.39
Sichuan	9,350.11	6,675.99	644	260.22	2,536.79
Guizhou	9,116.61	6,507.12	886.32	120.92	1,924.96
Yunnan	10,069.89	6,881.39	536.72	467.25	2,962.74
Tibet	8,941.08	7,512.25	389.88	217.95	1,420.78
Shaanxi	9,267.7	6,958.23	309.04	175.41	2,495.52
Gansu	8,920.59	7,008.4	403.57	32.14	2,142.35
Qinghai	9,000.35	6,316.64	564.08	62.93	2,859.48
Ningxia	9,177.26	6,450.79	978.99	89.19	2,483.06
Xinjiang	8,871.27	7,490.69	594.81	58.39	1,545.18

Source: National Bureau of Statistics of China (2007) *China Statistical Yearbook 2007*. Beijing: China Statistics Press.

Table A.10 The quantity and composition of per capita disposable income of rural citizens in 2006

	Per capita net income	Income from wages and salaries	Net income from household operation	Property income	Transfer income
National average	3,587.04	1,374.8	1,930.96	100.5	180.78
Beijing	8,275.47	5,047.39	1,957.09	678.81	592.19
Tianjin	6,227.94	3,247.92	2,707.35	126.37	146.29
Hebei	3,801.82	1,514.68	2,039.64	107.72	139.78
Shanxi	3,180.92	1,374.34	1,622.86	74.51	109.21
Inner Mongolia	3,341.88	590.7	2,406.21	84.81	260.16
Liaoning	4,090.4	1,499.47	2,210.84	141.8	238.3
Jilin	3,641.13	605.11	2,556.7	187.74	291.58
Heilongjiang	3,552.43	654.86	2,521.51	145.69	230.38
Shanghai	9,138.65	6,685.98	767.71	558.17	1126.8
Jiangsu	5,813.23	3,104.77	2,271.37	178.51	258.58
Zhejiang	7,334.81	3,575.14	3,084.28	311.6	363.8
Anhui	2,969.08	1,184.11	1,617.76	52.78	114.43
Fujian	4,834.75	1,855.53	2,481.62	113.52	384.09
Jiangxi	3,459.53	1,441.34	1,863.5	35.13	119.57
Shandong	4,368.33	1,671.54	2,409.78	127.6	159.4
Henan	3,261.03	1,022.74	2,108.26	40.37	89.66
Hubei	3,419.35	1,199.16	2,095.15	25.91	99.13
Hunan	3,389.62	1,449.65	1,743.39	42.49	154.09
Guangdong	5,079.78	2,906.15	1,693.64	220.87	259.12
Guangxi	2,770.48	974.32	1,705.75	22.45	69.96
Hainan	3,255.53	555.72	2,486.94	49.44	163.43
Chongqing	2,873.83	1,309.91	1,349.57	27.29	187.07
Sichuan	3,002.38	1,219.51	1,586.54	52.84	143.5
Guizhou	1,984.62	715.49	1,112.81	36.93	119.38
Yunnan	2,250.46	441.81	1,631.6	82.19	94.85
Tibet	2,434.96	568.39	1,410.51	156	300.06
Shaanxi	2,260.19	848.26	1,219.33	52.56	140.04
Gansu	2,134.05	637.37	1,291.85	52.56	152.27
Qinghai	2,358.37	653.3	1,374.36	100.66	230.05
Ningxia	2,760.14	823.09	1,662.07	53.35	221.63
Xinjiang	2,737.28	254.07	2,323.01	58.69	101.51

Source: National Bureau of Statistics of China (2007) *China Statistical Yearbook 2007*. Beijing: China Statistics Press.

Table A.11 The quantity and composition of per capita consumption expenditure of urban citizens in 2006

	Per capita consumption expenditure (Yuan)	Food	Clothing	Family appliance, facilities and services	Medicare	Transport and communication	Education, culture and entertainment	Housing	Others
National average	8,696.55	3,111.92	901.78	498.48	620.54	1,147.12	1,203.03	904.19	309.49
Beijing	14,825.41	4,560.52	1,442.42	977.47	1,322.36	2,173.26	2,514.76	1,212.89	621.74
Tianjin	10,548.05	3,680.22	864.89	634.39	1,049.33	1,092.87	1,452.17	1,368.2	405.99
Hebei	7,343.49	2,492.26	849.58	460.27	737.43	875.43	827.72	864.92	235.88
Shanxi	7,170.94	2,252.5	1,016.69	441.82	589.97	825.18	1,007.92	830.38	206.48
Inner Mongolia	7,666.61	2,323.55	1,168.93	464.55	555	928.48	1,052.65	802.26	371.19
Liaoning	7,987.49	3,102.13	846.91	362.1	767.13	797.64	853.92	909.42	348.23
Jilin	7,352.64	2,457.21	907.61	318.65	671.44	815.02	890.22	984.95	307.56
Heilongjiang	6,655.43	2,215.68	971.44	319.37	634.3	665.01	843.94	755.32	250.37
Shanghai	14,761.75	5,248.95	1,026.87	877.59	762.92	2,332.83	2,431.74	1,435.72	645.13
Jiangsu	9,628.59	3,462.66	886.82	647.52	600.69	1,203.45	1,467.36	997.53	362.56
Zhejiang	13,348.51	4,393.4	1,383.63	615.45	852.27	2,492.01	1,946.15	1,229.25	436.37
Anhui	7,294.73	3,091.28	869.55	336.99	441.42	788.25	869.23	694.17	203.83
Fujian	9,807.71	3,854.26	784.71	525.65	513.61	1,232.7	1,321.33	1,233.49	341.96
Jiangxi	6,645.54	2,636.93	725.72	451.32	357.03	600.16	894.58	742.93	236.87
Shandong	8,468.4	2,711.65	1,091.22	526.29	624.06	1,175.57	1,201.97	838.17	299.48
Henan	6,685.18	2,215.32	919.31	431.02	520.57	762.08	847.12	737	252.76
Hubei	7,397.32	2,868.39	877.01	401.22	517.19	763.14	997.74	752.56	220.08
Hunan	8,169.3	2,850.94	868.23	513.63	632.52	965.09	1,182.18	871.7	285
Guangdong	12,432.22	4,503.86	719.26	633.03	707.86	2,394.66	1,813.86	1,254.69	405
Guangxi	6,791.95	2,857.4	477.67	360.62	401.06	785.01	850.9	826.86	232.43
Hainan	7,126.78	3,097.71	375.42	405.81	369.33	1,154.87	791.24	743.6	188.8

Chongqing	9,398.69	3,415.92	1,038.98	615.74	705.72	976.02	1,449.49	954.56	242.26
Sichuan	7,524.81	2,838.22	754.93	505.83	449.87	1,009.35	976.33	728.43	261.85
Guizhou	6,848.39	2,649.02	832.74	446.53	329.77	775.07	938.37	627.23	249.66
Yunnan	7,379.81	3,102.46	745.08	335.14	600.08	1,076.93	754.69	585.35	180.07
Tibet	6,192.57	3,107.9	734.83	211.1	221.7	694.21	359.34	612.67	250.82
Shaanxi	7,553.28	2,588.91	768.47	478.58	612.3	824.46	1,280.14	746.59	253.84
Gansu	6,974.21	2,408.37	854	403.8	562.74	703.07	1,034.42	716.35	291.46
Qinghai	6,530.11	2,366.42	724.96	420.31	542.93	753.07	793.72	653.04	275.66
Ningxia	7,205.57	2,444.98	874.39	480.7	578.75	774.57	846.72	890.97	314.49
Xinjiang	6,730.01	2,386.97	953.03	364.11	472.35	765.72	819.72	698.66	269.45

Source: National Bureau of Statistics of China (2007) *China Statistical Yearbook 2007*. Beijing: China Statistics Press.

Table A.12 The quantity and composition of per capita consumption expenditure of rural citizens in 2006 (Yuan)

	Per capita consumption expenditure	Food	Clothing	Housing	Family appliances, facilities and services	Transport and communication	Education, culture and entertainment	Medicare	Others
National average	2,829.02	1,216.99	168.04	468.96	126.56	288.76	305.13	191.51	63.07
Beijing	5,724.5	1,878.95	451.63	859.37	303.46	698.14	844.08	575.8	113.06
Tianjin	3,341.06	1,212.62	265.3	664.43	122.41	441.32	315.59	263.24	56.14
Hebei	2,495.33	915.5	167.87	531.66	115.84	285.7	265.38	166.34	47.03
Shanxi	2,253.25	867.65	227.61	305.02	98.29	224.23	339.75	142.66	48.03
Inner Mongolia	2,771.97	1,082.07	184.6	352.85	98.02	361.83	398.47	232.76	61.38
Liaoning	3,066.87	1,162.53	242.98	509.66	112.22	337.08	354.59	267.86	79.94
Jilin	2,700.66	1,082.28	191.16	343.97	105.11	295.99	346.79	256.28	79.07
Heilongjiang	2,618.19	923.7	198.96	560	79.26	267.05	279.69	253.84	55.68
Shanghai	8,006	3,023.53	417.57	1,658.07	481.04	779.88	919.94	549.44	176.52
Jiangsu	4,135.21	1,728.99	223.26	641.06	199.48	465.17	544.14	232.3	100.8
Zhejiang	6,057.16	2,218.88	368.68	1,202.02	288.25	664.81	731.65	459.39	123.47
Anhui	2,420.94	1,045.19	138.37	378.65	116.8	237.15	290.74	165.02	49.02
Fujian	3,591.4	1,621.92	213.31	563.85	167.33	431.4	333.55	162.26	97.79
Jiangxi	2,676.6	1,312.28	131.02	373.42	105.68	250.93	287.51	159.14	56.62
Shandong	3,143.8	1,191.32	198.12	548.05	158.73	352.19	408.84	221.8	64.75
Henan	2,229.28	911.48	159.77	443.59	105.08	220.83	198.58	140.55	49.38
Hubei	2,732.46	1,278.88	146.69	377.28	135.53	246.07	292.34	172.44	83.24
Hunan	3,013.32	1,463.33	137.69	420.96	129.8	249.7	341.7	196.54	73.6
Guangdong	3,885.97	1,887.17	151.15	633.99	148.6	443.46	303.37	197	121.23
Guangxi	2,413.93	1,196.07	79.91	424.88	110.09	239.48	198.17	123.91	41.45
Hainan	2,232.19	1,191.09	75.15	252.34	87.86	205.68	238.47	110.92	70.68
Chongqing	2,205.21	1,150.98	113.28	254.17	117.98	186.57	189.73	159.68	32.83

Sichuan	2,395.04	1,216.19	133.3	328.58	114.13	203.63	196.64	160.31	42.26
Guizhou	1,627.07	838.42	88.56	265.54	64.91	122.47	138.13	76.76	32.28
Yunnan	2,195.64	1,071.13	93.62	435.87	83.81	157.25	177.89	138.16	37.91
Tibet	2,002.24	965.83	184.85	467.79	125.14	104.3	64.27	54.37	35.69
Shaanxi	2,181	850.2	138.59	340.63	94.88	216.66	296.07	195.61	48.36
Gansu	1,855.49	865.99	97.23	251.79	78.69	174.6	228.43	127.35	31.41
Qinghai	2,178.95	938.5	170.81	366.36	94.69	255.82	118.66	192.77	41.33
Ningxia	2,246.97	929.15	159.1	414.65	104.32	226.41	168.85	187.6	56.89
Xinjiang	2,032.36	810.74	187.03	371.56	73.04	209.46	157	189.69	33.85

Source: National Bureau of Statistics of China (2007) *China Statistical Yearbook 2007*. Beijing: China Statistics Press.

Table A.13 Number of health agencies and medical workers in 2006

	Health agencies						Medical workers			
	Number of health agencies	Hospitals	Health centers	Clinics	Disease prevention and control centers (epidemic prevention stations)	Mother and child health care centers	Number of medical workers	Hygienic personnel	Practicing (assistant) physician	Registered nurse
China	308,969	19,246	40,791	212,243	3,548	3,003	5,619,515	4,624,140	1,994,854	1,426,339
Beijing	4,877	541	164	3,902	28	18	166,276	126,903	52,795	45,647
Tianjin	2,367	218	183	1,633	24	23	78,631	62,057	25,266	20,010
Hebei	17,733	874	1,965	13,778	192	183	279,663	234,133	106,086	57,952
Shanxi	9,776	916	1,585	6,442	147	133	178,994	149,371	68,145	44,694
Inner Mongolia	7,958	474	1,346	5,101	140	113	120,575	102,336	50,409	27,601
Liaoning	15,876	956	1,065	12,198	131	111	273,374	216,457	94,321	76,796
Jilin	9,696	590	796	5,461	71	72	161,438	128,471	59,060	40,267
Heilongjiang	8,181	901	935	5,510	196	143	191,945	151,916	64,895	45,542
Shanghai	2,519	260	49	1,879	22	24	138,002	109,009	45,511	42,216
Jiangsu	17,143	1,061	1,407	9,833	153	107	334,508	275,368	114,590	85,955
Zhejiang	14,230	606	2,188	7,322	100	87	255,057	214,622	94,524	66,615
Anhui	9,288	699	1,886	5,313	130	116	204,498	169,181	69,421	50,392
Fujian	9,652	370	937	7,695	93	88	124,909	106,586	46,051	35,910
Jiangxi	10,210	489	1,543	7,240	124	112	142,682	119,761	51,436	37,870
Shandong	17,016	1,168	1,774	11,254	178	150	395,897	336,669	146,391	103,843
Henan	14,629	1,201	2,091	9,915	182	166	374,924	300,712	115,481	82,850
Hubei	10,052	575	1,195	7,116	114	95	265,298	217,950	90,149	70,608

Hunan	15,331	812	2,430	10,971	151	137	248,018	204,011	87,853	58,187
Guangdong	16,953	1,008	1,427	12,551	131	122	408,972	332,829	130,551	114,445
Guangxi	9,977	460	1,280	7,539	104	102	162,725	133,924	56,661	46,756
Hainan	2,337	190	312	1,633	28	26	38,199	30,787	12,195	11,508
Chongqing	6,613	361	1,088	4,884	43	41	96,742	79,805	37,511	21,269
Sichuan	24,015	1,178	5,012	16,294	207	202	285,785	240,444	114,694	63,730
Guizhou	6,147	394	1,460	3,715	105	79	95,654	82,324	41,147	23,641
Yunnan	10,020	649	1,410	7,204	150	148	145,621	121,424	56,476	39,837
Tibet	1,349	97	666	432	81	55	10,746	8,895	4,310	2,000
Shaanxi	11,631	851	1,748	8,111	124	116	168,190	139,065	60,566	40,703
Gansu	12,022	381	1,351	9,649	106	99	99,431	85,581	36,018	22,985
Qinghai	1,643	136	399	790	56	22	23,509	20,119	8,575	6,739
Ningxia	1,553	131	238	1,022	26	21	27,852	23,591	10,991	7,652
Xinjiang	8,175	699	861	5,856	211	92	121,400	99,839	42,775	32,119

Source: National Bureau of Statistics of China (2007) *China Statistical Yearbook 2007*. Beijing: China Statistics Press.

Table A.14 The number of people participating in basic pension insurance, unemployment insurance and basic medical insurance in 2006 (10,000 persons)

	Basic pension insurance			Unemployment insurance		Basic medical insurance for urban employment		
	Total	Employees	Enterprise employees	Total	Beneficiaries	Total	Employees	Retirees
China	18,766.3	14,130.9	12,618.0	11,186.6	326.5	15,731.9	11,580.3	4,151.5
Beijing	603.6	442.6	442.6	482.2	3.1	679.5	515.7	163.9
Tianjin	328.2	215.5	208.3	216.7	3.6	344.2	218.2	126.0
Hebei	747.5	551.5	447.1	470.8	13.4	615.9	457.3	158.6
Shanxi	486.9	374.1	302.4	296.0	5.2	353.8	271.7	82.2
Inner Mongolia	356.6	265.5	238.1	223.5	5.0	316.2	223.0	93.1
Liaoning	1,248.8	865.8	790.2	614.1	25.9	959.3	651.9	307.4
Jilin	480.2	341.4	330.5	224.4	10.2	376.3	275.1	101.2
Heilongjiang	801.0	564.5	505.1	457.5	17.8	708.2	515.3	192.9
Shanghai	891.7	577.3	515.6	476.4	18.5	1,023.3	732.3	291.0
Jiangsu	1,469.8	1,141.7	1,059.3	901.1	22.7	1,274.3	935.8	338.5
Zhejiang	1,052.6	881.7	814.4	504.4	6.5	730.6	557.7	172.9
Anhui	495.2	361.4	353.3	362.6	17.9	441.2	316.5	124.7
Fujian	456.1	362.5	304.1	293.1	6.8	370.1	284.9	85.2
Jiangxi	415.0	303.3	287.8	241.0	4.9	313.3	226.8	86.5
Shandong	1,368.0	1,106.3	883.3	789.7	30.3	996.1	796.1	199.9
Henan	863.8	655.6	572.9	682.8	28.0	704.1	530.9	173.3
Hubei	850.8	630.3	570.1	395.5	12.0	565.3	398.7	166.6
Hunan	751.6	541.8	386.1	386.3	10.2	560.5	398.0	162.4
Guangdong	1,972.3	1,728.8	1,581.5	1,208.2	16.7	1,421.1	1,223.1	197.9
Guangxi	302.7	225.6	225.6	222.3	8.1	302.0	213.3	88.7

Hainan	132.0	94.0	74.3	59.1	2.3	91.0	65.3	25.6
Chongqing	317.3	209.4	197.3	193.0	4.8	257.5	160.1	97.4
Sichuan	842.7	597.7	491.2	400.0	16.3	734.5	486.7	247.8
Guizhou	193.2	139.1	124.6	131.1	1.5	199.2	141.4	57.8
Yunnan	267.4	183.6	175.0	183.0	6.4	331.5	232.7	98.8
Tibet	7.6	4.4	4.4	7.5		16.5	11.4	5.0
Shaanxi	391.5	280.2	280.2	326.5	14.1	377.1	265.7	111.4
Gansu	201.2	143.4	138.7	160.5	7.5	195.8	144.1	51.7
Qinghai	62.5	45.1	45.1	34.0	1.0	64.5	42.5	22.0
Ningxia	72.3	55.6	55.6	38.3	1.2	73.1	53.3	19.9
Xinjiang	313.3	222.4	213.0	205.4	4.8	335.8	234.6	101.2

Source: National Bureau of Statistics of China (2007) *China Statistical Yearbook 2007.* Beijing: China Statistics Press.

Table A.15 The share of education expenditure and health expenditure in local fiscal expenditure and GDP in 2000 and 2005

	Share of education expenditure in local fiscal expenditure		Share of education expenditure in local GDP		Share of health expenditure in local fiscal expenditure		Share of health expenditure in local GDP	
	2000	2005	2000	2005	2000	2005	2000	2005
National average	0.1567	0.1483	0.0164	0.0203	0.0465	0.0404	0.0049	0.0055
Beijing	0.1356	0.1378	0.0242	0.0212	0.0644	0.0620	0.0115	0.0095
Tianjin	0.1650	0.1520	0.0188	0.0182	0.0465	0.0429	0.0053	0.0051
Hebei	0.1772	0.1742	0.0145	0.0169	0.0420	0.0460	0.0034	0.0045
Shanxi	0.1696	0.1527	0.0232	0.0244	0.0464	0.0421	0.0064	0.0067
Inner Mongolia	0.1203	0.1154	0.0212	0.0202	0.0368	0.0306	0.0065	0.0054
Liaoning	0.1272	0.1181	0.0141	0.0181	0.0331	0.0285	0.0037	0.0044
Jilin	0.1374	0.1175	0.0197	0.0205	0.0360	0.0328	0.0052	0.0057
Heilongjiang	0.1283	0.1353	0.0151	0.0193	0.0356	0.0356	0.0042	0.0051
Shanghai	0.1382	0.1111	0.0185	0.0200	0.0535	0.0317	0.0072	0.0057
Jiangsu	0.1986	0.1543	0.0137	0.0141	0.0551	0.0449	0.0038	0.0041
Zhejiang	0.1813	0.1830	0.0130	0.0172	0.0632	0.0513	0.0045	0.0048
Anhui	0.1669	0.1647	0.0178	0.0218	0.0362	0.0351	0.0039	0.0047
Fujian	0.1912	0.1880	0.0158	0.0170	0.0498	0.0437	0.0041	0.0039
Jiangxi	0.1707	0.1559	0.0190	0.0217	0.0462	0.0387	0.0052	0.0054
Shandong	0.1926	0.1697	0.0138	0.0134	0.0461	0.0371	0.0033	0.0029
Henan	0.1736	0.1678	0.0151	0.0177	0.0388	0.0375	0.0034	0.0039
Hubei	0.1564	0.1526	0.0135	0.0182	0.0518	0.0400	0.0045	0.0048
Hunan	0.1463	0.1408	0.0138	0.0189	0.0342	0.0280	0.0032	0.0038
Guangdong	0.1340	0.1438	0.0150	0.0147	0.0442	0.0360	0.0049	0.0037
Guangxi	0.1730	0.1721	0.0218	0.0258	0.0450	0.0425	0.0057	0.0064
Hainan	0.1502	0.1601	0.0186	0.0271	0.0437	0.0431	0.0054	0.0073

Chongqing	0.1356	0.1245	0.0160	0.0198	0.0428	0.0311	0.0051	0.0049
Sichuan	0.1434	0.1299	0.0162	0.0190	0.0485	0.0458	0.0055	0.0067
Guizhou	0.1577	0.1793	0.0320	0.0472	0.0549	0.0496	0.0111	0.0130
Yunnan	0.1505	0.1596	0.0319	0.0352	0.0540	0.0585	0.0114	0.0129
Tibet	0.1164	0.1099	0.0594	0.0815	0.0540	0.0383	0.0276	0.0284
Shaanxi	0.1415	0.1554	0.0232	0.0263	0.0305	0.0340	0.0050	0.0058
Gansu	0.1464	0.1572	0.0280	0.0349	0.0428	0.0416	0.0082	0.0092
Qinghai	0.1065	0.1196	0.0276	0.0374	0.0413	0.0522	0.0107	0.0163
Ningxia	0.1328	0.1218	0.0304	0.0322	0.0386	0.0337	0.0088	0.0089
Xinjiang	0.1642	0.1400	0.0230	0.0279	0.0558	0.0499	0.0078	0.0099

Source: National Bureau of Statistics of China (2007) *China Statistical Yearbook 2007*. Beijing: China Statistics Press.

Table A.16 The proportion of export and import to GDP in 2000 and 2006

	The proportion of export to GDP		The proportion of import to GDP	
	2000	*2006*	*2000*	*2006*
National average	0.208	0.364	0.188	0.298
Beijing	0.400	0.384	1.258	1.216
Tianjin	0.436	0.612	0.431	0.566
Hebei	0.060	0.088	0.025	0.039
Shanxi	0.062	0.069	0.027	0.042
Inner Mongolia	0.057	0.036	0.098	0.064
Liaoning	0.192	0.244	0.145	0.173
Jilin	0.057	0.056	0.060	0.092
Heilongjiang	0.037	0.109	0.039	0.057
Shanghai	0.461	0.874	0.534	0.876
Jiangsu	0.249	0.591	0.192	0.455
Zhejiang	0.267	0.511	0.115	0.194
Anhui	0.059	0.089	0.032	0.070
Fujian	0.273	0.432	0.176	0.224
Jiangxi	0.049	0.064	0.018	0.042
Shandong	0.150	0.212	0.092	0.132
Henan	0.024	0.042	0.013	0.020
Hubei	0.037	0.066	0.025	0.058
Hunan	0.037	0.054	0.019	0.024
Guangdong	0.788	0.919	0.670	0.685
Guangxi	0.060	0.059	0.022	0.051
Hainan	0.128	0.104	0.077	0.111
Chongqing	0.052	0.077	0.041	0.048
Sichuan	0.029	0.061	0.024	0.041
Guizhou	0.035	0.036	0.020	0.020
Yunnan	0.050	0.067	0.027	0.056
Tibet	0.080	0.061	0.012	0.029
Shaanxi	0.065	0.064	0.041	0.030
Gansu	0.035	0.053	0.013	0.081
Qinghai	0.035	0.066	0.015	0.015
Ningxia	0.102	0.106	0.036	0.055
Xinjiang	0.073	0.187	0.064	0.051

Source: National Bureau of Statistics of China (2001) *China Statistical Yearbook 2001*; and National Bureau of Statistics of China (2007) *China Statistical Yearbook 2007*. Beijing: China Statistics Press.

Table A.17 Land area of different provinces in 2006

	Total area of land (10,000 km²)	Per capita area of land (m²)	Total area of arable land (1,000 hectare)	Per capita area of arable land (m²)	Area of forest (10,000 hectare)	Per capita area of forest (m²)	Coverage rate of forest (%)
China	960.00	73.42	130,039.20	9.95		13.38	18.21
Beijing	1.64	10.66	343.90	2.24	37.88	2.46	21.26
Tianjin	1.18	11.31	485.60	4.66	9.35	0.90	8.14
Hebei	18.77	27.40	6,883.30	10.05	328.83	4.80	17.69
Shanxi	15.63	46.59	4,588.60	13.68	208.19	6.21	13.29
Inner Mongolia	118.30	495.81	8,201.00	34.37	2,050.67	85.95	17.70
Liaoning	14.80	35.06	4,174.80	9.89	480.53	11.38	32.97
Jilin	18.70	68.85	5,578.40	20.54	720.12	26.51	38.13
Heilongjiang	45.40	118.85	11,773.00	30.82	1,797.50	47.05	39.54
Shanghai	0.63	3.54	315.10	1.77	1.89	0.11	3.17
Jiangsu	10.26	13.73	5,061.70	6.77	77.41	1.04	7.54
Zhejiang	10.18	20.78	2,125.30	4.34	553.92	11.31	54.41
Anhui	13.94	22.78	5,971.70	9.76	331.99	5.42	24.03
Fujian	12.14	34.34	1,434.70	4.06	764.94	21.64	62.96
Jiangxi	16.69	38.71	2,993.40	6.94	931.39	21.60	55.86
Shandong	15.71	16.99	7,689.30	8.31	204.64	2.21	13.44
Henan	16.70	17.80	8,110.30	8.65	270.30	2.88	16.19
Hubei	18.59	32.56	4,949.50	8.67	497.55	8.71	26.77
Hunan	21.18	33.48	3,953.00	6.25	860.79	13.61	40.63
Guangdong	17.98	19.56	3,272.20	3.56	827.00	8.99	46.49
Guangxi	23.67	50.79	4,407.90	9.46	983.83	21.11	41.41
Hainan	3.54	42.75	762.10	9.20	166.66	20.13	48.87

(Continued overleaf)

Table A.17 (continued)

	Total area of land (10,000 km²)	Per capita area of land (m²)	Total area of arable land (1,000 hectare)	Per capita area of arable land (m²)	Area of forest (10,000 hectare)	Per capita area of forest (m²)	Coverage rate of forest (%)
Chongqing	8.24	29.45	1,399.20	5.00	183.18	6.55	22.25
Sichuan	48.50	59.06	9,169.10	11.17	1,464.34	17.83	30.27
Guizhou	17.62	47.24	4,903.50	13.15	420.47	11.27	23.83
Yunnan	39.40	88.54	6,421.60	14.43	1,560.03	35.06	40.77
Tibet	120.24	4,340.79	362.60	13.09	1,389.61	501.66	11.31
Shaanxi	20.58	55.32	5,140.50	13.82	670.39	18.02	32.55
Gansu	45.44	175.17	5,024.70	19.37	299.63	11.55	6.66
Qinghai	71.75	1,321.36	688.00	12.67	317.20	58.42	4.40
Ningxia	6.64	111.41	1,268.80	21.29	40.36	6.77	6.08
Xinjiang	166.49	828.31	3,985.70	19.83	484.07	24.08	2.94

Source: National Bureau of Statistics of China (2007) China Statistical Yearbook 2007. Beijing: China Statistics Press.

Note: The data of the appendix tables was collected by Mr Song Jin, and all tables were compiled by Li Shi.

Bibliography

Chinese

Assessment Team for the Work of Experiments on New Rural Cooperative Medical Insurance. *China's New Rural Cooperative Medical Insurance in Development: An Assessment Report*. Beijing: People's Medical Publishing House, 2006.

Cai Fang. A Rethink of the Reform on Basic Pension Insurance in China, *Economic Perspectives*, 2008 (7).

Cai Renhua. Invest in Sanitation to Promote Health, *Qiushi*, 2003 (13).

Center for Statistics Information, Ministry of Health. *A Bulletin on Health Development in China in 2003–2007*, 2008.

Chen Jiagui (ed.). *China Social Security System Development Report (1997–2001)*. Beijing: Social Sciences Academic Press, 2001.

Chen Jiagui and Wang Yanzhong (eds). *China Social Security System Development Report (2001–2004)*. Beijing: Social Sciences Academic Press (China), 2004.

Chen Jiagui and Wang Yanzhong (eds). *China Social Security System Development Report (No. 3)*. Beijing: Social Sciences Academic Press, 2007.

China Development Research Foundation. *China Development Report 2007: Eliminate Poverty during Development*. Beijing: China Development Press, 2007.

China Development Research Foundation. *A Book of Public Budgeting*. Beijing: China Development Press, 2008.

China Disabled Persons' Federation. *Report on Main Data about the National Monitoring of Disabled People in 2007*. http://www.foredu.com.cn (accessed April 6, 2009).

China National Committee for Ageing. *Follow-up Survey on Urban and Rural Aged Populations in China*. http://www.cpirc.org.cn (accessed April 6, 2009).

China National Health Development Research Center. *Report on Total Health Spending in 2007*, 2008.

China Social Insurance Research Institute. *China Social Security Framework*. Beijing: China Labour and Social Security Publishing House, 2000.

China Social Insurance Research Institute. *Beveridge Report*. Beijing: China Labour and Social Security Publishing House, 2008.

Department of Training and Employment, Ministry of Labor and Social Security. *An Explanation and Analysis of Positive Employment Policies*. Beijing: China Labour and Social Security Publishing House, 2003.

Ding Wenjie and Zhou Liquan. Existing Five Types of Violating Social Security Funds Make It Imperative to Improve the Supervisory System. *Economic Information Daily*, 10 January, 2008.

Ding Yuanzhu. *A Research of Conceptual Innovation in Social Administration*. A Compilation of CASS Papers, 2006.

Division of Development and Planning, Ministry of Education. *China Statistical Yearbook on Education (2006)*. Beijing: People's Education Press, 2007.

Division of Development and Planning, Ministry of Education. *A Concise Statistical Analysis of National Educational Development in 2007* [*R*], 2008.

Division of Planning and Finance, Ministry of Education. *Educational Achievements in China (1949–1983)* [*M*]. Beijing: People's Education Press, 1985.

Dong Keyong. *Public Governance and Institutional Innovation*. Beijing: China Renmin University Press, 2004.

Gao Shuguo and Yang Xiaoming. *A Report on Cultural Literacy of Chinese Population*. Beijing: Social Sciences Academic Press (China), 2004.

Ge Yanfeng and Gong Sen. *Medical Reform in China: Problems, Root Causes and Way Out*. Beijing: China Development Press, 2007.

Huang Yong Chang (eds). *Sanitary Conditions in China*. Shanghai: Shanghai Medical University Press, 1994.

Hu Jintao. *New Year Greetings*, 2008.

Institute of Population and Labor Economics (IPLE-CASS), Chinese Academy of Social Sciences. *Almanac of China's Population 2005*. Almanac of China's Population, 2006.

Institute of Population and Labor Economics (IPLE-CASS), Chinese Academy of Social Sciences. *Almanac of China's Population 2006*. Almanac of China's Population, 2007.

Jing Lin. *Practical Manual on Rural Cooperative Medical Insurance*. Chengdu: Sichuan Publishing House of Science & Technology, 1998.

Leading Group for the 2nd National Survey of Disabled People. *Bulletin on Main Data about the 2nd National Sampling Survey of Disabled People in 2006*. http://202.123.110.5/zizl/gacjr/content_459223.htm (accessed May 18, 2007).

Li Ling. 2006: The Turning point for Medical Reform in China. *Chinese Health Economics*, 2007 (4).

Li Shaoguang. *An Economic Analysis on the Deepening of Social Security Reform*. Beijing: China Renmin University Press, 2006.

Li Shi. *The Change of Income Distribution in China over the Past 30 Years of Reform and Opening: A Paper for the Forum on Economic Theories over the Past 30 Years of Reform and Opening and for the Centennial of the Birth of Sun Yefang*. Hong Kong: October 21–22, 2008.

Ma Zhenjiang. A Preliminary Discussion of the Rural Primary Healthcare System with Chinese Characteristics. *Chinese Health Economics*, 2000 (5).

Ministry of Agriculture, Ministry of Labor and Social Security, Ministry of Education, Ministry of Science and Technology, Ministry of Construction and Ministry of Finance. *National Program for Training of Migrant Workers in 2003–2010*, 2003.

Ministry of Civil Affairs and National Bureau of Statistics of China. *China Statistical Yearbook on Civil Governance 2007*. Beijing: China Statistics Press, 2008.

Ministry of Civil Affairs. *Development Program for the System of Helping and Protecting Vagrant Teenagers during the '11th Five-Year' Plan Period*. http://fss.mca.gov.cn, (accessed December 24, 2007).

Ministry of Civil Affairs. *Program for Development of the Community Service System During the '11th Five-Year' Plan Period*. http://www.sdpc.gov.cn (accessed November 9, 2007).

Ministry of Civil Affairs. *Statistical Bulletin on Civil Governance Development in 2007*. http://www.mca.gov.cn (accessed January 24, 2008).

Ministry of Civil Affairs. *Statistical Bulletin on Implementation of the '10th Five-Year' Plan for Disabled People*. http://www.cdpf.org.cn (accessed May 19, 2006).

Ministry of Construction. *Measures for Administration of Urban Low-Rent Housing*, 1998a.

Ministry of Construction. *Several Opinions on Vigorously Developing Affordable Housing*, 1998b.

Ministry of Education. *School Development Program during the '11th Five-Year' Plan Period for Special Education in Central and Western Regions (2008–2010)*. http://www. moe.gov.cn (accessed September 24, 2008).

Ministry of Finance. *Measures for Administration of Security Funds for Low-Rent Housing*. 2007.

Ministry of Human Resources and Social Security. *Statistical Bulletin on Labor and Social Security in 2007*, May 21, 2008.

Ministry of Labor and Social Security. *Statistical Bulletin on Labor and Social Security Development in 2006*. http://www.molss.gov.cn (accessed May 18, 2007).

Monthly Statistical Report on Civil Administration of May 2008. http://cws.mea.gov.cn (accessed April 6, 2009).

National Bureau of Statistics of China. *China Statistical Yearbook 2002*. Beijing: China Statistics Press, 2002.

National Bureau of Statistics of China. *China Statistical Yearbook 2006*. Beijing: China Statistics Press, 2006.

National Bureau of Statistics of China. *China Statistical Yearbook 2007*. Beijing: China Statistics Press, 2007.

National Bureau of Statistics of China. *Statistical Bulletin on National Economic and Social Development in 2007* [Z], February 28, 2008.

National Bureau of Statistics of China. *Beijing Statistical Yearbook 2008*. Beijing: China Statistics Press, 2008a.

National Bureau of Statistics of China. *China Statistical Abstract 2008*. Beijing: China Statistics Press, 2008b.

National Population and Family Planning Commission. *Statistical Bulletin on Awarding and Helping Rural Households Practicing Family Planning in 2006*. http://www.china-pop.gov.cn (accessed May 26, 2008).

Office of Inter-Ministerial Meeting on New Rural Cooperative Medical Insurance under the State Council. *Working Information on New Rural Cooperative Medical Insurance*, 2008 (2).

Organizing Committee of China Social Security Forum. *Establishing a Social Security System Covering both Urban and Rural Areas*. Beijing: China Labour and Social Security Publishing House, 2006.

Population Census Office under the State Council and the Department of Population & Employment Statistics (Social, Science and Technology Statistics) of NBS. *Main Data on the 5th National Population Census in 2000*. Beijing: China Statistics Press, 2001.

Research Group for Survey of Women Workers' Labor Protection, Beijing Municipal Working Committee for Children and Women. *Survey Report on Labor Protection of Women Workers in Beijing*. www.qianlong.com, 2002 (accessed April 6, 2009).

Research Group of the Research Office of the State Council. *Survey Report on Migrant Workers in China*. Beijing: China Yanshi Press, 2006.

Shang Xiaoyuan and Cheng Jianpeng. An Analysis of the Conditions of Orphans in China. *Youth Studies*, 2006 (10).

Song Wenjiong, Wu Ming, Li Weiping, Wang Pan and Wang Lin. Meet the Challenges of the 21st Century through Institutional Innovation: A Review and Remark of the Urban Health Reform over the Past 20 Years. *Health Economics Research*, 1999 (10).

Song Xiaowu. *Reform: Enterprises, Labor and Social Security*. Beijing: Social Sciences Academic Press, 2006.

State Council Information Office. *Draft Amendments to the Working Regulations on Rural People's Commune*, 1962.

State Council. *Notice Concerning Steadily Continuing the Urban Housing Reform (No.30, GUO FA [1991])*, 1991.

State Council. *Decision to Deepen the Urban Housing Reform (No.43, GUO FA [1994])*, 1994.

State Council. *Notice Concerning Further Deepening the Urban Housing Reform and Accelerating the Construction of Affordable Housing (No.23, GUO FA [1998])*, 1998.

State Council. *Opinion on Establishing the New Rural Cooperative Medical System*, 2003.

State Council. *The Status and Policy of Social Security in China (White Book)*, 2004.

State Council. *Development of Undertakings for the Elderly in China*. http://www.china.com.cn (accessed December 12, 2006).

State Council. *Guiding Opinions on Instituting Experiments on Basic Medical Insurance for Urban Residents*, 2007.

State Council. *Measures for Administration of Affordable Housing*, 2007a.

State Council. *Measures for Low-Rent Housing Security*, 2007b.

State Council. *Minimum Living Allowance System for Rural Residents*, 2007c.

State Council. *Several Opinions on Solving Difficulties in Housing of Urban Low-income Households (No.24, GUO FA [2007])*, 2007.

Statistical Bulletin on Health Development in 2007 in China. http://202.96.155.169, Ministry of Health (accessed May 21, 2008).

Statistical Bulletin on Labor and Social Security Development in 2007. http://www.molss.gov.cn, Ministry of labour and social security (accessed May 21, 2008).

Statistical Bulletin on National Implementation of Educational Funds. Website of the Ministry of Education at: http://www.moe.gov.cn, Ministry of Education (accessed December 15, 2008).

UNESCO. *Dakar Framework for Action, Education for All*, 2000.

US Social Security Administration. *Social Security Programs Throughout the World 1995* (Chinese version). Beijing: Huaxia Publishing House, 1997.

Wan Huanxun. *A Dictionary of Applied Education*. Beijing: Beijing Normal University Press, 1995.

Wan Yanzhong. International Cooperation in Social Security is Worth Attention. *Journal of Chinese Academy of Social Sciences*, July 31, 2008.

Wan Yanzhong. Problems about China's Public Health System and Way Out. *China Health Economics*, 2004 (11).

Wang Huanxun. *Ci Hai* ('An Encyclopedia of the Chinese Language'). Shanghai: Shanghai Lexicographical Publishing House, 2000.

Wang Mengkui. *China: Economic Development and Social Harmony*. Beijing: People's Press, 2006.

Wang Shaoguang. The Crisis and Opportunity Facing Public Health in China. *Comparative Studies*, 2003 (7).

Wang Shaoguang. Policy Orientation, Absorbing Ability and Health Justice. *Social Sciences in China*, 2005 (6).

Wang Yanzhong. *Labor and Social Security Issues in China*. Beijing: Economy & Management Publishing House, 2004.

Wang Yanzhong and Feng Liguo. Where China's Medical Health Reform Goes: The Resource Concentrating Effect and Improvement of 'Unburdening-type' Market-oriented Reform. *China Industrial Economics*, 2007 (8).

Wang Yanzhong and Zhang Chewei. *A Study of Unemployment Insurance in China*. Jinan: Shandong People's Press, 2004.

Wen Jiabao. Government Work Report. *Xinhuanet*, March 5, 2008.

World Bank Group. *Making Services Work for Poor People*. Beijing: China Financial & Economic Publishing House.

Xiao Donglian. *The Employment Crisis and Development Opportunity for Non-state Economy in China at the End of the 1970s*. http://www.usc.cuhk.hk (accessed May 8, 2008).

Xu Daowen. *Toward a Social Policy for Development*. Beijing: China Social Sciences Press, 2008.

Xu Lin and Zhang Hui. The Responsibility of the Government for Helping the Disadvantaged from the Perspective of the Current Status of Employment of Disabled People in Western China. *Journal of Henan Normal University (Philosophy and Social Sciences)*, 2006 (6).

Yang Wenzhong. Giving Full Play to the General Service Function of Unemployment Insurance. *China Social Security*, 2003 (11).

You Mingchun, Liang Liqun and Gao Peng. A Survey of the Connection between 'Three Security Lines' and Reemployment Policy. *Budget Management & Accounting Monthly*, 2005 (11).

Zhang Mingliang. *Help by Classifications and Total Protection so as to Advance Welfare Development of Children in China*. http://www.chain.net.cn (accessed September 8, 2008).

Zhang Xiulan and Xu Yuebin. Build China's Family Policy for Development. *China Social Sciences*, 2003 (6).

Zhang Xiulan, Xu Yuebin and James Midgley. *A Brief Discussion of China's Social Policy for Development*. Beijing: China Labour and Social Security Publishing House, 2007.

Zhao Dianguo. Establish a New Rural Pension Insurance System. *China Finance*, 2007 (6).

Zheng Gongcheng *et al. The Changes in and Evaluation of China's Social Security System*. Beijing: China Renmin University Press, 2002.

English

Anand, S. and Ravallion, M. Human Development in Poor Countries. *Journal of Economic Perspectives*, 7(1): 133–150, 1993.

Arts, W. and Gelissen, J. Welfare States, Solidarity and Justice Principles: Does the Type Really Matter? *Acta Sociologica*, 44: 283–299, 2001.

Bird, E.J. Does the Welfare State Induce Risk-Taking? *Journal of Public Economics*, 80: 357–383, 2001.

Chetty, R. and Looney, A. Consumption Smoothing and the Welfare Consequences of Social Insurance in Developing Economies. *Journal of Public Economics*, 90: 2351–2356, 2006.

Dryzek, J. and Goodin, R.E. Risk-Sharing and Social Justice: The Motivational Foundations of the Post-War Welfare State. *British Journal of Political Science*, 16 (1): 1–34, 1986.

Goodin, R.E. Vulnerabilities and Responsibilities: An Ethical Defense of the Welfare State. *The American Political Science Review*, 79(3): 775–787, 1985.

Hall, A. and Midgley, J. *Social Policy for Development*. Beijing: Social Sciences Academic Press, 2006.

ILO. *World Labour Report 2000*. Geneva: International Labour Office.

Kenworthy, L. Do Social-Welfare Policies Reduce Poverty: A Cross-National Assessment. *Social Forces*, 77(3): 1119–1139, 1999.

Li, Zhao. Changes in the Distribution of Wealth in China, 1995–2002, in Jim Davies (ed) *Global Distribution of Personal Wealth*. Oxford: Oxford University Press, 2008.

Lin, J.Y. Rural Reforms and Agricultural Growth in China. *American Economic Review*, 82: 34–54, 1992.

Nock, G.J. The Welfare State: An Affront to Freedom? *Canadian Journal of Political Science*, 21(4): 757–769, 1988.

Quadagno, J. Promoting Civil Rights Through the Welfare State. *Social Problems*, 47(1): 68–89, 2000.

Ranis, G. Human Development and Economic Growth. *Economic Growth Center Discussion Paper*, No. 887, 2004.

Ranis, G., Stewart, F. and Ramires, A. Economic Growth and Human Development, *World Development*, 28(2): 197–219, 2000.

Sen, A.K. *Development as Freedom*. New York: Anchor Books, 1999.

UNDP. *Human Development Report 2000*. Oxford: Oxford University Press, 2000.

UNDP. *Human Development Report 2007/2008*. Oxford: Oxford University Press, 2008.

Wang, Dewen. China's Urban and Rural Old Age Security System: Challenges and Options. *China & World Economy*, 14(1): 102–116, 2006.

Background reports

Gong Sen. *Governance Framework of China's Social Welfare System*.

Jia Kang and Wang Min. *Social Welfare Fund-raising and Public Finance Support*.

Kong Jingyuan. *Pension System of China*.

Li Shi and Luo Chuliang. *An Analysis of Urban and Rural Welfare Levels in China*.

Lin Minquan and Yu Jiantuo. *A Comparative Study of International Social Welfare Systems*.

Mo Rong. *Systems for Employment Promotion, Employment Assistance and Unemployment Protection*.

Ren Xingzhou. *Housing Security in China's New Social Welfare System*.

Wan Zhenyao and Tian Xiaohong. *The Minimum Living Allowance in China's New Social Welfare System*.

Zhang Li. *Public Education Services in China's New Social Welfare System*.

Zhang Shifei. *Social Welfare System for Particular Groups of Our Country*.

Zhang Zhenzhong, Wu Huazhang and Wang Xiufeng. *Health Security in China's New Social Welfare System*.

Zheng Bingwen. *Social Welfare Systems and Practices in Foreign Countries*.

Index

ROUTLEDGE INTERNATIONAL HANDBOOKS

Routledge International Handbooks is an outstanding, award-winning series that provides cutting-edge overviews of classic research, current research and future trends in Social Science, Humanities and STM.

Each *Handbook*:

- is introduced and contextualised by leading figures in the field
- features specially commissioned original essays
- draws upon an international team of expert contributors
- provides a comprehensive overview of a sub-discipline.

Routledge International Handbooks aim to address new developments in the sphere, while at the same time providing an authoritative guide to theory and method, the key sub-disciplines and the primary debates of today.

If you would like more information on our on-going *Handbooks* publishing programme, please contact us.

Tel: +44 (0)20 701 76566
Email: reference@routledge.com

www.routledge.com/reference

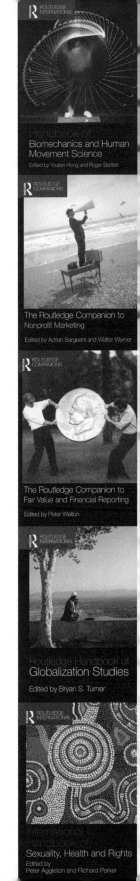